The Quest for
Community and Identity

New Critical Theory

New Critical Theory
General Editors:
Patricia Huntington and Martin J. Beck Matuštík

The aim of *New Critical Theory* is to broaden the scope of critical theory beyond its two predominant strains, one generated by the research program of
Jürgen Habermas and his students, the other by postmodern cultural studies.
The series reinvigorates early critical theory—as developed by Theodor
Adorno, Herbert Marcuse, Walter Benjamin, and others—but from more decisive post-colonial and post-patriarchal vantage points. *New Critical Theory*
represents theoretical and activist concerns about class, gender, and race,
seeking to learn from as well as nourish social liberation movements.

*Phenomenology of Chicana Experience and Identity: Communication and
Transformation in Praxis*
by Jacqueline M. Martinez

The radical project: Sartrean investigations
by Bill Martin

*From Yugoslav Praxis to Global Pathos: Anti-Hegemonic Post-post-Marxist
Essays*
by William L. McBride

New Critical Theory: Essays on Liberation
edited by William S. Wilkerson and Jeffrey Paris

*The Quest for Community and Identity: Critical Essays in Africana Social
Philosophy*
edited by Robert E. Birt

The Quest for Community and Identity

Critical Essays in Africana Social Philosophy

Edited by
Robert E. Birt

ROWMAN & LITTLEFIELD PUBLISHERS, INC.
Lanham • Boulder • New York • Oxford

ROWMAN & LITTLEFIELD PUBLISHERS, INC.

Published in the United States of America
by Rowman & Littlefield Publishers, Inc.
4720 Boston Way, Lanham, Maryland 20706
www.rowmanlittlefield.com

12 Hid's Copse Road
Cumnor Hill, Oxford OX2 9JJ, England

"Visions of Transcendent Community in the Works of Toni Morrison" from *Resisting State Violence: Radicalism, Gender, and Race in U.S. Culture*, by Joy James, Minneapolis: University of Minnesota Press, 1996. Reprinted by permission of the University of Minnesota Press.

"Paulette Nardal, Race Consciousness, and Antillean Letters" to be published in *Gendering Negritude: Race Women, Race Consciousness, Race Letters, 1924–1945*, by Tracy Denean Sharpley-Whiting, Minneapolis: University of Minnesota Press, 2002. Reprinted by permission of the University of Minnesota Press.

Portions of "The Revival of Black Nationalism and the Crisis of Liberal Universalism" from *We Are Not What We Seem: Black Nationalism and Class Struggle in the American Century*, by Rod Bush, New York: New York University Press, 1999. Reprinted by permission of the New York University Press.

British Library Cataloguing-in-Publication Information Available

Library of Congress Cataloging-in-Publication Data

The quest for community and identity : critical essays in Africana social philosophy / edited by Robert E. Birt.
   p. cm.—(New critical theory)
   Includes bibliographical references and index.
   ISBN 0-7425-1291-6 (alk. paper)—ISBN 0-7425-1292-4 (pbk. : alk. paper)
   1. Blacks—Race identity. 2. Identity (Philosophical concept) 3. Community—Philosophy. I. Birt, Robert E., 1952– II. Series.

HT1581 .Q47 2002
305.896'073—dc21   2001041695

Printed in the United States of America

♾™ The paper used in this publication meets the minimum requirements of American National Standard for Information Sciences—Permanence of Paper for Printed Library Materials, ANSI/NISO Z39.48-1992.

Contents

with all their philosophical and ideological diversity, most of our contributors would probably agree with Edward Said that the "purpose of the intellectual's activity is to advance human freedom and knowledge."[3] This purpose suffuses the writings of *all* of the writers in this anthology. At least implicitly, they find in the experiences and emancipatory struggles of Black people, and in current and previous intellectual reflections on those experiences and struggles, sources of inspiration for their own intellectual praxes.

Hence, one does not find among these writers the attitudes of certain fashionably superficial intellectuals who think that "there is nothing to be liberated from but liberation discourse itself."[4] Thinkers in this anthology are engaged in a liberatory project. There is a preponderance of concern among them for problems of relations between the self and others and for the perplexities of human (personal and collective) identity as it informs one's prospect of forming liberating communities where solidarity and individuality flourish. There is special concern for problems of social, political, and cultural values. Consistent with the legacy of Africana philosophy, one finds here projects that include "confrontation with unfulfilled democracy," colonial and neocolonial domination, ontological designation by race, and critiques of the human ravages of capitalism.[5] There is a passionate concern here for problems of justice, oppression, alienation, and relations among humans in society. Intellectual activity, whatever its intrinsic joys, is also valued as essential to the quest for social emancipation and a liberated human identity.

But these concerns—alienation, the relations among humans in society, the quest for social emancipation, and a liberated human identity—bring us to the thematic focus of this text. As is evident from the anthology's title, the thematic focus is on the problems and perplexities of community and identity in our times, especially as they pertain to the situations of Black people. Originally, this anthology was to be entitled *Community, Identity, and Freedom in African American Thought*. But the development of the text has led to a somewhat different outcome. Not all of the writers are African American, and some of the chapters focus on problems of community and identity in locations of the Black world other than North America. Moreover, while some writers focus on community as the theme through which to explore the perplexities of identity or freedom and while others focus on identity as the theme through which they examine notions of community and freedom, I am the only one who has specifically chosen freedom (which is treated as a quest for community, and for radically new and socially liberated modes of being-with-others) as the organizing theme for a chapter. The theme of freedom remains interwoven in treatments of the themes of community and identity. I take all three themes to be central to the entire Black intellectual and philosophical tradition. They essentially frame that tradition and express the core of what Du Bois once described as "our spiritual strivings."

Nonetheless, the chapters focus primarily either on the meaning and prospects of a liberated identity or on the meaning and prospects for an emancipated community. The writers' explicit emphases frame the design of the text. Accordingly, the volume is organized into four parts: (1) "Exploring Perplexities of Identity," (2) "In Quest of Community: Sociality and Situated Freedom," (3) "Historical Crises of Identity and Community," and (4) "Liberalism, Postmodernism, and the Quest for Community." Perhaps a brief overview of the whole can situate the text or at least clarify its design.

EXPLORING PERPLEXITIES OF IDENTITY

The very meaning of being a human subject with an identity is the focus of the first part of the volume. This is hardly surprising. Frantz Fanon notes that racial and colonial oppression ravages the psyches of its victims to the point where they feel compelled to continuously ask themselves: In reality, who am I? Indeed, the quest for human liberation is a quest for a liberated identity. Yet, the quest for identity is problematic. The writers in part 1 of this volume—Arnold Farr, Kevin Cokley, Clevis Headley, and Patrick Goodin—regard the quest for identity as both problematic and indispensable to the quest for personal and social freedom. They are sensitive to the ways in which racial identity (like all group identities) can enslave or liberate. Among the questions they ponder are: Do racial identities (even where formed in defiance of racism) allow of human freedom? Do such identities coincide or conflict with personal identities and desires for the realization of individuality? Are they unitary, fixed, and permanent? Are they hybrid, multiple, mutable, and dynamic? Is it possible to form a self-realizing racial identity that enhances community and solidarity?

Answers and philosophical approaches vary. There is not full agreement as to whether racial identity is compatible with a liberated life. Farr, Cokley, and Headley agree in their common opposition to essentialist identities, but they also argue for the possibility of self-actualizing, nonessentialist Black identities. Goodin defends racial identity against antiessentialist critique. No one argues for a fixed or given racial essence or Negro soul. All insist that human identities are human creations, and creativeness is essential to our authors' ideals of freedom.

Farr's "Racism, Historical Ruins, and the Task of Identity Formation" draws on Critical Theory, and especially on Walter Benjamin's notion of historical ruins, not only to critique racial essentialism, but also to indicate and affirm the possibility of a liberating nonessentialist racial identity. Benjamin's notion of historical ruins symbolizes in Farr's chapter the ravaging of Black psyches by centuries of slavery and racial oppression. But even with the ruins of history (e.g., alienation and loss of the past), a racial identity (based on shared experiences rather than an essentialist ontology) and solidarity are possible without negating individuality. Farr surmises that a nonessentialist racial identity may well function as a launching pad for self-creation.

Cokley's "To Be or Not to Be Black: Problematics of Racial Identity" is also an antiessentialist critique, but one that denies the validity of any racial identity. Preoccupation with racial identity leads to essentialist notions of Blackness that hinder, rather than help, the goal of Black unity. Black identity should be reframed as ethnic or cultural identity, which, Cokley surmises, is psychologically healthier, philosophically less problematic, and more conducive to group solidarity and community.

Headley's "Postmodernism, Narrative, and the Question of Black Identity" embraces postmodern discourse even though many critics deem it corrosive of subjectivity in general and Black identity in particular. But for Headley postmodernism offers a way of conceiving Black identity that liberates it from the "rhetoric of pathology" current in many discussions of it and offers ways of theorizing identity without conceiving it in terms of a historical recovery of a pure essence. He offers a "narrative conception" of identity as an alternative to modernist notions of a stable, unitary self. Narrative conceptions capture the complex, fluid, and dynamic factors that construct and structure Black identity.

Goodin's "Du Bois and Appiah: The Politics of Race and Racial Identity" introduces a note of difference through its critique of Anthony Appiah's antiessentialist theory of race and criticism of Du Bois. According to Goodin, Appiah begins with race as a "conceptual" problem rather than (like Du Bois) "with realities of racism, with the experience of suffering racism." Appiah erroneously conceptualizes race "on the level of speech and discourse"; overcoming the injuries of race thus becomes a matter of exposing race as a semantic or conceptual trick. But Goodin insists that oppression is not a conceptual trick. Nor is the meaning of race the same on the linguistic level as in experience. Lived social reality is such that people often experience their consciousness through race. The "experiential ties that bind people together," Goodin argues, "are grounded in essences, that is, reality"—a controversial claim, though he never ascribes an ontological status to these ties grounded in "essences." Yet, he does consider them as possible grounds for the creation of community.

IN QUEST OF COMMUNITY: SOCIALITY AND SITUATED FREEDOM

In the second part of the volume, which deals with community and sociality, the emphasis is also on creation and construction. Robert E. Birt and Lewis R. Gordon, whose chapters explore the existential conundrums of community, complement the writers of part 1 by their emphasis on sociality as an achievement. Humans create communities as they create identities. Thus, there is again no recourse to essentialism. Here, one finds common ground among the writers of both parts. But there is a greater coincidence of philosophical perspective between Birt and Gordon than among the writers in part 1.

Existential and Marxian philosophical perspectives implicitly inform Birt's "Of the Quest for Freedom As Community." This chapter is critical of collectivism but focuses its critique on liberal individualism's corrosion of human community. Since we cannot be individuals or human without community and since the negation of community and atomizing of human bonds are the most salient features of contemporary social unfreedom, the quest for freedom must become increasingly a quest for community. This entails a shift of focus from individualist notions of liberty to a vision of a cooperative community of freedom. This does not mean that *individuality* is to be denied, rather, a liberating community is an indispensable condition of its realization. Community involves human associations and relatedness in which individuality is dialectically interwoven with solidarity. But as the transcending praxis of community is diametrically opposed to the disintegrating forces of racism and the economic order, Birt surmises that the project of community is also a project of resistance. Creating community is central to the struggles of Blacks (and others) for self-determination and liberation as a people.

Gordon's "Sociality and Community in Black: A Phenomenological Essay" explores the meaning of community from an existential, phenomenological standpoint. This chapter confronts challenges to community raised by the human possibility of bad faith. Gordon notes a tension in Africana thought between a tendency to affirm Black community through collectivist models of solidarity and the tendency to affirm Black individuality in defiance of the racist assumption that "They're all alike." Gordon argues that although collective consciousness is often presented as a model against the lone individual, collectivity is *not* necessarily social while community is always social. Thus, it is erroneous to collapse community into collectives or to insist on a subordinated individuality as an essential condition of community. Gordon's chapter draws on the insights of Sartre ("bad faith"), Alfred Schutz ("sociality"), and Fanon ("sociogenesis") to advance a "rich" theory of community that articulates how sociality overcomes bad faith and how sociogenesis resists the tendency to displace sociality by collectivism. Gordon's chapter is grounded in an existential philosophic discourse of race and sociality.

HISTORICAL CRISES OF IDENTITY AND COMMUNITY

The more philosophically nuanced discussions of perplexities of identity and community in parts 1 and 2 are followed by more historical approaches in part 3. One might say that the writers in parts 1 and 2 explore the crises and quests for community and identity as *existential* crises and quests. The four writers in part 3, proceeding from perspectives of literary, sociological, and historical studies, place the existential crises and existential quest in a more explicitly historical and cultural context. Joy James and Tracy Denean Sharpley-Whiting explore the works of Toni Morrison and Nardal, respectively, to deepen our understanding of the historic crises of (and human quests for) identity and community. Rod Bush examines the recent revival of Black nationalism among contemporary Black youth as one response to contemporary crises of community. Paget Henry ends part 3 with an analysis and critique of commodified existence under global capitalism as a central source of our harrowing crises of community. I want to consider the four of them more closely.

The human quest for identity is ultimately inseparable from the quest for community. The interplay between the two quests may well be indispensable to the human quest for freedom and existential integrity in this postmodern era of fragmented sociality and a decentered subject. For James, community is essential to human wholeness, and its denial ultimately becomes a denial of human identity. James's "Visions of Transcendent Community in the Works of Toni Morrison" explores the cultural and philosophic dimensions of community in Morrison's literary nonfiction. In the process, we learn that community encompasses not only contemporaries, but also ancestors and inherited wisdom. Community is a continuum. James shows that the worldview informing Morrison's essays is based on "discredited knowledge" of African American cosmologies, including notions of transcendent community.

Community is central in Morrison's works because it entails the epistemological significance of the individual's connection to others. This concept of community is one that transcends time and space to include ancestors, contemporaries, and descendants. The presence of ancestors informs, empowers, and gives meaning to continued resistance to oppression.

While James's chapter assumes something of a cosmological perspective on community, Sharpley-Whiting's "Paulette Nardal, Race Consciousness, and Antillean Letters" takes a notably global perspective on identity through an exploration of race consciousness in Negritude. This chapter examines the Pan-Africanist dimensions of the Negritude movement of the 1930s and the pioneering work of Francophone Black women. Sharpley-Whiting argues that Negritude (despite essentialist inclinations) was a historically "progressive and self-actualizing alternative" to assimilationist ideologies of French colonialism. It was a liberatory movement of cultural resistance and the affirmation of Black consciousness whose treatment of race, identity, assimilation, and alienation remains of great contemporary significance. Of particular importance was the Parisian journal *La Revue du monde noir*. Sharpley-Whiting pays special attention to the thoughts of Nardal, who cofounded the journal with Aime Cesaire, Leopold Senghor, and Leon Damas. Nardal's essay "The Awakening of Black Consciousness" is philosophically explored as a work that jump-started the Negritude movement, helped radicalize Black consciousness, and formed the ideal of a *globalized* Black community.

Thus, we move from global consciousness to global community. We must not forget, however, that Black nationalism has been among the most powerful and persistent cultural and political traditions through which African Americans have striven for community and autonomous identity. Considering the international scope of Negritude, Garveyism, and Pan-Africanism, some form of Black nationalism has often been the *primary* expression of transnational Black identity and global community. It is not without reason that Bush offers historical reflections on the significance of contemporary Black nationalism.

Bush's "The Revival of Black Nationalism and the Crisis of Liberal Universalism" considers the post-1960s resurgence of Black nationalism among contemporary youth to be an indication of the crisis of liberalism. Nationalism offers conceptions of community and personhood widely divergent from liberal conceptions. It often critiques liberalism—for racism and liberalism are often complementary ideologies and liberal individualism is often corrosive to community. Yet, Black nationalism is neither monolithic nor unproblematic. There is a divergence in nationalism's understanding of community. Left nationalism envisions a community liberated *internally* as well as liberated from White domination. It advocates democracy and egalitarianism and is critical of capitalism and class privilege. Conservative nationalism, though distinct from liberalism, espouses a repressive ideal of community, an ideal designed to keep the community obedient to the narrow ideologies and politics of an elite. Bush finds in left nationalism the most promising vision of a free community with possibilities for liberated human identities.

But what of the "material conditions" inducing the social crises to which Black nationalism responds? Do not the global market and its deepening commodification of daily life subvert the sociality of community? These and other questions are addressed by Henry in his "Commodification and Existence in African American Communities." This chapter ponders the question of whether community is still possible under present economic conditions. It tries to address the *meaning* of community in light of the seemingly inexorable, socially disintegrating force of contemporary global capitalism. The growing commodification of daily life and the consequent erosion of the most intimate dimensions of personal and social existence indicate that the project of community among Blacks (and others) must also become a project of resistance to the social atomization of commodified life.

LIBERALISM, POSTMODERNISM, AND THE QUEST FOR COMMUNITY

Yet economic forces are also cultural forces, and cultural forces are often economic ones. Is commodified life not a cultural form even if corrosive to cultural life? In part 4, the chapters by Eddy Souffrant, George Carew,

Leonard Harris, and Richard A. Jones confront cultural (or sociocultural) challenges to community, especially the challenges of liberalism and post-modernism. The social chaos induced by global capitalism is hardly under-standable without comprehending the legitimating ideology of liberal indi-vidualism. Might not even postmodernism, with its deconstruction of the subject, be in part a cultural expression of late capitalism with its social dis-locations aggravated by electronic revolutions? Criticisms of liberalism in the previous parts are extended by Souffrant's critique, while for Carew it re-mains a point at issue whether liberalism (or liberal pluralism) still has a lib-erating role to play in the quest for social justice. Harris and Jones question what community can mean in this fragmented postmodern era, and both ponder the question: Is Black community still *possible* with our widening class divisions, the deepening fragmentation of Black identity, and the stub-born hegemony of liberal individualism?

Souffrant's "Black Philosophy As a Challenge to Liberalism" draws on African American philosophy (especially Du Bois) in his critique of liberal thought. He focuses on the perceived shortcomings of liberal thought con-cerning community or group membership. He argues that insofar as posses-sive individualism is a fundamental constituent of liberal theory, liberalism is "at worst unsympathetic to groups and at best relegates groups to a second-ary role." Liberalism tends to be blind even to the social bases of individual identity, which it prizes. Yet Souffrant sees possible remedies not only in Du Bois's critical social theory, but also in the liberal philosopher Dewey's no-tion of democracy as "associated living."

Democracy as associated living suggests that democracy is community. Are not democracy and community inseparable in our era? You can hardly realize one without the other. But the quest for its realization is not limited to the Black Diaspora. Carew's "Democracy, Transitional Justice, and Post-colonial African Communities" examines the problems of attempted passage from colonial status to democratic community in modern African societies. Carew's chapter proceeds from a "social constructivist" view of racial/ethnic identity. He explores the meaning of democratic community in culturally and ethnically diverse African societies, and he wonders how one can democra-tize a society in which social relations and ethnic identities are essentialized. Carew argues that reified identities must be made to regain moral autonomy. "Moral" ethnicities must be encouraged as alternatives to essentialized ones. Carew also examines the suitability of liberal conceptions of justice in the formation of democratic communities. While not wholly rejecting liberal thought, he finds liberal individualism unsuitable for multiethnic African so-cieties in which democratic community must allow group self-determination and a vision of collective freedom and the common good.

Group self-determination and moral commitment to the common good of the community are enduring themes of Black liberation discourse and popular struggles. But what kind of entities are communities? What kind of group should we commit ourselves to? These questions are explored by Harris in his chapter "Community: What Type of Entity and What Type of Moral Commitment?" Harris argues that communities are forms of association and that to view them as ontological entities is misleading. He tries to show why communities are better understood as associations by discussing how moral commitments are affected depending on whether we find it morally more compelling to fight for the liberation of a "raciated ethnicity" (like African Americans) or the liberation of the working class. Harris's chapter adds a philosophical dimension to old (sometimes sterile) debates over the priority of race and class.

But it is in Jones's concluding chapter "Theorizing Black Community" that we find explicitly and extensively addressed issues such as whether community is possible in our fragmented postmodern era or whether *Black* community remains possible amid growing class divisions and dislocations of Black identity. He questions what possibilities there might be for new visions of Black community and, assuming it still to be possible, what types of Black community we might deem desirable. In particular, Jones raises the fundamental question: What is community? He thereby brings into an explicit focus much that is implicit in the preceding chapters.

Jones's inquiry leads to an exploration of the "liberal" ideal of beloved community articulated by Martin Luther King's *Where Do We Go from Here?* This he contrasts with Cornel West's Christianized Marxist vision of community (with its critique of King) in *Prophesy Deliverance!* Finally, Jones considers Lucius Outlaw's *On Race and Philosophy* as a more tenable "third moment" between King and West, a position that theorizes transformative social praxis, synthesizing the best traditions of liberalism and socialism. He ponders the question: What might a Black community free of racism, sexism, and class oppression be theorized to be? Sensitive to the challenge of postmodernism, Jones argues that Black communities must be conceived in ways that transcend inherited traditions and that the formation of flourishing Black communities requires new conceptions of community that are nonassimilative, nonseparatist, and self-transformative. While engaging and critiquing postmodernism, this final chapter is deeply grounded in contemporary African American philosophy with a touch of Frankfurt School Critical Theory.

Jones's chapter ends the volume with emphases familiar throughout the whole. Liberation demands the affirmation of community, but not its reification. Communities are historical human associations, not eternal metaphysical essences. Similarly, identity is a human creation, not a metaphysical essence or "natural" entity. No one in this volume attributes absolute or metaphysical status to identity or community. One forms an identity as one forms community with others. Community and identity, inseparably intertwined aspects of human reality, are the outcomes of the never-ceasing movement of human praxis. They are expressions of human transcendence, human self-creation. The African American quest for community and identity is not some archaic pursuit, but ultimately a universal human quest for the realization of the human. It is this liberatory quest that animates the work of each of our authors.

Perhaps it is unwise to make claims about the extraordinary novelty of this volume. Historic earlier works by Outlaw, Harris, West, Gordon, James, Henry, Bernard Boxill, and innumerable others make it impossible even to claim the mantle of a pioneer in Africana philosophy. The themes of this text are not new as they have agitated Black thinkers and the Africana intellectual tradition for centuries. At the beginning, I conceded that we inherit a legacy and work within a tradition. Du Bois's reflections on double consciousness, Fanon's powerful existential analyses of colonized Black identity, Anna Julia Cooper's poignant inquiries and insightful wrestling with the question "What are we worth?" precede our own efforts to make sense of the possibility of a liberated Black identity. Similarly, their works (and those of other intellectual forebears) precede our own philosophical quest for a liberating community of freedom. We invent no new themes.

However, this volume brings together perennial themes in a concentrated form. The philosophical perspectives here are numerous and probably not extraordinarily novel. Feminism, poststructuralism, phenomenology, existential philosophy, Marxism, pragmatism, critical theory, multiculturalism, postmodernism, and all of the other well-known "isms" are found here. The writers go beyond philosophy in the conventional sense to explore works of literature, psychology, postcolonial studies, and other areas. But it is the concentrated *thematic focus* on the quest for a human identity and liberated human social existence in community as these are configured within the Black experience that is the special concern of this text. What our forebears reflected on sporadically throughout the vast array of their works, we devote concentrated attention to in a single volume. And within this concentrated focus, readers will discern a sense that, in this "postmodern" era marked by economic globalization and the crumbling of older forms of identity and human association, community and identity cannot simply be what they once were. Everything must be thought out anew. And this is what this volume's thinkers attempt to do.

If we invent no new themes, perhaps we can throw new light on historical themes. We seek to bring together in a single volume the *current* reflections of some thinkers on the themes of community and identity in light of the unsettling changes that the national (or *global*) Black community has undergone since the 1960s. This volume offers a concentrated focus on chosen themes, contemporary scholarly examinations of the work on these themes by past and present thinkers, and new and original inquiries into these issues, often by younger thinkers bringing insights from more recent philosophical trends. Perhaps this concentrated focus on a few central themes within the Black intellectual and philosophical tradition(s) will constitute an offering of some value to philosophical (and other) scholarship of the Black world and beyond.

NOTES

1. Frantz Fanon, *The Wretched of the Earth* (New York: Grove, 1968), 247.

2. Here, I should credit Lucius Outlaw's perceptive description of this dimension of the meaning of Africana philosophy. I would probably differ with him slightly in emphasizing a little more the "second order" reflection on experience in the constitution of Africana philosophy. See Lucius Outlaw, "Africana Philosophy," in *On Race and Philosophy* (New York: Routledge, 1996), 86.

3. Edward Said, *Representations of the Intellectual* (New York: Pantheon, 1994), 17.

4. Lewis R. Gordon, *Fanon and the Crisis of European Man* (New York: Routledge, 1995), 100.

5. Leonard Harris points out these concerns in the early 1980s as central, though not exclusive, features of African American philosophical and intellectual traditions. See Leonard Harris, ed., *Philosophy Born of Struggle: Anthology of Afro-American Philosophy from 1917* (Dubuque: Kendall-Hunt, 1983), xv.

I

EXPLORING
PERPLEXITIES OF IDENTITY

1

Racism, Historical Ruins, and the Task of Identity Formation

Arnold Farr

THE QUEST FOR IDENTITY AND SOLIDARITY

That the institution of slavery and the continuation of racism in its aftermath has had a traumatic effect on the self-consciousness of African Americans goes without saying. One of the symptoms of this traumatic experience is a feeling of homelessness and a loss or destroyed sense of self. The knowledge of having been uprooted from one's homeland and purged of all knowledge of one's language, customs, and ancestry leaves one longing for a self that one never was and for solidarity with one's people and place origin. That is, the quest for identity and solidarity with a people often causes one to long for an essentialist identity that is rooted in one's geographical origins or ancestry. One dreams of what one might have been, but, this "I that could have been" is now an impossibility due to certain historical factors. Hence, one is left longing for an imaginary self. This longing is quite natural to the extent that it is through one's conception of who one is that one finds one's way in the world. We organize our life projects in terms of our self-concept. Unfortunately for African Americans, the experience of racial discrimination fragments the ego to such a degree that one's self-conception may become pathologically distorted.[1]

Although the experience of racial discrimination leads to a pathologically distorted self-concept, there remains a healthy part of the psyche that seeks a stable identity and solidarity with a people. Nevertheless, due to the trauma of racial discrimination and the pathological instability that results from this type of dehumanization, this quest for identity and solidarity is also pathologically affected. There arises a conflict in the individual between his or her pathological self-concept and his or her attempt to transcend this conception

15

and find acceptance and solidarity in a community of like persons. This is the issue that I want to focus on in this chapter.

Naturally, our first inclination in our attempt to find or construct an identity for ourselves is to distance ourselves from the source of our pain, anguish, and pathological conception of ourselves. This flight often and unfortunately results in the reessentialization of Blackness and Whiteness. I use the term "reessentialization" because embedded in the racialized discourse that grounds acts of racism in the first place is an original racial essentialism or fixed racial identity that has been constructed by the oppressors. Originally, the very concept of race was a social–political construct wherein certain accidental, physical, and geographical differences were used as justification for mistakenly ascribing to groups who shared certain physical features other social and character traits that did not necessarily belong to all individuals who shared these accidental physical features.[2] The initial essentialist construction of race was for the purpose of political, social, and economic exploitation. In an attempt to escape early racist determinations or false identity markers forced on us by White racists, many African Americans have found it necessary to define Blackness ourselves. This is a necessary and legitimate move, but one that could be dangerous if such a move is made in the absence of critical self-reflection.

In the quest for identity and solidarity, we must be careful not to simply swap essentialisms. That is, the idea that there is an essential Black identity or that being Black means conforming to some abstract notion of Blackness is not at all liberating, but instead, it is oppressive.[3] It is possible for Blacks to oppress other Blacks by insisting that they conform to a set of criteria that determines one's Blackness. Such an act may destroy an individual's opportunity to flourish as a human being. If it is the case that the reessentialization of Blackness by Blacks is oppressive and destructive, what are our chances for establishing an identity and for establishing solidarity with other "Blacks" for communal and emancipatory purposes?

Identity and solidarity should not be established on the basis of an ahistorical essentialism, but rather, on a nonessentialist, historical basis. This will enhance Black solidarity while allowing individuals to freely determine themselves as individual persons. In the remainder of this chapter, I will develop a notion of racial identity that supports racial solidarity but does not entail the same pitfalls as an essentialist notion of racial identity.

THE RUINS OF HISTORY

In his ninth "Thesis on the Philosophy of History," Walter Benjamin writes:

> A Klee painting named "Angelus Novus" shows an angel looking as though he is about to move away from something he is fixedly contemplating. His eyes are

staring, his mouth is open, his wings are spread. This is how one pictures the angel of history. His face is turned toward the past. Where we perceive a chain of events, he sees one single catastrophe which keeps piling wreckage on top of wreckage and hurls it in front of his feet. The angel would like to stay, awaken the dead, and make whole what has been smashed. But a storm is blowing from Paradise; it has got caught in his wings with such violence that the angel can no longer close them. This storm irresistibly propels him into the future to which his back is turned, while the pile of debris before him grows skyward. This storm is called progress.[4]

It is with Benjamin's notion of historical ruins that we may gain some insight into a possible solution to the problem of Black identity and solidarity. My first task here is to provide a brief analysis of Benjamin's thesis, then secondly, to apply it to the situation of African Americans and our quest for racial solidarity.

The shock that is experienced by the angel of history as he looks at the past is due to the disclosure of a side of history that has hitherto been concealed. That is, the angel discovers that the notion of historical progress is false. He sees that what has paraded as progress is really barbarism.[5] The story of progress is a story that has been told by the victors of history. What has been concealed is the pain and suffering of the oppressed.

The most apparent meaning of Benjamin's thesis is that history is not necessarily progressive. What we call progress (particularly technological and economic progress) is enjoyed by one group of people at the expense of another. This level of analysis is quite interesting and informative, but there is another level of analysis that I want to explore that was not explored by Benjamin. Benjamin's analysis was directed at the forces of historicism, the capitalist forces of production and their dehumanizing consequences, and fascism. I want to situate the problem of identity formation and racial solidarity in the context of Benjamin's thesis on history. Although the problem of identity formation is not raised by Benjamin, his thesis on history provides a useful theoretical tool for examining the problem of identity with respect to an oppressed people.

It is helpful to read in conjunction with Benjamin's "Thesis on the Philosophy of History" Toni Morrison's essay "Playing in the Dark: Whiteness and the Literary Imagination" for the following reason. Like Benjamin's thesis, Morrison's essay discloses a presence, a reality that affects all of us but has been concealed by the victors of history. The difference is that Morrison focuses on American literature rather than history, although the two bear a striking resemblance with respect to the way in which White privileged identity is formed in contrast to Black identity or more specifically, for Benjamin, the way in which the identity of the oppressors is formed by presupposing then concealing the identity of the oppressed. Morrison notes that in many classic American novels White American identity is formed in opposition to an invisible Africanist presence.[6] The strong, noble, aggressive individual must tame the wild frontier and shape himself by becoming master of all that he sees (including Native Americans and Africans). White strength requires the illusion of Black weakness. White intelligence requires the illusion of Black ignorance. Hence, the identity of the dominant group is forged in opposition to the "Other."

This is an example of the original essentialism that I spoke of earlier. That is, the first meaning of Blackness was the construction of White oppressors. Whiteness had meaning only in opposition to Blackness. One determines who he is by contrasting himself to the "Other." White self-consciousness is formed in opposition to some essentialist notion of Blackness.

The consequences of essentialist racial determinations are quite serious. The most obvious consequence is that it provides the basis for racial discrimination. Groups may be discriminated against on the assumption that members of that group have in common certain properties that make them unworthy of respect, love, and fair treatment. Essentialist racial determinations also contravene the individual's right to flourish as a human being. In fact, victims of such an attitude are often denied any humanity whatsoever. African Americans know what it is like to be despised by others because properties have been attributed to us that do not belong to us. We know what it is like to be treated as a category and not as a person. Therefore, it is imperative that we ask why do we do this to ourselves.

The reessentialization of Blackness by Blacks is no less problematic and oppressive than the essentialist racial determinations forced on Blacks by White racists. Regardless of who forms the essentialist ideals or categories, to essentialize Blackness is to reject the freedom and humanity of the individual for the sake of some abstract categorization. To essentialize Blackness is to deny the individual certain opportunities and freedoms of expression on the basis of a socially constructed set of properties by which the individual must be bound.

How, then, do we deal with two fundamental yet conflicting drives in the human person? That is, the drive that each individual has to freely determine him- or herself as an individual with unique talents and style must be allowed to flourish coterminously with the human drive for solidarity with other individuals in a community. One may retort with respect to the latter drive that there is really no problem here to the extent that we all belong to the human community at large. However, this does not satisfy African Americans. Why? Here again we may consider Benjamin's angel of history.

The tendency on the part of some African Americans to determine one's Blackness on the basis of some abstract essentialist criteria is merely a natural response to the existential feeling of nothingness that many African Americans experience. It was through the institution of slavery and the subsequent racial discrimination that the humanity of African Americans (or at least the recognition of that humanity) was destroyed. Racism produces a pathological rejection of one's self, and it disrupts and destroys that which is human in the victim.

What is destroyed is one's ability for self-determination or self-actualization. The drive for free self-determination requires solidarity in a community of other self-determining beings, that is, the human community. However, through systems of domination such a community is destroyed. Indeed, racial discrimination destroys the human community to the extent that the victims of racial discrimination are denied their humanity. The denial of one's humanity leaves one with a feeling of nothingness or nobodiness.

The quest for solidarity by African Americans is an attempt to heal a broken humanity, it is an attempt to regain a feeling of worth and belongingness. The need to affirm others and be affirmed as Black is simply the need to have one's humanity affirmed by another. African Americans feel that they can only turn to each other for such an affirmation. This belief is based on a hermeneutics of suspicion with which African Americans view Whites. Not only are Black people suspicious of White people, but anything that appears to be a product of White culture is suspect. Hence, there arises a need for African Americans to clearly distinguish themselves from anything White even if it means the problematic construction of an essentialist Black identity.

As broken humanity, it would be absurd to think that African Americans can simply put the past aside and feel as if now their humanity has been fully accepted. Indeed, it is the past that has made us who we are. This statement is not a return to essentialism for reasons that I will explain in a moment. It is through solidarity with other African Americans that we are able to begin the necessary healing process that will allow us to regain our human dignity. This requires a recognition of our Blackness by ourselves and others in a way that has hitherto not been done. We must escape essentialist notions of Blackness in order to return to Blackness.

We are not Black because we share a certain set of essential or natural properties. We are Black because we share a history. That history is a history of ruins, brokenness, nothingness, a psychological, spiritual, and existential void. We are (as Morrison points out) the invisible Africanist presence against which White identity is formed. Blackness is not merely skin color, a style of music, a style of speech, and so on, it is most significantly a type of pain, a particular historical catastrophe. It is the type of pain that horrifies the angel of history in the Klee painting. The angel does not see the historical progress that is spoken of by the oppressors, but rather, he sees the pain and brutality suffered by African Americans. He sees Blackness and history as the mark of Black identity.

It is in terms of Benjamin's notion of the ruins of history that we may understand the problem of solidarity and find some solution to it. I recognize or identify another as Black in terms of a shared history. We call ourselves Black because we bear the marks of a historical event and attitude. We inherit a traumatized consciousness. We are the ruins of history, the broken and ostracized.

THE ETHICAL TASK OF SELF-CREATION (IDENTITY FORMATION)

When we think of history, we think of something that is contingent, not necessary. That is, things could have been otherwise. There are theories of history to the contrary, but in our day the notion that history is contingent seems to be the dominant view. I would argue that this view is correct if we take seriously the notion of human agency. To most of us, it would seem absurd to talk about invisible historical forces that made slavery necessary. However, there is no time to enter that debate here. My point here is that what we refer to as Black identity is the result of contingent, historical, political, economic human forces. As such, it harbors many possible ways of being, all of which stem from a common source that for African Americans is the institution of slavery and racial discrimination.

Racial discrimination presupposes the political and social construction of race. We must remember that the Africans that were sold into slavery were from many different tribes with many different languages, customs, belief, and religions. Africa is not a monolithic culture, but rather, is quite diverse. Hence, even an appeal to our African heritage does not produce a solidarity based on essentialism or some sort of homogenous culture. It is no secret that the concept of race was constructed by Europeans on the basis of a few shared characteristics among the Africans. Other properties or characteristics were constructed and attributed to them for political and socioeconomic purposes. The blackness of the skin of the Africans was just one of those insignificant accidental properties that they shared in common. However, this black skin was taken to be a signifier of other properties that justified the institution of slavery for White oppressors.

What then, is the task that lies before us as African Americans, as victims of racial discrimination? We must first realize that the very existence of systems of domination and discrimination are symptomatic of a fractured humanity. Humanity is fractured on two accounts. First, those who are the victims of systems of domination are a fractured humanity to the extent that they have been barred from those human activities that enhance fulfillment, well being, and self-actualization. Second, the oppressors represent a fractured humanity to the extent that in their treatment of others they destroy humanity in general. They act in an inhuman way toward other human beings. The task before us then is to strive to restore humanity in ourselves and in others. The restoration of humanity in oneself is nothing more than what I have called self-creation or identity formation, which is indeed, a uniquely human activity.

The problem of Black identity and self-creation is manifest at an individual and a group level. It has been stated that there already exist a Black identity and Black solidarity in terms of a shared history. However, this history is a history of ruins from which we are challenged to create ourselves. Self-creation is a matter of the way in which one responds to one's situation. My historical and social situation is the raw material of my existence wherein I begin my project of self-creation. There is no ready-made identity for me that I simply pick up and wear. My identity is formed through my response to my situation. We all find ourselves situated in a world with many possible ways of being, many possible ways of responding. These possibilities are what the phenomenologists refer to as the horizon of being. My identity is formed in terms of the choices I make from the possibilities that are before me. There are no black and white possibilities. That is, no thing is simply "a Black thing" or a "White thing." For example, neither tennis nor golf is a "White thing." They are possibilities for anyone interested in them.

It is the nature of oppression to shut the oppressed group off from possible ways of being in the world that are uniquely human possibilities. In other words, one is denied his or her position as a legitimate member of the species. Racism denies Blacks the right to flourish as human beings by viewing us as subhuman. The task that the oppressed person faces is the ethical task of claiming and developing his or her humanity. Any attempt to define the individual as a member of a group and in isolation from humanity in general is unethical and oppressive. The problem with this claim is that it sounds as if I am suggesting that the notion of Black identity is an unethical illusion. It is still not clear how one affirms one's Black identity while also affirming one's more general human identity. We have seen how Black identity may be affirmed on a historical basis. But how is this consistent with the demand that one freely determines oneself? That is, how is one to affirm a broad horizon of possibilities while maintaining solidarity with the Black community?

The history that African Americans share provides them with a shared situation. In existentialist terms one is always in a situation. However, it is one's situation that provides one with the context and raw material for self-creation. We do not simply live in a situation but we respond to our situation, we transform our situations and ourselves. The material with which we begin our process of self-creation is not material that has been provided by a privileged existence, but rather, it is fragmented material, leftovers, waste, ruins. Benjamin's angel of history wishes to gather unto himself the ruins of history and create from these ruins a thing of beauty. The angel recognizes the creative potential that lies in the ruins. What is it that differentiates the angel of history from contemporary African Americans?

The angel of history was unable to restore the ruins of history because he was being blown backwards into the future by the storm called progress. The storm from which we suffer today is the storm called race. It is the idea of race as an essential determination of personhood that prevents us from restoring the ruins of history. Like the storm called progress, the storm called race is a tool of destruction that was created by the oppressors for the purpose of surreptitiously blinding and paralyzing the oppressed. That is, the idea of progress conceals from us the devastation suffered by the oppressed—the ruins of history—while the essentialist idea of race conceals from us our potential for self-creation as human beings.

African Americans live, move, and have their being in the ruins of history. It is here where we identify ourselves as a people. As individuals, though, our interests, talents, and goals may be quite diverse. The idea of ruins is opposed to any notion of a fixed structure (or essence) in this case. Ruins are disorganized and dispersed piles of debris. It is the task of each individual to restore this debris, that is, to restore humanity, to mend broken pieces, to construct one's self from the wreckage of history. The identities that are formed by African Americans through this process may be quite diverse.

This brings me to what I call the task of ethical self-determination, which is nothing more than the freedom that individuals have to grow, develop, and flourish in ways that are possible for human beings given the proper conditions. Self-determination is an ethical task rather than a selfish pursuit to the extent that it has an intersubjective dimension. The emphasis that I have placed on the freedom of the individual to determine or create him- or herself seems to suggest some form of radical individualism. This is not the case. Self-determination does not drive a wedge between the individual and others; rather, it binds people together by offering them a vision of a future horizon wherein humanity itself may develop beyond its present stage. Ethical self-determination is not traditional individualism to the extent that the traditional notion of individualism puts the individual against other individuals in the context of a fight for dominance. Ethical self-determination recognizes an originary bond that we share as members of the human species and adumbrates the possibility of an emancipated future. The person who strives for ethical self-determination recognizes that even his or her awareness of him- or herself as an individual is rooted in intersubjectivity. That is, I am aware of myself as an individual only to the extent that I am not only aware of the way in which I differ from other people, but I am also aware of what I share in common with others. Individuality rides on the back of intersubjectivity.

Individualism understood as ethical self-determination requires not only awareness of what one is, but it also requires an awareness of one's possibilities. The possibilities for future development for the individual are always uniquely human possibilities. These possibilities are not properties that are possessed by a single individual, instead, they are shared by an entire species. The individual's consciousness of his or her potential presupposes consciousness of human potential in general. Hence, I am never merely aware of myself as an individual, but I am aware of myself as part of the human species. My potential for growth and development is the potential of the species. Whatever is possible for me is possible for humanity and vice versa.

The ethical dimension of self-determination qualifies as such only if three conditions are met. First, the growth and development of the individual is necessary. Second, the growth and development of the individual is not possible in isolation from other human beings. Third, the individual must not hinder the growth and development of other individuals for the sake of his or her own self-interest.

Ethical thinking implies the concept of a goal, an "ought." Therefore, self-determination, or in this context identity formation, is a task, something to be accomplished. Thus, there is no ready-made essential identity that one naturally fits into. We have before us the task of creating ourselves. Under the institution of slavery and systems of oppression, African Americans were not allowed to exercise the basic human need of self-determination. The task of overcoming systems of oppression includes overcoming psychological dispositions that were produced by these systems of oppression. That is, it has been instilled in African Americans that we are not capable of free self-determination. This way of thinking persists in the African American community in the form of a reessentialized notion of Blackness. This reessentialized Blackness is a remnant of a slave mentality and a fear of freedom.

RECONSTRUCTION AND HORROR

The fear of freedom that is experienced in the African American community may be best understood by a return to Benjamin. The angel of history in the Paul Klee painting looks at the pile of ruins before him with horror. This horror reveals the trauma involved in looking at the ruins. Suppose that the angel of history is Black. What the angel sees in the pile of ruins is his own expulsion from the human race. He sees what appears to be the impossibility of ever reclaiming personhood. He wants to go back and fix and repair the things that have been broken, even though the task appears to be insurmountable and overwhelming. However, the wind that propels the angel backwards is far too violent, so much so, that he eventually loses hope.

The reessentialization of Blackness by Blacks is a giving up in the face of what appears to be an impossible task. This new reessentialized Blackness at least allows one to seek the comfort of bad faith.[7] Once an essentialist notion of Blackness is accepted, one manages to escape the apparent impossible task of self-creation. This position eventually proves to be hopeless as well as oppressive.

Human individuals may have a multiplicity of interests that are not completely determined by race. Nevertheless, present social structures seem to suggest that these interests are racially determined. While it may be the case that members of a specific race may be predisposed to certain types of music, clothing, foods, and so on, it is not the case that there is some hidden natural law that determines these interests. It is quite conceivable that a Black youth raised in Harlem may be interested in the music of Johann Sebastian Bach while a White youth raised in the suburbs may be moved by the music of James Brown and Aretha Franklin. Unfortunately, many of us were raised to distinguish between "White" and "Black" music. To listen to "White" music is to attempt to be White. Many African American youth who have the potential to become powerful intellects are choked out by pressure from peers who think that reading William Shakespeare, Ralph Waldo Emerson, or Plato is a waste of time and "is for Whites anyway." Hence, many African Americans are afraid that if they pursue interests or express themselves in ways that have not been sanctioned by other African Americans as "Black ways of being" they betray the race. These individuals are prohibited by other African Americans from flourishing in ways that are appropriate for human beings.

African Americans face the difficult task of reconstructing themselves from the ruins of history. The future emancipation of African Americans depends on the seriousness with which individuals approach this task of reconstruction or identity formation. That we start with ruins, a disordered pile of debris, means we all start from a position that is a little different from others. Nevertheless, it is the particular ruins that stand as our starting place and bind us together as African Americans.

REDEMPTIVE VISION AND IDENTITY FORMATION

Although the notion of historical ruins is a helpful pedagogical metaphor, it has the potential to be misleading. That is, it seems as if the history that African Americans share is rather bleak. However, the notion of historical ruins should not be considered only in terms of its negative connotations. The history that African Americans share is not only a history of pain and agony. Anyone who has lived in the African American community is well aware of this. African Americans share not only pain, but a common joy as well. It is our common pain and joy that bind us together as a race in a way that is historical, social, and communal rather than natural or essential. Historical ruins always entail moments of hope, joy, love, and possible redemption. It is with respect to this notion of possible redemption that I turn to another important aspect of Benjamin's thought.

The theme of redemption runs through all of Benjamin's philosophical works. Redemption as discussed by Benjamin combines the Jewish notion of messianic redemption with the Marxist concept of revolutionary praxis. Unlike the Christian notion of redemption or messianism (which stresses internal salvation), Benjamin's notion of redemption does not allow for any differentiation between external and internal salvation.[8] It is only through the redemption of history that individuals are redeemed internally and externally. That is, redemption is not merely the internal salvation of the individual, it is also the redemption of a situation or condition that is the product of human agency. Redemption of our historical situation requires a critical view of history.

This critical view of history Benjamin calls materialistic historiography, or in more Marxist terms, historical materialism. This view is contrasted with historicism that views history as a progressive continuum. The critical view of history that Benjamin advocates recognizes the discontinuity in history. Indeed, it is the perspective of the oppressed. Benjamin writes:

> Materialistic historiography, on the other hand, is based on a constructive principle. Thinking involves not only the flow of thoughts, but their arrest as well. Where thinking suddenly stops in a configuration pregnant with tensions, it gives that configuration a shock, by which it crystallizes into a monad. A historical materialist approaches a historical subject only where he encounters it as a monad. In this structure he recognizes the sign of a Messianic cessation of happening, or, put differently, a revolutionary chance in the fight for the oppressed past.[9]

Consciousness of the discontinuity of history is an awareness that history is not a continuum. The angel of history does not see history as a continuum in terms of progress, but rather, he sees history as one single catastrophe. History is crystallized before the angel. That is, the notion that history is a progressive continuum portrays history as a perpetual movement from one event or stage to another. However, once the movement of history is crystallized into a thought that no longer flows from one thought or event to another, a feature of history is revealed that was hitherto concealed. One sees that what has remained constant in history is the domination of one group by another. "Progress" has always produced pain for the oppressed. This point has been made already. The point that I wish to stress here is that what is also revealed in this view of history is the potential for revolutionary praxis.

Benjamin refers to this view of history as crystallized as "now time" (*Jetztzeit*).[10] "Now time" does not merely refer to the present, but also to the making present of the past. It is through memory that the past is made present. This "memory" is contrasted to the "forgetting" of which the oppressors are guilty. Ultimately, a battle is waged between the oppressors and the oppressed "over who will control the historical past as it lives on in the memory of humanity."[11] With respect to this battle for control of the historical past, Susan A. Handelman writes:

> The belief in science and progress led to a devaluation of the past and orientation toward the future. In the nineteenth century, the consciousness of modernity became radicalized, and the past and present bitterly opposed. The search for the new now valorizes transitory phenomena and represents a desire for a kind of

fulfilled present moment (as in Benjamin's "now time"). This present is a subversive force which seeks to explode the continuum of tradition and history.[12]

While the oppressors want to insist on forgetting the past and marching on toward their future "destiny," the oppressed bear the marks of the past in their pain that is very present. However, since the past is always present to the oppressed, there is always the possibility of redeeming the past through revolution in the present. Hence, the oppressed hold on to the past in hope for redemption. To the oppressed, history is contingent and is not driven by unseen, necessary forces. History is the product of human agency and as such can be redirected by human agents through revolutionary praxis. Once history is seen as discontinuous and contingent, the victors of history lose their power over the oppressed. Benjamin writes: "Historicism contents itself with establishing a causal connection between various moments in history. But no fact that is a cause is for that very reason historical. It became historical posthumously, as it were, through events that may be separated from it by thousands of years."[13]

The historicist ascribes the element of necessity to contingent historical events after the fact. Every historical event could have been otherwise. Events unfold in the way that they do because of human agency and not because of historical necessity. When the oppressed take this view of history, they become aware of their own agency and their potential to act against what appears to be the flow of history. From this standpoint then one can see in each moment of history glimpses of possible redemption.

Benjamin continues: "A historian who takes this as his point of departure stops telling the sequence of events like the beads of a rosary. Instead, he grasps the constellation which his own era has formed with a definite earlier one. Thus he establishes a conception of the present as the 'time of the now' which is shot through with chips of Messianic time."[14] The most interesting thing about this passage is its implications for the formation of a historical identity. The historian that Benjamin mentions here is the oppressed, or for that matter, the angel of history. Since the historian no longer sees history as a sequence of events determined by necessary forces, he or she is able to extirpate from history certain moments or events that he or she identifies with and that are no longer merely the past, but rather, form a constellation that is very present to him or her. To the extent that a historical event or moment exists only in terms of human groups and their activities, the historian in extirpating from history a moment or an event also extirpates from history and identifies with a group of people. The pain, hopes, joys, and mission of that people are embodied in the present in the life of the historian. The historian carries with him or her the dream of emancipation that was also embodied by a former era.

Contemporary African Americans share with African Americans of the past an emancipatory interest. This interest binds us together in terms of a common pain and joy as we contemplate possible redemption. African Americans of past eras are bound to contemporary African Americans to the extent that as they looked toward the future they envisioned us as the redemptive moment in African American history. Contemporary African Americans are bound to those of a past era insofar as our redemption is grounded in the efforts and visions of past eras. However, as we look toward the ruins of the past we weep as we see the catastrophe that has been our history, and we sing with joy as we contemplate the moments of "messianic time"—moments of possible redemption that beat in the breast of our ancestors. With our backs toward the future, we must reconstruct the past so that our story is retold and that in the retelling of our story the future is given a shape that it would otherwise not have. This means that who we are is yet to be seen.

NOTES

1. This claim is based on some studies that I did on neurosis several years ago. The works of Karen Horney, Abraham Maslow, and Otto Fenichel were particularly important for my studies. A passage from the work of Maslow may make clear the link between the psychoanalytic theory of neurosis and my description of pathological self-conception: "that neurosis seemed at its core, and in its beginning, to be a deficiency disease; that it was born out of being deprived of certain satisfactions which I call needs in the same sense that water and amino acids and calcium are needs, namely that their absence produces illness. Most neurosis involved, along with other complex determinants, ungratified wishes for safety, for belongingness and identification, for close love relationships and for respect and prestige." See Abraham Maslow, *Toward a Psychology of Being* (New York: Van Nostrand Reinhold, 1968), 21.

2. One of the common strategies used by racists to justify racism is to claim that physical type determines character. It was believed that these views could be supported by science. For an interesting critique of this way of thinking, see Tzvetan Todorov, *On Human Diversity: Nationalism, Racism and Exoticism in French Thought*, trans. Catherine Porter (Cambridge, Mass.: Harvard University Press, 1994); see also Sander L. Gilman and Nancy Leys Stepan, "Appropriating the Idioms of Science: The Rejection of Scientific Racism," in *The Bounds of Race: Perspectives on Hegemony and Resistance*, ed. Dominick Lacapra (Ithaca, N.Y.: Cornell University Press, 1991), 72–103

3. In her essay "Black Identity: Liberating Subjectivity," bell hooks writes: "Narrowly focused black identity politics do a disservice to black liberation struggle because they seek to render invisible the complex and multiple subjectivity of black folks. . . . The contemporary crisis of identity is best resolved by our collective willingness as African Americans to acknowledge that there is no monolithic black community, no normative black identity. There is a shared history that frames the construction of our diverse black experiences." See bell hooks, "Black Identity: Liberating Subjectivity," in *Killing Rage: Ending Racism* (New York: Henry Holt, 1995), 247. Racial essentialism, whether it be done by White racists or Blacks, functions to deny the subjectivity of individual

Blacks. For the sake of liberation, racial essentialism must be rejected by African Americans. This point is also made by Michael Eric Dyson, "Essentialism and the Complexities of Racial Identity," in *Multiculturalism: A Critical Reader*, ed. David T. Goldberg (Oxford: Blackwell, 1994), 218–229.

4. Walter Benjamin, *Illuminations*, trans. Harry Zohn, ed. Hannah Arendt (New York: Schocken, 1968), 257–258.

5. In his seventh "Thesis on the Philosophy of History," Benjamin writes: "There is no document of civilization which is not at the same time a document of barbarism. And just as such a document is not free of barbarism, barbarism taints also the manner in which it is transmitted from one owner to another." See Benjamin, *Illuminations*, 256. History as told from the perspective of the victors is barbaric to the extent that it conceals the truth, that is, it refuses to recognize and disclose the abuse that certain groups have suffered at the hands of the victors. We will see later that there is a battle for history between the victors and the oppressed.

6. With respect to American literature, Morrison writes: "Through significant and underscored omissions, startling contradictions, heavily nuanced conflicts, through the way writers peopled their work with signs and bodies of this presence—one can see that a real or fabricated Africanist presence was crucial to their sense of Americanness." See Toni Morrison, *Playing in the Dark: Whiteness and the Literary Imagination* (New York: Vintage, 1993), 6.

7. The notion of "bad faith" is developed by Jean-Paul Sartre, *Being and Nothingness*, trans. Hazel Barnes (New York: Washington Square, 1956), chapter two. According to Sartre, human beings have the potential to negate themselves by lying to themselves. This idea is used in an analysis of racism by Lewis Gordon, *Bad Faith and Antiblack Racism* (Highlands N.J.: Humanities, 1995). In toto, "bad faith" refers to an attempt by an individual to escape an unpleasant or threatening situation by pretending that he or she has transcended the situation. That is, the person in bad faith forms a concept of him- or herself that is not the real embodied self in the situation. With respect to the reessentialization of Blackness, many African Americans are in bad faith to the extent that they attempt to form a concept of Blackness that is an abstract, reified concept of Blackness that does not take seriously the concrete situation that we are in.

8. This view of redemption is characteristic of Jewish thought and is shared by Benjamin and his friend and fellow Jew Gershom Scholem. With respect to Scholem's understanding of this matter, Susan A. Handelman writes: "Scholem argues that the distinguishing characteristic of Jewish messianism is that its activist stirrings are directed outward, in contrast to the Christian tendency to make redemption first and foremost an inward affair." See Susan A. Handelman, *Fragments of Redemption: Jewish Thought and Literature in Benjamin, Scholem, and Levinas* (Bloomington: Indiana University Press, 1991), 155.

9. Benjamin, *Illuminations*, 262–263.

10. Benjamin, *Illuminations*, 261.

11. Richard Wolin, *Walter Benjamin: An Aesthetic of Redemption* (Los Angeles: University of California Press, 1994), 50.

12. Handelman, *Fragments of Redemption*, 153–154.

13. Benjamin, *Illuminations*, 263.

14. Benjamin, *Illuminations*, 263.

2

To Be or Not to Be Black: Problematics of Racial Identity

Kevin Cokley

There is a saying that it is not so important what name you are called, but what name you respond to. In terms of so-called Black people, this statement speaks to a sometimes tempestuous racial consciousness that has served to both unify and divide Black people in the United States. Indeed, this tempestuous racial consciousness has been metaphorically referred to as a psychological storm.[1] While the issue of identity is important to all people as a function of being human, it is particularly salient for African Americans because of enslavement, which sought to eradicate all vestiges of an African identity. Self-identification has been an emotionally charged issue that has haunted African Americans for over 400 years. To many, it speaks to the ideology, philosophy, and politics of an individual. Indeed, it represents an individual's essence. The ability to define oneself and one's reality represents a fundamental, existential requirement for being fully human. In an existential sense, to be fully human requires that an individual or people exhibit agency. By agency it is meant that an individual or people have the freedom to be self-defining and self-determining.

The ideological battles surrounding a Black racial identity have at times been very acerbic. Particularly problematic about these ideological clashes is the sentiment felt by some that one is either "Black" or "not Black." Whether used literally or figuratively, the sentiment poses many problems and impediments toward intragroup racial unity. The thesis that is advanced in this chapter is that subscribing to a Black racial identity often leads to Black racial essentialism, which is, more often than not, rooted in some form of what Audrey Smedley calls a racial worldview.[2] While it may be possible to have a racial identity that is not rooted in a racial worldview, the probability is very low that this in fact is the case. Because of the history and reality of race-based prejudice and discrimination, it is most likely that a strong Black racial identity will often times rely on essentialist notions of Blackness. While a strong Black racial identity is deemed psychologically healthy by most Black psychologists, Black racial essentialism is more ambiguous in terms of its benefits to African Americans.

Most discussions surrounding the pitfalls of racialized thinking analyze its impact on intergroup relations (i.e., Black–White relations). Very few discussions analyze the pitfalls of racialized thinking on intragroup relations (i.e., Black–Black relations). This chapter reviews the history of the construct of race and racial self-identification in the African American community. The impact of a Black racial identity within the African American community is also explored. Specifically, I argue that the emphasis of a Black racial identity over an African cultural/ethnic identity is fraught with problems and ultimately leads to an orthodoxy of Black racial essentialism. Black racial essentialism prohibits the intragroup unity that it seeks, whereas an African ethnic/cultural identity is psychologically more healthy, philosophically less problematic, and more facilitative of group solidarity.

HISTORY OF THE RACE CONSTRUCT

In the context of human history, the term "race" is fairly new, having only been introduced into the European vocabulary in the eighteenth century. Prior to this time period, there is no evidence of its usage among Africans anywhere in the Diaspora. This is a significant point because Africans preceded Europeans historically by thousands of years without ever developing an ideology or social system based on physiognomy. This is not to say that Africans were not involved in wars, systems of servitude, and other acts of mistreatment against fellow Africans. (Hu)mans' mistreatment of other (hu)mans is characteristic of the past 5,000 years of history in most societies and cultures.[3] However, the rigid and exclusionist ideology of race evolved exclusively with Europeans in North America.[4] While Africa was a diverse continent in terms of the different ethnic groups, languages spoken, and spiritual systems practiced, there was a cultural unity[5] that allowed for an African worldview that did not facilitate a spirit of conquest, exploitation, and enslavement of people based on such an arbitrary physical marker as skin color. However, a historical survey of European thought and culture reveals a worldview that has justified acts of aggression against African and other indigenous people in the name of expansion and exploration.[6] This justification was clothed in the language of rugged individualism and survival of the fittest, the latter of which fuels the White supremacist ideology of superiority.

Specifically, how did the term "race" and the subsequent racial classifications become a part of scientific consciousness? The concept of race became codified in the late eighteenth century as a result of a racial taxonomic classification first developed by Carolus Linnaeus (who was also known as Carl von Linné). Stephen J. Gould provides a historical account that starts with Johann Friedrich Blumenbach, a German anatomist and naturalist who was mentored by Carolus Linnaeus.[7] Blumenbach invented the most influential of all racial classifications in his seminal work *On the Natural Variety of Mankind.* He initially divided all humans into four groups (based on Carolus Linnaeus's four-race classification): Caucasian, Mongolian, Ethiopian, and American. Blumenbach deviated from Carolus Linnaeus, his mentor, by adding a fifth race: the Malay race. Blumenbach's taxonomy was hierarchical and defined primarily by physical beauty, whereas Linnaeus's taxonomy was defined primarily by geography, with no explicit rank ordering. According to Blumenbach, the closer a racial group lived to the Caucasus Mountains, the more physically attractive (and implicitly, more superior) they were in comparison to other races.

Although the language that Linnaeus used to characterize each race undeniably had racist overtones (i.e., Americans and Europeans were ruled by habit and custom, while the African was ruled by caprice), the overt geometry of his model was neither hierarchical nor linear.[8] In short, Linnaeus's taxonomy, in spite of its obvious biases, made no attempt to infer psychological and behavioral traits from physical characteristics. In light of this, Blumenbach's actions became even more consequential. The significance of Blumenbach's actions are best summed up by Gould:

> Blumenbach's apparently small change actually records a theoretical shift that could not have been broader, or more portentous, in scope. This change has been missed or misconstrued because later scientists have not grasped the vital historical and philosophical principle that theories are models subject to visual representation, usually in clearly definable geometric terms. By moving from the Linnaean four-race system to his own five-race scheme, Blumenbach radically changed the geometry of human order from a geographically based model without explicit ranking to a hierarchy of worth, oddly based upon perceived beauty, and fanning out in two directions from the Caucasian ideal. The addition of a Malay category was crucial to this geometric reformulation—and therefore becomes the key to the conceptual transformation rather than a simple refinement of factual information within an old scheme. Blumenthal's addition of the Malay race was not a minor, factual refinement but rather a device for reformulating an entire theory of human diversity. With this one stroke, he produced the geometric transformation from Linnaeus' unranked geographic model to the conventional hierarchy of implied worth that has fostered so much social grief ever since.[9]

The problem with this racial taxonomy, of course, is that the boundaries between races are not so clear cut. Biologically speaking, the genetic variability (i.e., genotype) within racial groups is almost as great as, if not equal to, the genetic variability between racial groups.[10] In fact, it has been estimated that almost two-thirds of African Americans have European blood and another two-fifths have American Indian blood,[11] while other estimates are more conservative, usually estimating the contribution of genetic material of Europeans and American Indians to be around 20 percent to 30 percent.[12] The ambiguity and tenuousness of the race construct is reflected in the facts that there is no consensus within the scientific community on the number of races[13] and that the physical expression of genes (i.e., phenotypes) that usually defines races can vary tremendously within races.[14] Echoing the sentiments of James Shreeve, "there are no traits that are inherently, inevitably associated with one another."[15] For example, the epicanthic folds (i.e., slanted eyes) that are normally associated with Asians are also found among the Khoisan tribe of southern Africa.[16] The point is that race, contrary to popular belief, is not a biological truth but rather a social construction that historically has been used and contemporarily is still being used to justify White supremacy and oppression. The unscientific way in which Blumenbach's racial taxonomy developed supports the notion that race is socially, rather than biologically, constructed.

Out of this racial taxonomy eventually evolved a racialized worldview. Smedley defines the following as constituent elements of a racial worldview:

1. Humans (universally) are classified as exclusive and discrete biotic entities
2. An inegalitarian ethos that requires the ranking of human groups against one another is imposed
3. That the outer physical characteristics of different human populations are but surface manifestations of inner realities (i.e., behavioral, intellectual, temperamental, moral, and other qualities)
4. All of the aforementioned qualities are inheritable
5. That each exclusive group (i.e., race) was created unique and distinct by nature or by God, so that the imputed differences, which are believed to be fixed and unalterable, can never be bridged or transcended[17]

Smedley states that the term "race" came to be widely used in the English language during the latter part of the eighteenth century. And further contends that by the nineteenth century, all human groups could be subsumed arbitrarily into some "racial" category, depending on the objectives or goals of those establishing the classifications.[18] Thus, the somewhat dubious nature of the validity of race becomes highlighted by two facts: (1) its conspicuous absence from the worldview and cultural practices of ancient Africans, and (2) its recent development on the landscape of human history, as manifested in European thought and cultural practice.

BRIEF HISTORY OF SELF-DESIGNATION OF AFRICAN AMERICANS

Americans of African descent have gone through several names used to represent the "race." In 1619, when the first Africans were forcibly brought to Jamestown, Virginia, their self-referent was "Africans."[19] It must be noted that even though the enslaved Africans represented many different ethnic groups and many different languages, there was always the recognition that Africa was their common motherland. This was evidenced by the names given to their churches and organizations, such as the African Episcopal Church and the African Masonic Lodge No. 459. In fact, the first Black religious organization established was the First African Baptist Church in Savannah in 1787.[20] Other names that reflected their African identity include the African Free School, the Children of Africa, and the Sons of Africa.[21]

After realizing that their chances of returning to their precious motherland were remote, and to distinguish house servants from field servants, enslaved Africans began to call themselves "Colored."[22] This term was used throughout much of the nineteenth century. It was during this period that the National Association for the Advancement of Colored People was formed. Sometime during this period the term "negro" (a Portuguese adjective meaning "black") hit full stride. Booker T. Washington played a major role in getting the United States to use the word "negro" instead of "Colored."[23]

W. E. B. Du Bois attempted to bring some respect and dignity to the term by leading a massive effort to change "negro" to "Negro."[24] By 1930, the White media had started capitalizing the term. "Negro" was the term of choice until the revolutionary 1960s, when there was an explosion of Black consciousness and Black pride fueled by the civil rights movement, Black power movements, and African independence. "Black" became the preferred racial self-designation, and sayings like "Black is beautiful" and songs like "Say it loud, I'm Black and I'm proud" were in vogue.

In late 1988, the president of the National Urban Coalition proposed that the upcoming yearly summit be called the "African American" summit rather than the "Black" summit, because the name change would set a new agenda centered within a cultural context.[25] Along the way, there have been excursions of "Afro-American," "Afric-American," and there is a minority that prefers simply "African."

Thus, as Joseph E. Holloway notes, the debate on identity has come full circle, from "African" through "colored," "Negro," "Afro-American," and now "African American."[26] These changes in terminology reflect changes in consciousness, moving from a "strong African identification to nationalism, to integration, and attempts at assimilation back to cultural identification."[27] The ambiguity surrounding self-identification of African Americans is evidenced by a recent study by Suzette Speight, Elizabeth Vera, and Kimberly Derrickson. They examine the relationships among racial self-designation, racial identity attitudes, self-esteem, and demographic variables in a sample of 232 African Americans. Results revealed that there are significant differences in preferences for particular racial labels: 41 percent prefer "Black"; 30 percent, "African American"; 16 percent, "Afro-American"; 7 percent, "American"; 1.3 percent, "Negro"; and .9 percent, "African."[28] In a study on racial group concept and self-esteem in Black children, Maxine L. Clark contradicts conventional wisdom when she finds that there is no apparent relationship between the children's conception of themselves as racial beings and their self-esteem.[29] Notwithstanding the theoretical and methodological issues surrounding the ways self-esteem has been defined and measured,[30] racial identity and self-designation have been and continue to be important, complex, and divisive issues among African Americans.

WHAT CONSTITUTES A BLACK RACIAL IDENTITY?

Using Smedley's racial worldview theoretical framework, I want to examine more closely what typically constitutes a Black racial identity. It should be noted that while it is possible that one can have a Black racial identity without subscribing to any of these elements, the greater probability is that one subscribes to one or more of the elements.

The first element of a Black racial identity consists of the belief that humans (by virtue of their skin color and other physiognomic features) are exclusive and discrete biotic entities. Essentially, this means that there is some point embedded in skin color that delineates so-called Black people from non-Black people. This belief is a reductionistic conceptualization of what constitutes humanness that runs counter to the theme of interconnectedness of all life forms in an African cultural worldview.

The second element of a Black racial identity consists of the belief that all races are not equal. This belief necessarily entails a ranking of races against one another. Again, this hierarchical, competitive ideology runs counter to a traditional African cultural worldview. Instead, one finds a cooperative, communal ethos[31] that does not find it necessary to rank races for any purposes.

The third element of a Black racial identity consists of the belief that the outer physical characteristics of different races really represent surface manifestations of inner realities. In other words, black skin is correlated with high morals, high intellect, humane behavior, and so on. It must be acknowledged that the converse of this is also sometimes believed to be true, that is, black skin is correlated with low morals, low intellect, inhumane behavior, and so on. Out of this belief is born the admonition "Don't act your color!" Both propositions are problematic, because not all people with black skin exhibit high morality or humane behavior, just as not all people with black skin exhibit immorality or inhumane behavior.

The fourth element of a Black racial identity consists of the belief that the Black race inherited all of the aforementioned qualities (for better or for worse). Relatedly, the fifth element of a Black racial identity consists of the belief that the Black race was created unique and distinct by God, so that the differences between races are fixed and unalterable. This deterministic view of human groups truncates the range of African humanity in such a way that it either exaggerates the virtuous qualities of all black-skinned people or underestimates the moral qualities and possibilities of all black-skinned people. Again, both propositions are problematic, and ultimately lead to philosophical and psychological quandaries for African Americans.

BLACK RACIAL ESSENTIALISM DEFINED

Essentialism is the doctrine that objects have essences or properties that are immutable. By extension, racial essentialism would be the doctrine that humans are divided into biologically discrete races that have essential traits (i.e., intelligence, temperament, morality, and so on) that define and delimit the nature of their being.

Following this line of reasoning, Black racial essentialism is the doctrine that Black people have essential attributes that define the nature of all Black people. Black racial essentialism then goes one step further to state that not only do Black people have these essential attributes, but also that all Black people should be ideologically aligned. In this sense, Black racial essentialism is related to what has been called ontological Blackness, a term that connotes categorical, essentialist, and representational languages depicting Black life and experience.[32]

Although a causal relationship is not explicitly stated between essential attributes and ideology, an implicit correlation is sometimes drawn that allows for Black racial essentialists to spew vitriolic criticisms of "not being Black" (or some derivative thereof) against those who are ideologically at odds with them. Whether this statement is used literally or figuratively, it is problematic for the goal of Black unity.

Cornel West makes the following observation:

What is black authenticity? Who is really black? First, blackness has no meaning outside of a system of race-conscious people and practices. After centuries of racist degradation, exploitation, and oppression in America, being black means being minimally subject to white supremacist abuse and being part of a rich culture and community that has struggled against such abuse. *All black people with black skin and African phenotype are subject to potential white supremacist abuse.* Hence, all black Americans have some interest in resisting racism—even if their interest is confined solely to themselves as individuals rather than to larger black communities. . . . Hence any claim to black authenticity—beyond that of being a potential object of racist abuse and an heir to a grand tradition of black struggle—is contingent on one's political definition of black interest and one's ethical understanding of how this interest relates to individuals and communities in and outside black America. *In short, blackness is a political and ethical construct.*[33]

While West is correct in his assertion that Blackness is a political and ethical construct, his analysis of the condition of Black people is limited because of his preoccupation with race as opposed to culture. In his widely publicized book *Race Matters*, not once does he mention Africa or how the condition of Black people might be related to a historical ignorance and cultural amnesia.

Similarly, Michael Eric Dyson, a self-proclaimed cultural critic, is correct when he states that "[t]o this day, the narrative of racial unity has survived mainly as a rhetorical strategy of black intellectuals, artists, and leaders to impose provisional order on the perplexing and chaotic politics of racial identity."[34] However, his analysis is also incomplete in that it assumes that Black culture (here Dyson equates Black with only African Americans) has "its fragile origins in slavery."[35] In reality, Dyson's self-proclaimed moniker as a cultural critic is a misnomer, because he is really a racial critic masked in the vernacular of popular culture. In his quest to explicate Black identity, he falls short in articulating the African cultural retentions of African Americans that many argue represent the essence of Africans in America.

While West, Dyson, and other similarly minded "public intellectuals" eschew ideological thinking, particularly that which leads to Black racial essentialism, they appear to be oblivious to their own ideological propensity to ontologically define African Americans using the tripartite identity model of race, gender/sexual orientation, and class, as well as a primarily American nationalistic frame of reference, while leaving out culture (i.e., not popular culture). It must be pointed out that any model of African American identity will be heavily influenced by its author's experiences and personal belief system. That in and of itself does not make the model any more valid or virtuous than any other model. It simply means that the model is vulnerable to the same human biases that all human intellectual endeavors are subject to.

The primary thesis of this chapter is that Black racial essentialism prohibits the intragroup unity that it seeks. While the goal of creating a collective Black consciousness that will facilitate Black unity is laudable, some of the methodology that is employed in obtaining this goal leads to what West calls the "pitfalls of racial reasoning."[36]

Much, if not most, Black racial essentialist thinking subscribes to some version of what Smedley has called a racial worldview. In terms of Smedley's constituent elements of a racial worldview, Black racial essentialists are particularly drawn to the belief that the outer physical characteristics of different human populations (i.e., the melanin that provides the presence of color) are equivalent to the surface manifestations of inner realities. In other words, the very presence of black or white skin means that an individual is prone to thinking, acting, and feeling a certain way.

Stephen Asma speaks to this issue in some detail. He makes the following observations:

> What all this means for racial thinking is that a theoretical framework is established by which internal essences can manifest themselves in the phenomenal experiential realm. . . . The external becomes an expression of the internal. More precisely, the inner becomes the outer. Thus, Hegel's discussion of physiognomy and phrenology in the Phenomenology takes on significance for our exploration of internal and external metaphors.
>
> Physiognomy, Hegel claims, links the inner conscious character of the individual to its embodied organic shape in a necessary and "lawful" fashion. He claims that the outward shape of the individual "stands as an expression of his own actualization established by the individual himself, it bears the lineaments and forms of his spontaneously active being."[37]

At this point comes the heart of the problem. It seems, then, that a preoccupation with a racial identity invariably leads to categorical and ideological thinking. When a Black individual expresses a differing or dissenting viewpoint from the Black racial essentialist on an issue that is deemed particularly important in the lives and well being of Black people, that individual first becomes racially castigated. If this does not cause a change in his viewpoint, he then becomes racially ostracized. In other words, if after verbal chastisement the individual does not come around to the Black racial essentialist way of thinking, he or she is denied the right and privileges, if you will, of membership into the "Black" community. The presumption is that one's Blackness prescribes how one should walk, talk, think, feel, and act. When one violates any of these norms, one is punished by the Black racial essentialist orthodoxy.

Social–psychological empirical studies conducted on majority and minority influences in problem solving and decision making have found that when groups are dominated by majority influences, there is an overwhelming tendency to engage in convergent thinking, that is, uniformity of thought.[38] This phenomenon is also popularly known as "group think."

In terms of problem solving, convergent thinking generates fewer and less creative solutions.[39] However, when groups have both majority and minority influences, the minority presence generates divergent thinking, that is, diversity of opinions.[40] In problem solving, divergent thinking generates both a greater number of solutions to problems as well as more creative solutions.[41] When this is applied to issues concerning the Black community, such as identity and nihilism, Black racial essentialist thinking has a tendency to be convergent. This convergence, in addition to not welcoming new perspectives and generating creative solutions that could help the Black community, breeds enmity within the community. In other words, the convergent thinking stifles communication and diversity of ideas and creates latent or manifest resentment that infects the entire Black community.

This resentment is particularly resonant with Black women, as they are often times asked to overlook instances of sexist attitudes and behavior for the greater good of racial allegiance. One example would be the Clarence Thomas and Anita Hill fiasco. Many Black racial essentialists (e.g., Louis Farrakhan), in supporting Clarence Thomas, reasoned that he had to be supported and even defended from the racialized onslaught he was getting in the White media. This support came in spite of his rather lackluster record dealing with African Americans. In spite of concrete evidence that Thomas was not telling the truth, many Black racial essentialists chose to overlook Thomas's questionable moral integrity and dubious existential connections to the African American community all in the name of racial solidarity.

If Black racial solidarity is ever justified, it should only be when it is principled, not ideological. Principled racial solidarity would entail a deep, abiding, and critical love for one's socially ascribed racial group (i.e., more correctly referred to as ethnic group) that is based on a culturally sensitive moral consciousness that provides a guiding sense of right conduct. This right conduct is understood within the context of norms, beliefs, and values of the culture. For example, behavior and values that do not advance the best interests of the group (i.e., rugged individualism) should be critiqued and ultimately negatively evaluated. Ideological racial solidarity usually entails a deep, steadfast, and noncritical love for one's socially ascribed racial group that is based on the tenets of blind racial allegiance. Ideological racial solidarity can also entail a shallow, conditional, and noncritical love for one's socially ascribed racial group that is also based on the tenets of blind racial allegiance.

For example, many African Americans' response to O. J. Simpson was that of a hero, someone who had withstood the onslaught of racism with his head bloodied, but unbowed. This response was shallow and noncritical in that once again, here was an African American man who had very dubious existential connections to the African American community, yet he was not held accountable for this. The response was conditional because before Simpson could endear himself to the hearts of African Americans, he had to change his image from a raceless American icon to a pro-Black African American man who had been a victim of a White racist cover-up.

Relatedly and ironically, Christopher Darden, one of the lawyers for the prosecution, was lambasted on many Black radio stations and in Black newspapers as being an "Uncle Tom" and a tool for White racism. This response by the Black racial essentialist was shallow and noncritical because the essentialist failed to take into consideration Darden's commitment to improving the quality of life for the African American community by prosecuting drug dealers who were destroying Black communities. While it may be argued that it was Darden's complaining about Johnny Cochran's tactics that made him lose favor in the Black community, the more probable reason is that he dared to challenge the conventional "Golden Rule" of Black racial essentialist thinking. The unspoken "Golden Rule" states that when a prominent African American comes under attack from "the White Man," regardless of the validity of the accusation, all Black people should be aligned based on a racial imperative, rather than a moral and ethical imperative.

Another salient example would be many African Americans' response to Mike Tyson when he was convicted of raping Desiree Washington. The response was deep and steadfast because, unlike Simpson, Tyson was perceived as being existentially connected to African Americans, therefore he was worthy of the intensity of support that he had. The response was noncritical because the evidence of Tyson's pervasive disrespect of Black women, as evidenced by the several well-documented instances of verbal and physical mistreatment, was ignored. Even if the facts surrounding the alleged rape are ambiguous and conflictual, Tyson's history of disrespect toward Black women should have raised the critical consciousness of his supporters to the point where Tyson would not have been presented as merely the victim of a racist White society with double standards.

These three examples show that the problem with ideological racial solidarity is that there is no moral accountability for behaviors that negatively impact the Black community. Black racial essentialism, in addition to fostering resentment among Black people, has no internally regulated mechanisms of moral accountability for the behavior of Black people by Black people. Thus, focusing on a Black racial identity lends itself to the racial worldview that one's black skin represents a surface manifestation of some inner reality of behavior, temperament, morality, ideology, and so on, and is thus worthy of racial allegiance.

I propose that instead of focusing on the slippery slope of a Black racial identity, a more useful and appropriate dialogue would use ethnicity as the primary referent point. Discourse about African Americans as an African ethnic group provides a sensitivity and responsiveness to historical, temporal, and political contexts that not only distinguishes African Americans from other ethnic groups, but also binds African Americans across time and space with other African ethnic groups. Ethnicity centers one in both the deep and surface structures of culture.[42] The deep structure of culture includes a group's epistemological, axiological, and cosmological orientation. The surface structure of culture includes those very visible and superficial aspects of culture, such as the type of foods typically eaten, music listened to, and religion practiced. *Race, while useful in understanding a particular group's social standing, centers one in a reactionary metaphysics that does little to elucidate the group's ethos or character.*

Black racial essentialists argue that essentialism is the only true solution to intragroup unity. They argue that there has to be a standard of Blackness that members of the Black community are held to if Black people are going to be uplifted from their marginalized and "unconscious" states to reach the pinnacle of Black achievement, progress, and consciousness that we aspire to. Black racial essentialists believe that this standard of Blackness is intrinsically and sufficiently moral, such that alternative conceptualizations of Blackness are threatening to the "homeostasis" they believe is created by essentialism.

Essentialist thinking is easily supported by documenting the many instances that White people have mistreated and aggressed against otherwise peaceful Black people. Because there is a clearly documentable pattern of White on Black aggression in the United States and various parts of the world,[43] Black racial essentialists sometimes argue that there is obviously something inherent in the nature (i.e., biogenetics) of White people that causes these acts of inhumanity. Conversely, there must be something in the nature of Black people that prevents them from such acts of inhumanity against White people. Therefore, essentialists' authoritative claims to "Blackness" are spuriously supported, in part, by history. Simply put, Black people have not, do not, and will not commit large-scale genocidal acts of aggression against White folks. For the Black racial essentialist this means that there is a protocol of Blackness that serves as the blueprint for Black behavior, Black attitudes, and even Black cognitions. A failure to adhere to this protocol of Blackness means chaos, confusion, and the continued demise of the Black community. In other words, if one really and truly allows oneself to rediscover his or her Blackness and to "be Black," "act Black," "think Black," and "feel Black," his or her very nature (i.e., race) will cause him or her to do those things that will ultimately benefit the Black community. Thus, Black racial essentialism is necessary for Black unity because it not only provides standards for measuring appropriate conduct and thinking, but it also provides historical and contemporary evidence that supports its claims.

My rebuttal is best expressed by the very simple statement that Black racial essentialism, or ontological Blackness, signifies the Blackness that Whiteness created.[44] Much, if not most, of the argument posed by the Black racial essentialist is reactionary in nature. This is certainly understandable given, as the Black racial essentialist correctly points out, the history of racial relations throughout the world. But while it is understandable, it is still inexcusable, for it lacks the very principled and ethical reasoning that it has so precisely noted is lacking in much of White people's attitudes and behavior toward Black people.

This reactionary ideology falls short of being labeled "Black racism" proper because Black people cannot and should not own a term that is so based in the history of European people's aggression against African people. However, this reactionary ideology can be criticized to the extent that by internalizing the White oppressor's racial mentality that outer traits = inner reality, the Black racial essentialist commits a similar faux pas against his community. That is to say, Black racial essentialist notions of what constitutes "Blackness" delimits and demoralizes the African American community by restricting divergent thought similarly to the way that White racial essentialist notions of "Whiteness" delimits and demoralizes the African American community through acts of racism, prejudice, and discrimination. Both actions restrict the African American's basic human right to be self-determining.

It must also be noted that some Black racial essentialists will use the rhetoric of Black pride to justify their reactionary ideology. Racial essentialist pride should not be confused with cultural pride. Racial essentialist pride entails a pride based in a doctrine that Black people have essential traits that not only define and delimit the nature of their being, but also the nature of their doing. An example of racial essentialist pride would be having pride in African American sprinters' dominance in track events because of the belief that "brothers are just naturally fast." Cultural pride is recognition and admiration of the many contributions people of African descent have made to the world. An example of cultural pride would be having pride about the creativity and brilliance of African American artists and musicians.

All racial pride is not essentialist pride, however. In fact, much of what is dubbed Black racial pride is really cultural pride. Additionally, Black racial essentialism is sometimes masked in the rhetoric of certain strands of African-centered or Afrocentric ideology. While espousing a philosophy that is based on the ancient Egyptian moral virtues of MAAT and African philosophy and culture, some African-centered proponents exhibit the same type of racial essentialist thinking that manifests itself in a rigidity and intolerance for alternative viewpoints. The lesson to be learned is that the truest expression of African-centered thinking does not have to be intolerant, because as the cardinal virtues of MAAT teach us, just as we should pursue truth, justice, reciprocity, and propriety, so should we also pursue balance, harmony, and order. Or, as Asa G. Hilliard states more correctly, we should seek "to become one with MAAT, the cosmic order."[45]

CONCLUSION

Racial identity politics have plagued African Americans for many years. The issue of self/group identification has brought with it emotionally laced categorizations of who is a legitimate member of the Black community. I have argued that an inherent characteristic of these categorizations is a racial worldview based on the belief that one's outer characteristics represent some inner temperamental, moral, behavioral, and ideological essence. For African Americans to even engage in the debate over what constitutes Blackness or

African Americanness presupposes that there is an objective answer that is both definable and measurable by some criteria.

Thinking that is dominated by race brings about conceptual confusion and ideological posturing that ultimately hurts, rather than helps, the African American community. A preoccupation with a racial identity invariably leads to ideological thinking, which has been shown to impede the very unity in the African American community that it seeks. An emphasis on an African ethnic/cultural identity results in the careful examination of much more than the "what" in identity, but the "who." In other words, in explicating the psychology of African Americans, a focus on African ethnicity would cause certain kinds of questions to be asked, namely: Are there certain behaviors, beliefs, values, customs, and traditions that represent the deep structure of African culture?

Thinking that is informed by ethnicity tempers Black racial essentialist tendencies by acknowledging that there can be any number of ethnic groups based on genetic traits and geographical location. Generally speaking, ethnically minded people have fewer essentialist tendencies and therefore are more likely to demonstrate principled, rather than ideological, group allegiance, while racially minded people are more prone to essentialist tendencies and therefore are more likely to demonstrate ideological racial allegiance.

NOTES

1. T. A. Parham, *Psychological Storms: The African American Struggle for Identity* (Chicago: African American Images, 1993).

2. A. Smedley, *Race in North America: Origin and Evolution of a Worldview* (San Francisco: Westview, 1993).

3. Smedley, *Race in North America*.

4. Smedley, *Race in North America*.

5. C. A. Diop, *The Cultural Unity of Black Africa* (Chicago: Third World Press, 1978); and M. K. Asante and K. W. Asante, *African Culture: The Rhythms of Unity* (Trenton, N.J.: African World Press, 1990).

6. M. Ani, *Yurugu: An Afrocentric Critique of European Cultural Thought and Behavior* (Trenton, N.J.: African World Press, 1993).

7. S. J. Gould, "The Geometer of Race," *Discover* (November 1994): 9.

8. Gould, 1994, 66–69.

9. Gould, 1994, 66–69.

10. K. A. Appiah and A. Gutmann, *Color Conscious: The Political Morality of Race* (Princeton, N.J.: Princeton University Press, 1996); and M. Wetherell and J. Potter, *Mapping the Language of Racism: Discourse and the Legitimation of Exploitation* (New York: Columbia University Press, 1992).

11. Appiah and Gutmann, *Color Conscious*.

12. J. Shreeve, "Terms of Estrangement," *Discover* (November 1994).

13. Smedley, *Race in North America*.

14. Shreeve, "Terms of Estrangement."

15. Shreeve, "Terms of Estrangement," 58.

16. Shreeve, "Terms of Estrangement."

17. Smedley, *Race in North America*, 27.

18. Smedley, *Race in North America*.

19. J. E. Holloway, *Africanisms in American Culture* (Bloomington: Indiana University Press, 1990).

20. Holloway, *Africanisms in American Culture*.

21. Holloway, *Africanisms in American Culture*.

22. G. Smitherman, *Black Talk: Words and Phrases from the Hood to the Amen Corner* (Boston: Houghton Mifflin, 1994); and Holloway, *Africanisms in American Culture*.

23. Holloway, *Africanisms in American Culture*.

24. Smitherman, *Black Talk*.

25. Smitherman, *Black Talk*.

26. Holloway, *Africanisms in American Culture*.

27. Holloway, *Africanisms in American Culture*, xix–xx.

28. S. L. Speight, E. M. Vera, and K. B. Derrickson, "Racial Self-Designation, Racial Identity, and Self-Esteem Revisited," *Journal of Black Psychology* 22 (1996).

29. M. L. Clark, "Racial Group Concept and Self-Esteem in Black Children," in *African American Psychology: Theory, Research, and Practice*, ed. A. K. Burlew et al. (Newbury Park, Calif.: Sage, 1992).

30. W. Cross, *Shades of Black: Diversity in African-American Identity* (Philadelphia: Temple University Press, 1991); and W. W. Nobles, "Extended Self: Rethinking the So-called Negro Self-Concept," *Journal of Black Psychology* 2 (2) (1976).

31. L. J. Myers, *Understanding an Afrocentric World View: An Introduction to an Optimal Psychology* (Dubuque: Kendall-Hunt, 1988); and W. W. Nobles, "African Philosophy: Foundations for Black Psychology," in *Black Psychology*, ed. R. Jones, 2nd ed. (New York: Harper and Row, 1988).

32. V. Anderson, *Beyond Ontological Blackness* (New York: Continuum, 1995).

33. Cornel West, *Race Matters* (Boston: Beacon, 1993), 25–26, emphasis mine.

34. Dyson, 1993, xv.

35. Dyson, 1993, xvii.

36. West, *Race Matters*.

37. S. Asma, "Metaphors of Race: Theoretical Presuppositions behind Racism," *American Philosophical Quarterly* 32 (1) (1995): 22.

38. C. J. Nemeth, "Differential Contributions of Majority and Minority Influence," *Psychological Review* 93 (1986).

39. Nemeth, "Differential Contributions."

40. Nemeth, "Differential Contributions."

41. Nemeth, "Differential Contributions."

42. A. G. Hilliard, *The Maroon within Us: Selected Essays on African American Community Socialization* (Baltimore, Md.: Black Classic Press, 1995).

43. Ani, *Yurugu*.

44. Anderson, *Beyond Ontological Blackness*.

45. Hilliard, *Maroon within Us*, 102.

REFERENCES

Anderson, V. *Beyond Ontological Blackness*. New York: Continuum, 1995.

Ani, M. *Yurugu: An Afrocentric Critique of European Cultural Thought and Behavior*. Trenton, N.J.: African World Press, 1993.

Appiah, K. A., and A. Gutmann. *Color Conscious: The Political Morality of Race*. Princeton, N.J.: Princeton University Press, 1996.

Asante, M. K., and K. W. Asante. *African Culture: The Rhythms of Unity*. Trenton, N.J.: African World Press, 1990.

Asma, S. "Metaphors of Race: Theoretical Presuppositions behind Racism." *American Philosophical Quarterly* 32 (1) (1995): 13–29.

Clark, M. L. "Racial Group Concept and Self-Esteem in Black Children." In *African American Psychology: Theory, Research, and Practice*, ed. A. K. Burlew et al. Newbury Park, Calif.: Sage, 1992.

Cross, W. *Shades of Black: Diversity in African-American Identity*. Philadelphia: Temple University Press, 1991.

Diop, C. A. *The Cultural Unity of Black Africa*. Chicago: Third World Press, 1978.

Dyson, M. E. *Reflecting Black: African American Cultural Criticism*. Minneapolis: University of Minnesota Press, 1995.

Gould, S. J. "The Geometer of Race." *Discover* (November 1994): 65–69.

Hilliard, A. G. *The Maroon within Us: Selected Essays on African American Community Socialization*. Baltimore, Md.: Black Classic Press, 1995.

Holloway, J. E. *Africanisms in American Culture*. Bloomington: Indiana University Press, 1990.

McLeish, K. *Key Ideas in Human Thought*. Rocklin, Calif.: Prima, 1993.

Myers, L. J. *Understanding an Afrocentric World View: An Introduction to an Optimal Psychology*. Dubuque: Kendall-Hunt, 1988.

Nemeth, C. J. "Differential Contributions of Majority and Minority Influence." *Psychological Review* 93 (1986): 23–32.

Nobles, W. W. "African Philosophy: Foundations for Black Psychology." In *Black Psychology*, ed. R. Jones. 2nd ed. New York: Harper and Row, 1988.

———. "Extended Self: Rethinking the So-called Negro Self-Concept." *Journal of Black Psychology* 2 (2) (1976): 15–24.

Parham, T. A. *Psychological Storms: The African American Struggle for Identity*. Chicago: African American Images, 1993.

Shreeve, J. "Terms of Estrangement." *Discover* (November 1994): 57–63.

Smedley, A. *Race in North America: Origin and Evolution of a Worldview*. San Francisco: Westview, 1993.

Smitherman, G. *Black Talk: Words and Phrases from the Hood to the Amen Corner*. Boston: Houghton Mifflin, 1994.

Speight, S. L., E. M. Vera, and K. B. Derrickson. "Racial Self-Designation, Racial Identity, and Self-Esteem Revisited." *Journal of Black Psychology* 22 (1996): 22, 37–52.

West, C. *Race Matters*. Boston: Beacon, 1993.

Wetherell, M., and J. Potter. *Mapping the Language of Racism: Discourse and the Legitimation of Exploitation*. New York: Columbia University Press, 1992.

3

Postmodernism, Narrative, and the Question of Black Identity

Clevis Headley

> Almost everyone has something passionate to say about identity. Identity discourses are ways of speaking about one's perceived and desired location in the social world. They are complex and deceptive because they appear to be statements of fact and exhortations to act, when they are, in fact, expressions of virtual state (e.g., "wanting-to-be" or "wanting-not-to-be"). Assertions such as "I am a good citizen" or "I am black and proud" are not so much reality claims as they are affirmations, or voicings of a wish. The statement "black is beautiful" expresses a similar wish for black to be beautiful in a social universe where this category is demeaned.
>
> —Bennetta Jules-Rosette, *Black Paris: The African Writers' Landscape*[1]

Talk of identity predictably provokes intense reactions and emotions. Many persons who consider questions of identity inescapable are equal in intensity to those who are weary of identity discourse. But one thing is sure: There is no easy way to suppress the desire by most human beings to pursue actively the "infinite process of identity construction." But why talk about identity? Why is identity important? Identity, minimally speaking, is important precisely because, among other things, it serves as a rudder by which individuals navigate the turbulence generated by their social, cultural, and political environments. The significance of identity also emerges from the social imperative of being able to impose some order and coherence on one's existence. Understanding oneself, in terms of claiming an identity, is a means by which we announce ourselves to the world. Nevertheless, claiming an identity need not imply any kind of essentialist, dogmatic, or objectivist understanding of self.

Realist portraits of identity oftentimes dissipate in the face of the fluidity of identity. The realist begins with the assumption of a specific ontology, namely a totality of objectivist entities that are discourse-independent; these entities are called identities. Next there is the application of the bivalent logic of excluded middle. Each identity either has or has not the properties in virtue of which it is the specific kind of identity it is and not some other identity. Finally, the realist invokes a truth-based epistemology. The world constituted by identities is described in terms of the principle of correspondence, in which traits or properties correspond to groups of individuals, and statements are either true or false, depending on whether the characteristics they correspond to are really the traits that definitively demarcate one identity from another in the world. This objectivist portrait collapses as soon as it is confronted by the intermingling and creolization of a different identity in the same individuals or groups of individuals. The real world identity permutations violate any suggested neat essentialist portrait of identity.

This chapter focuses on the postmodernist's take on identity and its relevance or irrelevance for Black identity. Here, I follow bell hooks in warning against too quick a rejection of postmodernism in the context of Black identity. As she writes:

> Criticism of directions in postmodern thinking should not obscure insights it may offer that open up our understanding of [Black] experience. The critique of essentialism encouraged by postmodernist thought is useful for [Blacks] concerned with reformulating outmoded notions of identity. We have too long had imposed upon us, both from the outside and the inside, a narrow constricting notion of blackness. Postmodern critiques of essentialism which challenge notion of universality and static over-determined identity within mass culture and mass consciousness can open up new possibilities for the construction of the self and the assertion of agency.[2]

Most recently, Jim Sleeper, in "Toward an End of Blackness," urges Black Americans "to surrender their racial [identity] for the good of all Americans."[3] Ironically enough, Sleeper sees Blacks as providing a good example for other Americans: All Americans need to surrender identities structured on the basis of race, ethnicity, gender, and so on. "America needs blacks," Sleeper maintains, "not because it needs blackness but because it needs what they've learned on their long way out of blackness—what others of us have yet to learn on the journeys we need to take out of whiteness."[4]

The underlying thrust of Sleeper's position is the end of racial identity, both Black and White. Appeals to racial identity subvert the natural functioning of the social order; indeed, such appeals notoriously derail the teleological movement of America itself. As one writer puts it, Sleeper thinks that blacks must take the first step and "abandon the crutch of blackness in order to put America back on the road to progress."[5] Curiously enough, all of this talk of going "beyond," that is, going beyond race in order to go beyond racism, does not signal a new perspective on things. "The narrative of beyond—beyond identity, beyond race, beyond racism—is in many ways a revision of the Enlightenment narrative of the universal subject which gradually sheds all particularity and contingency to emerge into the light of its true being."[6] But there is a certain fuzziness or rather confusion in Sleeper's position. Seemingly rejecting a biological conception of race, he fails to realize that race still claims currency since it remains an effective social and cultural category of exclusion and inclusion, as well as being a category of immense analytical importance.

In this chapter, I set out to do a number of things. First, I examine the different critiques of postmodernism by a number of Black thinkers. Next, in order to clarify what I consider distorted readings of postmodernism, I present an extremely brief discussion of postmodernism, focusing on Jacques Derrida and Michel Foucault. In the fourth section, I briefly discuss how postmodernism relates to conceptions of identity, which leads to an examination of an alternative narrative conception of Black identity that draws on the work of Alasdair MacIntyre. Finally, I discuss the issue of race, showing why it is not the case that the idea of Black identity necessarily requires or presupposes a biological conception of race. This section concludes with a favorable discussion that connects certain sociocultural aspects of race with specific elements of a narrative account of identity.

THE PROBLEM WITH POSTMODERNISM

Certain Black thinkers deny the relevance of postmodernism for Black identity. Not only do they view postmodernism as a threat to Black identity, they fear that it can also lend comfort to neoconservative ideologies that resurrect reactionary appeals to individual responsibility as a way of deflecting racial critiques of the status quo. The idea is that the "celebration of agency among the oppressed has served as an entry way to postmodern analysis, which in turn has proven to be the back door to reemphasizing individual responsibility."[7] Let us examine the claims of a few of these thinkers.

Jon Michael Spencer charges that there is a postmodern conspiracy to eliminate racial identity. He informs us that,

[t]here is today a pattern in our public discourse that is aimed in part at reversing the impetus to implement multicultural education. Much of this kind of discourse is coming from intellectuals involved in what I call *the postmodern conspiracy to explode racial identity*. This conspiracy is the postmodern equivalent to the earlier "melting pot" theory, which postulated that all Americans should melt into a single cultural identity. What makes the postmodern version just as disturbing as its "melting pot" precursor is that it too seeks to leave black people and other peoples of color with no alternative but . . . to be "white."[8]

Clearly, Spencer does not pay attention to the postmodernist emphasis on the other, and on marginality, difference, and alterity.

Joyce A. Joyce, in a popular essay in *New Literary History*, scolds Black thinkers who mischievously involve themselves with poststructuralism. Before pursuing a more detailed examination of Joyce's position, some clarification is warranted with regard to her reference to poststructuralism and my emphasis on postmodernism. Although it is possible to develop construals of poststructuralism and postmodernism that are not immediately compatible, this chapter emphasizes the family resemblances between them. Hence, in focusing on the philosophical aspects of both poststructuralism and postmodernism, it is urged that there is no obvious substantive conflict between the use of postmodernism in this chapter and Joyce's use of the term "poststructuralism." The critical idea here is the embracing of the inscrutability of reference and the rejection of the idea of the stability of the referent. Similarly, both positions are philosophically committed to the rejection of a representationalist view of knowledge, that is, the idea that knowledge is a matter of having accurate representations of an external world.

Joyce expresses strong disapproval of what she calls "the poststructuralist sensibility," which "does not adequately apply to Black American literary works."[9] Irritatingly baffled, Joyce does not understand the motivations of those Black thinkers who flirt with postmodernist ideas. Unnerved and exasperated, she confesses, "I do not understand how a Black critic aware of the implantations of racist structures in the consciousness of Blacks and whites could accept poststructuralist ideas and practices."[10] She holds that Black thinkers who engage in strategies to deconstruct "race," including "the subject," as core conceptual categories, are not only dismantling their very own literary traditions, but also, even more regrettably, their own identity as Blacks. Again, she sternly insists that, "It is insidious for the Black literary critic to adopt any kind of strategy that diminishes or . . . negates his blackness."[11] The message is clear: Deconstructing race and the subject are destructive acts that entail the demise of Black identity.

Nancy Hartsock accuses postmodernism of subverting the aspirations of marginalized peoples. She specifically accuses postmodernist thinkers of corroding the otherwise liberatory visions of oppressed groups. According to her, when those previously denied subjecthood have started "to demand the right to name ourselves, to act as subjects rather than objects of history . . . [, j]ust when we are forming our own theories about the world, uncertainty emerges about whether the world can be theorized."[12]

Hartsock is suspicious of postmodernist claims celebrating the impossibility of obtaining a systematic understanding of the world. Instead of embracing this kind of epistemological limit, she insists on the liberatory importance of marginalized peoples being able to gain a systematic understanding of the world. Projects of emancipation, in her view, should minimally seek to secure a deliberate apprehension of the physical, as well as the nonphysical, obstacles that arbitrarily restrict freedom. According to Hartsock,

> postmodernism, despite its stated efforts to avoid the problems of the European modernism of the eighteenth and nineteenth centuries, at best manages to criticize these theories without putting anything in their place. For those of us who want to understand the world systematically in order to change it, postmodernist theories at their best give us little guidance. Those of us who are not part of the ruling race, class, or gender, not a part of the minority which controls our world, need to know how it works. Why are we—in all our variousness—systematically excluded and marginalized? At their worst, postmodernist theories merely recapitulate the effects of Enlightenment theories—theories that they deny marginalized people the right to participate in defining the terms of their interaction with people in the mainstream. Thus, I contend, in broad terms, that postmodernism represents a dangerous approach for any marginalized group to adopt.[13]

Hartsock connects the positing of the traditional transcendental epistemological subject with the oppositional exclusion of an alien Other. Put differently, the transcendental subject existing outside history, culture, and language opposes an inferior Other, an Other shamefully rooted in history, culture, and language, totally imprisoned in the flux of contingency, in the rhythm of temporality. The latter remains voiceless whereas the former speaks in the name of a disembodied reason. Hartsock puts the manner as follows: "Most fundamentally, I want to argue that the philosophical and historical creation of a devalued Other was the necessary precondition for the creation of the transcendental rational subject outside of time, and space, the subject who is the speaker in Enlightenment philosophy."[14]

Hartsock clearly thinks that Black thinkers should avoid flirting with postmodernism. For she apparently fears that postmodernism is corrosive to Black subjectivity, and consequently, Black identity. Far from embracing the postmodernist's attack against the subject, Hartsock demands a more progressive subjectivity for those formerly dehumanized and excluded from the modernist space of transcendental subjectivity. She states:

> [R]ather than getting rid of subjectivity or notions of the subject, we need to engage in the historical and political and theoretical process of constituting ourselves as subjects as well as objects of history. We need to recognize that we can be the makers of history and not just the objects of those who have made history until now. Our nonbeing was the condition of being of the "majority," the center, the taken-for-granted ability of one small segment of the population to speak for all; our various efforts to constitute ourselves as objects . . . were fundamental to creating the preconditions for the current questioning of universalistic claims.[15]

Hartsock's position is stronger than the other critics in that, although she de-
nounces postmodernism, she ironically expresses views that are consistent
with postmodernism.

Here, I want to focus on certain theoretical developments in postmodern
philosophy. To start, postmodern philosophy rejects the traditional attempt
to submit difference to identity, that is, to privilege identity over difference.
Similarly, whereas the metaphysical tradition tends to favor totality, unity,
and homogeneity and to suppress or marginalize contingency, temporality,
particularity, and difference, postmodernism emphasizes otherness, alterity,
singularity, difference, and even incommensurability. Instead of seeking to
erase the voice of the other, or the voice of those long treated as being
"voiceless," postmodernism can be reasonably construed as being supportive of giving voice to the other and to those long denied the opportunity to
speak for themselves.

bell hooks effectively captures the understandably exaggerated claims
that result in hasty dismissal of postmodernism. She cautions against the
harsh reception of postmodernism in the context of theorizing Black identity. Indeed, she maintains, that instead of fearing postmodernism, we
should see it as offering a way beyond essentialist notions of Black identity, as well as a way of understanding the constitutive nature of Black
identity. She writes:

> Part of our struggle for radical black subjectivity is the quest to find ways to con-
> struct self and identity that are oppositional and liberatory. The unwillingness to
> critique essentialism on the part of many [Blacks] is rooted in the fear that it will
> cause folks to lose sight of the specific history and experience of [Blacks] and
> the unique sensibilities and culture that arise from that experience. An adequate
> response to this concern is to critique essentialism while emphasizing the sig-
> nificance of the "authority of experience." There is a radical difference between
> a repudiation of the idea that there is a black "essence" and recognition of the
> way black identity has been specifically constituted in the experience of exile
> and struggle.[16]

Notice, again, that a more careful reading of postmodernism by Hartsock
would have indicated the similarities between her views and the claims of
postmodernism with regard to Black identity as this issue has been so far discussed in this chapter. I have said enough to establish the serious concern of
certain Black thinkers regarding the possible corrosive effects of postmodernism on Black identity. Obviously, one's take on this issue is contingent on
one's understanding of postmodernism. Hence, it is precisely because of this
unavoidable factor that we need to examine the claims of postmodernism regarding the subject.

DERRIDA ON THE SUBJECT

Derrida is the target of much criticism on the grounds that he carelessly celebrates the death of the subject. Ironically, he does not philosophize at the
level of naturalism, hence his attack does not assault the idea of the empirical subject. But he performs the deconstruction equivalent of an exorcism to
dethrone the ghostly transcendental ego, a being without a language, history, or culture. He vigorously opposes the idea of an autonomous Cartesian
subject strategically located outside the world, as well as rejecting the idea
that this Cartesian epistemological subject can survey the world by means of
an undisturbed and uninterrupted perception of it. The subject, he maintains, is not outside language but depends on language. According to him:

> Now if we once again refer to the semiological difference, what was it that Saus-
> sure in particular reminded us of? That language is not a function of the speak-
> ing subject. This implies that the subject (self-identical or even conscious of self-
> identity, self-consciousness) is inscribed in language, that he is a "function" of
> language. He becomes a *speaking* subject only by confronting his speech . . . to
> the system of linguistic prescriptions taken as the system of difference.[17]

This move displaces the idea of the subject as positioned outside language, the subject as a self-identical entity. To this extent, his radical attack
is both a formal and a technical attack against the traditional notion of the
philosophical subject, a subject that according to philosophers as varied as
René Descartes, Immanuel Kant, and Edmund Husserl is needed precisely
to serve as the a priori condition of meaning and intelligibility. Derrida supports the technical philosophical attack against the subject; but he opposes
the interpretation that deconstruction attacks empirical human subjects. He
writes:

> I have never said the subject be dispensed with. Only that it should be decon-
> structed. To deconstruct the subject does not mean to deny its existence. There
> are subjects, "operations" or "effects" of subjectivity. This is an incontrovertible
> fact. To acknowledge this does not mean, however, that the subject is what it
> says it is. The subject is not some extralinguistic substance or identity, some
> pure cogito of self-presence; it is always inscribed in language. My work does
> not, therefore, destroy the subject; it simply tries to resituate it.[18]

The crucial point here is that there is no call for the end or, rather, the death
of the subject. There is, rather, an attempt to refashion and relocate the subject within language.[19] In situating the subject within language, Derrida des-
ignates it as a set of relationships or contingencies. Thus, the subject is a system of relations determined by language or rather inscribed within language.
He writes: "The subject of writing does not exist if we mean by that some

sovereign solitude of the author. The subject of writing is a system of relations between strata: the Mystic pad, the psyche, society, the world. Within that scene, on that stage, the punctual simplicity of the classical subject is not to be found."[20]

Derrida delicately treads a thin line between the inflated traditional notion of the subject as a self-identical entity and the more careless view that sanctions a complete denial of the subject altogether. His concern is not to eliminate decisively and completely the subject but, rather, to deflate the philosophical concept of the subject. His real position is a form of ontological deflationism. Consistent with his view is the idea that the subject is not a reservoir of consciousness, namely, a determinate self-presence. From a deflationary perspective, Derrida tells us that there is "no subject who is agent, author, and master of *différance*."[21] And he goes on to state that "the subject, and first of all the conscious and speaking subject, depends upon the system of differences and the movement of *différance*. [I]t is not present, nor above all present to itself before *différance*."[22]

At this time, I want to connect Derrida's notion of the subject as being partly a relational construction of signification practices and not a extralinguistic, philosophical substance with Foucault's approach to the question of the subject.

FOUCAULT ON THE SUBJECT

Foucault joins in the poststructuralist attack against the traditional metaphysical subject, and he too supports a certain construal of the subject, being one of the many products of discourse and other social and political practices. According to him, "[w]e should discover how it is that subjects are gradually, progressively, really and materially constituted through a multiplicity of organisms, forces, energies, materials, desires, thoughts etc. We should try to grasp subjection in its material instance as a constitution of subjects."[23] The constructedness of the subject, and not its invisibility or impossibility, is at the center of Foucault's poststructuralist dethroning of the subject's alleged pregivenness or preexistence. Emphasizing this fact is not a move to blunt political engagement but, rather, to underscore the very politics inherent in the construction of the subject. "The individual," writes Foucault, "is not a pre-given entity which is seized on by the exercise of power. The individual, with his identity and characteristics, is the product of a relation of power exercised over bodies."[24]

Historicity is another component of Foucault's idea of the subject. While acknowledging that subjects emerge from various historical projects and contexts, he denies the existence of a metaphysical subject, a permanent posit, a stable center of consciousness, or a stable entity that serves as the foundation of different discourses. For example, the outlines of the subject characteristic of Stoicism are radically different from the modern, self-expressive subject. According to him, "[o]ne has to dispense with the constituent subject, to get rid of the subject itself, that is to say, to arrive at an analysis which can account for the constitution of the subject within a historical framework . . . , without having to make reference to a subject which is either transcendental in relation to the field of events or runs in its empty sameness throughout the course of history."[25]

For Foucault, then, the real issue does not concern the existence of a subject but whether or not this subject is the determinant of a field of constitution. It would be incorrect to claim that Foucault encourages political apathy by interpreting his notion of "the ends of man" as meaning the literal death of the subject. The term "man," in Foucault's view, need not be interpreted biologically. He treats the term "man" in a technical manner. Hence he posits it as the product of a particular context or, rather, a specific historical vocabulary. We recall his account of the emergence of the human sciences in the eighteenth century. In *The Order of Things*, he attributes this development to the way in which the idea of "man" served as part of a specific historical epistemological problematic that made it possible for the subject to become an object of inquiry. Thus, from this perspective, "[o]nly by understanding . . . talk of 'man' as designating a foundational concept of Kantian anthropology can we make sense of [Foucault] saying that 'man is a recent invention, a figure not yet two centuries old.'"[26] Foucault is not literally saying that the human race is only 200 years old; such a claim would be inescapably absurd. What he is saying is that the concept of "man" is a technical philosophical concept of recent origins; and his version of the "disappearance" of man emerges from the decentering of this traditional hyperrational subject, a decentering common to the fields of psychoanalysis, linguistics, and ethnology. In this regard, Foucault's announcement of the end of man concerns the fact that the technical concept "man" can no longer function neutrally as the center of representational thinking, as the secured anchor connecting language to the world.

To summarize, the preceding considerations demonstrate that postmodernism rejects the modern philosophical conception of the subject and the metaphysical essentialist view of identity that it sustains. What it clearly emphasizes is the constitutivity of subjectivity rather than the notion of a pregiven subject. The significant existential consequences of debunking a substance ontology of subjectivity and of subjecthood mean that there is no sense to be made of a predetermined self or, for that matter, of the self as a substance. Rather, the postmodernist self is a projection in the sense that it is not given but achieved in the transcendence common to the horizon of human choice and freedom. In dethroning the traditional metaphysical subject, a certain conceptual space is made available to talk intelligently about previously suppressed and marginalized subjects from the perspectives of gender, race, class, nationalism, and sexuality. There is also made possible the opportunity to talk about an individual claiming allegiance to multiple subjectivities.

Now, we need to consider the question: Is postmodernism antagonistic to identity? My answer is, "No." What postmodernism is antagonistic toward is the modernist notion of identity or, rather, of subjectivity.

A GENERIC POSTMODERN CONCEPTION OF IDENTITY

Stuart Hall suggests that there are at least two ways that we can theorize identity. First, we can start by saying that modernist theories of identity are essentialist in the sense of viewing identities as claiming ahistorical or acultural essences. In this view, the essence of identities precedes their manifestation in the world.

The second construal of identity is postmodernist. This conception does not think of identity in terms of metaphysical essences, nor in terms of unity and homogeneity; while not rejecting the existence of identities, it considers identities as being socially constituted and as real. The self, according to a postmodernist, is ambiguous, contradictory, and even multiple. But it is never an abiding unity. For Hall, a postmodernist notion of identity

recognizes that, as well as the many points of similarity, there are also critical points of deep and significant *difference* which constitute "what we really are": or rather—since history has intervened—"what we have become." We cannot speak for very long, with any exactness, about "one experience, one identity," without acknowledging its other side—the differences and discontinuities which constitute [identity]. Cultural identity, in this second sense, is a matter of "becoming" as well as of "being." It belongs to the future as much as to the past. It is not something which already exists, transcending place, time, history and culture. Cultural identities come from somewhere, have histories. But, like everything which is historical, they undergo constant trans-formation. Far from being externally fixed in some essentialized past, they are subject to continuous "play" of history, culture and power. Far from being grounded in a mere "recovery" of the past, which is waiting to be found, and which, when found, will secure our sense of ourselves into eternity, identities are the names we give to the different ways we are positioned by, and position ourselves with, the narratives of the past.[27]

Although I endorse Hall's construal of postmodern identity, I do not wish to imply that this construal captures the necessary and sufficient conditions for any conception of postmodern identity.

I contend that if postmodernism construes identity dynamically and emphasizes the antagonistic and oppositional struggles of identity formation, then it is not at all corrosive to Black identity. I also contend that a narrative conception of Black identity can escape apocalyptic and nihilistic versions of postmodernism. Narrative immediately suggests the importance, in identity discourse, of acknowledging that "[h]uman beings are creatures formed in communities marked by allegiance to a normative story."[28] Another way of framing this idea is to say that "[a]n identity discourse is the enunciation of a cultural narrative."[29] There is the danger of being vulnerable to the charge of embracing the idea of metanarrative when talking about narrative. Here, the appeal to narrative acknowledges no association with the idea that there is a *telos* to Black culture and personality or that there is some overarching meta-narrative that extends intelligibility to the lives of individual Blacks precisely because they are part of some overarching project.

Narrative extends the power of speaking to those who were once considered "people without voice." For example, "[T]he literary value of slave narrative is most often perceived to lie in its power to 'find a voice' or 'write the self' of the previously silent and invisible slave. . . . [T]he slave narrative not only chronicles the freeing of the slave and calls for an end to slavery for others; it also wrenches open a gap in the racial order that has denied the subjectivity of the slave and performatively instantiates the transformation of slave into subject"[30] Another writer states that: "The practice of Narrative functions to allow traditionally marginalized and disempowered groups, such as women and people of color, to reclaim their voices. In addition, by laying claim to personal narrative (i.e. the telling of one's own story), oppressed peoples are able to create their own sphere of theorized existence, and thus remove themselves from the marginalized position to which the dominant society has relegated them."[31] Narratives have offered, and continue to offer, Blacks the opportunity to dismantle the "discursive constraints that have rendered [them] invisible."

More significantly, it is my contention that a narrative conception of identity, and of Black identity particularly, offers an alternative to the theorizing of social identity as emerging from narrow-minded "economic interest groups, social classes, or political organizations," under the assumption that "ethnic groups are not biologically and culturally self-perpetuating."[32] On the narrative conception of identity, we shall see that an identity is partly constituted by an extended conversation regarding the content of that identity. Identities, therefore, are open. In other words, they are subject to revision and restructuring; they are never complete in the sense of having achieved a final definition. Finally, framing identity in terms of narrative nicely accommodates the multiple contexts that shape the identities of social actors. For example, Patricia Hill Collins makes the case for a Black feminist consciousness, an identity constituted by multiple narratives. The multiplicity of Black feminist identity emerges from the "intersection of race, gender and class oppression."[33]

Here, I should note that certain thinkers have denied the existence of Black narrative and narrative identity. Laurance Thomas argues that group success is contingent on group autonomy. He maintains that "[a]n identifiable group of people has autonomy when its members are generally regarded by others not belonging to the group as the foremost interpreters of their own historical–cultural traditions."[34] Thomas is confident that Blacks lack group autonomy precisely because they do not have a narrative. A narrative, he states, is "a set of stories which defines values and entirely positive goals, which specifies a set of fixed points of historical significance, and which defines a set of ennobling rituals to be regularly performed."[35] The narrative conception of Black identity being developed in this chapter exposes the excessive historical blindness inherent in Thomas's position. For Thomas clearly believes that African Americans are a people totally lacking in cultural capital. At this point, I will sketch a theoretical framework of narrative identity, following MacIntyre's narrative conception of identity.

MACINTYRE ON EPISTEMOLOGICAL CRISES

Modernist approaches to Black identity tend to describe Black identity in terms of self-hatred. One reason for this failure of perspective is that these approaches assume the existence of a unitary Black subject. In making this assumption, modernist approaches explain deviations from the alleged core Black self as pathological. Indeed, in some cases, there is reference to a "collectively damaged Black psyche." I maintain that these approaches fail precisely because they cannot adequately explain identity crises without attributing pathologies to Blacks. In viewing Black identity in unitary terms, as a presence, many thinkers consider any unsettling of this presumed center of consciousness to be destructive. They refuse to interpret certain events as offering Blacks the occasion to reshape or rethink their identity. Nevertheless, in order to avoid having to impose seemingly pathological traits on Blacks, I urge that a plausible conception of Black identity should start with an explanation of an identity crisis.

MacIntyre models his notion of identity crisis on the phenomenon of an epistemological crisis. The comparison is quite simple: Individuals experience identity crises when they are no longer able to make sense of their being-in-the world, that is, their existence in a cultural world.

An epistemological crisis, according to MacIntyre, develops because of the debilitating and irritating incoherence within a subject's conceptual scheme. Put differently, deep skepticism about one's earlier, reliable conceptual scheme often induces an epistemological crisis. MacIntyre writes:

> For it is not only that an individual may rely on the schemata that have hitherto informed all his interpretations of social life and find that he or she has been led

into radical error or deception, so that for the first time the schemata are put in question—perhaps for the first time they also in this moment become visible to the individual who employs them—but it is also the case that the individual may come to recognize the possibility of systematically different possibilities of interpretation, of the existence of alternative and rival schemata, which yield mutually incompatible accounts of what is going on around him. Just this is the form of *epistemological crisis* encountered by ordinary agents.[36]

MacIntyre also resourcefully connects the notion of an epistemological crisis with the idea of an identity crisis. An individual suffers an identity crisis because the "dramatic narrative . . . through which [the agent] identified his [own positionality within society and specifically his relation to the other members of his cultural group] has been disrupted by radical interpretative doubt."[37] I should note that the radical doubt initiating an epistemological crisis is not a mechanical Cartesian doubt that entails an agent having to submit all of his beliefs to radical doubt. "The agent who is plunged into an epistemological crisis, according to MacIntyre, knows something very important: That a schema of interpretation he has trusted so far has broken down irremediably in certain highly specific ways. . . . [D]oubts are formulated against a background of what [an agent] takes to be-rightly-well-founded beliefs."[38] This account clearly implies that an identity crisis, like an epistemological crisis, plunges an agent into a certain state of existential vertigo. The existential trauma suffered by an agent leads him or her to seek alternative ways of understanding the world so as to reclaim some semblance of normalcy. Differently construed, our identities function as social roles that we perform. As a consequence of performing these roles in our everyday lives, that is, of acting out our identities, our behavior becomes habitual and predictable. This existential serenity often leads to a certain complacency regarding the different aspects of our lives. That is, we take many things for granted, assuming that they will always remain as they are. But eventually, some specific event rudely intrudes and disrupts our complacency. At these times, when events beyond our control force us to suspend our previously habitual lives, individuals suffer under the cruel agony of an identity crisis and, ultimately, of an epistemological crisis.

Consider the following example of the conditions that can plunge a Black individual into a crisis of identity. The existential intrusion that can precipitate an identity crisis for a Black individual can take the form of racially motivated physical violence or even of being confronted by blatant expressions of racial hatred. I want to examine the use of racist language to cause harm.

Consider the Black family living in a predominantly White neighborhood. This family believes that its entry into the community will be uneventful. However, the first serious disagreement with a White neighbor can lead to racial harassment and, ultimately, the physical destruction of property. Here, a Black middle-class family, proudly considering itself successful, to the extent that it has transcended race, is painfully reminded that the dominant society still sees it as Black, meaning that it has not transcended race. Consequently, an interpretation of the world premised on the transcendence of race proves ineffective.

We can apply this insight to a broader historical context. Can we not argue that the Black experience in the new world is, in part, an effort to manage an extended epistemological crisis?[39] If we assume that prior to the experience of slavery Blacks were threatened by limited and manageable epistemological uncertainty regarding their understanding of their social worlds then, in the new world, the horrible experience of racial subordination placed Blacks in the unflattering situation of having to continuously find new ways of understanding and interpreting ever changing antagonistic conditions of existence.

On this view, a temporary turning away from things African is not necessarily a sign of self-hatred, as earlier models of Black identity suggest, but may very well represent strategic attempts by Blacks to deal effectively and creatively with highly exasperating and unstable circumstances, such as slavery, institutionalized racism, and cultural marginalization. Here, individuals can experience identity crises without necessarily suffering permanent psychological harm, although they may be more vulnerable to identity crises than others. Indeed, such exposure may very well generate individuals with highly inflated egos. Now that I have finished my examination of the relationship between epistemological crises and identity crises, I want to take a more detailed look at MacIntyre's conception of identity.

MACINTYRE AND IDENTITY

We construct new dramatic narratives, MacIntyre contends, to resolve epistemological crises as well as identity crises. New narratives reconstruct past events in manifold ways, and at certain times, strategically incorporate new events within already existing schemes of interpretation. To this extent, they provide an individual with a new understanding of his or her social world. He states that

> [w]hen an epistemological crisis is resolved, it is by the construction of a new narrative, which enables the agent to understand *both* how he or she could intelligibly have held his or her original beliefs *and* how he or she could have been so drastically misled by them. The narrative in terms of which he or she at first understood and ordered experiences is itself made into the subject of an enlarged narrative. The agent has come to understand how the criteria of truth and understanding must be reformulated. He has had to become epistemologically self-conscious and at a certain point he may have come to acknowledge two conclusions: the first is that his new forms of understanding may themselves, in turn, come to be put in question at any time; the second is that, because in such

crises the criteria of truth, intelligibility and rationality may always themselves be put in question . . . we are never in a position to claim that now we possess the truth or now we are fully rational.[40]

After the resolution of an epistemological crisis, one inevitably appreciates the fact that identities cannot be unilaterally structured in the sense of being anchored in absolute truths. Furthermore, one also comes to appreciate the constant threat of instability common to all identities, given the fact that identities mutate in response to theoretical ruptures and foundational shifts emerging from the unpredictable dialectical encounters between agents and the external world. Identities, far from being closed or completed, claim a certain creative and inviting openness, consistent with the obvious indeterminacy and flux characteristic of human existence.

Well-adjusted identities, that is, identities that result from narratives that constructively and intelligently arrange events in the world, enable individuals to understand why a past conception of self requires critical assessment. MacIntyre argues that Hamlet is a good example of an individual who has successfully reconstructed his identity by employing a scheme of interpretation that enables him to make sense of events that were previously disruptive. Again, it bears noting that, in contrast to a one-dimensional conception of Black identity, practices of redescription and reinterpretation are evident in the experience of African Americans. African Americans have perceptively rethought and reinterpreted their understanding of self and world in the face of fluid historical, social, and political conditions. This activity by Blacks renders Black identity heterogeneous and multiple, rather than fragmentary or nonexistent.

I want to examine in greater detail MacIntyre's account of the relation between identity and tradition in order to avoid attributing to him a naive conception of tradition. He not only describes the relation between identities and traditions, but he also offers a dynamic conception of tradition. First, I should note that MacIntyre correctly rejects the Burkean notion that construes traditions as stable and static. Instead of contrasting the healthy functioning of a tradition in terms of its stability, MacIntyre maintains that a tradition is an extended argument about some specific subject matter. Tradition serves as the background that generates and sustains coherent, meaningful, and persuasive argumentation. He states that "all reasoning takes place within the context of some traditional mode of thought, transcending through criticism and invention the limitations of what had hitherto been reasoned in that tradition."[41] Far from being an uncontested display of stability and conformity, a flourishing tradition exhibits argumentative and substantive debates about its internal good.

In applying these insights to identities, we need not construe identities as existing in nature, as being natural kinds, or as being unitary and stable, conveniently supporting a structural isomorphism between descriptions of identities and actual identities. Rather, we should characterize the theorizing about identities as constituting a tradition of argumentation.

Again, one main feature of African American history is the debate about the nature of Black identity. This debate constitutes a tradition of argumentation over the meaning of Black identity or what it means to be Black. As MacIntyre writes:

> For what constitutes a tradition is a conflict of interpretations of that tradition, a conflict which itself has a history susceptible of rival interpretations. If I am [African American], I have to recognize that the tradition of [being Black] is partly constituted by a continuous argument over what it means to be [an African American]. Suppose I am an American: the tradition is one partly constituted by continuous argument over what it means to be an American and partly by continuous argument over what it means to have rejected tradition. If I am an historian, I must acknowledge that the tradition of historiography is partly, but centrally, constituted by arguments about what history is and ought to be.[42]

MacIntyre's situating of identity within the context of a tradition offers another way to explain identity crises without having to view individuals caught in their midst as being clinically pathological. We constantly observe traditions in trouble. The frequent dogmatic and heated debates regarding identity within different ethnic communities indicate traditions under strain. MacIntyre's position nicely captures these varied phenomena: "A tradition . . . not only embodies the narratives of an argument, but is only to be recovered by an argumentative retelling of that narrative which will itself be in conflict with other argumentative retellings. Every tradition therefore is always in danger of lapsing into incoherence and when a tradition does so lapse it sometimes can only be recovered by a revolutionary reconstruction."[43]

Confronted with a tradition under debilitating stress and facing the danger of fragmentation, we see why certain Black thinkers consider postmodernism a grave threat to Black identity. They fear that, if postmodernism sanctions the demise of identity, it disempowers Blacks by rendering their efforts at continual identity formation and preservation meaningless. These thinkers consider postmodernism the latest corrosive assault on Black identity. Hence, it threatens to initiate a new and possibly prolonged epistemological crisis. But, as we have seen so far, we should not uncritically accept this charge.

The narrative conception of identity underscores the extent to which the sociocultural world nurtures and sustains our identities. Through the power of narratives, we construct our sociocultural worlds and creatively cast meaning on the varied events in the external world. Thus, we should not be surprised to discover that identities emerge from this narrative activity. And it is also by virtue of their narrative character that identities impart meaning and offer individuals ways to make sense of and answer questions such as: Who am I? All of this is to say that our identities reflect, among other things, our goals, anticipations, expectations, hopes, fears, and so on—things shaped by social and cultural experiences, or better yet, our being in the world. Since these things cooperate in constructing our identities, it is not at all surprising to note that, as stated before, identities are the products of narratives. Indeed, at the risk of repetition, MacIntyre refers to human beings "as characters in enacted narratives." Clearly, narrative imparts consistency, intelligibility, and "unity" to identities. However, the narrative conception of identity requires no unitary subject with a set of determinant predicates. One's sense of self emerges in the process of narratively structuring events in one's life. To remove individuals from the cultural world of daily existence, and then proceed to treat them as lacking a culture, a history, and a language, inevitably deprives them of the "unity" that renders their lives meaningful. This deprivation emerges from the loss of the narrative structure or framework that is required in order to understand the actions, wishes, and desires of individuals.

Clearly, then, the narrative construal of Black identity portrays the Black subject as a cumbered self, namely, a self situated appropriately within the context of a narrative tradition that is an extended conversation of what it means to be Black. Unlike the modernist notion of the self as unencumbered, as standing outside the stream of culture, language, and history, the postmodernist idea of a constructed subject, which I have linked to a narrative conception of Black identity, provides a means for rescuing Black identity from the modernist fantasy of an essentialist self waiting to fulfill its metaphysically inspired *telos*.

RACE AND IDENTITY

Failure to consider the concept of race in the context of theorizing Black identity would be an egregious omission. Race merits a critical discussion in order to consider its compatibility with the narrative conception of Black identity. Here, the case will be made that the narrative conception of identity outlined earlier can accommodate the relevant facts of race that pertain to Black identity.

The concept of race, many thinkers claim, is not only semantically defective, but also ontologically deficient. Even biology cannot rely on this concept precisely because there are no biological races in the sense of distinct groups of people with sets of unique genetic traits. Most recently, Walter Benn Michaels argues that the very notion of cultural identity requires a notion of race and that even notions of culture claiming not to be race based, in the biological sense, require a notion of race. He finally concludes by stating that all construals of cultural identity are theoretically dependent on prior, and often hidden, notions of race.

Michaels uses the example of the American Indians.[44] He argues that if we construe identity in terms of culture, then we should allow individuals to engage freely in different practices without accusing them of betraying their cultural heritage. Charges of cultural betrayal indicate the presence of a biological notion of culture. Without biological assumptions about race culture, the idea of cultural betrayal becomes meaningless. One cannot betray what one does not have any obligation to protect. "Our current notion of cultural identity," he writes, "both descends from and extends the earlier [biological] notion of racial identity."[45] And he adds that cultural identity is "the project of lining up [one's] practices with [one's] genealogy."[46] Ironically, however, although those supporting a cultural notion of identity insist that they are only talking about culture and not about anything biologically innate, Michaels suspects that they inevitably maintain that someone lacking the culture of his group lacks something that necessarily defines his or her identity, and that it is possible to reclaim what is lacking. So, he challenges those holding a cultural view of ethnicity to explain precisely the sense in which a culture belongs to someone, other than on a racial basis, if that person does not already observe the practices of the culture.

Michaels further maintains that "[t]he modern concept of culture is not, in other words, a critique of racism; it is a form of racism."[47] How does he establish that "accounts of cultural identity that do any work require a racial component?" His answer is that identity is a form of racial ontology.

> But why does it matter who we are? The answer can't just be the epistemological truism that our account of the past may be partially determined by our own identity, for, of course, this description of the conditions under which we know the past makes no logical difference to the truth or falsity of what we know. It must be instead the ontological claim that we need to know who we are in order to know which past is ours. The real question, however, is not which past should count as ours but why any past should count as ours. . . . The history we study is never our own; it is always the history of people who were in some respects like us and in other respects different. When, however, we claim it as ours, we commit ourselves to the ontology of "the Negro," to the identity of "we" and "they," and the primacy of race.[48]

Michaels insists on emphasizing that notions of cultural and ethnic identity can only do significant work by presupposing that objective, biologically based cultural differences are constitutive of identity and ethnicity.

He goes on to argue that notions such as cultural loss and retention are contingent on the prior deceptive assumption of the biological validity of race. Without race, it would be meaningless to talk about one losing one's culture for, otherwise, one would be free to engage in as many practices as one chooses without suffering the fate of being labeled a traitor to one's culture. Michaels writes:

> It is only the appeal to race that makes culture an object of affect and that gives notions like losing our culture, preserving it, stealing someone's else culture, restoring people's culture to them, and so on, their pathos. . . . Without race, losing our culture can mean no more than doing things differently from the way we now do them and preserving our culture can mean no more than doing things the same—the melodrama of assimilation disappears.[49]

Michaels concludes that, to the extent that a position depends on the category of "cultural identity," this position has done little more than "rescue . . . racism from the racists."[50]

At this point, I wish to respond to Michaels's claim that all attempts to salvage any conception of race are engaged in mythmaking. If a cultural notion of race is the same as mythmaking, that is, a falsehood, then any notion of identity similarly grounded on the bogus notion of race would be equally false. He states that,

> [t]he undeniable fact that people's belief in the biological reality of race has real consequences does not suffice to make race real: women, as Tzvetan Todorov reminds us, were hanged as witches, and yet there were no witches. So the non-biological reality of race cannot be adduced as a consequence of people's mistaken belief in its biological reality, and without some positive account of what a nonbiological race might be, anti-essentialist celebrants of racial difference are condemned to resorting to the biological categories they mean to repudiate."[51]

There is much that is misleading in Michaels's deceptive analogy between the ontological emptiness of the concepts of witches and of race. According to him, if the notion of race were truly a valid biological category, then we would be justified in using this concept. But since race is biologically invalid, there can be no justifiable use of this term, for there is no way to escape its ontological difficulties. Similarly, the attempt to justify race on the grounds that people believe in race will not work, according to Michaels. This attempt fails precisely because it resembles the claim that there are witches simply because people believe that witches exist.

I think that Michaels's position is extremist. His failure to appreciate the constitutivity of race emerges from his general employment of positivistic semantics. The positivist notion holds that in order for a word to be meaningful it must have empirical content. In applying this strategy to the terms "witches" and "race," he argues that there are no races in precisely the same way in that there are no witches. However, viewed from a distinctive sociocultural perspective, it is clear that witches do not exist in that there are no mainstream or widely institutionalized cultural and social practices determinately conferring reality to the idea of witches. To the contrary, there are many clusters of social and cultural regimes and sites of power reinforcing racial meaning, hence the reality of race. For example, when individuals are asked to declare a religious affiliation, there is no formal recognition of being a witch that is seen as a legitimate choice analogous to the declaration of being a Christian, a Jew, a Muslim, or a Buddhist. With race, things are quite different. Individuals are at times appropriately asked to volunteer a racial identification. This information makes it possible to monitor civil rights violations. Indeed, in some cases we also have good reasons for distributing certain goods on the basis of race.

I now turn briefly to examine the way in which the narrative conception of Black identity can directly accommodate a sociocultural notion of race without presupposing the biological validity of race. Once again, I am going to utilize MacIntyre's development of the interdependence between narrative and identity.

The intelligibility of narrative requires a setting, which is the theoretical space that sustains the analytical coherence of narrative. Hence, in advocating a narrative conception of Black identity, we need to place this conception of identity within its appropriate setting. It is inescapable that we must situate concerns about Black identity within the setting of race. Here, we need not understand race in the biological sense of racial essence but, rather, in the sense of the multiple discourses that traditionally have been used either to frustrate the possibilities of a Black identity or used by Blacks themselves to affirm a Black identity. Indeed, Black identity discourse in its own right claims a certain critical history. MacIntyre writes that

> I use the word "setting" . . . as a relatively inclusive term. A social setting may be an institution, it may be . . . a practice, or it may be a milieu of some other human kind. But it is central to the notion of a setting as I am going to understand it that a setting has a history, a history within which the histories of individuals agents not only are, but have to be, situated, just because without the setting and its changes through time the history of the individual agents and his changes through time will be unintelligible.[52]

In situating Black identity within the setting of racial discourse, without interpreting race biologically, we are in a position to appreciate another element that sustains narrative intelligibility. We recall the tendency to theorize Black identity in terms of Black self-hatred, reading Black identity as mainly determined by racism. What I want to suggest is that these thinkers mistakenly identify constraints on Black identity for Black identity itself. On the narrative view, all identities must accommodate certain constraints. The greatest constraint confronting Black identity is racial negation. However, it is my contention that Blacks must deal with the cultural and social reality of race even if it is the case that they are not the chief architects in constructing a world on the basis of racial designations. Hence, the constraint of race plays a significant role in the theorizing of Black identity. Indeed, human existence is always objectively limited as well as delimited by constraints, and for the Black individual, race in its negative guise—White supremacy, and vulgar racialist theories of history, culture, crime, and intelligence—is an omnipresent constraint. MacIntyre claims, "We enter upon a stage which we did not design and we find ourselves part of an action that was not of our making. Each of us being a main character in his own drama plays subordinate parts in the dramas of others."[53]

Another crucial element involved in narrative is storytelling. I have already commented on this issue. However, in this context, I need to reexamine this issue for the purpose of showing why it is the case that a narrative conception of Black identity avoids the problems associated with a biological notion of Black identity, and also the problem of having to argue that if identities are created, then they are illusionary and unreal in the sense of being false.

The narrative approach enables us to view Black identity in a manner consistent with the postmodernist's concern to displace modernist notions of an essentialist subject. Narrative requires storytelling in the structuring of identity. This element of narrative is particularly relevant to Black identity. The literary tradition of African Americans testifies to the importance of Blacks telling stories about their experiences both in slavery and in freedom. In this literary tradition, one finds numerous narratives and autobiographies that serve as ways of informing generations of younger Blacks about the experiences and the realties of being Black in the world. These narratives and autobiographies pass on to younger generations ways of understanding the world, ways of seeing the world, strategies of survival, and, most importantly, ways of forming conceptions of self, namely, identity. The slave narrative, according to Charles Davis and Henry Louis Gates Jr., is "the very generic foundation which most subsequent Afro-American fictional and nonfiction narrative forms [are] extended, refigured, and troped," more specifically, "the basis on which an entire narrative tradition has been constructed."[54]

Indeed, as stated earlier, there is no need to attempt to locate Black identity in a pure, originary African essence. A more sensible approach is to see Black "identity discourse as conversations among concrete social actors [responding] to specific historical situations."[55] For example, the new Black historiography[56] of the 1970s—which one can correctly argue substituted "thick descriptions" of Black identity for "thin descriptions" of Black identity[57]— "treated blacks as healthy subjects rather than maimed objects; emphasized collective strength rather than individual weakness; made black culture and the black community its central focus."[58] In emphasizing the importance of resistance, this new historical writing reconceives Black identity in that it calls into question "the theses of the damage and deficit" regarding Black identity. Another achievement of this new historiography is that it places Black identity within the stream of history, hence frustrating the tendency to articulate Black identity as a deprived marginal identity. Situating Black identity within a certain historical framework enables us to appreciate Black "heroic agency."

According to Leslie Owens, Blacks "have often perceived [resistance] as an inner stance coiled to preserve identity."[59] Finally, the Black historian John Blassingame writes that "free slaves by passing their unique set of cultural themes from generation to generation . . . were able to resist most of white teaching, [and] set themselves apart from white society, and mold their own cultural norms and group identity."[60] Here, I should note the intimate connection between identity and community. Toni Morrison has done much to articulate a nonessentialist conception of Black identity. "Identity," in her fiction, "is always provisional; there can be no isolated ego striving to define itself as separate from community, no matter how tragic or futile the operations of that community might be. Individual characters are inevitably formed by social constructions of both race and gender, and they are inseparable from these origins."[61]

Besides written documents, there is also the oral tradition of Black culture. There is simply no way to avoid the profound impact of the stories of courage, resistance, and struggle that the elders have transmitted and continue to relay to younger Blacks. Jewel Amoah writes that "[s]torytelling and the history of the oral tradition enable one to reconnect with one's past and one's ancestors in the process of asserting one's voice in the present. Ideally, this combination of reconnection and assertion will allow for the creation of a more equitable position in the future. The point is that story—one's personal narrative—is essential to one's identity and one's sense of self."[62]

Clearly, the critical importance of stories in shaping Black identity cannot be underestimated. Consciousness of being Black requires access to shared stories that record the complexity of existing in a world that is not always accommodating of Black identity. I turn one final time to MacIntyre to describe the crucial importance of stories in the formation of identities:

> We enter human society, that is, with one or more imputed characters—roles into which we have been drafted—and we have to learn what they are in order to be able to understand how others respond to us and how our responses to them are apt to be construed. It is through hearing stories . . . that children learn or mislearn both what a child and what a parent is, what the cast of characters may be in the drama into which they have been born and what the ways of the world are. Deprive children of stories and you leave them unscripted, anxious stutterers in their actions as in their words. Hence there is no way to give us an understanding of any . . . [group], including our own, except through the stock of stories which constitute its . . . dramatic resources.[63]

Once again, the prevalence of storytelling in Black culture more than validates the narrative status of Black identity. Amoah writes: "The practice of storytelling . . . is deeply rooted in African-American culture. It is a tradition based on the continuity of wisdom, and it functions to assert the voice of the oppressed. Storytelling is not merely a means of entertainment. It is also an educational tool, and for many, it is a way of life. For others, it is the only way to comprehend, analyze, and deal with life."[64]

NARRATIVES AND TRUTH

Before concluding, I want to critically engage an objection to the narrative conception of Black identity developed in this chapter. The objection takes on the following character. If Black identity is partly sustained by constructing narratives or through storytelling, then it should be possible to determine the objective truth of such narratives and stories. Hence, the questions: Who decides which narratives are correct? How do Blacks distinguish true stories from false stories? These questions take on a certain urgency because of the belief that a failure to determine the objective truth of the narratives structuring Black identity would open the door to a vicious self-refuting relativism. This relativism, far from securing and strengthening Black identity, would render it vulnerable, making it possible for any one to construct any fantastic narrative or any bizarre story. This fear stems from the conviction that narratives of identity should be faithful to the world; they should record the world as it is and not become victim to flights of fantasy, which ultimately can lead to a self-deception.

What this challenge demands is a correspondence between narratives and the objective facts constituting the social world. On this view, narratives of identity, like scientific theories, should be true descriptions of the world, true statements that correspond to the facts of the social world as it really is.

My response to the realist challenge of objectively determining the truth-value of narratives is to model narratives on a holist conception of scientific theories. This move entails assessing narratives in antirealist terms, namely, in accordance with their pragmatic value in enabling individuals to confront the problems of human existence and not in metaphysical realist terms of directly mirroring or corresponding to determinate objective features of the world. Hence, in my view, narratives of identity function like tools or instruments for the purpose of enabling individuals to develop strategies for coping with the various factors of nonbeing that threaten either to impoverish the quality of human existence or to corrode habitual ways of thinking and acting that have proven to offer existential comfort.

In defending a postmodernist narrative conception of Black identity, I do not view identities as being direct observational reports of the sociocultural

world. Far from being neutral descriptions of an external world, and hence
as being similar to realist scientific theories, I view identities as the products
of human efforts to understand ways of being in the world or rather styles of
existence. Identities are not chronicles precisely because they involve creativity and imagination, which is to say that they emerge from efforts to link
the past, the present, and the future. They are as much about imagination as
memory. Notice, however, that neither imagination nor memory necessarily
renders the process of identity formation deliberately hallucinatory.

I do not interpret the postmodernist attack against the idea that experience
can yield incorrigible foundations of knowledge and truth as the enthusiastic embrace of relativism. Rather, it is the denial that there are certain givens
in experience, which, being unmediated, provide neutral, incorrigible principles of knowledge. Postmodernists maintain that experience is theory-
laden, forcing them to embrace epistemological holism. Epistemological
holism holds that the justification of a statement is always in terms of another
statement or a set of statements in conjunction with experience. Raw experience cannot serve as the indisputable justification of each statement of a
theory in isolation.

CONCLUSION

I want to conclude by summarizing the narrative conception of Black identity developed in this chapter. I have argued that postmodernism need not
be interpreted as uncompromisingly antagonistic toward Black identity. The
modernist approach to the self, an approach firmly committed to the idea of
a unitary, stable subject has encouraged metaphysical essentialist notions of
identity. In the case of Blacks, identity then becomes the product of biology
or some other foundational principle. Once we appreciate the postmodernist's claim that the subject is the product of certain discursive practices
and power relationships, then we can more readily acknowledge and embrace a narrative conception of identity. In this case, we can conceive Black
identity not as static nor as already totally completed but rather as dependent
on the stories individuals tell about themselves and their understanding of
their place in the world.

Consequently, the concerns raised by certain Black thinkers, such as
Spencer, Joyce, and Hartsock, concerning the alleged threat that postmodernism poses to Black agency and political emancipation are exaggerated.
For, as I have argued here, we can develop a narrative conception of Black
identity that is compatible with postmodernism. Instead of treating Black
identity in homogeneous terms, this conception of Black identity can extend
considerable benefit to Blacks. It can contribute to a better understanding of
such things as community and identity without seeking theoretical support

from or being dependent on a notion of sameness. On this more extensive conception of Black identity, we can liberate Black identity from earlier notions that were unable to accommodate differences of gender and class within the context of an effective political agenda.[65] For example, a nationalist notion of Black identity will inevitably privilege masculinity and view gender as counterproductive to a collective racial agenda. Appreciating the more dynamic aspect of Black identity will certainly contribute to more constructive and practical political initiatives that realistically account for differences of gender and class without arbitrarily privileging either of them.

NOTES

1. Bennetta Jules-Rosette, *Black Paris: The African Writers' Landscape* (Urbana: University of Illinois Press, 1998), 240.

2. bell hooks, "Postmodern Blackness," *Postmodern Culture* 1 (1) (1990): 10.

3. Salim Muwakkil, "Deconstructing Blackness," *In These Times*, 16 June 1997, 25.

4. Jim Sleeper, "Toward an End of Blackness: An Argument for the Surrender of Race Consciousness," *Harper's Magazine* (May 1997): 44.

5. Muwakkil, "Deconstructing Blackness," 27.

6. Samira Kawash, *Dislocating the Color Line: Identity, Hybridity, and Singularity in African American Literature* (Stanford, Calif.: Stanford University Press, 1997), 20.

7. Daryl Scott, *Contempt and Pity: Social Policy and the Image of the Damaged Black Psyche, 1880–1996* (Chapel Hill: University of North Carolina Press, 1997), 191.

8. Jon Michael Spencer, "Trends of Opposition to Multiculturalism," *Black Scholar* 23 (2) (1994): 2.

9. Joyce A. Joyce, "The Black Canon: Reconstructing Black American Literary Criticism," *New Literary History* 18 (2) (winter 1987): 342.

10. Joyce A. Joyce, "'Who the Cap Fit': Unconsciousness and Unconscionableness in the Criticism of Houston A. Baker, Jr. and Henry Louis Gates, Jr.," *New Literary History* 18 (2) (winter 1987): 379.

11. Joyce, "Black Canon," 341.

12. Nancy Hartsock, "Foucault and Power: A Theory for Women?" in *Feminism/Postmodernism*, ed. Linda Nicholson (New York: Routledge, 1990), 163–164.

13. Nancy Hartsock, "Rethinking Modernism: Minority vs. Majority Theories," in *The Nature and Context of Minority Discourse*, ed. Abdul Jan Mohamed and David Lloyd (New York: Oxford University Press, 1990), 20–21.

14. Hartsock, "Rethinking Modernism," 21.

15. Hartsock, "Rethinking Modernism," 34.

16. hooks, "Postmodern Blackness," 11.

17. Jacques Derrida, *Speech and Phenomena*, trans. David Allison (Evanston, Ill.: Northwestern University Press, 1972), 145–146.

18. Richard Kearney, *Dialogues with Contemporary Continental Thinkers* (Manchester: Manchester University Press, 1984), 125.

19. Arkady Plotnitsky writes: "It is true that Derrida's analysis does not simply destroy the subject, but situates and resituates it—to the extent, finally very limited, that

subjectivity can be retained, outside of the necessity of accounting for its functioning elsewhere. That *deconstruction* does not simply destroy the subject was perhaps the main point used in the appropriation—the domestication and democratization—of deconstruction by way of ethical subjectivity, which is often not attentive enough to this point." See Arkady Plotnitsky, *Reconfigurations: Critical Theory and General Economy* (Gainesville: University Press of Florida, 1993), 58.

20. Jacques Derrida, *Writing and Difference*, trans. Alan Bass (Chicago: Chicago University Press, 1978), 227.

21. Jacques Derrida, *Positions*, trans. Alan Bass (Chicago: University of Chicago Press, 1981), 28.

22. Derrida, *Positions*, 9.

23. Michel Foucault, *Power/Knowledge: Selected Interviews and Other Writings by Michel Foucault*, ed. C. Gordon (London: Pantheon, 1980), 97.

24. Foucault, *Power/Knowledge*, 73–74.

25. Foucault, *Power/Knowledge*, 117.

26. Alan Schrift, *Nietzsche and the Question of Interpretation: Between Hermeneutics and Deconstruction* (New York: Routledge, 1990), 80.

27. Stuart Hall, "Cultural Identity and Cinematic Representation," *Framework* (36) (1989): 70.

28. Richard Bondi, "Elements of Character," *Journal of Religious Ethics* 12 (2) (fall 1984): 201.

29. Jules-Rosette, *Black Paris*, 241.

30. Kawash, *Dislocating the Color Line*, 28, 29.

31. Jewel Amoah, "Narrative: The Road to Black Feminist Theory," *Berkeley Women's Law Journal* 12 (1997): 85.

32. Virginia Domínques, *White by Definition: Social Classification in Creole Louisiana* (New Brunswick, N.J.: Rutgers University Press, 1986), 9.

33. Patricia Hill Collins, *Black Feminist Thought: Knowledge, Consciousness, and the Politics of Empowerment* (New York: Routledge, 1990), 10; see also Amoah, "Narrative."

34. Laurance Thomas, "Group Autonomy and Narrative Identity," in *Color, Class, Identity: The New Politics of Race*, ed. John Aythur and Amy Shapiro (Boulder, Colo.: Westview, 1996), 179–190; reprinted in *Reflections: An Anthology of African American Philosophy*, ed. James Montmarquet and William Hardy (Belmont, Calif.: Wadsworth/Thomson, 2000), 218.

35. Thomas, "Group Autonomy and Narrative Identity," 219.

36. Alasdair MacIntyre, "Epistemological Crises, Dramatic Narrative and the Philosophy of Science," *The Monist* 60 (4) (October 1977): 454, emphasis mine.

37. MacIntyre, "Epistemological Crises," 455.

38. MacIntyre, "Epistemological Crises," 458.

39. For a good discussion of the different threats of nonbeing faced by African people in recent times, see Paget Henry, "African and Afro-Caribbean Existential Philosophies," in *Existence in Black: An Anthology of Black Existential Philosophy*, ed. Lewis Gordon (New York: Routledge, 1997).

40. MacIntyre, "Epistemological Crises," 455.

41. Alasdair MacIntyre, *After Virtue* (Notre Dame, Ind.: University of Notre Dame Press, 1984), 222.

42. MacIntyre, "Epistemological Crises," 460–461.

43. MacIntyre, "Epistemological Crises," 461.

44. Walter Benn Michaels, "Race into Culture: A Critical Genealogy of Cultural Identity," *Critical Inquiry* 18 (summer 1992).

45. Michaels, "Race into Culture," 658.

46. Michaels, "Race into Culture," 679.

47. Michaels, "Race into Culture," 683.

48. Michaels, "Race into Culture," 682.

49. Michaels, "Race into Culture," 684–685.

50. Michaels, "Race into Culture," 684n40.

51. Walter Benn Michaels, "Posthistoricism," *Transition* 70 6 (2) (1996): 9.

52. MacIntyre, *After Virtue*, 206–207.

53. MacIntyre, *After Virtue*, 213.

54. Charles Davis and Henry Louis Gates Jr., eds., *The Slave Narratives* (New York: Oxford University Press, 1985), xxxiv.

55. Jules-Rosette, *Black Paris*, 242.

56. Herbert Gutman, *The Black Family in Slavery and Freedom* (New York: Pantheon, 1976); Lawrence Levine, *Black Culture and Black Consciousness* (New York: Oxford University Press, 1978); George Rawick, *From Sundown to Sunup: The Making of a Black Community* (Westport, Conn.: Greenwood, 1972); and John Blassingame, *The Slave Community* (New York: Oxford University Press, 1972).

57. For a clarification of "thick descriptions" and "thin descriptions," see Clifford Geertz, "Thick Descriptions: Toward an Interpretive Theory of Culture," in *The Interpretation of Cultures*, ed. Clifford Geertz (New York: Basic, 1973).

58. Peter Novick, *That Noble Dream: The "Objectivity Question" and the American Historical Profession* (New York: Cambridge University Press, 1988), 484.

59. Quoted in Novick, *That Noble Dream*, 486.

60. Blassingame, *Slave Community*, 41

61. Barbara Hill Rigney, *The Voices of Toni Morrison* (Columbus: Ohio State University Press, 1991), 38.

62. Amoah, "Narrative," 91.

63. MacIntyre, *After Virtue*, 216.

64. Amoah, "Narrative," 84.

65. Although not dealing specifically with nationalist notions of Black identity, Kevin Gaines, in his study of uplift ideology, has masterfully exposed the limitations of early notions of Black leadership and identity with regard to gender and class. See Kevin Gaines, *Uplifting the Race: Black Leadership, Politics, and Culture in the Twentieth Century* (Chapel Hill: University of North Carolina Press, 1996).

4

Du Bois and Appiah: The Politics of Race and Racial Identity

Patrick Goodin

Several scholars, among them Stuart Hall,[1] K. Anthony Appiah,[2] Anna Stubblefield,[3] and Robert Gooding-Williams[4] have recently put forward what they have variously called "sociohistorical," "nonessentialist," or "social constructionist" conceptions of racial identity. They sharply contrast such conceptions of racial identity from what is called "racial essentialism," the view that races exist in the order of nature, that they are not conventional but "real." For these scholars, there is a radical separation and opposition between these two views. Stubblefield is especially unequivocal on this point. According to her, "those who would attempt to answer the question 'what is race?' must either choose between an essentialist and a non-essentialist stance or be condemned to struggle endlessly and fruitlessly between them."[5] Yet, the meaning of this distinction is by no means perfectly clear. What status does this distinction have? Is it intelligible? What does it entail politically?

Of these four scholars, only Appiah has published, in addition to his positive account of racial identity, a fairly detailed proof that races constructed essentially do not exist. In this chapter, I want to engage the problematic of the essentialist–nonessentialist distinction in Appiah's work, particularly as it appears in his essay "Race, Culture, Identity: Misunderstood Connections."[6] I focus on this essay in part because it includes both his negative proof that there are no races and his positive proof of racial identity, thereby enabling one to see how Appiah intends to combine these two proofs into a comprehensive whole. I am also particularly interested in this essay because Appiah engages the great W. E. B. Du Bois, a pivotal and controversial figure in the history of the debate concerning race, who is described by Stubblefield as having "adopted an ultimately essentialist approach."[7]

A little over 100 years ago, Du Bois first delivered at the founding meeting of the American Negro Academy and later that same year published the essay "The Conservation of Races." In this essay, Du Bois defends a sociohistorical understanding of race—according to which the human race can be divided into groups or races, each of which is determined by the striving for certain ideals. Each group has a particular or peculiar message that it and only it can contribute. Also, the scientific–biological conception of race is rejected in favor of a sociohistorical conception.

Nearly ninety years after the publication of Du Bois's work, Appiah criticizes Du Bois in "The Uncompleted Argument: Du Bois and the Illusion of Race" for not having a truly sociohistorical conception of race. In fact, Appiah asserts, underneath Du Bois's sociohistorical conception proposed both in "The Conservation of Races" and in subsequent essays, lay the vestiges of the scientific–biological conception that Du Bois supposedly rejected as untenable. About nine years later, though, in "Race, Culture, Identity; Misunderstood Connections," Appiah amends this earlier observation, concluding that there is more to Du Bois's sociohistorical conception than he initially realized. In fact, Appiah goes so far as to claim that what Du Bois was after is Appiah's own notion of racial identity. What accounts for this change in Appiah's view of Du Bois?

This chapter divides into three parts. I begin with a fairly detailed account of Appiah's proof that there are no races. Next, I give an account of his argument for racial identity as the replacement for the concept of race. Then, I present my own observations of Appiah's engagement of Du Bois and explore the political meaning of race and racial identity as well as the politics of the movement from one to the other. In this final section, I also make some observations about certain features shared by the social constructionists and nonessentialists and about the very idea of social construction itself. A careful look at Appiah's work and at the constructionists in general will hopefully shed some useful light on the meaning of community and identity not only among Black people, but among Black scholars as well.

THE NEGATIVE ACCOUNT: THERE IS NO "ESSENCE" IN RACE

Appiah begins his essays with three examples, each of which he characterizes as involving some sort of conceptual ambiguity regarding the meaning of "race." The first example involves an American of Chinese descent who finds him- or herself labeled "Oriental." The second example involves a dark-skinned person who arrives in America from Sicily and who is labeled "Caucasian." The final example concerns a person born of a White father and a Black mother who altogether confounds the notion of labeling. Appiah places all three examples in the late nineteenth and early twentieth centuries and uses them to make clear the threefold purpose of his essay. "Seventy years ago," he asks," how would you have explained to someone from outside the modern West what the English word 'race' meant?"[8] In response to this puzzle, Appiah explains "why American social distinctions cannot be understood in terms of the concept 'race,'"[9] and shows that replacing the notion of race with the notion of civilization is not helpful. Finally, he proposes that "for analytical purposes that we use instead the notion of racial identity."[10]

Appiah begins with race as a conceptual problem, a problem about the ambiguous meaning of the term. His initial approach to the problem is significant because it is on the level of the conceptual—a theoretical meaning—that he presents his ultimate solution to the problem of race. He does not begin with the realities, experiences, or suffering of racism. In other words, he does not begin where Du Bois began. Instead, he regards it as simply a conceptual problem, one whose solution can be found by turning to the philosophy of language and in particular to theories of meaning.

According to Appiah, "In the 1920s, there were—and there are still today—two very different and competing philosophical notions of what it is to give an adequate account of the meaning of a word or expression."[11] These two theories are respectively the "ideational" and the "referential" views of meaning. The ideational view, as the term itself suggests, deals with our ideas about a term and considers under what sorts of circumstances we apply it. By contrast, the referential view deals with the referent of the term, that is, that in reality to which it refers. Is it possible to find or construct a definition of race that can satisfy either the ideational or the referential theory of meaning? If it is possible on either theory, there can or will be races; if it is not possible, there cannot or will not be races. To determine the possibility or the impossibility of races, Appiah constructs a sociohistorical analysis of the term, at the end of which no viable candidate is found. On the basis of this negative result, Appiah concludes that there are no races.

The sociohistorical analysis Appiah constructs reveals itself as follows: On the basis of passages from the works of Thomas Jefferson and Matthew Arnold, Appiah derives a notion of race that reflects in some sense the ordinary (and perhaps the racist or the racialist) opinion as to what race is. That notion, according to Appiah, is reflected in what he calls "racialism," the view that "we could divide human beings into a small number of groups called 'races,' in such a way that the members of these groups shared certain fundamental, heritable, physical, moral, intellectual and cultural characteristics with one another that they did not share with members of any other race."[12] These divisions between groups of human beings are built into nature. On this view, each group shares an essence. There are then, so to speak, essential differences between groups. Once one knows the group to which one belongs, one knows not only the physiology, but also the corresponding capacities for moral, aesthetic, and cultural development.

Now, the respectability of this view of race/races, according to Appiah, is derived from its association with science, and in particular with the new science of biology then emerging in the mid-nineteenth century. Charles Darwin had published *The Origin of Species by Natural Selection or the Preservation of Favored Races in the Struggle for Life*, the core of which turns on two notions. First, that organisms develop by "descent with modification."[13] Second, that the "mechanism of modification was natural selection,"[14] that is, the selective survival of characteristics that give individuals advantages in the "struggle for life." According to Appiah, there were various problems with Darwin's theory, for example, an "underdeveloped theory of inheritance"[15] and how to account for the possibility of variation. But Darwin's theory when it was complemented with Gregor Mendel's work on genes put "the theory of natural selection on sound footing."[16] Together, they laid and clarified the foundation of the modern scientific view of organisms and their development.

For Darwin, states Appiah, species and subspecies and hence races were "essentially classificatory conveniences. . . . [Darwin] was, in philosophical jargon, a nominalist about species, holding the boundaries between species were not marked 'in nature,' and if species were not marked in nature then varieties or subspecies (which is what, in his view, races were), being even less distinct from one another than species, were presumably classificatory conveniences also."[17]

This is the key move that Appiah makes—Darwin's theory combined with Mendelian genetics put the science of biology on firm footing. This is essentially the modern scientific view. In this view, differences between groups of human beings are not based in nature, they are rather to be understood nominalistically as merely ways of classifying. If races are understood purely nominalistically, then not only can science not provide support for the "racial essence" view of Jefferson and Arnold, it also contradicts them.

According to Appiah, "once we have the modern genetic picture we can see that each person is the product of enormous numbers of genetic characteristics, interacting with each other and the environment, and that there is nothing in the theory of evolution to guarantee that a group that shares one characteristic will share all or even most others."[18] On the basis of the modern genetic picture, rigid lines cannot be drawn between groups of human beings determining the "things we care about. . . . [O]nce we have the modern theory of inheritance, you can see why there is less correlation than everyone expected between skin color and things we are about: people are not the product of essences, but of genes interacting with each other and with environments and there is little systematic correlation between the genes that fix color and the like and the genes that shape courage or literary genius."[19] I take this to mean that Appiah understands genes as fixing everything, including "courage."

On the basis of this sociohistorical analysis of the term "race," no viable candidate is found that can satisfy the requirements of either the ideational or the referential theory of meaning. Appiah therefore concludes that there are no races.

THE POSITIVE ACCOUNT: BEYOND RACE TO RACIAL IDENTITY

Believing that he has successfully gotten rid of the notion of race through his sociohistorical analysis of the concept, Appiah shifts to his positive construction. He begins anew, as it were, with Du Bois. Appiah notes that in Du Bois's 1940 autobiography *Dusk of the Dawn*, Du Bois writes that "the meaning of 'race' conceived in [a] sociohistorical term"[20] is circumscribed by the label "the social heritage of slavery: the discrimination and the insult."[21] What binds Black people together—what makes them belong to the same race is not some physiological constellation, but rather some social constellation of meaning. The physiology—the "badge of color"—is not what determines a race. It plays no role whatsoever. It is, so to speak, purely external. Du Bois, it seems, has already substituted racial identity for race. One may wonder at this point how it is possible to constitute groups on the level of social meaning and leave the color behind or regard it only as a badge. What, in other words, is the relationship between a badge and a construction of a group on the level of social meaning? This I shall answer later.

Appiah, in any case, agrees with Du Bois's understanding of race. He thinks Du Bois is correct with regard to his characterization of what constitutes a race, but "his approach is misleading." The framework by means of which Du Bois arrived at the correct characterization is flawed. Appiah, however, does not perform "exegesis" on Du Bois's work: he takes another tack and provides a completely sociohistorical account of racial identity. He does not try and patch up Du Bois but instead abandons entirely Du Bois's framework. He does not begin where Du Bois begins, but he does make Du Bois's "badge of color" his own point of departure. Could he have begun otherwise?

I hope to make clear shortly that according to Appiah the fundamental defect of Du Bois's account is that he grounds his characterization of race on an essentialist analysis or essentialism and on the notion that there are essences. But Appiah's analysis of what binds Black people together, in contradistinction, will not in any way be essentialistic. He must shape an account of racial identity that does not in any way depend on any sort of essentialism; it must be one variety or another of nominalism. He must show how labels can do things, can do damage all by themselves, without being grounded in any sort of essence.

How does Appiah do this? He begins with an example taken from American history. The label "African" was once applied to people who would later be called "Negro" and then "colored," "black," "Afro-American," "African

American," and a few others. Historically, of course, each label has a certain signification and consequently produced certain effects for the person so labeled. These are historical facts. To trace the history of the labels is to also trace the history of the changing constellation of effects.

Once labels are applied, they "come to have their social effects" and "not only social effects but psychological ones as well,"[22] according to Appiah. For him, the crucial point about labels and their social effects is that they shape what he calls "identification, the process through which an individual intentionally shapes her project—including her own life plans and conception of the good—by reference to available labels, available identities."[23] But how are these mere labels able to do these things all by themselves? To give an account of this, Appiah turns to a species of nominalism called "dynamic nominalism," put forward and articulated by Ian Hacking in a piece entitled "Making People Up."

Dynamic nominalism may be characterized as the idea that "numerous kinds of human beings and human acts come into being hand in hand with our invention of the categories labeling them."[24] This brand of nominalism is a way of showing how labels by themselves created "kinds" of human beings where there were not these kinds before. On this view, what kind of human being it is possible for one to become depends on the available labels and categories. One cannot become a certain human being prior to the invention of the label. The range of the labels in existence determines the range of the kind of human being one can become.

Perhaps the most significant feature of this dynamic nominalism is that it shows how labels pick out and/or perhaps create a type that did not exist prior to the label or the invention of the label. At any historical moment, our choices are circumscribed by the range of available labels and identities. In addition to this, according to Appiah, an important distinction must be made between the two different sorts of labels and identities.[25] One sort is characterized, for example, by waiter, doctor, teacher—each of which is unintelligible apart from some political certification process. The certification is never based on some, so to speak, natural antecedent property. The other sort of label is characterized by Black, straight, gay, female, and so on. These all require antecedent properties that determine ascriptions of the label. The sort of label-identity that is crucial for Appiah is, of course, the latter. They are the ones that we fight over. They are the ones that generate heated debates as to the antecedent properties necessary for the ascription—as to the criteria for ascription. They are also the ones regarding which the same label can be employed but different antecedent properties can be picked or different criteria held. But once one is labeled X, certain effects follow whether or not one has antecedent properties or agrees to the label.

Appiah concludes his positive argument for racial identity and indicates explicitly how Du Bois is correct in his characterization but wrong or misleading in his approach.

Du Bois' analytical problem was, in effect that he believed that for racial labeling of this sort to have any obvious real effects that it did have—among them, crucially, his own identification with other black people and with Africa—there must be some real essence that held the race together. Our account of the history of the label reveals that this is a mistake: once we focus, as Du Bois almost saw, on the racial badge—the signifier rather than the signified, the word rather than the concept—we see both that the effects of labeling are powerful and real and that false ideas, muddle and mistake and mischief, played a certain role in determining both how the label was applied and to what purposes.[26]

For labels to have real effect, essences are not at all needed or necessary. All one needs is to "understand the sociohistorical process of construction of the race" and one sees "that the label works despite the absence of an essence."[27]

Now, according to Appiah, with the theory of dynamic nominalism, one sees that one does not need essences—as Du Bois thinks—to understand how labels do real damage or have real effects. The multiplicity of kinds of groups of human beings are not bound together by essences. That is why "Du Bois so often found himself reduced, in his attempts to define race, to occult forces: if you look for a shared essence you won't get anything, so you'll come to believe you've missed it because it is super-subtle, difficult to experience or identify, in short, mysterious."[28]

In the remainder of this second part of his essay, Appiah does primarily two things. First, he fleshes out the notion of identity understood in a dynamic–nominalistic fashion, including the multiplicity of identities. Second, he argues that culture cannot be substituted for race. I say this to indicate that for all intents and purposes the argument for the replacement of race with racial identity is complete at this point.

CIVILIZATION VERSUS RACIAL IDENTITY

In the previous section I gave a relatively detailed account of Appiah's argument. It was necessary because Appiah says as much by what he does and by his manner of argumentation as by what he explicitly says. It was important, then, to display the manner and mode of his thought.

With this in view, I want to examine more closely Appiah's treatment of Du Bois and his supplanting of Du Bois's "civilization" with "racial identity." I want to begin with the observation that Appiah understands and presents the racial problem, the issue of race, as a conceptual–analytic problem (one need not argue too strenuously that for Du Bois, race is decidedly not a conceptual problem). His solution takes place on the same level. Is Appiah correct in understanding race as a conceptual problem or as primarily a conceptual problem? If not, then Appiah's solution will not provide us any real relief.

The racialist position, typified in the writings of Jefferson and Arnold, against which Appiah argues, is presented as an essentialist position and Appiah's criticism of Du Bois is that Du Bois remains unwittingly committed to a brand of essentialism in his own concept of "civilization." But any essentialist position, Appiah argues, cannot approach the race problem as a conceptual problem but instead must approach it as a fact of nature. Appiah's refutation of the racialist turns decisively on the understanding that the current/best science no longer views race as "natural" but rather as a way of grouping people that is no more than a conceptual "convenience." In other words, science now views race nominalistically. Appiah's solution, then, is not so much a solution but a "dis-solution." He has solved the problem by dissolving it.

In dissolving the race problem, however, Appiah ends up making claims about the human being that pretty closely resemble essentialist claims. The human being—he says—"person,"[29] "people,"[30] is or are the product not of essences but of genes interacting with one another and with environments. Appiah ends up characterizing the human being more rigidly than he intends, since not only does he make the human being a function of "genes interacting with one another and environments,"[31] but also makes genes, by extension, fix everything—color, courage, and literary genius. Is the materialistic schematic that Appiah employs to refute racial essentialism merely some sort of scaffolding that one can throw away once his point that there are no races has been made? Is the schematic content neutral? It may not be.

In moving from his argument against races to his argument for racial identities, Appiah does not link in a continuum these two parts of his work. In other words, he does not specifically provide a bridge between these parts. It is as if the genetics theory that serves as proof for Appiah's argument against race must fall away once the point has been made. This may, however, be just an appearance. Can Appiah really abandon in his positive construction the materialistic scheme he relies on in the first part of his essay?

In turning to the part of his essay in which he offers his positive construction, Appiah develops a nominalistically understood concept of racial identity. Is there a coincidental parallelism between the scientific proof used to show that there are no races and the sociopolitical concept of racial identity used to show that racial labels can have real effects without being grounded in some sort of essence? A careful reading of the sociohistoric argument of the first part of Appiah's essay and the sociopolitical argument in the second shows that the latter is nothing but the former made positive. Is this positive "remaking" intelligible? It is not easy to understand how one put together the apparent freedom inherent in the construction of identities with the determinism that seems to characterize the genetic picture of the human being.

In constructing his sociohistorical account of racial identity, Appiah starts with Du Bois's "badge of color," with Du Bois's racial label grounded in some sort of essence. But why begin with what Appiah characterizes as a misconceived notion? Would it have been possible for Appiah to begin else-where? It may not be entirely accidental that Appiah starts with Du Bois's racial label, determined as it was on the basis of bitter experience. The label makes no sense without the experience, that is, the experience must precede the label. Only with this code determination can Appiah determine that the label has a certain affect. But when Appiah wants to show how other labels have certain affects, he goes to history, that is, he demonstrates the affects that they have had. Is it the case, though, that these labels, like Du Bois's "badge of color," can only have some affect when they become the rhetori-cal embodiment of some concrete experience? Yet, Appiah's argument showing that labels have affects in and of themselves amounts to a history of the effects of labels. On the basis of the history of labels, Appiah concludes that labels can and do affect, that is, do real damage.

The argument seems to amount to this—labels have the power to affect because they have had the power in the past. Simply put, labels have the power to affect because they have had the power to affect. But can Appiah's historical view of the effect of labels be made equivalent to an account of what labels can do in and of themselves—as he wants and according to his own argument must do—without going to history, to experience, or to some form of essentialism? Appiah's replacement of "essence" with "the sociohis-toric construction of race" replaces the palpableness of concrete experience with its depth and complexity with the atemporal horizontal continuum of constant, never-ending sociohistoric construction. The transmuting of expe-rience vis-à-vis labels blinds him to the real ground of labels.

Unlike Du Bois, Appiah begins not with experience, not with the reality of racism, but with the labels, which are either clear or ambiguous, which once having come into being lose their connection to the concrete experience that made them intelligible in the first place. Freed from their mooring in experi-ence they seem to take on a life of their own. Hence one can deal with them purely on the level of the linguistic. But the meaning of race on the linguis-tic level is not the same as the meaning of race on the experiential level. This difference of meaning accounts, I believe, for the utter lack of pathos in Ap-piah's essay, whereas one senses and feels it palpably in Du Bois's work.

In a sense (to use a cliché), Du Bois is correct that the experiential ties that bind people together are grounded in essences, that is, reality. And not only are these essences real, they must be grounded in some sort of bodily char-acteristic or characteristics. But here we have to go back to the first part of Appiah's essay and in a sense become aware of the real issue: Is the human being reducible to pure physiology or not? Appiah's argument relies on the assumption that the human being is pure physiology and yet it is not entirely clear that he consistently holds to this assumption.

I want to end this chapter by remarking on two issues in particular: what Appiah shares about race with the other social constructionists mentioned at the beginning of this chapter, and what a social constructionist understanding of race implies for the idea of community among Black intellectuals.

With regard to the first issue, it seems to me that what Appiah shares with the other social constructionists is this lack of emphasis on the concrete experience, the experiential. Race for these thinkers is construed as something constructed on the level of "speech" or "discourse," "semantically," and this discourse itself can do damage.[32] The issue then becomes a matter of exposing this trick on the semantic level and thus freeing us morally. But we may ask: Is oppression a conceptual trick, a discursive fraud fundamentally? And therefore: Is the solution an "unmasking"?[33] In any case, if race has been a discursive, conceptual trick, how does one reconcile this understanding of it with the concrete suffering of people so designated? It seems to me, at the very least these are fundamentally different and not easily reconcilable.

This leads to the second issue, namely that of community among Black intellectuals. For if the divide is as I have laid it out, the two positions imply two different ways of construing community. A community formed on the basis of a shared legacy of suffering seems at odds with one formed on the basis of a shared realization that race has been nothing but a discursive fraud. Again, how would we reconcile them? Of one thing, however, we may be sure—a fundamentally different sociopolitical constellation separates Appiah from Du Bois. What would a social constructionist construal of race have meant to the Du Bois of *The Conservation of Race* and *Dusk of Dawn*? What allows us at present to raise the question of race on this very abstract conceptual level?

NOTES

Versions of this chapter were presented at the 1997 American Philosophical Association meeting in Philadelphia, the 1998 Society for the Advancement of American Philosophy Conference at Marquette University, and the New York chapter of the Society for the Study of Africana Philosophy.

1. See Stuart Hall, "New Ethnicities," in *Stuart Hall: Critical Dialogues in Cultural Studies*, ed. David Morely and Kuan-Hsing Chen (London: Routledge, 1996).

2. See K. Anthony Appiah, "Race, Culture, Identity: Misunderstood Connections," in *Color Conscious: The Political Morality of Race*, K. Anthony Appiah and Amy Gutmann (Princeton, N.J.: Princeton University Press, 1996).

3. See Anna Stubblefield, "Racial Identity and Non-essentialism about Race," *Social Theory and Practice* 21 (3) (fall 1995).

4. See Robert Gooding-Williams, "Race, Multiculturalism and Democracy," *Constellations* 5 (1) (1998).

5. See Stubblefield, "Racial Identity," 341.

6. The four scholars are in some way familiar with each other's work and also even engage some of each other's work, for example, Stubblefield cites Appiah, Appiah mentions Hall's critique of his earlier work, and Gooding-Williams explicitly relies on the works of Appiah and Stubblefield.

7. See Stubblefield, "Racial Identity," 341.

8. Appiah, "Race, Culture, Identity," 31.

9. Appiah, "Race, Culture, Identity," 32.

10. Appiah, "Race, Culture, Identity," 32.

11. Appiah, "Race, Culture, Identity," 33.

12. Appiah, "Race, Culture, Identity," 54.

13. Appiah, "Race, Culture, Identity," 65.

14. Appiah, "Race, Culture, Identity," 65.

15. Appiah, "Race, Culture, Identity," 66.

16. Appiah, "Race, Culture, Identity," 66.

17. Appiah, "Race, Culture, Identity," 67.

18. Appiah, "Race, Culture, Identity," 68.

19. Appiah, "Race, Culture, Identity," 68.

20. Appiah, "Race, Culture, Identity," 75.

21. Appiah, "Race, Culture, Identity," 75, who is quoting from W. E. B. Du Bois, *Dusk of the Dawn: An Essay toward an Autobiography of a Race Concept* (New York: Harcourt, Brace, 1940).

22. Appiah, "Race, Culture, Identity," 78.

23. Ian Hacking, "Making People Up," in *Reconstructing Individualism, Autonomy, Individuality, and the Self in Western Thought*, ed. Martin Sosna (Stanford, Calif.: Stanford University Press, 1987), 236; see also Ian Hacking, *The Social Construction of What?* (Cambridge, Mass.: Harvard University Press, 1999).

24. Hacking quoted by Appiah, "Race, Culture, Identity," 78.

25. Appiah, "Race, Culture, Identity," 70.

26. Appiah, "Race, Culture, Identity," 81.

27. Appiah, "Race, Culture, Identity," 81.

28. Appiah, "Race, Culture, Identity," 81.

29. Appiah, "Race, Culture, Identity," 68.

30. Appiah, "Race, Culture, Identity," 72.

31. Appiah, "Race, Culture, Identity," 72.

32. See Stubblefield, "Racial Identity," 345; and Gooding-Williams, "Race, Multiculturalism and Democracy," 25.

33. Hacking, *Social Construction of What?*, 53.

II

IN QUEST OF
COMMUNITY: SOCIALITY
AND SITUATED FREEDOM

5

Of the Quest for Freedom As Community

Robert E. Birt

Why not the simple attempt to touch the other, to feel the other, to explain the other to myself? Was not my freedom given to me . . . in order to build the world of the *You?*

—Frantz Fanon, *Black Skin, White Masks*[1]

The primary aspiration of all history is a genuine community of human beings.

—Martin Buber, *Paths in Utopia*[2]

The individual is the social being.

—Karl Marx, *Writings of the Young Marx on Philosophy and Society*[3]

Is not the quest for freedom in our time essentially a quest for community? Or must it not become so? And what is the historic significance of this quest for the experiences of Black people and our present or future emancipatory strivings? Inasmuch as the struggle for freedom is social, it seeks a liberated social condition. It seeks to alter radically our way of being-with-others, to liberate us from self-estrangement and reified social relations. Yet, the surpassing of self-estrangement and social reification is possible only through an upsurge of common freedom. To the extent that we give social form to this upsurge we thereby create community.

Most humans desire freedom. We are *human* by virtue of our freedom. It is freedom that constitutes the *being* of the human. Freedom is no mere property that we have, but rather the peculiar mode of being that we *are*. As the dimension of transcendence and possibility, it is the very structure of

88 Robert E. Birt

existence. For this reason, Frantz Fanon describes freedom as "what is most human in man."[4] And Jean-Paul Sartre infers more explicitly that "man is freedom";[5] that "freedom is impossible to distinguish from the *being* of human reality."[6] Things may have their being ready-made, but *being* human is an activity of becoming. Our being *is* becoming. For in the absence of a fixed nature or predetermined essence, we humans can (even must) invent ourselves. Is not this human capacity for self-creation the most unique manifestation of human freedom?

But this freedom is not the disembodied, atemporal liberty of gods or spirits. It is not the asocial liberty of the liberal imagination. Though we humans can invent ourselves, we can do so only through choices and actions conditioned by our social existence. Human freedom is situated freedom, and we are beings in situation. Whatever may be the case with gods, a nonsituated *human* freedom is an existential impossibility. But being in situation implies the sociality of existence. For an essential aspect of lived situations is the human relation with others. The self is not a monad, nor freedom an isolated subjectivity. As Simone de Beauvoir correctly observes, "the existence of others as a freedom defines my situation and is even the condition of my own freedom."[7] One cannot be a self without others, but is always an existing individual in relation to others. Our freedom—hence our very *being*—is an active relation of self to others and the world.

Yet, our social existence is often unfree; our relations with each other reified by social oppression. Freedom may characterize human existence, but existential freedom is often denied in social practice. Human being is transcendence. But in a situation of social oppression this transcendence is denied and thwarted, is "condemned to fall uselessly back upon itself."[8] Yet deny transcendence and life becomes suffused with the smell of death. Our relations with others become reified and deprived of reciprocity. Hence, Fanon notes a "mummification" of cultural life and individual thought among victims of colonialism.[9] And Martin Luther King Jr. observes that America's racial caste system "substitutes an 'I–it relationship for an I–thou' relation, and ends up relegating persons to the status of things."[10] While common freedom is the true meaning of human sociality, and mutual recognition the real meaning of being with others, oppression works to reduce us to pure facticity and to impose on human relations the twisted form of a relation between things.

Yet, we are not things. And we are violated by the reification of our relations. But freedom cannot be realized through flight or by an inward withdrawal of the self. Freedom is realized through resistance to that which denies it, through defiance of social alienation, and (most importantly) through a transcending social praxis that discovers and invents new forms of association in which our transcendence is affirmed rather than denied, in which reciprocity and recognition replace estrangement and atomization. In short, freedom realizes itself in community, and the human being creates him- or herself in and through the creation of community.

Community is the expression of freedom in a social mode. For this reason, Sartre describes it as common freedom. Its essential characteristic is the "resurrection of freedom." And its mode of being is "that of a developing action" that "can be conceived only as the ubiquity of freedom positing itself."[11] Community is created by this "developing action," this common praxis whereby freedom "posits" itself. Of course, this self-positing freedom is no self-contained essence or Fichtean ego. It is a free association of fraternal, self-active individuals among whom bonds of mutual recognition have formed. And the recognition that thereby replaces reification is "simultaneously recognition of everyone of his freedom . . . *through* the freedom of the other, and an affirmation of membership in the group."[12] In community, individuals can recognize themselves in each other, and can each find in the other an affirming incarnation of his or her own freedom. When we create community, our way of being-with-others is transformed and oriented toward "a creative and life-affirming intersubjectivity."[13] Transcendence is expressed in relatedness, individuality in association. Insofar as the established order is grounded in reified relations, the creation of community is *a revolutionary* praxis, its realization is an essential aim of a liberatory quest for freedom.

But this suggests that our quest for freedom requires a rethinking of freedom. It requires a shift of focus from individualist notions of liberty so deeply rooted in American culture to an emphasis on the communality of freedom—indeed, to a vision of a cooperative community of freedom. A revisioning of freedom is crucial because a really human experience of freedom is hardly possible without community, and also because one of the most salient features of contemporary social unfreedom is precisely the negation of community and the atomizing of human bonds. A genuine liberatory struggle must vigorously resist this negation and atomization. Henceforth, the affirmation of freedom is also an affirmation of community, an affirmation of the right to community.

Now this revisioning of freedom is in sharp contrast to predominant notions of freedom in America. In America, freedom is commonly seen as a purely personal or private experience. It is a possession of atomized individuals. This view is deeply informed by traditions of liberal individualism that emerged in the early modern era of adolescent capitalism.[14] Its historical–social origin is the modern profiteering, market-driven society. Its philosophical pedigree can be traced to the works of Thomas Hobbes and John Locke. This is the same tradition that frames our legal conceptions of civil rights and personal liberties. In liberal thought, the individual is not part of any social whole. Community is largely seen as artificial and even as harmful to individual liberty. Liberal thought classically pictures the individual as a presocial (or asocial) being whose liberty first exists in a presocial state of nature and who only later (perhaps reluctantly) enters society. This atomic individual "is free inasmuch as he is a proprietor of his person and capacities."[15] Hence, one finds not only a property-centered (bourgeois) conception of freedom, but also a proprietary view of the self. The self is a commodity, and one's own body a possession. One easily discerns in this the seeds of individualist alienation from self and others. C. B. MacPherson notes that liberal "freedom is a function of possession."[16] In America, freedom is usually conceptualized in terms of rights, and rights are thought to be solely the possession of individuals.

The shortcomings of liberal individualism are numerous and have been often critiqued. But of special concern for the oppressed is its disabling false consciousness about the realities of liberal society. As Harold Cruse notes, this America that idealizes the rights of the individual above all else, is still a nation dominated by the social power of "groups, classes, in-groups and cliques."[17] There are few rights that any individual has that are not backed up by the power of some group. Cruse hastens to add that if an individual Black person has proportionately fewer rights, it is because his or her ethnic group has proportionately less power. Hence, those Blacks who have "accepted the full essence of the Great American Ideal of individualism are in serious trouble trying to function in America."[18] The problem is transparent. Oppressed people are not oppressed first as individuals, but as a group or a people. It is by means of our violation as a people that individuality is denied. The "stunted individuality" that Max Horkheimer claims to find among victims of race and class oppression is obviously a result of the collective violation of the human subject.[19] Our *invisibility* as subjects and our presence in the American mind as *problem* people are part of a regime of group oppression, of our racial reification as a people. For this reason King argues that since "we have been oppressed as a group . . . we must overcome that oppression as a group."[20] Without a community of resistance, members of an oppressed group can neither achieve nor defend their rights as individuals.

Yet, the issue goes deeper still. If situated freedom constitutes the very *being* of the human, then sociality is intrinsic to our existence. Existential freedom cannot realize itself without social freedom, nor can the human being be human without others. Thus, the most essential human right is the right to be human: to be human in a human community. The individualist tradition is not wrong in desiring freedom for the individual. It errs because it does not see that individuality is social. Thus, it repeatedly makes the mistake (against which Karl Marx so frequently warns us) of "establishing society . . . as an abstraction over against the individual." Liberalism forgets that even the expression of an individual life is also "an expression and assertion of social life."[21] Without this social life individuality becomes a mirage.

Like community, individuality is an achievement. It is largely through each other that we become individuals. And an essential condition of the individual's fullest realization is a free and flourishing community.[22] In the dimension of individuality, freedom is intrinsically social. Philosophers have long known this. King writes that the "self cannot be a self without other selves." For "all men are interdependent."[23] And we may recall that famous postulate of Georg Hegel that self-consciousness "exists in itself and for itself" insofar as it "exists for another self-consciousness"—that "it *is* only by being acknowledged and recognized."[24] Implicit in these reflections is the mutuality of selfhood and the possibility of intersubjective community. Freedom is inseparable from this mutuality (though not simply reducible to it). And if King and Hegel are both right, the creation of human identity is as much a communal as a personal project. The self discovers and constitutes itself in relation to other selves. Hence, we may concur with Calvin O. Schrag that "community is constitutive of selfhood," and that "if we cannot find a proper setting for the we-experience, then the location of the I-experience will elude us also."[25]

Community in its various forms and manifestations is the most "proper setting" for the "we-experience." We *form* this "we-experience" in our formation of community. Here one finds the positive reciprocity that Sartre describes as what one person expects of another "if their relation is human," and in which "that which is Other than me *is also the same.*"[26] Community involves human association, bonds, and relatedness in which individuality is dialectically interwoven with fraternal relations of solidarity. It is not that idea of society (pilloried by Fanon) "where each person shuts himself up in his own subjectivity." For this would lead to a desiccated life, a spiritual desert in which grows the custom "of very seldom meeting man."[27] In community, we become aware of our bond with each other, aware that we owe to each other our common humanity. Community is the antithesis of the liberal view of society as a "contractual association of egoistic satisfaction-maximizers."[28] For that is hardly an "association" at all, but an inert collectivity of alienated atoms. Though a fine description of capitalist life, this is hardly a description of community. Capitalism is ever inclined to acknowledge "individuals" only, but only as atoms or commodities, not persons. But then it is interhuman relations in community that allow us to become persons. As the institutionalized "relativism of egoistic self-interest,"[29] capitalism can only erode community. Thus, in the name of individual rights the "rapacious individualism of capitalist civilization prohibits the flowering of individuality."[30] Community is no mere collection of egos united (or conflicted) by interests. In community, there is a bond between human beings, not only for practical purposes and interests, but also because of a sense of belonging and mutual understanding. "Man becomes an I through a You,"[31] Martin Buber writes. To negate the social is to pulverize the personal.

Yet, community is not collectivism. Its unity is not uniformity. "Collectivity is not a binding but a bundling together."[32] This, too, is an atomizing of the human. For "if individualism understands only a part of man, collectivism understands man only as a part."[33] But community is cooperative self-creation, which requires self-creative freedom of its members. It constitutes its "common praxis through the individual praxis of the agents of whom it is composed."[34] Individuality is neither denied nor given as an atomic individualism. Real community must preserve the Other in his or her Otherness and uniqueness. It must leave room for one to be oneself. "[I]f the individual is a pure zero," de Beauvoir writes, "the sum of those zeros . . . is also a zero."[35] If there is to be mutual recognition, then individuality must be real. If "that which is Other than me *is also the same,*" this is possible because there remain both the Other and I. We do not disappear as unique individuals. There is a oneness that affirms plurality. Cornel West correctly distinguishes the "norm of individuality which reinforces the importance of community" from a "doctrinaire" individualism "which . . . denigrate the idea of community."[36] Critiques of the latter need not mean negation of the former. We cannot create community through a collectivism that negates the individual. To erode the personal is to disintegrate the social. Freedom is irreducibly individual and ineffaceably social. As individuality and sociality—which are inextricable and irreducible dimensions of human existence—are unrealizable without community, any negation of community is an erosion of freedom. Freedom realizes itself neither in atomism nor collectivism, but in community.

This emphasis on the communality of freedom is of great historic significance to the experience, thought, and liberatory strivings of America's Black people. Since the time of slavery and the terrors of the Middle Passage, freedom has been the bright shining star of Black aspirations. "[F]ew men," W. E. B. Du Bois notes, "ever worshiped Freedom with half such unquestioning faith as did the American Negro for two centuries."[37] Freedom was the hope of slaves and the dream of their subjugated descendants. But it is often forgotten that the forebears' dream of freedom nearly always entailed a vision of community. The strivings for freedom among slaves commonly assumed a communal form. In defiance of the social erosion of bondage, slaves created new cultural forms that synthesized African and European forms. Thus, they created (in defiant affirmation of their irreducible transcendence) not only a limited sphere of life independent of the master's control, but also a self-perpetuating community of resistance. An African American culture could hardly exist today without the cultural self-creation of slaves. John Blassingame notes that these cultural forms and activities "led to cooperation, social cohesion, tighter communal bonds, and brought all classes of slaves together in common pursuits."[38] Forms of association, religious activities, familiar bonds, personal loyalties and devotions, and communal celebrations were affirmed within the slave communities despite their denial by the masters.

The quest for freedom persisted as a communal quest for some time after slavery. One historian notes that the aspiration for freedom during Reconstruction revealed "a desire for independence of white control, for autonomy *both as individuals and as members of a community.*"[39] Some former slaves now preferred the cities. For they believed that in cities the new "freedom was freer" partly because of the greater availability of Black social institutions and associations, which were features of community life that allowed Blacks to express themselves autonomously as a people and as individuals.[40] The great explosion of Black churches, schools, economic experiments, towns, and social institutions reveals the extent to which the pursuit of freedom was a communal pursuit. To win freedom from White domination, to affirm oneself as a people and as human subjects, one had to form associations and create community.

And yet we need not reach back so far as the nineteenth century to see the importance of community in the quest for freedom. Du Bois's mission involved more than a demand for rights as understood in the liberal tradition. One can hardly understand his quest for freedom without his vision of Pan-African (often socialist) solidarity, or his advocacy of a Black cooperative commonwealth.[41] Then there was the strong communal spirit of the movements of the 1960s. Can one really understand King's idea of freedom without his vision of an interracial "beloved community"? Nor should we forget his emphasis on the need for cooperative effort to create, to reinvent a self-liberating *Black* community. We ought especially to recall his advice that Blacks should "work passionately for group identity" without group exclusiveness; that we seek unity without uniformity since this "group unity can do infinitely more to liberate the Negro than any action of *individuals.*"[42]

The emphasis on the communality of freedom was even more pronounced among Black leftists and nationalists. Malcolm X advised his comrades to at least consider cooperative or socialist alternatives before being "incorporated, or integrated or *disintegrated* into this capitalist system."[43] In the works of Fanon there is high regard for African communal forms, the value of village assemblies, of "communal criticism," and all the democratic and cooperative activities whereby "the community triumphs, and . . . spreads its own light and reason."[44] Such thinking has been deeply influential in American Black liberatory discourse. And were not the Student Nonviolent Coordinating Committee's freedom schools and the various projects of the Black Panther Party efforts to plant the liberatory seeds of common freedom? America's Black left and nationalist movements often articulate their idea of freedom in terms of communal self-determination. Thus, in the first point of the Panthers' Ten-Point Program it is written: "We want freedom. We want the *power to determine the destiny of our Black community.*"[45] Freedom is obviously not conceived in the image of an alienated individualism. Rather, this is a freedom that presupposes community, seeks its realization through community, and perhaps even realizes itself as communal freedom.

Yet, we should neither oversimplify the historical picture of our liberatory quest, nor paint too flawless a portrait of its communal vision. Lewis R. Gordon notes in chapter 6 that some elements within the movement advanced "community" through collectivist motifs of a subordinated individuality.[46] But a genuine experience of community cannot be realized in this way, for community develops on the basis of autonomy and mutual recognition. To deny individuality is to subvert the social. Community then degenerates into reified collectives. Yet, the mainstream of the movement often manifested the reverse side of this error. The civil rights movement surely evoked a powerful communal spirit, and to some extent transformed Blacks and others into a deeply idealistic community of fraternity and resistance. But the "Great American Ideal of individualism" formed the frame of reference of most of the (mainly middle-class) leaders who defined the movement's aims. Thus, a movement that inspired community held an ideology that threatened to dissolve community once the movement achieved its aims.[47]

But these shortcomings do not discredit the idea of a communal vision of freedom or reduce its importance in Black peoples' historic quest for human liberation. The most advanced leaders and visionaries within the civil rights movement knew that *at least* the liberal freedoms guaranteed by law to everyone else had to be won for people of color. Otherwise, we would have the perpetual peonage of racial caste. Of course, such rights have proven inadequate for the elimination of racism. As such rights belong only to *individuals*, they hardly suffice to liberate a people. They cannot even be equally extended to all Blacks, since class privilege (money, education, and so on) is needed to fully actualize many of them. Yet if not sufficient for liberation, they were (are) certainly a necessary condition. One had to achieve them before one could transcend them. And the most advanced thinkers and activists within the civil rights movement knew that neither legal rights nor liberal individualist ideology could achieve the liberating life of a transcendent community. Eventually, liberation would require the transcendence of liberalism.

Black leftists and nationalists were even less susceptible to the seductions of liberalism. And not all held to collectivist conceptions of community. They often argued for unity without uniformity. A difference was discernible between the creation of a cooperative society and construction of a collectivist order. One could oppose possessive individualism and a corrosive profit motive without negating individuality and democratic values. Here, we may recall the insight of Fanon who, after excoriating the individualism of elites while extolling the liberatory potential of African communalism, still insists that pretexts (e.g., economic progress) "must not be used to push man around, to *tear him from himself and his privacy*."[48] Community is common freedom, freedom in a social mode. One can never create community while negating the freedom of its members. The most insightful members of the left understood this.

Yet, the world changes. Historical significance does not prove contemporary relevance. Today, many people doubt that historic visions of a community of freedom can sustain us in these fragmented "postmodern" times. Do such visions still exist? Is Black (or other) community still possible? Or is the quest for community a vain pursuit, possibly based on archaic forms of human association and identity that cannot be restored and whose attempted restoration can lead only to stifling social repression?

Now I have argued that sociality is intrinsic to the being of the human (as situated freedom), but that it requires community for its free and disalienated realization. Thus, the question of whether community is at all possible is a question of whether the human being is possible. A definitive answer cannot be given to this question, for humanity's future is not guaranteed. The future must be made. Our fate is not predetermined. But the affirmation of community is the affirmation of humanity, the creation of community essential to the "world process of humanization."[49] If this is obstructed by conditions of postmodern times, then we must affirm our humanity in defiance of the times. Not for us then is the jaded wisdom that says that there is no possible alternative to the existing order. If need be, we affirm the necessity of the impossible. It is a question of creating a future, of deciding whether we are committed to a community of human freedom. To create community is to make the human.

Of course, communities are historical. Historical visions can sustain and inspire us as part of our historical project of making the human through the free creation of community. It is as sacred icons, idols, and formulae that they constrain, stifle, and repress. It is not a matter of rigidly adopting an antique model of sociality or of embracing some archaic ideal as inscrutable doctrine. As community is no atemporal abstraction, we can concur with Buber that it "should not be made into a principle."[50] Since communities are historical, their realization does not occur once and for all time, but have taken (and continue to take) historically variable forms. The task is to create new forms of community that address the needs of our time. And since even the most vibrant communities are susceptible of falling into new reifications, communities must continually invent, reinvent, and transcend themselves.

The challenge to invent and reinvent community is of special urgency for Black peoples in our time. For we face an excruciating crisis of community that is inseparable from our crises of identity. What endangers us is our growing loss of community, our loss of a sense of community. The great battles of the 1960s, drawing on an already existing framework of institutions and communal networks of support, evoked immense solidarity and cooperative effort. But with the movement's defeat of de jure segregation, the cooperative efforts began to subside, and there began a gradual erosion of those feelings of bonding and communal networks of support that sustained us as a people before the emergence of the movement.

Something of what we lost (or are losing) is pictured in literary reminiscences of our writers. bell hooks recalls that there were in the rural southern community of her youth Black elders who expressed maternal and fatherly concern for all children (not only natural offspring), schools in which children affirmed themselves and bonded with each other, and teachers who "had taught your mama, her sisters, and her friends . . . who knew your people . . . and shared their insight, keeping us in touch with generations."[51] Similar pictures of Black communality in larger urban settings can be equally striking. We can hardly forget the picture of Harlem's communality in James Baldwin's eloquent recollections of "church suppers and outings, and . . . after I left the church, rent and waistline parties where rage and sorrow sat in darkness and did not stir, and we ate and drank and talked and laughed and danced and forgot about the 'man.' We had the liquor, the chicken, the music and each other, and had no need to pretend to be what we were not. This is the freedom that one hears in some gospel songs . . . and in jazz."[52]

Hemmed in by material poverty, imprisoned by racial caste, the Black world described by hooks and Baldwin was often rich in communal spirit and throbbing with a vibrant sociality. Therein human beings affirmed themselves and each other in defiance of the corrosive forces of oppression. They affirmed themselves as community in resistance to a tyrannical atomization. Yet, hooks recalls, with a note of nostalgic sadness, how her cohesive little world was altered, how it became unraveled by the process of desegregation that was the aftermath of the civil rights movement. Lost (or vanishing) was that marginal space within which Blacks (though confined) "were truly caring and supportive of one another." Is liberation or disintegration the final outcome of the great battles of the 1960s? Today, hooks believes that "black people are experiencing a deep collective sense of loss."[53]

Could it be that our bonds of solidarity are dissolving? Or that the precious space of communal freedom, first forged by our forebears in the dark dungeons of slavery, is finally eroding into oblivion? The margin of beleaguered freedom has not vanished, but it faces desiccation. Since communities are historical, it would be foolish to expect that our communal bonds would remain unchanged. Moreover, the bonds that sustained us before the movement were informed (or *deformed*) by the racial caste domination that the movement sought to end. These bonds were bound to be altered or loosened once the movement loosened (without dissolving) the crippling tentacles of caste. Nor should we forget the limitations of the movement itself. The civil rights movement neither transcended liberalism nor offered a radical critique of the existing order. Cruse argued in 1966 that the movement could not become revolutionary until it articulated goals transcending the limited objectives of racial integration. Most of its leaders failed to see that "social equality for the *entire* Negro group" and "an unqualified capitalism are contradictory and incompatible."[54] Unwittingly, the movement may have helped pave the way for widening class divisions even as it expanded our rights.

Thus, "integration" could become disintegration or assimilation. In the absence of a social vision of freedom surpassing the liberal rights of citizens, this outcome could hardly be avoided. Instead of King's egalitarian beloved community, we get rationalist liberalism in blackface. In the place of group solidarity and identity, we are offered assimilation into a still largely racist mainstream, a process that often deepens wounds to African American psyches already ravaged by centuries of caste. To the extent that integration is equated with assimilation, with the surrender and dissolution of the self into the White "mainstream," it neatly coincides with the penetration of Black communities on a hitherto unprecedented scale by the acquisitive consumerist values of the market and the dismemberment (or commodification) of our cultural and personal lives. Our daily lives are more deeply affected, disrupted, and disoriented by the atomizing force of capital than in the darkest days of de jure segregation. We see not only widening class divisions among our people, but also the atomizing of communal bonds by the corrosive power of the market and its profiteering ethos. We become more fragmented as a people as our social spaces shrivel.

In a capitalist society driven by profit and polluted by a poisonous culture of consumerism, a culture that promotes acquisitiveness and the pursuit of private gain over any common good, the shriveling of communal bonds is essential to the status quo. Our growing class divisions since the 1960s and the unprecedented saturation of our communities with the psychology and values of the marketplace have induced a shift of emphasis away from such nonmarket values as care, solidarity, and mutual support. Sensitivity, creative thought, independence of soul, and other features of individuality so crucial to personal realization and a thriving community of freedom are inevitably given short shrift in the Hobbesian world of the corporate market. The "experience of relational love, of a beloved black community"[55] that bell hooks recalls with such tender, nostalgic longing, can hardly be sustained in a system that increasingly leaves no other nexus between humans but "naked self-interest," and that resolves all "personal worth into exchange value."[56] Human relations are patterned after market relations, and love is treated like a commodity to be traded or sold on the market. In this system, "my brother is my purse, my friend part of my scheme for getting on."[57] Can we really expect to nurture communal bonds under these circumstances? Is there any wonder that things fall apart?

Of course, we are revealing no new discoveries, nor any especially profound ones. Capitalism has always sought to reduce everything and everyone to economic categories, and we have always been especially vulnerable to its social predations.[58] Was it not the profit motive that engendered slavery and the horrors of the Middle Passage? Has the market not always negated solidarity and friendship, compassion and love? Yet, in this era of globalization, our everyday lives are probably more directly and intimately subject to the corrosion of capital than in previous generations.[59] The system is more totalitarian than before, more "one-dimensional" than when it was so described by Herbert Marcuse. More than ever, it seeks to "claim the *entire* individual" to such an extent that "the subject which is alienated is swallowed up by its alienated existence."[60] The erosion of our communal bonds makes us more susceptible than before to this debilitating alienation. It may be an irony of history that the full development among us of the totalitarian logic of this alienation was stymied by the totalitarian regime of racial caste from which our movement partially freed us.[61]

Moreover, communities are being shattered today as the labor of millions is eliminated by electronic revolutions within a profit-driven economy and when vast multitudes are displaced from economic and societal life. Thus, people are increasingly disconnected, detached, estranged, and alienated. When people become disconnected and detached, and when communities dissolve and beget a social abyss, the result is not greater freedom. It is dehumanization. We achieve no actualization as individuals, no realization of intellectual, emotional, or spiritual potentialities. People become like atoms; powerless units of impotent self-interest at the mercy of giant corporate and political powers. Horkheimer writes that the individual's emancipation "is not emancipation from society, but the deliverance of society from atomization."[62] Yet, the present economic order is institutionalized atomization. It threatens the decimation of Black (and other) communities in America and throughout the world. Combined with the vicious reifications of American racism, it portends havoc and devastation for our communities and our personal lives.

Yet, we humans are not mere products of circumstances, nor need we be passive victims of history. We can rethink and reshape our circumstances. We can reexamine and transform our social existence. We cannot return to the past, but we can build the future. With our legacy of struggle, we can reclaim our communality. All social bonds are not broken, and we can create them anew. Nor are we all awash in that sea of nihilism so somberly described by Cornel West. It may be that our collective condition "has been and is characterized by continued displacement, profound alienation and despair."[63] But it is also one of solidarity and hope, of that stubborn resistance to disintegration and despair that allowed a depreciated people to achieve "an unassailable and monumental dignity."[64] It may be that our social existence is threatened, but this is simply another urgent challenge to realize our sociality in the creation of new communities of freedom.

Of course, we may be charged with begging the question of whether Black communities are still possible. But a definitive answer to the question cannot be given. Again, history offers no guarantees. History is a sphere of possibilities. And while everything is not possible, it is only in our praxis of liberatory struggle that we learn what is or is not possible. First, we must decide whether we wish any longer to exist as a people. If we decide in the affirmative, then we must commit ourselves to the creation of community. And if we are correct that the quest for freedom today is essentially a quest for community, then our commitment to community is our way of seeking to bring into fruition centuries of liberatory struggle cemented by the sweat and toil of forebears and contemporaries. It is our way of continuing on a new level the struggles of the 1960s and earlier without simply seeking to bring back the past. Since we become human in our communal relations, it is a question of affirming our humanity.

Yet, the current struggle presents new difficulties and demands that call for a rethinking of the entire liberatory project. Our emancipatory struggles can no longer fight *only* against racism. Nor is it enough to contest racism *and* sexism only. For the growing class divisions among African Americans is one of the singular developments that call into question the possibility of a Black community. It remains to be seen whether our common history of suffering and struggle, or resistance to current racist attacks on our rights and our humanity, will be enough to bind us as a community. We can no longer evade the issue of class or the question of what kind of socioeconomic conditions are needed for the realization of community.

My reflections here have hopefully indicated that the existing economic order is a mortal obstruction to community, and that prevailing individualist notions of liberty do not allow for an adequate understanding of freedom. Without a fundamental transformation of the socioeconomic order, the realization of a community of freedom is ultimately impossible. Without an inspiring vision of a new society and new modes of freedom surpassing the limits of liberal individualism, new movements for liberation are doomed to disorientation and defeat. The failure of the mainstream of the civil rights movement (with a few exceptions) to radically critique the individualist ideology and capitalist social relations was a severe shortcoming that limited the reach of the movement. And there were critics who warned that "without an anticapitalist ideology the Negro movement is doomed to be rolled back into submission."[65] Yet, that movement did succeed in expanding our rights and reducing the scale of overt violence and brutality against our people. But there is little that we can achieve today with an idea of freedom that does not surpass individualist notions of liberty or with political orientations that do not challenge class privilege. To realize the liberatory aims of the 1960s we must transcend the limitations of the 1960s.

But we have no blueprints awaiting us. And perhaps it is just as well. This is a time for inventions, for making discoveries. We must create a new vision of freedom, of communal freedom, and a cooperative ideal of human sociality.

The historic African American idea of self-determination—communal self-determination—may prove essential in this. But if this idea is not to be equated with the private interest of self-seeking individuals or the narrow class interests of an aspiring Black bourgeoisie (e.g., by being identified with Black capitalism), it must be bound to a democratic and anticapitalist social philosophy. We must acknowledge that our aims cannot be achieved without a radical change in the entire socioeconomic order. Any system of organized acquisitiveness that sets people against each other by forcing them to fight for their livelihoods and that allots four-fifths of society's wealth to less than a tenth of the people is a system inherently corrosive of community. The Panthers were justified in demanding "an end to the robbery by the CAPITALIST of our Black Community."[66] For a people cannot sustain itself as a community without resources and control of its economic destiny. Either the community cannot survive at all or its self-determination is compromised and its communal life deformed by material servitude to the masters of wealth. Clearly, we must work out new concepts and a different philosophy of life.

A revisioning of self-determination in terms of the idea of the cooperative or communalism may offer a path forward. hooks claims that there "are no examples of cooperative black communities," and that "liberal individualism has so deeply penetrated the psyches of black folk in America . . . that we have little support for a political ethic of communalism that promotes sharing resources."[67] Yet, there is a tradition of communalism among Blacks, however eroded it may now be by the individualist culture and aggressive global capitalism. Du Bois proposes a "cooperative commonwealth" for African American communities to enhance democratic self-determination and also to provide an alternative to Black capitalism that he rightly feared would insert "into the ranks of the Negro race a new cause of division, a new attempt to subject the masses of the race to an exploiting capitalist class of their own people."[68] In the late 1960s, leftist Black nationalist writer Robert L. Allen was inspired by Du Bois to propose communal property relations (and radical political organizing) both to aid in creating an enduring anticapitalist movement and to help promote Black self-determination while "strengthening family and group ties and building a stronger sense of community among black people so that all become dedicated to the welfare of the group."[69] United with a general struggle for self-determination, such projects may help to engender a new vision of freedom and sociality that radically contests the existing order.

Yet, it is not one or another experiment that is central to our liberatory quest. Nor is it a matter of seeking panaceas. As Fanon puts it, "those tasks which increase the sum total of humanity . . . demand true inventions."[70] The historic moment calls for discoveries, for the reinvention of community, society, and democracy. What is essential is a radical reorientation of our social thought and practice, of our ethics and politics, and our creation of a new social vision of human possibility. Eventually, society itself must be reconstituted in a radically democratic manner on the basis of a democratically governed, cooperative economy. This will not happen immediately. Yet, it must remain an objective of persons of a genuinely humanistic social conscience. What our people—indeed humanity—must achieve is, in C. L. R. James's words, "a sense of the primacy of their own personality, with an equally remarkable . . . capacity for social co-operative action."[71] The quest for a life of freedom and for a cooperative community of freedom is essentially a liberatory quest for a more complete human existence. There lies the heart of "our spiritual strivings," and we dare not seek for less.

NOTES

1. Frantz Fanon, *Black Skin, White Masks*, trans. Charles Lamm Markmann (New York: Grove, 1967).

2. Martin Buber, *Paths in Utopia* (Syracuse, N.Y.: Syracuse University Press, 1996).

3. Karl Marx, *Writings of the Young Marx on Philosophy and Society*, ed. Loyd D. Easton and Kurt Guddat (New York: Anchor, 1967).

4. Fanon, *Black Skin, White Masks*, 222.

5. Jean-Paul Sartre, *Existentialism and Human Emotions* (New York: Philosophical Library, 1957), 23.

6. Jean-Paul Sartre, *Being and Nothingness* (New York: Pocket, 1956), 60.

7. Simone de Beauvoir, *The Ethics of Ambiguity* (Secaucus, N.J.: Citadel, 1980), 91.

8. de Beauvoir, *Ethics of Ambiguity*, 81.

9. Frantz Fanon, *Toward the African Revolution* (New York: Grove, 1967), 34.

10. Martin Luther King Jr., "Letter from the Birmingham Jail," in *A Testament of Hope: Essential Writings and Speeches of Martin Luther King, Jr.*, ed. James H. Washington (San Francisco: HarperCollins, 1986), 293.

11. Jean-Paul Sartre, *Critique of Dialectical Reason* (London: New Left, 1976), 401. Of course, Sartre develops his theory of community in terms of a theory of the praxis of groups, especially the "group-en-fusion" and the "pledged group." My reflections here are partly informed by his theory of community (groups) as radical, transcending praxis, marked by positive reciprocity, in which "freedom frees itself from alienation and affirms itself as common efficacy." For a fuller discussion of Sartre's theory of community, see Robert E. Birt, "The Prospects for Community in the Later Sartre," *International Philosophical Quarterly* 29 (2) (June 1989): 139–149.

12. Sartre, *Critique of Dialectical Reason*, 435, emphasis mine.

13. Calvin O. Schrag, *The Self after Postmodernity* (New Haven, Conn.: Yale University Press, 1997), 88.

14. Liberalism in this broad sense encompasses both "liberals" and "conservatives" as these terms are commonly understood in ordinary political discussion in America. It includes economic policies and ideologies commonly described as "neoliberal" by European and Latin American critics. And I am especially thinking of the

Anglo American tradition of liberalism most famously represented in philosophy by Locke, Hobbes, J. S. Mill, and others.

15. C. B. Macpherson, *The Political Theory of Possessive Individualism* (Oxford: Oxford University Press, 1962), 3.

16. Macpherson, *Political Theory of Possessive Individualism*, 3. Here, I am also reminded of Locke's idea of each man's "property in his own person" that "nobody has any right to but himself." See John Locke, *The Second Treatise of Government* (New York: The Liberal Arts Press, 1952), 17. Can we not detect germs of self-estrangement in this proprietary conception of one's own person that Locke devises in defense of private property? Do I have an external relation to my body as property? Or am I embodied existence and agency?

17. Harold Cruse, *The Crisis of the Negro Intellectual* (New York: Quill, 1967), 7.

18. Cruse, *Crisis of the Negro Intellectual*, 8.

19. Max Horkheimer, *The Eclipse of Reason* (New York: Continuum, 1992), 129.

20. Martin Luther King Jr., *Where Do We Go from Here: Chaos or Community?* (Boston: Beacon, 1967), 125.

21. Karl Marx, "Private Property and Communism," in *Writings of the Young Marx on Philosophy and Society*, ed. Loyd D. Easton and Kurt Guddat (New York: Anchor, 1967), 306.

22. We can also affirm the other side of this dialectical relation by recalling Fanon's comment about the individual in the revolutionary quest for national liberation. Thus, just as a liberating community is an essential condition for the individual's liberation, the social liberation that creates a community of freedom can exist "only to the precise degree to which the individual has irreversibly begun his own liberation." See Fanon, *Toward the African Revolution*, 102–104.

23. King, *Where Do We Go From Here?*, 180–181.

24. Georg Hegel, *Phenomenology of Mind* (New York: Harper and Row, 1967), 230.

25. Schrag, *Self after Postmodernity*, 77–78.

26. Sartre, *Critique of Dialectical Reason*, 131, 189.

27. Frantz Fanon, *The Wretched of the Earth* (New York: Grove, 1968), 47, 313.

28. Robert Paul Wolff, *The Poverty of Liberalism* (Boston: Beacon, 1968), 185.

29. Lewis Gordon, *Her Majesty's Other Children* (New York: Rowman & Littlefield, 1997), 235.

30. Cornel West, *Prophesy Deliverance! An Afro-American Revolutionary Christianity* (Philadelphia: Westminster, 1982), 123.

31. Martin Buber, *I and Thou* (New York: Scribner's, 1970), 80.

32. Martin Buber, *Between Man and Man* (New York: Macmillan, 1965), 31.

33. Buber, *Between Man and Man*, 200. Obviously, "individualism" versus "collectivism" is a false dichotomy. Both are forms of atomization. One suppresses individuality (though in the name of the individual) through its very denial of community. The other suppresses community (though in the name of community) through its very denial of individuality. Reverse sides of the same reification, their common antithesis is community.

34. Sartre, *Critique of Dialectical Reason*, 67.

35. de Beauvoir, *Ethics of Ambiguity*, 103.

36. West, *Prophesy Deliverance!*, 17.

37. W. E. B. Du Bois, *The Souls of Black Folk* (New York: Bantam, 1989), 4.

38. John Blassingame, *The Slave Community* (New York: Oxford University Press, 1972), 42.

39. Eric Foner, *Reconstruction: America's Unfinished Revolution* (New York: Harper and Row, 1988), 78, emphasis mine.

40. Foner, *Reconstruction*, 81.

41. W. E. B. Du Bois, *Dusk of Dawn: An Essay Toward an Autobiography of a Race Concept* (New York: Schocken, 1971), 197–220.

42. King, *Where Do We Go from Here?*, 123–125. Though obviously a defender of individual freedom (noting in protest that even the most cultivated Black is denied individuality by the racist), King did not believe in liberalism's asocial, atomic individual. He understood that individuality is social and that personal and social liberation required cooperative effort.

43. Malcolm X, "At the Audubon," in *Malcolm X Speaks: Selected Speeches and Statements*, ed. George Breitman (New York: Grove Weidenfeld, 1965), 121, emphasis mine.

44. Fanon, *Wretched of the Earth*, 47–48.

45. Huey P. Newton, *To Die for the People* (New York: Vintage, 1972), 3.

46. This would probably have been more common among some Black leftists and nationalists.

47. Of course, this is a criticism made by Cruse and other nationalists and leftists. It is implicit in the comment from Malcolm X cited earlier. Yet, King became increasingly aware of the limitations of liberal freedoms protected by law (however indispensable these may be), and was increasingly critical both of liberal individualism and the dictatorship of profiteers and the profit motive. More radical elements within the civil rights movement preceded King in arriving at this understanding.

48. Fanon, *Wretched of the Earth*, 314, emphasis mine.

49. Fanon, *Toward the African Revolution*, 146.

50. Buber, *Paths in Utopia*, 134.

51. bell hooks, *Yearning: Race, Gender, and Cultural Politics* (Boston: South End, 1990), 33.

52. James Baldwin, *The Fire Next Time* (New York: Dell, 1970), 60.

53. hooks, *Yearning*, 35–36.

54. Cruse, *Crisis of the Negro Intellectual*, 367.

55. hooks, *Yearning*, 36.

56. Karl Marx, *The Communist Manifesto* (New York: Penguin, 1967), 82.

57. Fanon, *Wretched of the Earth*, 47.

58. A philosophical exploration of the interplay between the essentializing reifications of racism and the atomizing alienations of capital could radically deepen the understanding of our self-estrangement and the devastation of Black communal life. But such cannot be done in this chapter.

59. This is a point made by Angela Davis in her analysis of the need for anticapitalist critiques in present liberatory projects. See Angela Davis, *African-American Philosophers: 17 Conversations*, ed. George Yancy (New York: Routledge, 1998), 28.

60. Herbert Marcuse, *One-Dimensional Man* (Boston: Beacon, 1964), 10–11.

61. Of course, Jim Crow segregation was part of the same system of economic exploitation. But as a caste system that severely limited our mobility and involvement in the dominant society, it limited too the full cultural and economic penetration of

Black communities by that society. Moreover, it was within the repressive caste system that postslavery, pre-1960s communal bonds were formed (partly for mutual support and common defense against the system), and these limited the atomization and co-optation of the dominant society.

62. Horkheimer, *Eclipse of Reason*, 135.

63. hooks, *Yearning*, 26.

64. Baldwin, *Fire Next Time*, 21.

65. Cruse, *Crisis of the Negro Intellectual*, 367.

66. Newton, *To Die for the People*, 3

67. bell hooks, *Killing Rage, Ending Racism* (New York: Henry Holt, 1995), 165.

68. Du Bois, *Dusk of Dawn*, 208.

69. Robert L. Allen, *Black Awakening in Capitalist America* (Garden City, N.Y.: Anchor, 1969), 277. The reader might recall Fanon's similar proposals for cooperatives, decentralized and democratically governed, as part of the project of national reconstruction after colonialism. Buber also proposes communes or cooperatives specifically for the purpose of reviving community in technically advanced capitalist societies. See Buber, *Paths in Utopia*.

70. Fanon, *Wretched of the Earth*, 312–313.

71. Quoted in Anthony Bogues, *Caliban's Freedom: The Early Political Thought of C. L. R. James* (London: Pluto, 1997), 150.

6

Sociality and Community in Black: A Phenomenological Essay

Lewis R. Gordon

There is a tension in the literature on community in the Africana context. There is the claim of a fundamental communal reality rooted in African cultural norms. This view is found in both positive and insidious dimensions in works ranging from Frantz Fanon's defense of African communalism in *The Wretched of the Earth* to the unanimism that undergirded Placide Tempels's ethnophilosophical *Bantu Philosophy*.[1] It is a view that also undergirds popular movements, as is clear in Black Panther ideology in North America and Bobo Dread Rastafarian communes in Jamaica. There is also the heroic dimensions of this communal spirit, as demonstrated in Herbert Gutman's classic *The Black Family in Slavery and Freedom*, and there is no mistaking the force of communal spirit in the civil rights movement of the 1950s and the antiapartheid movement of the 1960s through the 1980s, where the complex array of cultural and spiritual resources that cemented Black peoples (along with many non-Black peoples) through their understanding of *struggle*.[2]

The reality of struggle, however, often advanced community through motifs of collectivity and subordinated individuality. Individuality carried the annoying tendency of difference and normative contradictions to collectivities. What good is a struggle that demands criteria for authentic membership that may run counter to the very being of some individuals in struggle—especially where the norm requires denial of their status *as individuals* to begin with?

A continued concern of antiracist struggle is, after all, exemplified by outrage at the cliché "They're all alike." Such a concern is a leitmotif of much Africana existential literature, but with the paradoxical project of simultaneously demonstrating Black individuality and the shared reality of Blacks, especially on the level of "experience." Fanon's *Black Skin, White Masks* is an excellent example of this dual project. It can also be found in writings by

Richard Wright, from *Native Son* through to *Outsider*, and by Ralph Ellison, from the complex portrait of invisibility in *Invisible Man* to the struggle with idiosyncrasy in *Going to the Territory*.[3] Such struggles emerge in nineteenth-century writings as well, as can be found in Anna Julia Cooper's *A Voice from the South*, where Cooper struggled with the structural collapse of self into oneness and the continued assertion of individual and group "worth."[4]

My own work could easily be characterized as my negotiating my way through such dual realities by demonstrating that they need not be contradictory. A constant source of error, I have shown, is the tendency to collapse community into collectives. Not all collectives are communal ones. That being so, what are the unique features of collectives that are? The response that I have advanced is sociality. The reason that some collectives are not communal is because they fail to meet the condition of sociality. No community lacks sociality. Some communities *lose* their sociality, however, and collapse into collectives guided by self-deception. Where the collapse of sociality is the aim, a fusion of resentment and hate often emerges, which leads, inevitably, to performative contradictions since even "fusion" requires *others*, which a fight against sociality hopes to eliminate.

Such is my position. Specialists in philosophy would see straightaway that such a position is informed by ideas rooted in the phenomenological tradition. It is a tradition that I have found vital for creative insights into philosophical dynamics of the Africana people's condition in the modern and contemporary world. That being so, the rest of this chapter will be devoted to spelling out some of the insights it offers not only for our understanding of some central problems faced by Black communities, but also the understanding of the very sociality through which these problems can be understood as problems themselves.

PHENOMENOLOGY

By phenomenology, I mean reflective thought on what can be called objects of thought. An object of thought emerges as such through suspension of certain kinds of interests in the world. In the everyday world, I walk to the store with an interest in the thing I would like to purchase. I drive to work in order to complete the tasks I have for that day. And I work because I either like my job or, given my class status, must do so in order to survive. In that world, I meet people with expectations of conversation, to learn from them, to know what's going on, to strike a deal, to be, perhaps, a little less lonely. This world of interests and purpose is familiar among phenomenologists as the "natural attitude."

The phenomenological moment begins when we suspend those sorts of interests. By suspension, we put to the side those types of questions. It is not that we eliminate them; we simply do not make them our focus. Thus, through such suspension, we may wonder what it means to walk to the store, or instead of focusing on my interest in the thing to be purchased, I focus on the thing itself. I may think about what it means to drive to work. I may wonder what it means to "work." I may ponder what it means to "meet people," "strike deals," or what it means to be "lonely." As I suspend or "bracket" certain interests, I find myself approaching these objects of thought as "phenomena." Phenomena, as most phenomenologists know, are objects of thought or, better yet, objects of consciousness. I am conscious of these phenomena, and the form of this consciousness—indeed, consciousness itself—is "directed" or "intentional": consciousness is, always, consciousness *of* something. Without something of which we are conscious, we are left with, in a word, "nothing."

"Nothing." In *Being and Nothingness*, Jean-Paul Sartre explores this consequence of the intentionality of consciousness.[5] He presents, first, as is well known, an "ontological" argument. If consciousness must be consciousness of something, and if consciousness by itself constitutes nothing, then the form of intentionality already points beyond itself. Indeed, even "beyond" connotes the limitations of idealism, where the world is reduced to an idea, for without transcendence, "beyond" makes no sense. An ironic consequence of this observation is that it raises a form of argument that undergirds the brand of phenomenology against which Sartre rallies his brand of phenomenology—namely, Husserlian transcendental phenomenology. The argument that even "beyond" makes no sense without the possibility of transcendence is one that goes back to Immanuel Kant's transcendental reflections on experience in his *Critique of Pure Reason*, and at its core is an insight that affected Edmund Husserl's *Ideas* and *Cartesian Meditations*—namely, at the core of such argument is that sense must make, in a word, "sense."[6] The appeal to meaningful conditions requires more than the *validity* of such appeals but their *viability* in projects of achieving, say, "rigorous" intellectual work. The transcendental argument is premised on the necessary and universal conditions for an idea, conditions that make the idea "objective," so to speak. But does not such a notion of objectivity presuppose a rationality to reality that fails to account for the negative moment that stimulates such reflection?

Sartre, it is well known, proposes a radical *existential* phenomenology. The existential turn goes to the heart of intentionality as a point toward that simultaneously embodies a standing apart. *Ex sistere*—the Latin etymology of "existence" means to stand apart—and *existence*, the French cognate, is to exist and to live. To stand apart, the existential moment, challenges any *preceding* necessity, any preceding meaning. Thus, how can a transcendental presupposition be at the heart of such reflections? Sartre's way out is simply not to address it. He *performs* transcendental phenomenological works without reflecting on them as transcendental. The "existence" of which he speaks is presented, for instance, as an "object" of phenomenological investigation—even though as such it is understood by readers who may lack the mediation offered by analysis. Since they, too, exist, they "see" the point as they stand apart from it in the paradoxical epistemological act of being drawn to a concept by differentiating themselves from it, the act, that is, of what Sartre calls "nihilation."

Case in point: If consciousness by itself is nothing, what, then, emerges when consciousness reflects on consciousness? The formal move Sartre makes is to point out the embodied prereflective moment that is objectified by the reflective moment. Thus, reflective consciousness reflects on prereflective consciousness as its object. In effect, we have a negation reflecting on a negation. This negation on a negation raises serious questions of whether it could deny itself as a negation and whether it could reduce itself to a negation. The denial and the reduction carry dangers, he argues, of "bad faith."

Bad faith is a lie to the self. It is a lie to the self that involves an effort to hide from one's freedom. One's freedom is at the heart of the absence of a sedimented thing that we expect to conjoin us to the things of which we are conscious. We seek two "things"—the object of consciousness *and* consciousness. But consciousness, Sartre argues, is not a "thing," so in such instances there is simply one "thing"—the object of consciousness. Freed from "thingness," we find ourselves facing a slippage of the self. Our selves are not fully contained but, instead, always "ecstatic," always, that is, facing its possibilities and its past. Motivations abound on why such distantiation might be unbearable, and many of us seek retreat in various directions. We could retreat into a pit of thinghood, where we convince ourselves that we are, literally, full of ourselves. Or we could deny all; we can convince ourselves that we are so free from "thingness," that we can transcend *everything*. Such paths, as is well known among Sartre scholars, are called a retreat to facticity (thingness) and a retreat to transcendence (absolute freedom).

Sartre complicates matters by adding a requirement to consciousness. A "requirement" to consciousness should already render Sartre's antitranscendental appeals suspect. Nevertheless, his requirement is straightforward. Consciousness, he argues, must be embodied. The logic of embodied consciousness makes sense simply because without being embodied, consciousness cannot be somewhere, and without being somewhere, consciousness cannot be a point of view, and without being a point of view, there can be no position from which to be conscious *of* anything. Every "there" requires a "here."

"Here" is where "I" am located. That "place," if we will, is an embodied one. It is consciousness "in the flesh." In the flesh, I am not only a point of view, but I am also a point that is viewed. I see, hear, and smell, and I am seen, heard, and (let us say without embarrassment) smelled. The one who sees, hears, and smells me is the Other. And I do the same to him or her. Both of us, however, can be aware of another phenomenon—the experience of being seen, heard, and smelled. Implicit in that experience is the Other as a subjective point of view to whom I am presented as a self-aware object. Sartre identifies several forms of bad faith or self-lie connected to these relations. The first is sadism.

Now, sadism by itself is not a form of bad faith. One can engage in sadistic sexual play, for example, which means that one has, in principle, taken the position that one's role is not absolute, is not, in existential parlance, "serious." The spirit of seriousness is a bad faith attitude that involves a collapse of values into material conditions of the world. With such an attitude, values are "caused" by and are "in" the world in forms similar to the release of energy from a split atom. Put differently, the serious spirit treats values as ontological features of the world. Values lose their force as judgments and become ossified reality; they "are" the way the world "is." The bad faith sadist is, therefore, serious. Sadistic sexual play is not bad faith because in such an instance the erotic charge emerges for the sake of *playing*, which requires recognizing that one *chooses* the rules of the game.

Choice is an activity whose importance is so central to our subsequent discussion that I should take a moment to discuss its meaning here. A condition of one's freedom is that one is able to choose. Yet, choosing and having options are not identical. Choices may work in accordance with options, but one may choose what is not a live option. The choice, then, turns back on the chooser and lives in the world of negation. There, the choice, at best, determines something about the chooser, although it fails to transform the material conditions imposed on the chooser. Theories that fail to make the distinction between choice and option carry the danger of using the genii as the model for human choice. For the genii, and, for that matter, God, there is no schism between choice and option, so whatever he or she chooses *is*, absolutely, what *will be*.

The sadist can, at best, *play* God, but the sadist cannot *be* God. The sadist who is not playing situates himself on the level of God. Such an obvious lie to the self affirms such sadism as a form of bad faith. The sadist of which Sartre speaks is one that is not playing. Such a sadist desires to be the only eyes that function as eyes, the only standpoint of sight. Such a being "becomes" the point of view from which others are seen and thus manifests a desire to see without being seen, since a consequence of being the *only* point of view is the absence of others'. To do that, the sadist must control the sight of others, force them never to function as a point of view. His credo? "I am the only point of view." Solipsism is, thus, another feature of serious sadism.

Then there is the serious masochist. Such a figure seeks to be by being seen. The nothingness of consciousness carries no "reality" sufficient to found being. It is better to be the object of consciousness. The masochist throws him- or herself beneath the eyes of the sadist, and where there are no willing sadists, the masochist attempts to create one. The irony here is that in his or her desire to be the pure object, to be a saturated existent, to be at the mercy of the sadist and thus "give up" agency, the masochist ends up manifesting agency. The masochist ends up attempting to "fix" the sadist's vision and, hence, the sadist's freedom. We could think of the serious sado-masochistic paradox: "Beat me! Beat me!" pleads the serious masochist, to which the serious sadist replies, with narrowed eyes and a wry grin, "No."

The serious sadist wants to deny *others'* point of view, a task that would render others patently not-*others*. The world that he desires is a world without what phenomenologists in the Schutzean tradition call "sociality."[7] Sociality is the intersubjective world, the world of "others," a world that requires the self *and* others, and the self as other to those other selves. The serious sadist's sadism could not be acted out, could not even emerge, without others. Similarly, serious masochism is a point of view with the interest of not being a point of view. Only the masochist could pull off this lie to the masochist, which renders the masochist's efforts performative contradictions.

What Sartre leaves out of his argument, but we shall here consider, is this. If the precondition of sadism is another subjectivity and the precondition of masochism is a subjectivity that seeks to fix other subjectivities, then intersubjectivity is the precondition of these forms of bad faith. The argument is, in other words, transcendental. Seen in this way, the orthodox interpretation of sociality as a "psychological" phenomenon fails to appreciate the importance of the nonpsychological foundations of the psychological appeal. In other words, it could only be purely psychological *in bad faith*. In Husserlian phenomenology, the point was put differently: Psychological explanations are *relative* to the "factual" appeals of the natural sciences, appeals that are not absolute by virtue of their failure to raise radical questions of their own assessment. A psychologistic explanation of social reality is, in other words, blatantly *not* phenomenological, and by bringing in the natural sciences as modes of legitimation, they commit another phenomenological sin: They reintroduce the causal nexus of the natural attitude, a nexus that should have been suspended at the moment of initial reflection.[8]

THE PROBLEM OF SOCIAL REALITY

That sociality could not be denied without contradiction is the message we gain from the analysis of bad faith. Sociality is so much at the heart of human relations—indeed, their "relationality" through which emerges their "historicity"—that we might as well add another definition of bad faith. Bad faith is the denial of sociality. Since bad faith is also a lie to the self, then to lie about sociality is also a self lie. What type of self could be such that it is at one with social reality? It is none other than human reality. In denying our sociality we deny our humanity.

At this point, all would seem fine and good but for a problem raised by the phenomenological approach. If sociality is linked to our humanity, does this mean that we must always be among others in order to be human? I recall a student informing me that he preferred "cooperative" housing during his years of study. I responded that such a way of living would have driven me crazy. In order to appreciate people, I need to be away from them now and then with some regularity. For my fellow human beings to be staring me in the face without a reprieve, with "no exit," as Sartre would say, would truly be hell.

Yet, it would be remiss for my student to have concluded that I was anti-social, anticommunal, or a misanthrope. Paradoxically, an antisocial human being or a misanthrope could ironically manifest his or her ire through *intense* association with others. The intensity could be such that the *sui generis* dimensions of each human being would be lost. With such a loss, one need not pay the sort of attention to others as one would when each emerges as an individual human being. Karl Jaspers, in his *Philosophy*, points to this saturation as simply *Dasein*, simply being there. His preferred existence (*Existenz*), which calls on us to look at each other as irreplaceable. Although not premised on Husserlian and Sartrean phenomenology, Jaspers's observation affirms its insight: The irony of sociality is that although it is the world of others, it is also a world of *irreplaceable* others.[9]

Realization of the irreplaceability of others is particularly acute in social relations that have attained the status of community. When, for instance, a member of one's community dies, the loss is such that one no longer feels "whole," and although others may attempt to fill the gap, such efforts are ultimately artificial. What others who come on the scene become are new irreplaceable others to be cherished on their own terms. Paradoxically, then, communities are social relations that heighten each member's understanding of every other member's value and uniqueness. Such understanding leads to relations that are empathetic without egoism: I am my communal Other and I understand that I am that Other's Other, which means we are equally related yet distinct. I am thus able to place myself, on the level of understanding, into that Other's situation while recognizing that I am in that relation on the level of what we share but ultimately different by virtue of who I am. That is why a twentieth-century, New World Black man such as Bob Marley could sing in "Slaver Driver": "I remember on the slave ships / How they brutalized our very souls." That is why, during the invasion of Ethiopia, Blacks all across the world suffered invasion. That is how, in spite of the impossibility of ever *experiencing* bondage in ancient Egypt, every contemporary Jewish person is able to connect across the world and over the ages during Passover. Examples need not be dramatic.

Throughout the 1970s, Franky Crocker, the famed radio host of WBLS in New York City, opened his evening program at 8:00 P.M. with the Nat King Cole version of Eddie Jefferson's "There I Go." It was a ritual that linked nearly the entire Black community of New York City. Young children, adolescents, and adults listened attentively to the opening verse "There I go, there I go, there I go" and to Crocker's opening remarks. The song was known by heart, and part of what it meant *to be* a Black person in New York City was "experienced" through this ritual. Similar to solidarity during times of war or Jewish Passover ceremonies there was awareness not only of participating in something that formed an identity relation with others, but also of *being in that identity relation*. Listening to Crocker's opening remarks, one was aware of the rest of the city listening as well. Irreplaceability is a condition through which there are socially created phenomena to which I could refer in thought, memory, or imagination. The irreplaceable dimension of actors in the social world suggests a remarkable aspect of sociality and socially created phenomena. They are not simply here or there. They are *achieved*.[10]

That sociality is an achievement raises a problem that is peculiarly phenomenological. Recall the phenomenological approach. We suspend certain interests in order to examine their phenomenal features. I want to give this approach another name. I want to call it "ontological suspension," which means that we are less concerned with what something "is" and more concerned with its "thematization," its meaning. With a rock, a chair, or a tree, one could suspend ontological commitments and simply study its meaning. If one is uncertain, one could consult the "others" for information regarding such an object. Could one do so with a person? Another human being? If one does so, does not that leave one simply with a flat surface? Could one intend a person without, say, moral commitments? How do moral commitments differ from ontological commitments when we focus on personhood? And finally, how can the "Other" appear as "Other" without *being* an Other? In the course of my investigations, a curious possibility emerges that is absent from my investigations of rocks, chairs, and trees. Interrogation shifts from third-person resources—resources of a set of explanations, of knowledge, of ways of the world offered in support of certain judgments—to the second person. Such an Other is no longer "such an Other" but, instead, *You*.

RACE STUFF

The "You" with which I have concluded the last section is peculiarly absent in many discussions of race and racism. Although the racist's basis for such a violation is obvious—he or she does not want to recognize some people as *You*—a difficulty emerges in cases where there are antiracists who make a similar violation: the same people continue to be ignored in the discourse of antiracist reasonability. When many race theorists write about race, it seems as though they are not writing to racialized people. Race talk has that flavor of "Hey, take a look at this!" The problem is that "this" tends to be "them."

There is much that many of us, including those who theorize about race, claim to want to know but in fact do not really want to know about racial reality. The trajectories are familiar: The concept of race, for instance, is without natural scientific foundation and should therefore be abandoned. Race is divisive, so for the sake of unity, it should be abandoned. Race is a social construction, so it should not be granted the same credence as things that are supposedly not social constructions. This last claim tends to ally itself with the first, since things that have natural scientific foundations tend to be treated as things that are not social constructions. And then there are the blatant racist versions of each of these trajectories: Race *is* scientifically redeemable through measurements of normal versus abnormal groups of people, with, of course, the abnormal being those designated inferior "races." Race is divisive, so *Black* and other *colored* people should abandon their identities in favor of the abstract, supposedly "neutral" identities. Race is a social construction, so colored races should abandon their race attachments.

Why do I call these racist positions? Although I have not offered a definition of racism, it could easily be seen here that the latter set presents "neutrality" and "normal" as terms devoid of racial significance when in fact they are highly charged racial terms. Because, say, Whites are normative in an anti-Black society, it becomes superfluous to identify them when other groups are not mentioned. Put bluntly: The appeal to many so-called racially neutral terms—"man," "woman," "person," "child," and "one"—often signify Whites except where stated otherwise. They have a prereflective parenthetical adjective—"(White) man," "(White) woman," "(White) person," "(White) child," and "(White) one." It is not the case that these terms "must" signify these subtextual markers. If that were so, then our position would exemplify the spirit of seriousness. It is that our life world, so to speak, is such that these are their significations. To advance the claim, then, that we should abandon the other designations in favor of the so-called racially neutral ones in no way threatens the unholy alliance between the racially favored group and normativity.

But what about the first set? How do they fare, given our criticism of their reactionary offshoots? From a phenomenological standpoint, the obvious flaw with the first appeal is that to reject race on *scientific* grounds is not a *phenomenological* critique, and, furthermore, it achieves at best a claim to scientific modes of assessment. It tells us that something is "wrong" with race and racism, but it does not transcend mere factual conceptions of error. The other objections, about divisiveness and social constructivity, fail phenomenologically because they simply scratch the surface. After all, divisiveness by itself is not an evil. One could easily think of some alliances that should be divided. And social constructivity itself is not necessarily fictitious. One could easily think of things that rely on social reality for their existence without being fictions. Is language, for instance, fictitious? How about community? Friendship?

What is more, there are instances of appeals to scientific validity that are hypocritical. For example, commentators who reject race because of its scientific invalidity have not scrutinized the type of race questions that many scientists ask. In "Anthropological Measurement," Fatimah L. C. Jackson presents a reading of scientific treatments of race that challenge much that is presumed by both conservative and liberal proponents of a scientific resolution of racial rationalizations.[11] The standard criticism, found in writers like K. Anthony Appiah and Naomi Zack, rejects race on the basis of its failure to achieve an isomorphic relation between morphological differences and genetic difference.[12] People who look different may share genes, and people who look alike may be genetically different. The conservative position uses old racial morphological categories of Caucasoid, Mongoloid, and Negroid and then struggles through mixtures of these three. And "origins" range from monogenesis in Africa and then spontaneous differences of genes and appearance to polygenesis with different genes and appearances on each continent. Thus, there would be Asian races, European races, African races, (once) Australian races, North American races, and South American races. Now, an implication of these ways of thinking is that one takes positions on race *because* of the scientific information available. We already see, however, a divide in understanding the relationship between race and racism here. For it should be clear that one could take the position that there are distinct sets of races *and* that we should respect them equally. One could then, as many of our predecessors did in the nineteenth century, fight against racism while believing in the existence of races. And one's belief in the origins of races could be either monogenic or polygenic.

Jackson argues, however, that the type of question we have been asking about genetics are dead wrong, and their wrongness is unfolding in one of the largest natural scientific efforts to chart the course of the human species: the human genome project. What this project is revealing is that *all* human genes originated from the same region: southeast Africa. During the period of our evolution, when human beings were in a single region, conditions were ripe for the maximum diversity of our gene pool. Subsequent patterns of movement and mating selections led to the focus on certain combinations of those genes in certain regions over others until the gene variations spread across the planet. What this means is that, from a genetic point of view, there is indeed one human species who originated from a single region. But here is the rub: Race critics have read this conclusion to mean that races do not exist. In one sense it is true. Races do not exist. *One* race exists. And that race is "Negro."

How could this be? The standard pitch is to say that there is one race, the *human* race. But "human," from a genetic standpoint, is determined by the genetic diversity of *homo sapien sapien*. Genetic diversity emerges at the point of "origin," which here means evolution. After evolving, environmental conditions and mating selections affect formations. Thus, in Negro is the genetic diversity that was subsequently reworked through such processes to create lighter Negroes—Negroes whom we have come to know as "Caucasoid" and "Mongoloid." Or put differently, if Negroes were to disappear, we will not be able to reproduce the genetic diversity of the human species. If all groups but Negroes disappear, it would still be possible to reproduce the genetic diversity of the human species.[13]

Now although this may strike some of us as odd, it is something that many people who have been designated Negroes have long been able to "see." The social constructivists may point out that one could pick a socially mediating document like a birth certificate of a member of any group known today as "White" or "northeast Asian" and notice the following consequence, should that birth certificate reveal two biological parents designated "Negro." Many of us would begin to "see" Negro features in that person. The hair, the lips, the buttocks, the feet; the way the person walks, talks—and, yes, dances and makes love—would take on new meaning in our race inflected social reality. The families of many people who have been designated Negroes, especially in North and South America, tend to be morphologically diverse, but regarded (for the obvious reasons of being biologically related) as genetically one. In effect, such families are microcosmic versions of the human species.

The question emerges: What do geneticists now "see" when they look at their fellow human beings? And correlatively: What would race theorists who have supported scientism now advocate, given the growing body of evidence of our most ambitious natural scientific mapping out of the human species? Will they begin to look in the mirror and accept themselves as simply lighter-skinned Negroes? Could they now begin to think of "human" as "maximum diversity"?

It is with such questions that the uniqueness of racial reality comes to the fore. In his profoundly misunderstood 1952 book *Black Skin, White Masks*, Fanon presents one of the best existential phenomenological treatments of this subject with the departing observation that between phylogenic explanations (the sort exemplified by natural scientific mapping out of the species) and ontogenic explanations (the sort exemplified by natural scientific portraits of an individual organism or theoretical study of an individual), there is *sociogeny*—that which emerges from the social world. The social world is here understood as a dynamic medium of historical, economic, semiotic, and intersubjective forces. From the standpoint of the social world, the natural scientific support for humanity's diverse gene pool being synonymous with what we call "Negro" will be of little consequence if it does not affect the lived reality of how people negotiate their way through the social world. If, that is, the social world is premised on there being people of different races and there being a major difference between Negroes and all other races, a difference of kinds, a difference that treats that group as subhuman, then the world would continue to "be" racially divided as such. An impact of social reality, then, is ontological; it transforms concepts and knowledge claims into lived concepts, into forms of being, into forms of life. The geneticist might demonstrate the existence of one race, but the social reality is multitudinous: races and their mixtures abound.

The usefulness of a phenomenological analysis becomes obvious: It explores the intersubjective framework of meanings and the impact of multiple intentions and sociality; it also presents interpretations that, at the same time, do not fall into the trap of bad faith. This is so because phenomenology distinguishes between interpreting ontological judgments and making them. By suspending the natural attitude, phenomenologists are able to explore the contours of the social world while keeping their contingency in mind. It is with these considerations in mind that I now move further into the complex world of race and racism.

RACISM, DEHUMANIZATION, INVISIBILITY

My first observation is that racism is a form of dehumanization, which is a form of bad faith—for to deny the humanity of a human being requires lying to ourselves about something of which we are aware. This observation debunks a misconception in many presentations of racism. Racism, it is said, emerges through an anxiety over the Other. The Other is supposedly a mark of inferior difference. The problem with this view is that it fails to deal with the meaning of "Other." Implicit in "Other" is a shared category. If one is a human being, then the Other also is a human being. "Here *I* am and there is another *human being*." Dehumanization takes a different form. There one finds the self, another self, and those who are not-self and not-Other. In effect, as Fanon points out in the seventh chapter of *Black Skin, White Masks*, there is a schema in which self-Other relations are between Whites and between Blacks, but White-Black does not signify a self-Other but a self-below-Other relation. Whereas a Black-White signifies a self-Other. For the Black, in other words, the White *is* another human being, but the structure of anti-Black racism is such that for the anti-Black racist, the Black is not another human being. The struggle against anti-Black racism is such, then, that it involves an effort to achieve Otherness. It is a struggle to enter the realm, in other words, in which ethical relations are forged.

So racism is a context marked by a paradox of being a human relation of inhumanity. It is a human act of denying the humanity of other groups of human beings. This human act can be structural (institutional) and situational (between individuals). Although the addendum "on the basis of race" is usually advanced, it is important to note that most racists advance the superiority or inferiority of a racial group without advancing a concept of race. They may, in other words, not know what races are—only that they do not like Black people or indigenous people, and so on. But more, that racism involves dehumanization situates it as a form of oppression. Oppression, often understood in terms of impositions of "power," is a function of the number of options a society offers its members. I speak of options because of the vagueness of appeals to power. Although many of us know power when we see it, defining power is another matter. Foucault, for instance, has spoken about power and knowledge as fused realities—"power/knowledge." But indeed, this does not tell us what power is, only that knowledge is one of its forms, or that one of the forms of knowledge is power. Worse, many discussions of power often speak more about *effects* of power the result of which is our gaining little understanding of what power may be.

It is my view that power-in-itself is an empty notion, and that words like "force," "power," "motion," "gravity," and "sadomasochism" are simply ways of talking about things that are able to put other things into being. For some commentators, it is institutions that have this "power," and for others, individuals do as well. From the standpoint of an oppressed individual, however, "power" makes no sense if it is of no consequence. Recall my discussion of the relation between choices and options. Where there are many options, choices can be made without imploding on those who make them. If a set of options is considered *necessary* for social well being in a society, then trouble begins when and where such options are not available to all members of the society. In effect, such options have an impact on *membership* itself. In a world where I only have two options, but everyone else has three, it is highly likely that my choices will exceed my options more quickly than would the others. Where there are only two options, I may use up two choices before I begin to make inward, abstract "choices," like "neither," or "I will choose X or Y *affirmatively* or *reluctantly*," and so on. Eventually, it becomes clear that to make more than two choices without collapsing onto myself and the *way* I make choices, I will need to expand my options. But to do so would put me in conflict with a world that has only given me two options. In effect, then, to live like everyone else places me in a situation of conflict. Here, we see the problem brought into philosophical focus. For, to live like everyone else, to live as "ordinary," as "normal," would require of me an "extraordinary" act.[14]

Think of Jim Crow or U.S. apartheid. Jim Crow, in limiting the options available for Blacks in the everyday negotiation of social life, increased the probability of Black social life being in conflict with American social life; it increased the probability of Blacks breaking the law on an everyday basis.

Such limited options forced every Black to face choices about the self that placed selfhood in conflict with humanhood. We could think, as well, of the debate on abortion. When abortion was illegal in the United States, many women faced no option but an illegal abortion when they made the choice of having an abortion. The consequence was that the meaning of being a woman in the society was also marked by a high probability of an encounter with the legal system or having one's reproductive activities carrying high associations with being in "trouble."

In the post–Jim Crow era, problems continue as the collapse of Blacks into pathologies is such that it limits the options available for Blacks in civil society. Many Blacks, for instance, in going about their everyday life, incur a constant risk of incarceration. The expression "driving while Black" (DWB) has become so much a feature of American society that it has made its way to National Public Radio (March 9, 1999). Blacks suffer the phobogenic reality posed by the spirit of racial seriousness. In effect, they more than symbolize or signify various social pathologies, they "become" them; in our anti-Black world, Blacks *are* pathology. The consequence is obviously claustrophobic. Under such circumstances, Blacks are forced to take extraordinary measures to live "ordinary" lives; an ordinary life, after all, should not involve expected encounters with the criminal justice system.

It is at this point that we encounter a feature of Black invisibility. Black invisibility involves a form of hypervisibility. The Black is, in other words, invisible by virtue of being much too visible. The Black is, in other words, not seen by virtue of being seen. "Being seen" is, however, ambiguous here. It means an act of reducing a feature of reality to absolute reality—of ontologizing that which is not ontological. In effect, it means to render something "present" through making something "absent." I want to call this phenomenon "epistemic closure." In an act of epistemic closure, one ends a process of inquiry. In effect, it is the judgment "say no more."

By contrast, epistemological openness is the judgment "there is always more to be known." Placed in the context of making judgments about groups, epistemic openness pertains to the anonymity that undergirds the social dimension of each social group. A social group is such that each member can occupy the role that exemplifies it. When the one encounters a member of that group and identifies, usually by virtue of the role the member performs, the social group to which he or she belongs, it is good practice to restrict judgments to the context and to the social role but not over the full biography of the individual who plays that role. Those aspects remain anonymous, nameless. Thus, to pass by *a* student and to recognize him or her as a student need not entail the role "student" to cover the entire scope of that student's life and being. Such is the case with many other social roles and groups. There is always *more* that one could learn about the individual who occupies that social role. In the case of epistemic closure, however, the identification of the social role is all one needs for a plethora of other judgments. In effect, to know that role is to know *all there is to know* about the individual. In effect, there is no distinction between him or her and the social role, which makes the individual an essential representative of the entire group. The group, then, becomes pure exterior being. Its members are literally without "insides" or hidden spaces for interrogation. One thus counts for all. The guiding principle of avoiding the fallacy of hasty generalizations is violated here as a matter of course. Blacks become both effect and cause, cause and effect, an identity without dynamism, without possibility.

EPISTEMIC LIMITATIONS OF RACE REPRESENTATIONS

Identifying the epistemological features of racial stereotypes raises a question for the phenomenologist who studies such phenomena: To know what people do when they make stereotypical judgments is one thing, but to look at such judgments phenomenologically raises questions of whether the phenomenological treatments are themselves devoid of such error. That the error of hasty generalizations occurs is one thing, but what would it mean to describe and to make judgments over such phenomena without being fallacious, and fallacious in a phenomenological sense—that is, without falling into reimposition of the natural attitude?

Here, I am advancing the metatheoretical question of "rigor." "Rigor" means that the process of gathering and interpreting phenomena must be guided by an understanding of the challenges raised by the subjects of study at hand. In this case, the subjects of study are human beings, and as human beings, they challenge the sedimented judgments we might make. In Sartrean language, they are "metastable" subjects, subjects who defy permanent, isomorphic relations with judgments we may make about them. Such defiance poses unique challenges to anyone who chooses to study or make knowledge claims about human beings. Such a challenge pertains, as well, to inquirers who might be members of the communities they study or interpret. Consider, for example, W. E. B. Du Bois's following autobiographical observation: "I became painfully aware [while studying Blacks in Philadelphia at the end of the nineteenth century] that merely being born in a group, does not necessarily make one possessed of complete knowledge concerning it. . . . I concluded that I did not know so much as I might about my own people."[15]

A member of a group does not live his or her everyday experience in a way that constitutes the reflection of study. To study one's lived reality requires a displacement and a new set of questions about that reality that render one's experiences at best data to be added to the stream of data to be interpreted. But more, the theoretical questions raised may be such that there is no precedent for them, which means that by raising them, one has placed oneself outside of a privileged sphere of knowledge. How one lives in a community is not identical with the sort of knowledge involved in how one *studies* a community.

Yet, an implication of resisting epistemic closure is that one should approach members of the relevant group with the spirit of inquiry, with, that is, realization that the Other has a point of view that can only be accessed by the mediation of expression (language, speech acts, and embodiment); there are hermeneutical considerations and the experiential considerations, in other words, of looking at hypervisible or oppressed people from the *inside*. These are concerns that Du Bois himself deploys in an essay at the end of the nineteenth century: "The Conservation of the Races," a paper that he presented to the American Negro Academy.[16]

"The Conservation of the Races" has received much discussion over the past two decades.[17] In the hullabaloo, there has not, however, been much discussion of its existential phenomenological dimensions. These dimensions come to the fore in both its context and its content. It is "inside," so to speak, to a community of Black intellectuals, that Du Bois brings forth his famous existential phenomenological reading of the nihilistic threat of denied membership as a struggle of twoness, of two souls, of double consciousness. Double consciousness raises not only the experience of seeing the world from an American point of view and a Black point of view, and from the point of view of the Black Diaspora, but also from the contradictions encumbered by such experience. Must "Black" be anathema to "American"? What Black folks *experience* are the contradictions of American society; it is an experience of what is denied, an experience of the contradictions between the claims of equality and the lived reality of inequality, between the claims of justice and the lived reality of systematic and systemic injustice, between the claims of a universal normativity and the lived reality of *White* normativity, between the claims of Blacks not having any genuine points of view and the lived reality of Blacks' points of view on such claims.

By raising the question of Blacks' points of view, Du Bois raises the question of an "inside" that requires an approach to social phenomena that puts the inquirer in a position to break down the gap between him- or herself and the subjects of study. For in principle, if the inquirer can imagine the Black point of view as a point of view that can be communicated, then already a gap between the inquirer and the Black subject of study has been bridged. The inquirer, whether White or Black, must work with the view of communicability and, simultaneously, a process of interrogation that will bring forth what Black subjects are willing to divulge. In short, the method presupposes agency, freedom, and responsibility, which transforms the epistemological expectations of inquiry. From the "outside," one could receive limited understanding. From the "inside," one could, as well, receive limited understanding. Combined, one receives "good" understanding and "solid," "rigorously acquired" information, information marked by the social reality of intersubjectivity—a subject studying other subjects who have addressed him or her as a subject as well—but never "complete" information. It is by staying attuned to the incompleteness of all epistemic projects with regard to human beings that one makes the approach rigorous, which leads to a conception of rigorous human study that is, as Michel Foucault once objected, "humanistic."[18] It is a method that reveals, when it comes to the human being, there will always be more to learn.

CONCLUDING

I write "concluding" since such investigations are always in process. I hope I have shown that phenomenology can be useful for the concerns of this volume. Thinking about community and identity is a tricky business, although in our times, perhaps because of the postmodernism and conservatism that often infuse discourses on community and the political correctness and nihilism that often infuse discourses on identity, the task at times carries a veneer of naiveté and a lack of sophistication. There is, even in such instances, much work to be done. On the pragmatic side, how we think of each other greatly affects how we treat each other, which means there is much epistemic and semiotic work to be done, whereby we look at knowledge claims and the signs and symbols through which such claims are meaningful. On the side of purely philosophical work, challenges raised by studying Africana people's realities tap into the complexity of thought in the present age. They give new meaning to what my mentor, Maurice Natanson, once described as "infinite tasks."[19]

NOTES

This chapter is based on Lewis Gordon, "A Phenomenology of Visible Invisibility: Racial Portraits of Anonymity," in *Confluences: Phenomenology and Postmodernity, Environment, Race, Gender*, ed. Daniel J. Martino (Pittsburgh: The Simon Silverman Phenomenology Center, Dusquesne University, 2000), 39–52, and chapter 4 of Lewis Gordon, *Existentia Africana: Understanding Africana Existential Thought* (New York: Routledge, 2000).

   1. Frantz Fanon, *The Wretched of the Earth*, trans. Constance Farrington (New York: Grove, 1963); and Placide Tempels, *Bantu Philosophy*, trans. Colin King (Paris: Présence Africaine, 1959).

   2. Herbert Gutman, *The Black Family in Slavery and Freedom (1750–1925)* (New York: Vintage, 1976).

   3. Frantz Fanon, *Black Skin, White Masks*, trans. Charles Lamm Markmann (New York: Grove, 1967); Richard Wright, *The Outsider* (New York: Harper and Row, 1953);

Richard Wright, *Native Son* (New York: Harper and Row, 1960); Ralph Ellison, *Invisible Man* (New York: Vintage, 1990); and Ralph Ellison, *Going to the Territory* (New York: Vintage, 1987).

4. Anna Julia Cooper, *The Voice of Anna Julia Cooper: Including "A Voice from the South" and Other Important Essays, Papers, and Letters*, ed. Charles Lemert and Esme Bhan (Lanham, Md.: Rowman & Littlefield, 1998).

5. Jean-Paul Sartre, *Being and Nothingness: A Phenomenological Essay on Ontology*, trans. Hazel Barnes (New York: Washington Square Press, 1956).

6. Immanuel Kant, *Critique of Pure Reason (Unabridged Edition)*, trans. Norman Kemp Smith (New York: St. Martin's, 1965); and Edmund Husserl, *Cartesian Meditations: An Introduction to Phenomenology*, trans. Dorion Cairns (Dordrecht: Martinus Nijhoff, 1960).

7. See Alfred Schutz, *Collected Papers*, vol. 1, *The Problem of Social Reality*, ed. Maurice Natanson (The Hague: Martinus Nijhoff, 1962); and, of course, Alfred Schutz, *The Phenomenology of the Social World*, trans. George Walsh and Frederick Lehnhert (Evanston, Ill.: Northwestern University Press, 1970); see also Maurice Natanson, *Anonymity: A Study in the Philosophy of Alfred Schutz* (Bloomington: Indiana University Press, 1986).

8. Husserl made this argument on many occasions, but see especially Edmund Husserl, "Philosophy As Rigorous Science," in *Phenomenology and the Crisis of Philosophy*, trans. Quentin Lauer (New York: Harper Torchbooks, 1965).

9. For example, see Karl Jaspers, *Philosophy*, 3 vols., trans. E. B. Ashton (Chicago: University of Chicago Press, 1969–1971); and Karl Jaspers, *Reason and Existenz: Five Lectures*, trans. William Earle (New York: Noonday, 1955).

10. The achievement of sociality is a Schutzean theme with many implications. For example, see my discussion of achieving sociality in Lewis R. Gordon, *Fanon and the Crisis of European Man: An Essay on Philosophy and the Human Sciences* (New York: Routledge, 1995), chapter 3.

11. Fatimah L. C. Jackson, "Anthropological Measurement: The Mismeasure of African Americans," *The Annals of the American Academy of Political and Social Science* 568 (March 2000): 154–171.

12. K. Anthony Appiah, *In My Father's House: Africa in the Philosophy of Culture* (New York: Oxford University Press, 1992); Naomi Zack, *Race and Mixed-Race* (Philadelphia: Temple University Press, 1993); and Naomi Zack, *Thinking about Race* (San Francisco: Wadsworth, 1998).

13. For a wonderful, detailed discussion of this argument, see Charles S. Finch III, *Echoes of the Old Darkland: Themes from the African Eden* (Decatur, Ga.: Khenti, 1996), especially chapter 1.

14. Much of what was just related is discussed in Lewis Gordon, *Bad Faith and Antiblack Racism* (Highlands, N.J.: Humanities, 1995); Gordon, *Fanon and the Crisis of European Man*; and Lewis Gordon, *Her Majesty's Other Children: Sketches of Racism from a Neocolonial Age* (Lanham, Md.: Rowman & Littlefield, 1997).

15. W. E. B. Du Bois, *The Autobiography of W. E. B. Du Bois: A Soliloquy on Viewing My Life from the Final Decade of Its First Century*, ed. Herbert Aptheker (New York: International, 1968), 98.

16. W. E. B. Du Bois, "On the Conservation of the Races," in *African Philosophy: An Anthology*, ed. Emmanuel Chukwudi Eze (Oxford: Blackwell, 1998), 269–275.

17. See Appiah, *In My Father's House*; and Lucius Outlaw, *On Race and Philosophy* (New York: Routledge, 1996).

18. Michel Foucault, *The Order of Things: An Archaeology of the Human Sciences* (New York: Vintage, 1994).

19. Maurice Natanson, *Edmund Husserl: Philosopher of Infinite Tasks* (Evanston, Ill.: Northwestern University Press, 1973).

III

HISTORICAL CRISES OF IDENTITY AND COMMUNITY

7

Visions of Transcendent Community in the Works of Toni Morrison

Joy James

AFRICAN AMERICAN INTELLECTUALS AND ACADEMIC QUESTIONS

The education of the next generation of black intellectuals is something that is terrifically important to me. But the questions black intellectuals put to themselves, and to African American students, are not limited and confined to our own community. For the major crises in politics, in government, in practically any social issue in this country the axis turns on issues of race. Is this country willing to sabotage its cities and school systems if they're occupied mostly by black people? It seems so. When we take on these issues and problems as black intellectuals, what we are doing is not merely the primary work of enlightening and producing a generation of young black intellectuals. Whatever the flash points are, they frequently have to do with amelioration, enhancement or identification of the problems of the entire country. So this is not parochial; it is not marginal—it is not even primarily self-interest.

—Toni Morrison, "African American Intellectual Life at Princeton: A
Conversation," *Princeton Today*

In her nonfiction essays, Toni Morrison's dissection of racist paradigms is framed by a worldview that testifies to African American ancestral spirits, the centrality of transcendent community, and her faith in the abilities of African American intellectuals to critique and civilize a racist society. Reading Morrison as a cultural observer and practitioner, I share a sensibility that privileges community and ancestors while confronting dehumanizing cultural representations and practices. I quote from Morrison's nonfiction to sketch a frame for viewing her observations on racist stereotypes and Black resistance. Even in its incompleteness, a sketch reveals clues for deciphering how Morrison uncovers and recovers ground for "discredited knowledge" in which traditional and contemporary cultural beliefs held among African Americans are connected to political struggles.[1] The outline of a conceptual site or worldview is not an argument for Black essentialism; recognizing the political place of African American cultural views, which manifest and mutate through time and location, constructs these views neither as quintessential nor universal to everyone of African descent. Likewise, a passionate interest in African American intellectual and political resistance to anti-Black racism is not synonymous with an indifference to non-African Americans or to accommodations to Eurocentrism and White supremacy.

Morrison explores the intellectual service of African American educators in ways compatible to the role of the African philosopher, as development within and through service is described by Tsenay Serequeberhan: "The calling of the African philosopher . . . comes to us from a lived history whose endurance and sacrifice—against slavery and colonialism—has made our present and future existence in freedom possible. The reflective explorations of African philosophy are thus aimed at further enhancing and expanding this freedom."[2] This call of the African philosopher or theorist, shared by the African American intellectual, predates imperialism, enslavement, and racism. If, as Morrison argues, the questions that African American intellectuals raise for and among themselves reverberate beyond Black communities, then exploring a worldview that presents service and community as indispensable, time and space as expansive, knowledge as intergenerational and responsive to the conditions of people, and community as a changing, transcendent but nevertheless shared and thorny tie, would frame responses to state violence and resistance to oppressive cultural practices.

Morrison's essays raise a number of questions about the possibilities for critiquing and developing curricular paradigms that acknowledge realities greater than those recognized by conventional academia. Worldviews contextualize educators' lives and shape how they develop curricula, pedagogy, and scholarship to talk about, or silence talk about, critical theory and racialized knowledge. Educators can challenge or reinforce academic relationships to the worldviews of alternative thinkers such as Morrison. For instance, teaching her writings without a critical discussion of racism and slavery is a perhaps not uncommon, appropriative act that reproduces racial dominance. In Morrison's work discussed below, one finds the demystification of racism tied to a deep commitment to the well being of African Americans. Educators who unravel these ties depoliticize the radical nature of her writings, and, in effect, repoliticize the work as compatible with intellectual paradigms that are indifferent to the racist practices of American society.

In the classroom, expanding the intellectual canon to include Morrison and other people of color, women, poor and working-class people, gay, lesbian, and bisexual people—for more inclusive and representative curricula does not subvert racialized hierarchies. Additive curricula do not inherently democratize education: in integrative reforms, the axis of the universe remains the same. For instance, bell hooks notes:

> A white woman professor teaching a novel by a black woman writer (Toni Morrison's *Sula*) who never acknowledges the "race" of the characters is not including works by "different" writers in a manner that challenges ways we have been traditionally taught as English majors to look at literature. The political standpoint of any professor engaged with the development of cultural studies will determine whether issues of difference and otherness will be discussed in new ways or in ways that reinforce domination.[3]

At best, additive curricula that offer no critique of the dominant worldview civilize racist practices; at worst, they function as decorative shields against critiques of Eurocentrism. Where analyses of Whiteness as a metaparadigm are absent, critiques of racialized oppression are insufficient to create a learning environment in which teaching critical work maintains rather than dismantles communal ties and subversive insights. More accurate representation of the diversity of intellectual life and work of transgressive African American intellectuals requires a context greater than the traditional academic paradigm. Perhaps the only way to attain greater accuracy and honesty is to stand on some terrain, within some worldview other than that legitimized by Eurocentric academe. Engaging in this "dangerous, solitary, radical work," we might finally confront the academic penchant for playing in the dark.[4]

TRADITIONAL WORLDVIEWS

> [In *Song of Solomon*] I could blend the acceptance of the supernatural and a profound rootedness in the real world at the same time with neither taking precedence over the other. It is indicative of the cosmology, the way in which Black people looked at the world. We are very practical people, very down-to earth, even shrewd people. But within that practicality we also accepted what I suppose could be called superstition and magic, which is another way of knowing things. But to blend those two worlds together at the same time was enhancing, not limiting. And some of those things were "discredited knowledge" that Black people had, discredited only because Black people were discredited therefore what they knew was "discredited." And also because the press toward upward social mobility would mean to get as far away from that kind of knowledge as possible. That kind of knowledge has a very strong place in my work.

> —Toni Morrison, "Rootedness"

Distinguishing worldview from superstition requires sketching the cosmology that grounds Morrison's work. Some Black writers posit a nonhegemonic perspective in which (1) community or the collective is central rather than individual achievement or individualism; (2) the transcendent or spiritual is inseparable from the mundane or secular; (3) "nature" is a force essential to humanity; and (4) feminine and masculine are complementary rather than contradictory components of identity and culture. These beliefs (considered illogical in conventional U.S. culture) are not exclusive to an "African-centered" viewpoint. There are similarities between traditional African cosmology and other cosmologies. For instance, in some traditional Native American worldviews, the concept of community also extends through time, for example, in Native American discussions of the seven generations.

What some call superstition or magic, John Mbiti describes as aspects of a cultural worldview in his book *Traditional African Religions and Philosophies.*

> Most [traditional] peoples . . . believe that the spirits are what remains of human beings when they die physically. This then becomes the ultimate status . . . the point of change or development beyond which [one] cannot go apart from a few national heroes who might become deified. . . . Man [or woman] does not, and need not, hope to become a spirit: he [or she] is inevitably to become one, just as a child will automatically grow to become an adult.[5]

Mbiti notes that historically African worldviews have maintained nonlinear time in which the past, present, and future coexist and overlap. (This view is also held in other cultures and in some scientific communities.) Traditional African cosmology sees the nonduality of time and space. Rather than suggest a monolithic Africa, Mbiti's work describes the diversity of religions throughout the continent. Yet he maintains that various organizing principles are prevalent despite ethnic and societal differences. The cosmology he documents rejects the socially constructed dichotomies between sacred and secular, spiritual and political, the individual and community that are characteristic of Western culture. This perspective reappears in African American culture.

Worldviews or values are not deterministic. One may choose. In fact, Mbiti, an African theologian trained in European universities, selects Christianity, depicting it as superior to traditional African religions, which he notes share Christianity's monotheism. We may elect to reject the traditional worldviews that shape African cultures, as Mbiti does. Or we may reaffirm these values, as Morrison does. Stating that "discredited knowledge" has "a very strong place" in her work, Morrison refuses to distance herself from a traditional African and African American cultural worldview, despite the fact that academic or social assimilation and advancement "would mean to get as far away from that kind of knowledge as possible." Without considering the validity of this discredited knowledge or academically marginalized belief system, some may portray Morrison's work as romantic, ungrounded mysticism. Outside of a worldview that recognizes the values mirrored in her work, it is difficult to perceive of Morrison as anything other than exotic. Her fiction is not mere phantasm. As her nonfiction explains, she writes within the framework of African American cultural values and political and spiritual perspectives.

Morrison's work clearly relies on African-centered cultural paradigms that are documented by anthropologists, theologians, philosophers, and sociologists. For centuries, these paradigms have been derided by Eurocentric thought and dismissed as primitive superstition. The invalidation of these frameworks is traceable to European colonization on several continents for several centuries. Historically, European racial mythology determined whether people whose physiology and ancestry were strikingly different were capable of creating theory, philosophy, and cosmology or were merely able to ape superstition. Today, the rejection of discredited knowledge, held by not-fully-assimilated African Americans, branches from this disparagement of the African origins of these views. As Congolese philosopher K. Kia Bunseki Fu-Kiau notes in *The African Book without Title*:

> Africa was invaded . . . to civilize its people. . . . [Civilization] having "accomplished" her "noble" mission . . . African people are still known as people without logic, people without systems, people without concepts. . . . African wisdom hidden in proverbs, the old way of theorizing among people of oral literature [cannot be] seen and understood in the way [the] western world sees and understands [a proverb]. . . . For us . . . proverbs are principles, theories, warehouses of knowledge . . . they have "force de loi," [the] force of law.[6]

People whose traditional culture is supposedly known to be illogical, without complex belief systems, are generally received in racialized societies as dubious contributors to intellectual life or theory. Spoken and unspoken debates about their epistemic subculture range ideologically from reactionary conservatism to progressive radicalism.

Morrison's writings are radical precisely because they reject the Eurocentric labels of primitive for African cosmology and the epistemological aspects of African American culture (all the while cognizant of the value of parts of European culture). Critiquing the racial stereotypes of White supremacy, she asserts the presence of traditional, communal culture as connected to Black and African ancestors. Challenging hegemonic paradigms, Morrison delineates and deconstructs the European American muse's addiction to ethnic notions. She issues two complementary calls that politicize the spirit: to resist the racial mythology embodied in the White European American imagination and to reconnect with the values rooted in traditional African American culture. Of these values, the one that provides the foundation for her work is that of African American community: in her writings, Morrison draws down the spirit to house it in community.

THE CENTRALITY OF COMMUNITY

Perhaps one of the most debated concepts is the viability of an autonomous African American cultural community. Irrespective of the arguments that discredit this concept, Morrison expresses a personal sense of responsibility to community, making it a cornerstone in her work. The individual's salvation, her or his sanity, comes through relationship to others. This knowledge resonates in Morrison's work, and it inspires and informs her political risk-taking and daring. The community she explores is neither a global nor a nation-state one, yet she does not deny the existence or significance of either. The vibrant collection of people that engages her is the African American community. And it is its synthesis of seeming polarities—maleness and femaleness, ugliness and beauty, good and evil, the spiritual and the mundane—that intrigues her.

In "Unspeakable Things Unspoken: The Afro-American Presence in American Literature," Morrison's analysis of her novels, particularly her comments on *Beloved* and *Song of Solomon*, illustrates her emphasis on community and the individual's relationship to it. In this essay, Morrison examines how language "activates" and is activated by outlining the context for the first sentences of each of her novels. She reminds us that this exploration into how she "practices language[s]" seeks and presents a "posture of vulnerability to those aspects of Afro-American culture" that shape her novels.[7]

Of those novels, *Beloved* is a striking example of her awareness of the destructive impact of unbalanced spiritual and political worlds on community. According to Morrison, *Beloved is* haunting because it works in part "to keep the reader preoccupied with the nature of the incredible spirit world while being supplied a controlled diet of the incredible political world."[8] An aspect of this incredible political world is this novel's inspiration in a specific historical tragedy, the story of an African American woman, Margaret Garner, who tried to flee slavery with her children in the nineteenth century.[9] After she was captured in Cincinnati, Garner killed her daughter to save her from slavery and then attempted to take her own life. In a videotaped interview with the BBC, Morrison describes how her own haunting by Garner's life and death ended when she wrote *Beloved*. The context for community and the resistance to oppression is the groundwork for Garner's story of the "unnatural" mother who may or may not have demonstrated the incredible depths of maternal love and political resistance, as fictionalized in *Beloved*. In life and in death, individuals remain connected to and grow within the life of the community.

This is true as well in *Song of Solomon*, where the essence of community directs Morrison's discussion of freedom and grace. In her essay she describes the insurance agent whose suicide fulfills his promise to fly from (no-)Mercy Hospital:

> The agent's flight, like that of the Solomon in the title, although toward asylum (Canada, or freedom, or home, or the company of the welcoming dead), and al-

though it carries the possibility of failure and the certainty of danger, is toward change, an alternative way, a cessation of things-as-they are. It should not be understood as a simple desperate act . . . but as obedience to a deeper contract with his people.[10]

Morrison explains: "The insurance agent does not declare, announce, or threaten his act. He promises, as though a contract is being executed faithfully between himself and others. Promises broken, or kept; the difficulty of ferreting out loyalties and ties that bind or bruise wend their way throughout the action and the shifting relationships." Dangerous but not desperate, the insurance agent embraces rather than flees his community. His notion of a contract is connected to a cultural understanding of community as transcendent; his flight transcends dualities that posit a divide between life and death. Morrison relates how his not-fully-comprehensible gift is acknowledged and received:

It is his commitment to them, regardless of whether, in all its details, they understand it. There is, however, in their response to his action, a tenderness, some contrition and mounting respect ("They didn't know he had it in him.") and an awareness that the gesture enclosed rather than repudiated themselves. The note he leaves asks for forgiveness . . . an almost Christian declaration of love as well as humility of one who was not able to do more.[11]

Exploring the relationship between community and individual, Morrison suggests that her novels involve the reader and narrator in communal ties. In the worldview of her literature, knowledge emerges from connection rather than alienation from other people. Wisdom arises in community, in spite of the flawed character of its constituents:

That egalitarianism which places us all (reader, the novel's population, the narrator's voice) on the same footing, reflected for me the force of flight and mercy, and the precious, imaginative yet realistic gaze of black people who (at one time, anyway) did not mythologize what or whom it mythologized. The "song" itself contains this unblinking evaluation of the miraculous and heroic flight of the legendary Solomon, an unblinking gaze which is lurking in the tender but amused choral-community response to the agent's flight.[12]

Morrison's own unblinking gaze fosters critical self-reflection in regard to African American communities. It would be simple yet simplistic to idealize the African American community as a haven of safety and harmony against dehumanizing racism. Nowhere do Morrison's essays argue for this perfected Black bliss. Everywhere in her literature there exists the reality of the grim, bizarre, and determined struggle in community that embodies both the rotting and the purifying. Rather than succumb to romantic idealism, Morrison admits that her "vulnerability would lie in romanticizing blackness rather than demonizing it; vilifying whiteness rather than reifying it."[13] Her deconstruction of Eurocentrism and Africanisms coexists with a critique of the limitations of Black community. Those limitations partly stem from African Americans' stunted abilities and our refusal to recognize and honor the ancestors and each other. For example, Morrison details how in *Song of Solomon*, the ancestral figure represented by Solomon, who embodies the African ancestors' flight toward freedom, is not readily recognized by community members: "The African myth is also contaminated. Unprogressive, unreconstructed, self-born Pilate [the female protagonist] is unimpressed by Solomon's flight."[14]

Rejection, alienation, and violence toward self, others, or the ancestors, however, do not negate the reality of these ties. Relationships are determinant. One cannot erase community. One decides only how to relate to the community, which includes self, others, ancestors, and future born. Morrison's commentary on *Beloved* and *Song of Solomon* suggests that our ancestors are indispensable to community. Through them, the past sits in the present and future, guiding descendants. The writings suggest that to the extent that we recognize our ancestors, seeking their advice and spiritual power, we deepen our ability to grow in community with them.

THE ROLE OF AFRICAN ANCESTORS

> When you kill the ancestor you kill yourself . . . nice things don't always happen to the totally self-reliant.
>
> —Toni Morrison, "Rootedness"

For some worldviews, the greatest spiritual development is tied to service to the community; in fact, in time through such work one will likely evolve into an elder and later an ancestor. Ancestors are communal members in these traditional worldviews.[15] The practice of honoring or worshiping ancestors is prevalent worldwide. The symbols of European American cultural icons are both physical and literary. For example, the ancestral spirits of Confederate soldiers and slave holders, in iconic statues in Memphis, Jackson, or Birmingham parks, inspire devoted visitors. The fervor of canonical reverence in universities belies the disdain that many European-descended Americans feel for ancestral worship. Popularized ancestors such as George Washington, Thomas Jefferson, and Elvis evince complex relationships to and facile representations of White American freedom and civilization that are dependent on enslaved or exploited African Americans. Increasingly, since the civil rights movement, American culture has jumbled the contradictory values embodied in ancestors who manifest oppositional worldviews: holidays, coins, and postage stamps pay tribute to Washington and Jefferson as well as

Ida B. Wells and Martin Luther King Jr. (although John Brown is rarely memorialized). All collectively comprise community. Extending through time and space to include our predecessors, contemporaries, and future generations, community here is not bound by physical or temporal limits; its relationships are transcendent. This transcendence is marked by the presence of ancestors.

Morrison uses the term "ancestor" to refer to living elders and ancestral spirits. (I reserve the term for historical figures). Arguing that "there is always an elder" in Black literature, Morrison maintains that a distinctive characteristic of African American writing is its focus on the ancestors: "These ancestors are not just parents, they are sort of timeless people whose relationships to the characters are benevolent, instructive, and protective, and they provide a certain kind of wisdom."[16] For Morrison, studying how African American writers relate to the ancestor(s) is revealing:

> Some of them, such as Richard Wright, had great difficulty with that ancestor. Some of them, like James Baldwin, were confounded and disturbed by the presence or absence of an ancestor. What struck me in looking at some contemporary fiction was that whether the novel took place in the city or in the country, the presence or absence of that figure determined the success or the happiness of the character. It was the absence of an ancestor that was frightening, that was threatening, and it caused huge destruction and disarray in the work itself. That the solace comes, not from the contemplation of serene nature as in a lot of mainstream white literature, nor from the regard in which the city was held as a kind of corrupt place to be. Whether the character was in Harlem or Arkansas, the point was there, this timelessness was there, this person who represented this ancestor.[17]

Speech about the ancestors not only enables critiques of historical oppression (such as the references to slavery made in *Beloved* and *Song of Solomon*), but it also establishes communal realities to support and reflect political–spiritual and secular–sacred traditions. Within this worldview, ancestors illuminate an avenue for liberation: listen, and you learn from them; acknowledge their contributions and legacies, and you share their power (which does not necessarily promise redemption). In their physical lives, our predecessors who attained the stature of elders helped others to develop as free human beings. As spiritual forces after death, they continue to guide human development. In this worldview, according to Congolese philosophy, knowledge is "the experience of that deepest reality found between the spiritualized ancestors and the physically living thinkers."[18]

As a living thinker, Toni Morrison is a mapper of recollection sites. Instructional and often inspirational calls to expansive community come from various locations of memory, which despite cultural variances point to unifying elements that are based on shared values. In my own recollection sites,

I remember the values of family, peers, and teachers. I recall the political work in the 1980s of friends and activists countering apartheid and U.S. imperialism in the Caribbean and Latin America, where Nicaraguans and El Salvadorans, fighting United States–funded contras and death squads, honored their dead by calling "Presente!" after their names were read in roll calls. I remember the teachings of activist elders and ancestors, the technique of seminary, and the spirit of African-based religious houses in Brooklyn and the Bronx. All these experiences politicized me and now remind me of the futility of traveling without faith or ancestral hope, and the liabilities of academic training that encourage ignorance of communal culture.

Morrison's writings present us with the knower who reaches beyond the straitjacket of Africanisms into the past, which is the present and future, to pull out both the African presence and the European American imagining of that presence. Morrison is only one of many African Americans following liberating traditions that acknowledge the ancestors as part of a spiritual and political place and practice. Calls to the ancestral presence and the primacy of historical African American figures appear in African American religion, politics, and art. This recognition is also in written (literary) and oral culture. For instance, the African American women's vocal group Sweet Honey in the Rock consistently honors the ancestors in song. Their "Ella's Song," dedicated to civil rights activist Ella Josephine Baker, uses excerpts from Baker's speeches: "We who believe in freedom cannot rest, until the killing of black men, black mothers' sons, is as important as the killing of white men, white mothers' sons."[19] In their introduction to the song "Fannie Lou Hamer," the group and its founder, Bernice Johnson Reagon, former Student Nonviolent Coordinating Committee activist and now director of African American culture at the Smithsonian, explicates their worldview:

> During the civil rights movement of the 1960s Fannie Lou Hamer became a symbol of the strength and power of resistance. We call her name today in the tradition of African libation. By pouring libation we honor those who provide the ground we stand on. We acknowledge that we are here today because of something someone did before we came.[20]

In the academic works of African American intellectuals, the ancestral spirits also appear. Angela Davis speaks of the ancestors in *The Autobiography of Angela Davis* and *Women, Race and Class*. Historian Vincent Harding pays tribute to the ancestors in *There Is a River—The Black Struggle for Freedom in America*.[21] Using "we" throughout his narrative history of African American resistance to enslavement over centuries, Harding merges past, present, and future. With the pronoun "we" he includes himself in the historical telling of our liberation struggles. Finding the historical accounts of Black radicalism in the United States to be limited by their abstractness, scope, and Eurocentrism, Harding's narrative both analyzes and celebrates the history of the African American freedom struggles. Using the metaphor of a river and the imagery of a poem by Langston Hughes, he describes as mentacide the dehumanizing practices that turned Africans into slaves, arguing that to enslave a people, one must first destroy their belief systems, their knowledge in themselves, and their understandings of physical and metaphysical power.

Morrison's work is very familiar within this worldview, framing the vision of African American artists and writers who assert that invoking the spirit honors the memories of ancestors. This act of conjuring also testifies to the prevailing wisdom that we, as a people, resist enslavement and genocide because of the spirits that politicize our lives. Reading as strangers in strange sites can politicize the spirit of our societies and instill some honest vigor in our intellectual and moral life. What prevents new, critical, and antiracist readings are the racist stereotypes that have been imprinted on American literary and academic minds.

AMERICAN AFRICANISMS

My work requires me to think about how free I can be as an African-American woman writer in my genderized, sexualized, wholly racialized world. To think about (and wrestle with) the full implications of my situation leads me to consider what happens when other writers work in a highly and historically racialized society.

—Toni Morrison, *Playing in the Dark*

Writers working in a highly racialized society often express fascination with Blackness that is both overt and covert. In *Playing in the Dark: Whiteness and the Literary Imagination*, Morrison maintains that Europeans and European Americans "choose to talk about themselves through and within a sometimes allegorical, sometimes metaphorical, but always choked representation of an Africanist presence."[22] She labels this practice and its arsenal "American Africanisms," which mirror European Africanisms. The term "Africanism" represents for Morrison

the denotative and connotative blackness that African peoples have come to signify, as well as the entire range of views, assumptions, readings, and misreadings that accompany Eurocentric learning about these people. . . . As a disabling virus within literary discourse, Africanism has become, in the Eurocentric tradition that American education favors, both a way of talking about and a way of policing matters of class, sexual license, and repression, formations and exercises of power, and meditations on ethics and accountability. [23]

As a literary and political tool, Africanism "provides a way of contemplating chaos and civilization, desire and fear, and a mechanism for testing the problems and blessings of freedom." The distinctive difference of the New World, she writes, is that its claim to freedom coexisted with "the presence of the unfree within the heart of the democratic experiment." It is arguably still the same. Morrison advises that we "investigate the Africanist character as surrogate and enabler" and the use of the "Africanist idiom" to mark difference or the "hip, sophisticated, ultra-urbane." Her own explorations inform us that within the "construction of blackness and enslavement" existed

> not only the not-free but also, with the dramatic polarity created by skin color, the projection of the not-me. The result was a playground for the imagination. What rose up out of collective needs to allay internal fears and to rationalize external exploitation was a [European] American Africanism—a fabricated brew of darkness, otherness, alarm, and desire that is uniquely American.[24]

Newly constructed beings and inhumanities, such as the White male as both exalted demigod and brutish enslaver, were sanctioned by literature. Morrison emphasizes the cultural aspects of dominance in order to critique the European American literary imagination: "Cultural identities are formed and informed by a nation's literature. . . . [W]hat seemed to be on the mind of the literature of the United States was the self-conscious but highly problematic construction of the American as a new white man."[25] In the formation of this new American identity, Blackness as embodied in the African was indispensable to elevating Whiteness. In this exaltation of Whiteness, the Africanist other became the device for "thinking about body, mind, chaos, kindness, and love; [and] provided the occasion for exercises in the absence of restraint, the presence of restraint, the contemplation of freedom and of aggression."[26] Within this framework, the boundaries of the conventional literary imagination were set to ignore or rationalize enslavement and freedom that was based on enslavement. Transgressing such boundaries is rarely encouraged. Those determined to see themselves without mystification, however, do cross these borders.

According to Morrison, an exceptional few and brave European American writers attempted to free themselves of their entrapment in Whiteness. She describes the courage in Herman Melville's tormented struggle to demystify Whiteness in *Moby Dick*.

> To question the very notion of white progress, the very idea of racial superiority, of whiteness as privileged place in the evolutionary ladder of humankind, and to meditate on the fraudulent, self-destroying philosophy of that superiority, to "pluck it out from under the robes of Senators and judges," to drag the "judge himself to the bar," that was dangerous, solitary, radical work. Especially then. Especially now.[27]

Today, this "dangerous, solitary, radical work" is discouraged by claims that race or discussions of racism politicize and so pollute literary work:

> When matters of race are located and called attention to in American literature, critical response has tended to be on the order of a humanistic nostrum—or a dismissal mandated by the label "political." Excising the political from the life of the mind is a sacrifice that has proven costly. I think of this erasure as a kind of trembling hypochondria always curing itself with unnecessary surgery.[28]

This surgery is also selective, usually performed only on those deviating from the dominant ideologies. Literary works derive their meaning from worldviews that intend political consequences. Worldviews carry cultural values as well as political agendas. Only by replicating or naturalizing the dominant political ideologies—in effect, reproducing the racialized hegemony—can writers claim to be apolitical. Morrison clearly identifies her work as a practical art with a political focus, writing in "Rootedness: The Ancestor as Foundation":

> I am not interested in indulging myself in some private, closed exercise of my imagination that fulfills only the obligation of my personal dreams—which is to say, yes, the work must be political. It must have that as its thrust. That's a pejorative term in critical circles now: if a work of art has any political influence in it, somehow it's tainted. My feeling is just the opposite; if it has none, it is tainted.[29]

These writings enable discussions in a society guarded against analyses of White supremacy. Her critical thought, despite increasing calls for the irrelevance of race, is particularly important in a society that routinely rejects such commentary as politically uncivil. Racial discourse seems to be pulled by marionette strings that work to curtail antiracist critiques. As Morrison notes in "Unspeakable Things Unspoken":

> For three hundred years black Americans insisted that "race" was no usefully distinguishing factor in human relationships. During those same three centuries every academic discipline, including theology, history and natural science, insisted "race" was the determining factor in human development. When blacks discovered they had shaped or become a culturally formed race, and that it had specific and revered difference, suddenly they were told there is no such thing as "race," biological or cultural, that matters and that genuinely intellectual exchange cannot accommodate it. In trying to come to some terms about "race" and writing, I am tempted to throw my hands up. It always seemed to me that the people who invented the hierarchy of "race" when it was convenient for them ought not to be the ones to explain it away, now that it does not suit their purposes for it to exist. But there is culture and both gender and "race" inform and are informed by it. Afro-American culture exists and though it is clear (and

becoming clearer) how it has responded to Western culture, the instances where and means by which it has shaped Western culture are poorly recognized or understood.[30]

African American culture exists within the worldviews that shape and inform it. This culture and its practices reappear in Morrison's work. For instance, typical of the African and African American call-and-response tradition, she receives the call to testify to worldviews that are greater than White myths and to demystify, and thereby resist, a Frankensteinian Blackness. Politicized by and politicizing the spirit, she issues her own charge to intellectuals and educators. This spirit is one of Black resistance to oppression, a resistance historically rooted in the African American community, its elders, and its ancestors. This spirit fuels current social debates. The worldview that shapes her politics is rooted to traditional African culture. This worldview coexists with and influences other perspectives within the dominant culture.

CONCLUSION

The ability to distinguish between humane culture and dehumanizing, racialized mythology presupposes critical thinking that is grounded someplace other than in the conventional academic mind. Because critical race thinking is rarely encouraged in racialized settings, we seldom ask how a people, manufacturing and depending on racist myths and ghosts in order to see their reflections in the world, lose more than they gain. It seems that hauntings cannot be restricted. Inevitably, the racially privileged caste and its entourage find themselves marked and demarcated, more obsessed and possessed than their demonized Africanist inferiors. Morrison's work clinically and coolly dissects this production and possession. It calls us to witness a literacy that predates and overcomes Africanism, individualism, and materialism. With this literacy, we read about spirit and power through time and space. This knowledge is made meaningful—or meaningless—by the worldviews we embrace, viewpoints that credit—or discredit—the questions raised by the nonfiction of Toni Morrison.

All educators reflect and articulate worldviews in which they reveal themselves as compromised or uncompromisable knowers, either reproducing or resisting dominance. (There seem to be at least three types of compromised knowers connected to academe—the unwittingly, the voluntarily, and the forcibly compromised). Bernice Johnson Reagon maintains that the uncompromisable knower is the one who straddles, standing with a foot in both worlds, unsplit by dualities and unhampered by a toxic imagination.[31] As I straddle and sometimes seem to fall from places in which an African American spirit world and European American racial mythology converge, I marvel at Morrison's grace, her ability to call out both the reactionary—the Africanisms of the racist mind—and the revolutionary—the African ancestors and communal commitments.

Whether it is reactionary, reformist, or revolutionary, movement for curricular change entails a spirit of political struggle. Three oppositional tendencies generally appear: advocacy for a romanticized past as intellectually civilized; acquiescence to hierarchical but relatively stable structures; and visionary projections toward the unknowable known as the promise and risk of future justice. Those of us who straddle walk between worlds, in a space where insight and agency arise from community. Between, in, and within these worlds, some intellectuals respond when called. Morrison is such a traditionalist, an uncompromisable knower, a straddler with deep communal ties. How else could she blend two worlds to stand, rooted as she is, politicized by and politicizing the spirit? In that rootedness she writes:

> There must have been a time when an artist could be genuinely representative of the tribe and in it; when an artist could have a tribal or racial sensibility and an individual expression of it. There were spaces and places in which a single person could enter and behave as an individual within the context of the community. A small remnant of that you can see sometimes in Black churches where people shout. It is a very personal grief and a personal statement done among people you trust. Done within the context of the community, therefore safe. And while the shouter is performing some rite that is extremely subjective, the other people are performing as a community in protecting that person.[32]

Because cultural remnants are markers for realities denied or suppressed in a racialized society, African American subjective and communal rites reveal the immeasurable distance between African ancestors and European/American Africanisms. Through her essays, which are unique and representative, political and spirit-filled, Toni Morrison invites us to struggle with these distinctions and differences in a polarized world.

NOTES

This chapter previously appeared in *Resisting State Violence: Radicalism, Gender, and Race in U.S. Culture*, by Joy James, Minneapolis: University of Minnesota Press, 1996. Reprinted by permission of the University of Minnesota Press.

1. Toni Morrison, "Rootedness: The Ancestor As Foundation," in *Black Women Writers*, ed. Mari Evans (New York: Doubleday, 1984), 342.

2. Tsenay Serequeberhan, *African Philosophy* (New York: Paragon House, 1991), xxi.

3. bell hooks, *Yearning: Race, Gender, and Cultural Politics* (Boston: South End, 1990), 131.

4. Toni Morrison, "Unspeakable Things Unspoken: The Afro-American Presence in American Literature," *Michigan Quarterly Review* (winter 1988): 88.

5. John Mbiti, *Traditional African Religions and Philosophies* (London: Heineman, 1969), 79.

6. K. Kia Bunseki Fu-Kiau, *The African Book without Title* (Cambridge: Fu-Kiau, 1980), 62–63.

7. Morrison, "Unspeakable Things Unspoken," 33.

8. Morrison, "Unspeakable Things Unspoken," 32.

9. The Garner story appears in Angela Davis, *Women, Race and Class* (New York: Vintage, 1983), 21, who is quoting from Herbert Aptheker, "The Negro Woman," *Masses and Mainstream* 11 (2) (February 1948): 11–12.

10. Morrison, "Unspeakable Things Unspoken," 28.

11. Morrison, "Unspeakable Things Unspoken," 28.

12. Morrison, "Unspeakable Things Unspoken," 29.

13. Toni Morrison, *Playing in the Dark: Whiteness and the Literary Imagination* (Cambridge, Mass.: Harvard University Press, 1992), xi.

14. Morrison, "Unspeakable Things Unspoken," 29.

15. Morrison, "Rootedness," 343.

16. Morrison, "Rootedness," 343.

17. Morrison, "Rootedness," 343.

18. Fu-Kiau, *African Book without Title*, 62.

19. Sweet Honey in the Rock, "Ella's Song," on *B'lieve I'll Run on . . . See What the End's Gonna Be* (Ukiah, Calif.: Redwood Records, 1977).

20. Sweet Honey in the Rock, "Fannie Lou Hamer," on *B'lieve I'll Run on . . . See What the End's Gonna Be* (Ukiah, Calif.: Redwood Records, 1977).

21. Vincent Harding, *There Is a River: The Black Struggle for Freedom in America* (New York: Random House, 1983).

22. Morrison, *Playing in the Dark*, 17.

23. Morrison, *Playing in the Dark*, 6–7.

24. Morrison, *Playing in the Dark*, 38.

25. Morrison, *Playing in the Dark*, 38.

26. Morrison, *Playing in the Dark*, 47–48.

27. Morrison, "Unspeakable Things Unspoken," 18.

28. Morrison, *Playing in the Dark*, 22.

29. Morrison, "Rootedness," 344–345.

30. Morrison, "Unspeakable Things Unspoken," 3.

31. Bernice Johnson Reagon, "'Nobody Knows the Trouble I See'; or, 'By and By I'm Gonna Lay Down My Heavy Load,'" *Journal of American History* 78 (1) (June 1991): 111–119.

32. Morrison, "Rootedness," 339.

8

Paulette Nardal, Race Consciousness, and Antillean Letters

Tracy Denean Sharpley-Whiting

> Should one see in the tendencies here expressed a sort of implicit declaration of war upon Western culture and the white world in general? We want to eliminate such ambiguity so as to leave no doubt. . . . Without it we would have never become conscious of who we really are.
>
> —Paulette Nardal

Coined between 1936–1937 by Martiniquan poet Aimé Césaire during the writing of his now celebrated *Cahier d'un retour au pays natal*, Negritude, as a poetics, a philosophy of existence, a literary, cultural, and intellectual movement, signified the birth of a new literature among Black Francophone writers, a "New Negro" from the Francophone world, a metaphorically rich Pan-Africanism in French. While the neologism is readily traceable to Césaire, the mapping of the concept of Negritude as the inauguration of a Black humanism, as a "theory of black cultural importance and autonomy"[1] was the stuff of a panoply of critical works.

Before the 1935 publication of *L'Etudiant noir*, a one issue journal sponsored by the Association des Etudiants martiniquais en France that featured, according to Georges Ngal, "les deux textes fondateurs du mouvement de la Négritude," ("The two founding texts of the Negritude movement")[2] Aimé Césaire and the Senegalese poet Léopold Sédar Senghor, there were a number of Francophonic novelistic and journalistic precursors that equally treated the themes of assimilation, colonialism, identity, and Black consciousness. These were most notably, René Maran's 1921 Prix Goncourt winning *Batouala: veritable roman nègre* with its incendiary anticolonialist preface, Suzanne Lacascade's 1924 *Claire-Solange, âme africaine*, and the journals, *La Race Nègre* (1927–1986), *Le Cri des Nègres* (1931–1935), *La Revue du monde noir*

(1931–1932), and the June 1932 publication of the Marxist–Surrealist pamphlet *Légitime Défense*. However, it was not until September 1931 that Senghor made the acquaintance of Césaire and the Guyanese Léon-Gontron Damas, the third voice of this poetic trilogy, thus setting the stage for their collective exploration of their conflicting identities, the "tormenting question" in the words of Senghor, of "who am I?", and their experiences of being Black, African and African-diasporic, and French.[3] For Césaire and Damas, "in meeting Senghor, [they] met Africa."[4] Through Damas and Césaire, Senghor's horizon was opened to the dynamism of the literary and cultural worlds of West Indians and African Americans living in Paris in the 1930s.

For their part, Césaire, Senghor, and Damas, the designated founders of this poetics in the French-speaking world, provide a conspicuously masculine genealogy of their critical consciousness, tracing "the awakening of their race consciousness" to the writers of the Harlem Renaissance, specifically Claude McKay, Langston Hughes, James Weldon Johnson, and Sterling Brown, Du Bois's journalistic organ for the National Association for the Advancement of Colored People (NAACP), *The Crisis*, Carter G. Woodson's *Opportunity*, medium for the National Urban League, and Alain Locke's 1925 anthology *The New Negro: An Interpretation*. As Senghor revealed, "[T]he general meaning of the word [Negritude]—the discovery of black values and recognition for the Negro of his situation—was born in the United States of America."[5]

But if African American writers of the 1920s radicalized the consciousness of these young and aspiring Francophone Black writers, if the race-conscious New Negro of the United States planted the seeds of Negritude in their collective imagination, then the three future Negritude poets also received inspiration from Cuban writer Nicolas Guillén, Haitian writers Jacques Roumain and Jean Price-Mars, and deployed as tools of critical engagement Frobenius and Delafosse's ethnology and Breton's surrealism.[6]

While a general consensus among the founding poets around Negritude's literary historiography and philosophical commitment to affirming Blacks' "being-in-the-world" exists, Césaire, Damas, and Senghor experienced and expressed their Negritudes differently. In a series of interviews with sociologist Lilyan Kesteloot at the 1959 Black Writers and Artists Conference in Rome sponsored by *Présence Africaine*, Césaire responded that he experienced his Negritude as the acknowledgment of "a fact, a revolt, and the acceptance of responsibility for the destiny of [my] race." For Senghor, Negritude represented "black cultural patrimony, that is to say, the spirit of its civilization," while Damas regarded it as the explicit "rejection of an assimilation that negated his spontaneity and as a defense for his condition as Negro and Guyanese."[7] The tones and styles of Damas's 1937 *Pigments* and Césaire's oft-analyzed *Cahier* (1939) are periodically anguish-ridden, volatile, critiquing slavery, the colonial system, the utter fallaciousness of the French program of assimilation, suffering from feelings of exile, evoking biting sarcasm, and searching for an identity and culture rooted in Africa, Blackness, and the West Indies.

In "Trève," Damas writes:

> Enough letting-go-of
> licking-up-to
> taking-the-leavings
> and
> of an attitude
> of super-assimilation.[8]

Tired of the mimetic existence lived by the colonized, knowing full well, in the prophetic words of Frantz Fanon, that "wherever he goes, the Negro remains a Negro,"[9] that assimilation requires a "negation of spontaneity," Damas revolts against the inauthenticity of this existence in "Solde":

> I feel ridiculous
> In their shoes
> in their dinner jackets. . . .
> I feel ridiculous
> among them an accomplice. . .
> hands hideously red
> from the blood of their
> ci-vi-li-za-tion.[10]

Damas realizes that the *devenir français* process necessitates loss, repression, rejection, negation. With their bloodied hands, the colonized will have murdered themselves in trying to assimilate into a culture, a *"ci-vi-li-za-tion,"* that denegrates indigenous cultures and peoples as it claims to civilize. The poet laments this loss in "Limbé," the Creole word for "Blues" or "Spleen":

> Give me my black dolls
> so that I may play with them
> the naive games of my instincts
> I become myself once more
> myself anew
> of that which yesterday I was
> Yesterday
> > Without complexity
> > > Yesterday
> when the hour of uprooting came . . .[11]

The poet wants to return to the precolonial Black world, an era of innocent games, where naiveté and spontaneity supposedly reigned before the physical uprooting of Black bodies for production, before European cultural and racial domination.

Damas's slow-burning ire reaches a boil in Césaire's *Cahier*:

> Because we hate you and
> your reason, we identify with the
> precocious dementia of the burning madness
> of tenacious cannibalism.[12]

Reason, Absolute Truth, Logic—the ideals of the European Enlightenment—are renounced by Césaire in favor of the madness, the illogical, the uncivilized, indeed cannibalistic tendencies, ascribed to blacks by Europeans. Césaire recognizes the Manichean nature of the colonial world. If the Negro is but a "jungle savage,"[13] "a corrosive element, the depository of maleficent powers,"[14] then Césaire, as he writes in the *Cahier*, "accepts, accepts, accepts . . . entirely without reserve" the lot of his race.[15] His revolt against Europe and alienated Antilleans consists partly of this acceptance.

Unlike Damas's and Césaire's wounds associated with exilic existence, that is, the state of "inhabit[ing] one place," as Michael Seidel notes in *Exile and the Narrative Imagination*, "and remember[ing] or project[ing] the reality of another,"[16] in this case, sub-Saharan Africa and the Antilles, Senghor's ancestral ties to Africa were solidly traceable and his cultural memory of Africa remained clearly, if not romantically, intact. Growing up in the rural villages of Djilor and Joal in Senegal, Senghor's two collections of poetry, *Chants d'ombre* (1945) and *Hosties noires* (1948), represent rather mythical "pilgrimages to the ancestral fountains," of his "childhood universe" interjected with anticolonialist tropes:

At the foot of my Africa, crucified these four hundred years
yet still breathing. . . .
Lord forgive those who made guerrillas of Askias
who turned my princes into sergeants.
Made houseboys of my servants, and laborers of my country folk, who turned my
people into proletariat
For you must forgive those who hunted my children like wild elephants . . .
You must forgive those who stole ten million of my sons in their leprous ships. . . .
Yes, Lord, forgive France, which hates all occupations
and imposes hers so heavily on me
That have made my Mesopotamia, the Congo, a vast
cemetery beneath the white sun.[17]

Senghor recounts France's crimes against Africa, while simultaneously imploring the Lord for forgiveness for France. Written after World War II, Senghor makes mention of the rather touchy subject of the German Occupation in this "Peace Prayer," a subject France is still grappling with today. Occupied, oppressed, humiliated by the Occupation, France hypocritically continued to shine its "white sun" over parts of the *dark continent*, gradually turning the idyllic Africa of Senghor's boyhood into a wasteland, a vast cemetery, as it emptied out the continent's natural resources, including Black boys and men to fight for its freedom. Senghor knew first hand the impact of France's liberation wars on Africa: he was drafted into the French army in World War II and detained in a prison camp until the end of the war; his elder brother was gassed while serving France in World War I.

Despite Negritude's cultural currency in the 1930s and 1940s, it has not been without its critics regarding its self-reflexive exoticism and its sociopolitical efficacy. Early on in "Orphée Noir" ("Black Orpheus"), his 1948 preface to Senghor's *Anthologie de la nouvelle poèsie nègre et malgache de langue française*, Jean-Paul Sartre described Negritude, much to the chagrin of Senghor and *Présence Africaine* editor Allioune Diop, as an "antiracist racism," as a negative stage in the dialectics of history invented to be destroyed in a move towards synthesis, a universal humanism.[18] Negritude was thus not for Sartre the answer to "the black problem" in France and the Francophone world, but a necessary step toward resolution. Writer and literary critic Wole Soyinka insists that Negritude was reactionary, advocating a return to the past and feeding into a notion of a Black Essence. In his essays "De la négritude" and "De l'Exotisme," René Ménil, one-time Negritude proponent, Marxist, philosopher, and cofounder with Aimé Césaire of the Martiniquan literary magazine *Tropiques*, equally critiqued Negritude as a form of Black exoticism, as an "appetitive self-consciousness," unable to free itself from its ideological straitjacket, its becoming other, hence contributing to continuing European imperialism in the Martiniquan context.[19] And, Marcien Towa, in *Poèsie de la négritude: approche structuraliste* (1983), writes that Césaire's Negritude was "ouvertement politique" ("openly political"), an "authentic revolutionary Negritude" as opposed to Senghor's "bon nègre" ("good Negro") Negritude.[20]

It is perhaps undeniable that in their zeal, their antiassimilationist stances, and their resistance to colonialism's cultural and political fleecing of the Black world, Negritude writers lapsed into a reductive essentialism, an evocation of a specifically "Black sensibility," "Black spirit," "Black soul." Yet every movement, concept, and poetics has its place and time in history. To Charles de Gaulle's declaration that "between America and Europe, there is only the ocean and some dust,"[21] to questions regarding the existence of culture in the Antilles and civilization in Africa, for the 1930s and 1940s, Negritude, with its affirmation of Blackness, vindication of Africa, promotion of a culturally engaged literature in the face of French assimilationist propaganda, *les missions civilisatrices* in Africa, and nauseating French paternalism, represented a radically progressive and self-actualizing alternative.

Negritude flew in the face of Cardinal Verdier's 1939 introduction to the anthology *L'homme de couleur* in which French colonial policy is praised as benevolent and humanitarian, indeed, humanizing:

> Nothing is more moving than this gesture of the Frenchman, taking his black brother by the hand and helping him to rise. This hierarchic but nonetheless real collaboration, this fraternal love stooping towards the blacks to measure their possibilities of thinking and feeling; this gradual initiation to all the arts of sciences; . . . helping them progress toward an improved physical, social and moral well-being. . . . This is . . . France's colonizing mission.[22]

Negritude would throw down an important gauntlet to French colonialism, exposing it as a "murderous humanitarianism"[23] in the words of the Paris Surrealist Group, as wholly self-serving in its "hierarchic collaboration," self-affirming in its "fraternal love." While Damas denounced French assimilationist policy in his 1938 ethnography *Retour de Guyane* as "the cunning instrument of domination,"[24] Léopold Senghor, also included in Cardinal Verdier's volume, methodically presented "that which the black man brings" to his world, to his culture, to humanity in his essay of the same title "Ce que l'homme noir apporte."

Hence, it was not until the 1950s that René Ménil took Negritude to task in "De la négritude."[25] And while Frantz Fanon recognized that the "black soul was but a white artifact" in the 1952 publication of *Peau noire, masques blancs*, within this same text writings by Negritude poets were scattered throughout.[26] Whatever its conceptual and practical shortcomings, in its engagement with issues of race, identity, color, assimilation, alienation, and exile, Negritude, as a race-conscious movement, raised questions that have continuing relevance in contemporary Black Francophone African and Caribbean letters and philosophical thought.

At this juncture I would like to shift the terrain of this chapter. While Senghor et al recite a curiously masculinist, albeit Pan-Africanist, literary historiography of Negritude, one Francophone woman intellectual in particular, however, played a pivotal role in shaping the philosophical commitments, indeed, the evolution of this literary movement in the 1930s. Paulette Nardal, as editor of *La Revue du monde noir* and hostess of weekly Sunday salons at her residence outside of Paris, was the veritable conduit through which the Negritude poets passed. The Martiniquan Nardal literally provided a cultured place (her apartment) and literary space (*La Revue du monde noir*) for male intellectual coming-of-age, as it was within the pages of the review and Nardal's apartment that Damas, Césaire, and Senghor read and mingled with Harlem Renaissance writers. Yet, Paulette Nardal's landmark essay "Eveil de la conscience de race chez les étudiants noirs" ("Awakening of Race Consciousness among Black Students"), published in the sixth and final issue of *La Revue du monde noir* in April 1932, marked the inauguration of three major and lasting components of Negritude thought, that is, Pan-Africanism, the affirmation of peoples of the African Diaspora and their cultural productions, and the validation of African civilizations.

Born in 1896 to a rather affluent Black family in François, Martinique, Paulette Nardal was the eldest of the four *soeurs* Nardal. Educated at the Colonial College for Girls in Martinique, she perfected her English in the British West Indies. She would later attend the Sorbonne, specializing in French and English literature and language. She taught English for a year in Martinique until she returned to Paris where she became a journalist. Nardal wrote articles for one of the long-standing Black newspapers, *La Dépeche africaine*, among others in Paris.[27]

In 1931, Paris became a safe haven of sorts for the African American community fleeing racial oppression in America. Josephine Baker was performing at the Casino de Paris and the Folies Bergères, and Langston Hughes, Claude McKay, Countee Cullen, Jean Toomer, Alain Locke, and Nella Larsen could be seen in cafes and at the various salons in the 1930s. This was also the year of the Exposition Coloniale at the Bois de Vincennes where Blackness was showcased, celebrated, and simultaneously exoticized. On the eve of all this cultural activity in Paris, the Sunday salons at 7 rue Hébert in Clamart, a suburb of Paris, began. Its hosts were Andrée, Jane, and Paulette Nardal. Drinking *thé à l'anglaise* and speaking in French and English, the hosts and their guests danced, discussed interracial and colonial problems, racist injustices, current events, examined the precarious position of men and women of color in France, and reflected on the attention to things black generated by the Exposition Coloniale.[28] It was under these circumstances, these lively intellectual and diasporic exchanges, that the idea for a monthly, bilingual, multiracial collaborative review was born under the directorship of the Haitian Dr. Léo Sajous, a specialist on Liberian issues, and Paulette Nardal. While Nardal helped to edit, translate, and arrange the journal, her title—general secretary—reflected a typically supportive feminine role. Dr. Sajous was director of the monthly. The offices for *The Review of the Black World* were located at 45 Rue Jacob in the student-filled Left Bank. According to Nardal, "This review, this movement, it was something that had to happen. It happened like that, like a sudden dawning. At this time, people were ready to read such a review."[29]

The first issue of the journal appeared in November 1931. Its Pan-Africanist and race-conscious raising objectives were boldly declared in "Ce que nous voulons faire":

> To give to the intelligentsia of the black race and their partisans an official organ in which to publish their artistic, literary and scientific works.
> To study and to popularize by means of the press, books, lectures, courses, all which concerns NEGRO CIVILIZATION and the natural riches of Africa, thrice sacred to the black race.

The triple aim which LA REVUE DU MONDE NOIR will pursue will be: to create among Negroes of the entire world regardless of nationality, an intellectual,
and moral tie, which will permit them to better know each other, to love one another, to defend more effectively their collective interests and to glorify their race.

By this means, the Negro race will contribute, along with thinking minds of
other races and with all those who have received the light of truth, beauty and
goodness to the material, the moral and the intellectual improvement of humanity.

The motto is and will continue to be:
For PEACE, WORK and JUSTICE.
By LIBERTY, EQUALITY and FRATERNITY.
Thus, the two hundred million individuals which constitute the Negro race,
even though scattered among the various nations, will form over and above the
latter a great Brotherhood, the forerunner of universal Democracy.[30]

With its grandiose mission, the managing editors sought out and published
articles, reviews, poetry, short stories, editorials, and letters to the editor in a
section called the "Negroes' Letterbox" on a variety of topics related to Africa
and the African Diaspora in Cuba, the United States, Liberia, Ethiopia, and
the Francophone Antilles. Articles such as "The Problems of Work in Haiti,"
"The Negroes and Art," "Reflections on Islam," "The Negro in Cuba," reprints
of ethnologist Frobenius's "Spiritism in Central Africa," and novelistic extracts
by Walter White and poetry by Claude McKay and Langston Hughes appeared within its pages.

As the review received part of its funding from the Ministry of the
Colonies, subjects of an overtly political nature were to be expressly
avoided. Its cultural emphasis has, thus, led critics, among them Etienne
Léro, who was initially inspired by the journal, to characterize *La Revue du
monde noir* as "rosewater," as apolitical, bourgeois, and assimilationist.[31]
Clearly, as the journal's aim states, the review targeted a particular class of
Blacks and their "partisans": the educated of the races. The articles found
within the review's six issues, specifically those written by Antilleans on the
Antillean situation vis-à-vis French culture, do indeed advocate a democratic
collaboration between "white, Western culture"[32] and the Black world. The
notion of a total abandonment of White, Western culture for all things African
represents, for Nardal, a return to "obscurantism," to the unknown. Moreover, she is not interested in "declar[ing] a war on upon Western culture and
the white world in general."[33] And yet, the review's very presence on the cultural scene as an instrument through which to "glorify their race" and "defend their collective interests," undermined White cultural hegemony and
signified a political and culturally politicizing intent. While the journal, com-
munitarian in its approach and aspirations, naively assumed that all Black
peoples, or at least those members of the Black intelligentsia to which it was
directed, had common interests, its goals, rather novel ones for the era, were

to globalize Negro consciousness. It never challenged the social constructivity of racial categories, rather it proudly donned the mantle of Negro-ness and endeavored to affirm the Negro's being in the world through cultural, artistic, and scientific works. Using the rhetoric of *Les Droits de l'homme,* of liberty, equality, and fraternity and the principles of the Enlightenment— "light of truth, beauty, goodness"—to foreground their Pan-Africanism, the editors of *The Review of the Black World* further endeavored to bring about a new humanism made up of enlightened minds of all races that displaced the normative model of democracy that was explicitly White. It is then no small wonder that the French police and colonial administrators, believing the contributors had ties to Communists and American Garveyites, kept abreast of the activities of the journal's contributors,[34] that the review, plagued by funding issues after colonial administrators withheld further monetary support, ceased publication after a mere six issues, and that in its sixth and final issue Paulette Nardal would write a politically charged philosophical and historical essay that would not only broach the subject of colonialism and its effects on the evolution of the modern Antillean writer, but also implore students and aspiring writers to engage with the "riches that the past of the black race and the African continent offers them." In effect, Nardal called dangerously for the awakening of race conscious in the psyche of cultural workers and intellectuals, a displacement of Frenchness as the embodiment of culture; she explicitly linked race and the experiences of racialized subjects to cultural productivity, a linking that would definitively formalize the course and commitments of Negritude in the latter part of the 1930s and 1940s.

In the opening sentence of the six-page article, Paulette Nardal asserts that she is concerned with this awakening among Antilleans in particular. Witnessing a modification in attitudes towards race and racial problems among the younger and older generations of Antilleans in 1930s Paris, Nardal writes: "A few years ago, we might even say a few months, certain subjects were simply taboo in Martinique. . . . One could not speak of slavery nor proclaim pride in being of African descent without being considered a fanatic or at the very least eccentric."[35] Just what brought on this marked transformation in the Antillean Negro's consciousness? Through a literary historiography, Nardal proceeds systematically to outline this evolution. Race consciousness among a number of Antilleans was stirred in the late nineteenth century. This racial stirring was initially brought on when the native left the colony for the metropolis. Exile and feelings of non-belonging, or as Nardal writes, "uprooting and ensuing estrangement," created a sensation of difference, oftentimes a *malaise.* The writer for the first time was forced to live his/her Blackness, experience his/her difference. However, the Antillean writer never explicitly articulated this conflict. Rather the writer seemed bent on immersing him/herself more deeply in the culture of the metropolis in order to avoid confronting this consciousness; the writer was content to imitate rather than create for fear of giving life to this difference through his/her art. Creativity would force the writer to confront his/her situation.

Nardal then compares and contrasts the development of race conscious literature among African Americans to that of Antilleans. In effect, because of the persistence and virulence of American racism, the African American writer has been consistently confronted with the "race problem," thus, their identity as Black. The African American like the Antillean passed importantly through the imitative phase because of their initial uprooting and forced immersion into a foreign and hostile environment; their creative expressions were necessarily imitative. In this category, Nardal would most likely include the writings of the Black poet Phyllis Wheatley. The African American writer then passes through Nardal's next phase: "literature of controversy and moral protest" amidst antislavery agitation.[36] Various fictional memoirs such as Harriet Wilson's *Our Nig, or Sketches from the Life of a Free Black* (1859), slave narratives such as Harriet Jacob's powerful *Incidents in the Life of a Slave Girl* (1861), and Frederick Douglass's classic *Narrative* (1845), which, for Nardal, attempt to appeal to a sense of morality, pity, and moral indignation, would necessarily characterize this stage of African American letters. From 1880 onwards, the African American writer enters into a period where she/he ascends to, in Nardal's words, "veritable culture."[37] Through W. E. B. Du Bois's social protest literature, Paul Lawrence Dunbar's "school of racial realism," and the poetry of Claude McKay and Langston Hughes, reprinted in the pages of the *Review*, Nardal insists that one can "observe that the Americans, having thrown off all inferiority complexes, tranquilly express their individual dark-skinned selves without fear or shame."[38]

The Antillean writers' broaching of racial themes in literary productions developed less rapidly. Nardal attributes this slower awakening to the cultural and historical differences between French and U.S. race policies. The ideals of the French Republic, its racial liberalism, and assimilation policy effectively obfuscated the very real issues of domination and its attendant results in the area of cultural production: alienation. The Antillean writer up until 1914 was consistently and consciously imitative, lapsing into the standard forms of exoticism practiced by European writers, as they wrote "lovingly of their native islands."[39] For Nardal, no race pride can be found in this literature; strangers celebrated the islands with more appreciation and real attachment than the indigenous poets and writers who continued to model "their artistic productions after those of the metropolis."[40] Ever diplomatic and measured, Nardal levels a veiled critique at the West Indian literary bourgeoisie. In effect, their literary productions have been hitherto mediocre, unimaginative, "no way inferior to those of the French writers," but certainly not distinguishable.[41] Taking his cue from Nardal, poet Etienne Léro, and a frequent contributor to *The Review of the Black World*, would acerbically write, just two months after Nardal's journal ceased publication in April 1932, "Misère d'une poésie" in the June 1932 Marxist-surrealist manifesto *Légitime Défense*:

> The West Indian writer, stuffed to bursting with white morality, white culture, white education, white prejudice, fills his little books with a swollen image of himself. Merely to be a good imitation of the white man fulfills both his social and his poetic requirements. . . . [H]e does not want to "make like a nigger" in his poems. It is a point of honor with him that a white person could read his entire book without ever guessing the author's pigmentation. . . . He will stifle his originality in order to be considered "civilized." Because of this borrowed personality, his poetry is hardly better than pastiche. . . . Some indigestible mix of French *esprit* and classical humanities has produced these babblers and the soothing syrup of their poetry.[42]

Nardal writes that between the period of conscious imitation of the literature of the metropolis by West Indian writers and the present, there was another stage in which theories by Marcus Garvey and the organization of the first Pan-African Congress incited commentary. Negro journals and studies on the history of Guadeloupe emerged and within René Maran's preface to *Batouala* "a generous indignation stir[red]."[43] However, Nardal finds these efforts perplexing on the question of race: "These works remain still," she writes, "the tributaries of white Western culture. In none of them is expressed faith in the future of the race and the necessity to create a feeling of solidarity between the different groups of Blacks disseminated throughout the globe."[44] Antillean writers still avoided racial subjects. Objective observation, rather than reflective subjectifying narratives dominated these writerly endeavors. Race was still a thorny issue for the writer who was still more interested in expressing his/her Frenchness, in *becoming French*. The idea that there was a future in Blackness, a "future of the race" and that there was a particular lived experience of Blackness that could somehow create feelings of transracial solidarity was beyond the comprehension of the Antillean writer. Race may exist; Blackness may exist, but it was not accorded a crucial role in the formation of an Antillean identity, hence a grand place in the scheme of Antillean letters.

Paulette Nardal then moves on to a discussion of the veritable awakening of race consciousness among Antilleans. Parallel to the aforementioned string of developments and commentaries, indicative of some stirring of race consciousness within the Antillean, was the veritable awakening of race consciousness, the desire to secure the future of the race in the annals of cultural history and the need for race solidarity among a group of Antillean women students:

> The women of color living alone in the metropolis, who until the Colonial Exhibition, were certainly less favored than their male compatriots who have enjoyed

easy successes, have long before the latter, felt the need of a racial solidarity that would not be merely material. They were thus aroused to race consciousness.[45]

In this passage, Nardal asserts clearly that Antillean women were at the vanguard of the cultural revolution that would later be called Negritude and identified as male. It was the women who recognized a need for racial solidarity, who had first experienced a veritable race consciousness; it was the women who "passed, just as their Black American counterparts, through a period of revolt."[46] In providing a literary historiography of race consciousness among Antilleans, Nardal's essay also reveals itself as an official record of Black women's collective cultural praxes in a Francophone Antillean and African context. She would again elaborate upon the Black feminine dimensions of this newly found and celebrated race consciousness among French-speaking Black intellectuals in the 1930s four years later in a June 1936 interview-essay, "Black Paris," with Eslanda Goode Robeson, Paul Robeson's wife. Nardal's text, in effect, demands that literary critics, historians, and philosophers reconsider Black Francophone women's contributions to Negritude's intellectual history.

In her chronicling of the evolution of race consciousness among the women, Nardal describes the curious situation of Black male privilege and Black female circumscription in matters of race, sex, and class. Unlike their Black and mulatto male counterparts in France, who threw themselves, successfully one might add, into the pursuit of French women, the educated women of color were isolated, ignored by fellow Antilleans, and unable to be fully accepted into French culture other than on certain defined interracial terms.[47] The desire for a community in Paris, their "uprooting," she continues, "had been the starting point of their evolution." While the celebrated literary men of the era sidestepped their responsibilities to become engaged writers, and a number of Antillean male students partook of the fruit of French (sexual) liberalism in full swing, these young race women threw themselves into the study of subjects on the Black race and on their respective countries.[48] What began as a descriptive essay, tracing the evolution of racial themes in the writings of the African Diaspora, winds down with earnest prodding on the continued need for academic, literary, scientific, and artistic engagements with questions of race. Nardal suggests optimistically that some Antillean writers are on the brink of entering into "the last phase" of the evolution noted in African American letters and that *The Review of the Black World* fully intends to publish these writers. However, the journal never fulfilled its promise. The funding by the Ministry of the Colonies had been withdrawn.

Yet, Paulette Nardal's prophetic last essay ushered in a stream of writing by Antillean and African students. Confronted with French metropolitan racism, a "Negro" identity had been forced upon Antilleans and Africans.

This imposition was doubly shocking for the Antillean who, according to Fanon in *Black Skin, White Masks*, thought that Negroes were Senegalese. Nardal's reaction was to encourage Antilleans to accept their being in the world as Blacks, as Negroes, extol it, research it, and write about it. Appearing to have heeded her call, three students whose names would be forever associated with Negritude changed their courses of study: the nineteen-year-old Aimé Césaire began to write on the theme of the South in African American literature; Damas examined African survivals in the West Indies; and Senghor, who was writing on Baudelaire, began to study African ethnography and languages.[49] Among the women she undoubtedly influenced was Martiniquan student Suzanne Roussy. In 1937, Roussy would return to Martinique as Suzanne Roussy-Césaire. Troubled by what she perceived as a cultural void and the continuing imitative nature of Martiniquan writing, she, along with her husband Aimé Césaire and René Ménil, cofounded *Tropiques* in 1941.

NOTES

This chapter is also to be published in *Gendering Negritude: Race Women, Race Consciousness, Race Letters, 1924–1945*, by Tracy Denean Sharpley-Whiting, Minneapolis: University of Minnesota Press, 2002. Reprinted by permission of the University of Minnesota Press.

1. Janet Vaillant, *Black, French and African: A Life of Léopold Sédar Senghor* (Cambridge, Mass.: Harvard University Press, 1990), 1.

2. Georges Ngal, <<*Lire*>> *Le Discours sur le colonialisme* (Paris: Présence Africaine, 1994), 13.

3. Vaillant, *Black, French and African*, 90.

4. Vaillant, *Black, French and African*, 91.

5. Léopold S. Senghor, "Problematique de la négritude," *Présence Africaine* 78 (1971): 12–14.

6. André Gide's *Voyage au Congo* was a French precursor to Black Francophone literary anticolonial resistance.

7. Lilyan Kesteloot, *Black Writers in French: A Literary History of Negritude*, trans. Ellen Conroy Kennedy (Washington, D.C.: Howard University Press, 1991), 119–120.

8. Léon G. Damas, "Trève," in *Pigments* (Paris: Présence Africaine, 1962).

9. Frantz Fanon, *Black Skin, White Masks*, trans. Charles Lamm Markmann (New York: Grove, 1967), 173.

10. Léon G. Damas, "Solde," in *Pigments* (Paris: Présence Africaine, 1962).

11. Léon G. Damas, "Limbé," in *Pigments* (Paris: Présence Africaine, 1962).

12. Aimé Césaire, *Cahier d'un retour au pays natal* (Paris: Présence Africaine, 1956), 47–48.

13. Fanon, *Black Skin, White Masks*, 12.

14. Frantz Fanon, *The Wretched of the Earth* (New York: Grove, 1963), 41.

15. Césaire, *Cahier*, 76–77.

16. Quoted in Marjorie Salvodon, "Contested Crossings: Identities, Gender, and Exile in *Le baobab fou*," in *Spoils of War: Women of Color, Cultures, and Revolutions*, ed. T. Denean Sharpley-Whiting and Renée T. White (Lanham, Md.: Rowman & Littlefield, 1997), 113.

17. Léopold S. Senghor, "Prière de paix," in *Hostie noire* (Paris: Seuil, 1948), 148–152.

18. See Kesteloot, *Black Writers in French*.

19. Michael Richardson, *Refusal of the Shadow: Surrealism and the Caribbean* (London: Verso, 1996), 1–30.

20. See Belinda Jack, *Negritude and Literary Criticism: The History and Theory of "Negro-African" Literature in French* (Westport, Conn.: Greenwood, 1990).

21. Quoted in René Ménil, *Tracées: Identité. Négritude, esthétique aux Antilles* (Paris: Éditions Robert Laffont, 1985), 27. The original statement was by de Gaulle: "Entre Amérique et l'Europe, il n'y a que l'Océan and quelques poussières!"

22. Cardinal Verdier, *L'homme de couleur* (Paris: Plon, 1939), xi.

23. The Surrealist Group in Paris, "Murderous Humanitarianism," in *Negro: An Anthology*, ed. Nancy Cunard (New York: Ungar, 1970), 353.

24. Léon G. Damas, *Retour de Guyane* (Paris: n.p., 1938), 97.

25. See his essay in Ménil, *Tracées*.

26. In "On National Culture," Fanon also challenged these "men of culture" to engage with the culture of today and leveled a subtle critique of Léopold Senghor after the 1959 Black Writers and Artist Conference in Rome in a footnote of that chapter. See Fanon, *Wretched of the Earth*.

27. See Eslanda Goode Robeson, "Black Paris," *Challenge* (June 1936): 9–12.

28. Louis Achilles, preface to *Revue du monde noir* (Paris: Jean-Michel Place, 1992), xv.

29. Achilles, preface to *Revue du monde noir*, xiii. Achilles was a relative of Nardal. Her words are taken from an interview he conducted with her in Martinique.

30. "Our Aim," in *Review of the Black World* (Paris: Jean-Michel Place, 1992).

31. See Louis Hymans, *Léopold Sédar Senghor: An Intellectual Biography* (Edinburgh: University Press of Edinburgh, 1971), 42–43.

32. Paulette Nardal, "Awakening of Race Consciousness," in *Review of the Black World* (Paris: Jean-Michel Place, 1992), 30. All citations are from a retranslation of this essay.

33. Nardal, "Awakening of Race Consciousness," 31.

34. Vaillant, *Black, French and African*, 95.

35. Nardal, "Awakening of Race Consciousness," 25.

36. Nardal, "Awakening of Race Consciousness," 26.

37. Nardal, "Awakening of Race Consciousness," 27.

38. Nardal, "Awakening of Race Consciousness," 27. Nardal does not mention any U.S. Black women writers in this essay. However, she does discuss a U.S. Black woman orator's recital in Geneva and Cambridge in the first issue of the journal.

39. Nardal, "Awakening of Race Consciousness," 28.

40. Nardal, "Awakening of Race Consciousness," 28.

41. Nardal, "Awakening of Race Consciousness," 28.

42. Etienne Léro, "Misère d'une poésie," *Légitime Défense* 1 (June 1932): 10–12.

43. Nardal, "Awakening of Race Consciousness," 28.

44. Nardal, "Awakening of Race Consciousness," 29.

45. Nardal, "Awakening of Race Consciousness," 29.

46. Nardal, "Awakening of Race Consciousness," 29.

47. See Eslanda Goode Robeson, "Black Paris," *Challenge* (June 1936): 10. Being ever the cultured woman, Nardal says "friend." But one could well imagine other less desirable terms of interaction. She further states that many of the French women pursued by men of color were from a lower socioeconomic class and that on the island those liaisons would have been frowned upon. The educated Antillean woman, much more sensitive to the class issue, according to Nardal, was less willing to interact with White men not of her class. Conversely, race prevented many educated French men from interacting with serious intentions with Antillean women. Writer Mayotte Capécia, in her award-winning *Je suis martiniquaise*, would express this same sentiment with respect to interracial relationships with Frenchmen. See Mayotte Capécia, *Je suis martiniquaise* (Paris: Corrêa, 1948).

48. Nardal, "Awakening of Race Consciousness," 30.

49. Vaillant, *Black, French* and *African*, 98.

9

The Revival of Black Nationalism and the Crisis of Liberal Universalism

Rod Bush

The concepts of community and identity are central elements in the thought and experience of the African American people. From the time that the status of slave became identified with Africans in the nation's laws, mores, and folkways, the elaboration of a sense of peoplehood among people of African descent in the United States was sharply etched vis-à-vis these themes.

The identity developed in the seventeenth century between Africans and slavery was the edifice upon which a racial division of labor was constructed. Following slavery the freed people in the South were accorded citizenship rights, but many Whites fought to maintain the prerogatives of White racial privilege, leading eventually to the reversal of radical reconstruction and the establishment of a counterrevolutionary harshly restrictive regime called Jim Crow.

The degradation of the humanity of African people among Whites perpetuated the separation of both enslaved Africans and free Africans from the dominant White culture. This experience of exclusion and humiliation reinforced the alienation that all people of African descent felt within the United States. The other side of this sense of alienation was an exceptional sense of community, a sense of peoplehood grounded in some notion of Pan-African identity that has come to be known as Black nationalism.

WHAT IS BLACK NATIONALISM?

Nationalism is an ideology which asserts the right of nationhood of a particular group, the cultural similarities of members of the nation, and draws boundaries for that group vis-à-vis others who are deemed outsiders. The central arguments of most forms of nationalism is that the political boundaries should be coterminous with cultural boundaries. Although the concept of a nation is much less self-evident than we commonly think, an influential definition from the Marxist traditions holds that a nation is: "A historically evolved, stable community of language, territory, economic life and psychological make-up manifested in a common culture."

Like other forms of nationalism, Black nationalism can be viewed as the reaction of a formerly disunited group to a sense of mutual oppression and humiliation. Prior to the African slave trade African people were organized around local cultural loyalties and traditions. In such societies, tradition as embodied in the wisdom of living elders or revered ancestors, is sacred. While the slave system destroyed the traditions of those whom they enslaved within a generation or two, it also endowed them with a sense of common experience and identity.

Black nationalism and Pan-Africanism emerged out of the awareness of people of African descent in the West, that the slave trade conferred an inferior status upon all Black people, whether slave or free. Black nationalism is thus the belief that all Black people suffer from oppression within White society, and that a common heritage of oppression provides the basis for a system of universal cooperation among Blacks, especially in racist societies such as the United States.

Because the originators of Black nationalism emphasized the need for Black people to rely primarily on themselves in vital areas of life-economic, political, religious, and intellectual in order to affect their liberation, a variety of types of nationalism corresponding to each of these areas emerged among the African American population. Unlike other ethnic groups in the United States, Blacks were believed to be different and historically separated from the rest of the citizenry. While some forms of Black nationalism involve the notion of territorial separatism, other forms emphasize more strongly the notion of cultural and spiritual autonomy, some the notion of economic cooperation, and others the notion of a political bloc within the American polity.

THE NATIONALIST REVIVAL

Nationalist consciousness has been a constant in the social psychology of the African American people. Black nationalism has long been an element in the structuring of Black political action and cultural standpoint, but its fortunes have fluctuated. In the 1960s a vigorous and vibrant Black Power movement took the nation by storm. It burned brightly for a decade, setting fire to a whole generation of Black youth. Powerful and vibrant organizations flourished briefly. But these organizations were repressed by a combination of violent attacks, harassment, and intrigue on the part of federal, state, and local law enforcement agencies.

In the 1990s Black Nationalism reemerged as a popular ideology among broad segments of the African American population, particularly among Black youth. For Black youth a nationalist orientation seemed a quite logical response to their own life experiences, having come of age during a profoundly racist conjuncture dominated by a political culture which glorified the White middle class, acquisitive individualism, and the reassertion of U.S. dominance of the world-economy. The reassertion of North American hegemony in the 1980s was a response to the malaise that had set in upon large segments of the society in the late 1970s when the social psychology of a hegemonic power was challenged as one national liberation movement after another came to power almost always against the resistance or active opposition of the United States (Vietnam, Mozambique, Guinea Bissau, Grenada, Nicaragua, Angola, and others). These political struggles against Third World countries intensified many White Americans' perception that they were under siege by an envious world populated by an inferior species some of whom had made their way to our own shores, and were now loitering on the corners of the Black and Latino inner cities. While the radical and nationalist mobilizations of the 1960s occurred amidst increasing opportunities for many elements of the national Black community, this period was notable for the increasingly bleak socioeconomic prospects of noncollege educated Black youth.

Since White liberalism has largely been in retreat during the lives of these young people, and Black liberalism has been treated with disdain, their isolation from the main currents of White middle-class life simply reinforced their perception that mean-spirited conservatism and aggressive racism were virtually uncontested within the White adult population. The White public's disenchantment with liberalism is clearly correlated with the decline of the United States from unchallenged preeminence in the world-economy. The resulting experience of economic squeeze was accompanied by a search for explanations for the changing fortunes of the nation, which in the minds of many led to a search for scapegoats.

The racial liberalism of the 1960s was no longer viable. The Black sociologist William Julius Wilson sought to reformulate the liberal position by arguing that race had declined in significance and that the primary problem facing the Black inner-city residents was the issue of class position.[1] While many Whites lauded this position as pathbreaking, innovative, and courageous, any school child recognized that Black and Latino group status was clearly associated with being poor. Most also recognized that ill will rather than "impersonal economic forces" were deeply implicated in the worsening conditions of their communities. They knew that most employers did not consider them as desirable candidates for employment, and that many White teachers did not consider them educable. They knew that they were feared and despised by much of the White public. They knew that many White politicians made political points by public denunciations of their alleged misdeeds and attitudes.

In this context it should not be surprising that this generation was so strongly attracted to larger than life images of Malcolm X whose militance and clarity of vision resonated profoundly with their own sense of justice denied. A culture of opposition which had crystallized among inner-city youth was intensified by insights from Malcolm X. The egalitarian elements in hiphop culture (being true to one's roots, taking care of homies, and so on) cut sharply against the grain of the prevailing selfishness and greed of the dominant culture. This egalitarian ethos cemented the solidarity within and between inner-city Black and often Latino youth, and their more middle-class sisters and brothers. For these youth, so scathingly demonized in public discourse, Malcolm X was a model of Black dignity, standing up to the racist system, telling it like it was. He was viewed as a prophet who articulated their righteous anger against White society's racism and hypocrisy. Finally, he was a personification of Black peoples' demand for peace, justice, and equality.

In the complex and confusing conjuncture in which the 1990s' Black nationalist revival occurred, Malcolm X's legacy was reinterpreted or nullified (most notoriously by Spike Lee's film), and Black nationalism as an ideology was increasingly appropriated as the sole intellectual and political property of proponents of a more elitist and conservative social praxis associated with those in the Nation of Islam whose bourgeois aspirations led them to participate in the conspiracy to kill Malcolm X.

J. Edgar Hoover and the Federal Bureau of Investigation (FBI) had made their point rather well. Those Black people who identified with and attempted to unite with the ideals, sentiments, and practices of the revolutionaries of the three continents should realize that they would be subjected to the same lethal disincentives that U.S. imperialism's iron fist offered to it's Third World opponents. Malcolm X, George Jackson, Fred Hampton, Alprentice Bunchy Carter, Jonathan Jackson, and even Martin Luther King Jr. were all victims of U.S. imperialism's iron fist. Many of the intellectuals who came of age during this period became full-time cadres in the movements, and did not pursue more traditional academic interests or a career in mainstream politics. As a consequence of these choices their impact on the politics and intellectual life of the larger society was moderated.

Thus in the 1990s we moved very quickly from the revolutionary political discourse of Malcolm X discovered by a new generation seeking to address their situation in U.S. society, to the controversial but nonrevolutionary discourse of Louis Farrakhan and Khallid Abdul Muhammad. The ascendance of these conservative Black nationalists who opposed racial domination and degradation but who lacked a structural or systemic critique of U.S. society elevated verbal militance and rhetorical bombast into an already superheated public discourse, forming a perfect foil for a White racist backlash that had gained the upper hand within the nation's polity since the Reagan counterrevolution of 1980. The Reaganites cynically exploited the liberal premises of individual rights, calling for a color-blind policy against racism, but deftly shifted the attack against a phenomenon which they identified as "reverse discrimination" (against White men) which was implicit in the color conscious remedies (like affirmative action) which had emerged from the struggles of the 1960s.

While nationalist consciousness is ever present among the racially oppressed, the centrality of racism to the political realignment toward the conservative right not only fanned the flames of nationalism among the poorest and less fortunate in the Black communities, but also among the Black middle class who, though at the height of their fortunes, were themselves tarnished by the sheer weight of the degrading myths about the Black underclass. The middle class were then pushed not only to express their resistance to these degrading stereotypes in nationalist terms, but were pushed as well to identify strongly with the less fortunate members of the Black community.

The assassinations and disruptions of the Counter Intelligence Program (COINTELPRO) left the more conservative activists and intellectuals in a position to grow both within the academy and within Black communities. Thus when nationalist consciousness began to grow among the broader Black community, they were in place to insinuate themselves as the *only* legitimate voices of Black nationalism. The important point is not so much that conservative Black nationalism has become a part of the popular discourse and social praxis within the Black community, the concern is that they view themselves as the *only* legitimate voice. Why is this important? It allows the conservative nationalists to play a prosystemic policing function within the Black community which the representatives of the White establishment can never do.[2] The attack on the memory of Malcolm X, and the actual removal of Malcolm X from the scene is inextricably combined with this particular notion.[3]

These conservative Black nationalists have claimed the mantle of leadership in the Black community because they correctly identified and acted upon some of the internal barriers to Black success and unity. They sympathized with the militance of youth but focused on the need for responsibility, self-respect, Black pride, and respect for one another. But the emphasis on self-improvement and internal cohesion has meant that much of their focus has been on exhortation, often substituting inspiring rhetorical militance for substantive programs and strategies for destroying the power of White capitalist hegemony and domination. They tell it like it is to Whites and Blacks, no matter how unpleasant their truths. But is this the basic challenge to the system which is needed?

There is considerable evidence in the writings and presentations of the Nation of Islam (NOI) spokespersons that this is a plea for entry into the system.

Its boldness stems from its potential for success as a strategy for increasing the competitive position of *some* Blacks within the system by making use of Black solidarity and racial uplift as resources for advancement. This is basically the strategy of Booker T. Washington but with an important element of Black pride and militant assertiveness as forms of social cohesion.

Following the military defeat of the revolutionaries of the 1960s and 1970s and the retreat of the popular mobilizations, a new generation of Black intellectuals came to increasing public prominence. This group of Black intellectuals were mostly Left and Left leaning, but mostly rejected the "extremism" of the radicals of the 1960s and 1970s.[4] While their "prudence" has ensured them a positive reception among progressive and Left-leaning Whites, this group has been much less successful than the more vociferous conservative nationalists in getting the attention of Black youth both in the academy and on the streets.

The Left liberal or social democratic intelligentsia often soft-pedaled their critique of White supremacy or balanced their critique of White supremacy with a corresponding critique of the nihilism of Black youth and the alleged follies of neonationalism. These essentially liberal measures were simply cannon fodder for the culture of racism which had so long been characteristic of U.S. society, adding momentum to the White racist backlash which had increasingly characterized U.S. political culture since the 1970s. Indeed the White racist backlash lent a great deal of credence to a militant but relatively conservative Black nationalism who undermined their trenchant and correct critique of White supremacy by indulging in the anti-Semitic sentiments of Euro–North American culture and by its adherence to that culture's masculinist and homophobic values.

Ironically the marginalization of the Black Left took place while the conditions of the Black masses worsened, and the attitudes of the White public changed from disdain to contempt. The politics of the White backlash which perhaps appeared to have been ineffectual to the liberal elite in the 1970s was now playing to full houses throughout the court rooms of White America. No doubt the oppositional stance of the revolutionaries clashed violently with the deeply racist and conservative culture of the White majority. The radicals had sought to change the terms of the debate from the need for tolerance to the need for the transformation of the structures and values throughout the entirety of U.S. society. This fundamental challenge inspired some Whites and evoked a deeply defensive posture among others. But the "true believers" were deeply antagonized and sought to stampede both the Black radical interlopers and their supplicant liberal friends in the public discourse. Does this mean the militance of the Black community was responsible for the ensuing ideological polarization as has been charged by a chorus of Left liberal intellectuals from William Julius Wilson to Jim Sleeper? Can tolerance alone deal effectively with the legacy of racial oppression in our country?

In truth the White backlash was simply an elaboration on the basic cultural framework of historical capitalism, which explained inequality in cultural/racial terms. The fact of contention between deeply racist and pro-civil rights views among Whites, and sometimes within the same individual is not an anomaly. As Wallerstein argues[5] racism and universalism are complementary ideologies which relate to different parts of the process of class formation within the capitalist world-economy. Racism is the ideology which justifies the allocation of some groups to lower positions in the social division of labor of the working class. In contrast to the means of reproducing a segmented working class, the intermediate strata are assimilated to a neutral universal culture. The ideology by which the intermediate strata are controlled is thus called universalism. If indeed racism and universalism are applied to two different classes, then the existence of racist ideas and pro-civil rights ideas in the same individual makes much more sense.

Liberals on the other hand believed that racism is a moribund ideology, a holdover from slavery, which would wither away under the processes of rationalization within the industrial society. Many on the Left held to a variant of the liberal position, emphasizing racism as a superstructural phenomena, a product of the false consciousness of the working class who lost sight of their real interests by partaking of the psychological salve of racial superiority.

But the evolution, deepening, and the centrality of the White backlash shattered the traditional liberal optimism about the inevitability of progress. The "declining significance of race" which William Julius Wilson had triumphally observed in the late 1970s was by now an obvious fiction. Even Nathan Glazer who had earlier split with the liberal establishment was to say that America had not proved to be receptive to the humanity of Black people and that the only way forward is to declare that "we are all multiculturalists now."

The meaning of this trajectory might be clearer if we examine more closely the concept of liberalism and liberal universalism.

LIBERALISM AND LIBERAL UNIVERSALISM

Initially liberalism emerged as a new philosophy emphasizing the rights of individuals against incursions on individual rights by the state. At this time states were under the control of nobles and kings throughout most of Europe and liberalism sought to protect the rights of the emerging middle classes (at this time the rising business class was caught between the feudal lords and the peasants). John Locke's *A Second Treatise of Government* sought to ensure the individual's right to their own property. He argued that this was the sole legitimate purpose of government. These classical liberals viewed the free and competitive market as the only means to the good life.

The political concept referred to as liberal democracy borrowed heavily from economic liberalism, and is largely a correlate of the consolidation of capitalist civilization and the maturation of capitalist centers in the twentieth century. It is almost exclusively a political phenomenon of the developed nation-states of the capitalist world-economy. The less developed or under-developed zones of the capitalist world-economy are seldom the site of liberal democratic governments because their subordinate role within the capitalist system means precisely that they are very limited in their responsiveness to any significant segment of their local populations. The states in these zones are strong enough to hold the grievances of their local populations in check, but not strong enough to place restrictions on the power of international capital, or the core states who will do the bidding of international capital.

Like the notions of economic liberalism, liberal democratic theory stressed that the purpose of the state as an association of independent individuals is to facilitate the happiness of its members. The state should not have projects of its own. Political liberalism also held that competing interests are the foundation of political life, giving rise to an emphasis on a system of checks and balances that is probably most developed in the United States. Liberal democratic theorists such as Hobbes, Locke, Montesquieu, and Madison who argued for the right of citizens to elect a representative government, however, for the most part defined citizens as male property owners of some substance.[6] Classical liberals thought laborers were incurably lazy, that only a large reward or fear of starvation would make them work. The higher ranks on the other hand were said to be motivated by ambition.[7]

The concept of liberal democracy is thus quite limited in its democratic aspect, contrary to what is commonly held. Listen to the patron saint of economic liberalism, Adam Smith:

> The understanding of the greater part of men are necessarily formed by their ordinary employments. The man whose life is spent in performing a few simple operations . . . has no occasion to exert his understanding. . . . He generally becomes as stupid and ignorant as possible for a human to become. . . . His dexterity at this own particular trade seems in this manner to be acquired at the expense of his intellectual, social, and martial virtues. But in every improved and civilised society, this is the state into which the labouring poor, that is, the great body of the people, must necessarily fall.[8]

Liberalism is essentially an elitist doctrine, but it is also sophisticated in its emphasis that the good society is one which guarantees the greatest happiness for the greatest number and thus deals with the grievances of the dissatisfied via a process of orderly change brokered by experts. But liberal society is distinguished from the old order since it responds to pressure for change by the lower orders. We should be mindful, however, that the universal franchise, for example, is of rather recent origin throughout the liberal democracies, an issue for southern Blacks until the passage of the Voting Rights Act in 1965.[9]

Thus liberal democracy has also evolved over the years, in response to the evolution of economic and political life, and the demands of various sections of the population. With industrialization, urbanization, and modernization, economic life was confronted with a set of new needs which led to the reevaluation of the use of state power within the economy. Business began to employ various government support, subsidies, and protections of various kinds. Within this context some segments of the population also sought protection against some of the hardships created by the new conditions.

Liberalism's emphasis on the process of orderly change administered by experts appears eminently reasonable. Liberalism's promise is for the potential integration of the excluded, but those who are excluded are integrated into the values and structures of those who are already included. This is an important condition, and is a masterful stabilizing process. The dangerous classes are not entitled to grievances as a class, but will be integrated one by one as soon as they meet the requirements set by the liberal experts. This is a well-developed system of plausible denial. The promise held out to the dangerous classes seems palpably real. One can reach out and touch it as soon *as one is ready*.[10] It is because of this promise that the tendency to confuse liberalism with democracy has held for so long.

But democracy is inclusive and egalitarian. Democrats have given priority to the inclusion of all, in contrast to the liberal emphasis on the good society being one in which the competent prevail. Democrats have often claimed that liberalism is simply a sophisticated form of privilege cloaked in the mask of universalism. My own focus on liberal universalism thus attempts to draw attention precisely to this sleight of hand. An examination of the relationship between what is called the American Century and liberal universalism might help to clarify this point.

The ideological complement of the rise of the United States to world hegemony was its articulation of a mature global liberalism which promised to spread the material and cultural benefits of the American model to the entire world. The hegemonic status of the U.S. state within the world-economy not only affected the mentalities of ordinary citizens, but the militants of the mostly White (communist and noncommunist) Left as well. Despite the position of the United States as the main defender of the capitalist status quo, notions of American exceptionalism led the mostly patriotic Left within the United States to envision the development of social democracy on a world scale at the behest of U.S. government intervention in the world. This grand vision seemed to be the apotheosis of liberalism, but it was also embraced by the powerful conservatives who viewed the *promise* of global social democracy as the most effective means of defending the capitalist nature of the world-economy in the then existing circumstances. The rise of the United States to the position of hegemonic power in the world-system thus coincided with what appeared to be the final triumph of liberalism over its conservative and socialist rivals.

Henry Luce of *Time* magazine had coined the phrase "the American Century" to describe this period of unprecedented world hegemony and prosperity for some. But by 1968 challenges to North American power seemed to emerge from behind every bush and the triumphant claims of the American century disappeared from the public discourse, except for those on the Right who sought to revive a somewhat narrower notion of American power as the policeman of the capitalist world.

In 1968 the liberal consensus had come unraveled and liberalism was under attack from the Left and from the Right. Wallerstein argues that 1968 constituted the first real challenge to liberalism since its rise to a dominant position in the nineteenth century. Wallerstein argues that liberalism has constituted the geoculture of the capitalist world-economy for the last 180 years.

The ideological divide of the modern world is traced by Wallerstein to the French Revolution. The proponents of the French Revolution opposed hereditary privilege and claimed the moral and juridical equality of all people. Despite the fates of the proponents of the French revolution these ideas gained legitimacy in large parts of the world and eventually everywhere. Conservatism was constituted as a rejection of these ideas. Conservatives sought to reinforce the authority of traditional institutions such as the church, patriarchal families, the local nobility, monarchy, and so on. Liberals did not think these institutions could stem the tide of popular grievances. Liberals thought that the legitimacy of these grievances should in principal be granted, but that the pace and scope of change should be managed by experts. In this way such change as did take place would not displace those with legitimate claims to power and wealth.

Liberalism thus emerged as a means of *managing* change, of rationally and effectively controlling the dangerous classes. Conservatives wanted to slow down change as much as possible. Socialists wanted to accelerate change toward an egalitarian and just society. Liberalism's triumph in the twentieth century according to this logic is that the socialists (in particular the radical socialists around Lenin and the Bolsheviks) attempted to co-opt the center (liberalism) by arguing that indeed they could manage change better than the liberals, since they inculcated the future. This is a complicated issue, which is often treated as a given, but suffice it to say that the de facto substitute of a strategy of managed change for the socialist project fostered an illusion that the dangerous classes could eventually gain equality through these means rather than via a process of self-emancipation. In this way liberalism triumphed over both its conservative and socialist opposition. It acquired a universal posture.

One of liberalism's central tenants was the notion of equality of opportunity, which ironically acted as a powerful justification for inequality. Liberalism was the ideology of capitalism at the height of its power. The upper strata of the subordinate zones of the world-economy were assimilated to this universalist ideology. It stood for tolerance of different cultures and nationalities, and the assimilation of a class of individuals into the worldview of the dominant North American power. This group while maintaining contact with their local communities of origin increasingly viewed themselves as part of a global class of cadres of a global system.[11] In this way their loosening of ties from their local communities entailed a weakening of those communities because of the loss of leadership thus entailed.

LIBERAL UNIVERSALISM AND THE DECLINE OF COMMUNITY

Liberal universalism thus constituted in and of itself a decline in community among subordinate ethnic groups, since the intermediate strata who would normally provide leadership to these groups were assimilated to a universalist ideology. In this context freedom was not concerned with the groups' right to self-determination, but with the right of these educated classes to be more independent of their group of origin. The movement of this new petite bourgeoisie away from the traditional politics of their communities leaves the field of competition for leadership to the old petite bourgeoisie of small shopkeepers, ministers, and self-employed professionals on the one hand and a class of organic intellectuals from the working class on the other. The community itself is increasingly ghettoized and is composed of a greater concentration of the most marginalized sections of the working class. Within such communities where integration is not at all likely, a fertile soil has existed for hundreds of years for the elaboration of nationalist narratives and a nationalist culture quite unlike those within the other realms of society.

Some within the Black community, though disdainful of Whites in general, have sought to construct a society parallel to White society in its values, institutions, and aspirations. Others, ostensibly less disdainful of Whites have sought to construct a society that is closely attuned to those parts of the Black world which evolved in part from its own culture but freely choosing and selecting from all cultures with which they have been in contact. This is not a purely Black world, but one much more working class in its culture, although partaking of multiple cultural influences, one might say polycultural.[12] At the same time much of the poorer segments of this world are increasingly isolated from the mainstream institutions which provided a connection to the formal economy and its labor markets.

This environment has in past years formed the context for the elaboration of a culture and polity far removed from the mainstream culture of the

United States. But this distinctive subculture or culture of opposition is not new, it has long been characteristic of Black working-class life. From the invisible institution (slave churches) to the maroons, to the slave rebellions, this political psychology has been an element of the culture of those segments of the Black population who have been least integrated into the mainstream of North American society.

On the other hand, the political and social strategy of conservative nationalism is largely based on the class interests of the petite bourgeoisie and the aspiring bourgeoisie of subordinate groups. The split within the Nation of Islam between Malcolm X and the Chicago leadership of the NOI illustrates these two versions of Black nationalism.[13] Despite the distinctions made here between conservative nationalism and radical or revolutionary nationalism, it should be clear that even conservative nationalists pose a democratic challenge vis-à-vis the White world. But the challenge centers around their right to be bourgeois, to reap the benefits which are the entitlement of all bourgeois. Garvey had asked where are our Black men of big affairs? And he decided that his mission in life was to constitute this class of Black people. But Garvey also opposed imperialism and monopoly capitalism rhetorically. But he was vulnerable to a neocolonial deal as was evident in some of his dealings within the U.S. domestic sphere.

The revolutionary nationalism of Malcolm X, W. E. B. Du Bois, Paul Robeson, the African Blood Brotherhood (ABB), and the Black Panther Party was altogether different. These leaders were anticapitalist and anti-imperialist, egalitarian and democratic. They envisioned a liberated community internally, as well as one independent of White Western domination. While the outlook of conservative nationalism is distinct from liberal individualism, their idea of community is repressive, not only to keep the troops in line, but to keep the community obedient to the narrow views of an elite. While conservative nationalism is distinct from liberal individualism, they are generally open to a comprador relationship with the power elites of the capitalist world-economy.

Identity is not a given. It is constantly created and recreated out of the social interactions of which people partake. These interactions are varied in nature reflecting relations of exploitation-oppression, subordination-dominance, and advantaged-disadvantaged. The relationships, however are not unilateral or simply linear. They are dialectical and thus contradictory. Oppression is never total, there is always resistance. Such resistance is always the basis of the construction of an alternative set of utopistics. The tradition of the field Negro revolt which Malcolm X raised to the level of theory is the linchpin of the Black radical tradition. This is a tradition which has learned from many traditions, but which is not simply a copy of any tradition. It is one of the strongest antisystemic traditions on the face of the earth today. This has to be appreciated.

But we would be mistaken if we reified two such starkly different aspects of the nationalist tradition. In a population suffering from centuries of a most humiliating racial oppression, nationalist consciousness is widespread, such that few people do not manifest some aspect of this nationalist consciousness in their political ideology. Thus the talented tenth egalitarianism of W. E. B. Du Bois, Martin Luther King Jr., and Paul Robeson also manifest a significant and meaningful degree of nationalist consciousness. If we look at the ideas promoted by these two segments of the African American national movement we obtain quite a different picture of the meaning of African American nationalism than the much more narrow vision promoted by the conservative nationalists, whose ideas are much closer to but not identical to the ideas of White conservatives.

CONSERVATIVE BLACK NATIONALISM

Some argue that conservative Black nationalists share the views of more traditional fascists. Classical fascism in Germany, Italy, and Japan functioned most consistently as a block on the militancy of the working class through active repression and delegitimation. These movements were most effective in waging combat against the revolutionary or protorevolutionary section of the working class. The Nation of Islam articulates much of the same kind of narrow nationalism as some of the fascists, but the more ominous aspects of their practice is their use of strong-arm tactics against revolutionary nationalists (especially Malcolm X), and their use as a police force in the war against drugs. Several commentaries have raised this issue. The African Peoples' Socialist Party (APSP) has been most consistent in this critique, raising the issue against the more general tendency of Black activists to cooperate with the police in the war on drugs. The APSP argue that the war against drugs is a ruse for the establishment of police state practices within the Black community, not so much to control drugs but to control a potentially insurgent Black community.

The demeanor of the Nation of Islam is a doubled-edged sword. On the one hand they come from the community so they are able to understand and communicate with the residents of the impoverished inner cities. But they can use this ability to communicate and their organizational capabilities to assist in the empowerment of the community, or they become an agent of social control for some other force, or of their own more narrow interests.

Their idea of freedom is oriented toward a notion of nation-building centered on the NOI's theocracy more so than on the empowerment of non-Muslim Black people. While the NOI has changed the policy of nonengagement advocated by Elijah Muhammad, its actions in the political arena are extremely self-centered. Their tendency to seek control of the coalitions in which they work is extremely dangerous for the overall health of these coalitions. Their tendency to resort to violence to get their way in these coalitions is just as effective as if they were police agents. According to David Muhammad, formerly the assistant to Khallid Abdul Muhammad, the NOI is actively seeking to develop a niche for themselves within the police departments of U.S. cities. He argued that they simply wanted their piece of the pie.

This is a very long way from nation-building. It is easy to rationalize this behavior as part of a strategy of nation-building, of situating oneself in the crucial arena for ultimately waging combat against the White devils' social system. But there is little indication that such a strategy is underway.

The most likely conclusion that we can draw from the evidence is that the NOI is being groomed as a hedge against the development and maturation of a revolutionary nationalist current in the tradition of the African Blood Brotherhood and the Black Panther Party. Within the context of a crisis of liberalism the elites of the dominant states are searching for means of stabilizing power relations and staving off challenges from the dangerous classes. The Black and Latino lower strata form the most conscious radical section of the lower working class, and attempts to bolster conservative or reactionary views within this sector is high on the agenda. Thus the implicit romance with Farrakhan and Khallid Abdul Muhammad must be seen in this light. In the United States the conservative nationalism of Louis Farrakhan holds the promise to control the dangerous classes. In this sense conservative nationalism is stepping into the breach to play the prosystemic function of liberalism among the candidates for the most antisystemic role within the United States.

THE TRADITION OF THE FIELD NEGRO REVOLT

I hold that the radicalization of social movements in the United States is in large part a consequence of the impact of radical Black nationalist movements. The development of seriously antisystemic (revolutionary) strands within the North American Left can be clearly related to the impact of the African Blood Brotherhood in the 1920s, Malcolm X in the 1960s, and the Black Panther Party and its descendants in the 1970s. All of these organizations attempted to go beyond radical nationalism, but finding themselves in uncharted waters, either attempted to rely on old formulas (the leadership of the African Blood Brotherhood liquidated its leadership responsibility and joined the Communist Party USA [CPUSA] on the assumption that we were on the verge of a world socialist revolution; the Black Marxists of the 1970s became part of the New Communist Movement and attempted to synthesize unsuccessfully the traditions of the Third International and Maoism, while often undervaluing the tradition of the Black liberation movement); or were not able to make the turn before they were destroyed (Malcolm X and the Black Panther Party).

The Free African Society founded by Richard Allen in 1787 was one of the early organizations of the Black freedmen. Allen was later to found the African Methodist Episcopal Church in 1816 in response to the racism of the White churches. The institutional church which emerged among the Free Africans was the counterpart of the "invisible institution," the clandestine church which was the site of the formation of social and religious organization among the enslaved Africans in the United States. African American religious practice emerged in the interstices of co-optation and resistance.

Thus despite the Black Muslim–influenced 1960s' argument that Christianity was the White man's religion given to Africans to make them good slaves, the reality is much more complex. Christianization of the enslaved Africans in the United States was not a given. Slave owners feared that the Christianization of the slaves would imply that they were equal to Whites, and this would undermine the slave system. Religious leaders wanted converts so they argued to slave owners that Christianization of the enslaved Africans would make them better slaves.

Christianization did finally prevail, but African American Christianity, though drawing doctrinally from White Christianity, was marked by the perceptions and culture of the enslaved African. The invisible institution focused on the freedom struggle and on elaborating a concept of freedom and justice which came to be the common sense of the enslaved African population. The institutional churches, particularly the African Methodist Episcopal and the African Methodist Episcopal Zion churches were also a focal point of the elaboration of the freedom struggle for enslaved Africans. Afro-Christianity developed as a distinct form of religious practice from White Christianity and provided an important ideological and organizational base for the transformative activities of the African American people.

The desire to establish an independent nation was a consequence of the belief of large numbers of free Black people that their experience outside of the slave states was marked by racist treatment, almost tantamount to the treatment of their enslaved brethren. Slavery required the integration of the enslaved Africans with the White slave owners. But it was the nonslave North which took the lead in the establishment of segregated institutions. These institutions existed in practically every sphere: including schools, churches, hospitals, jails, hotels, and public conveyances. Blacks in the North were also subject to pogroms, not to mention the possibility of being enslaved because of the stipulations of the 1850 Fugitive Slave Act.

The Negro Convention Movement was the most effective forum for Afro-American protest in the antebellum period. Until the 1850s the advocates of moral suasion and the absorption of Blacks into the larger society predominated within the convention movement. With the fugitive slave law of 1850, the Kansas–Nebraska Bill of 1854, the Dred Scott Decision of 1857, and the general proliferation of scientific racist theories the attitude of Blacks about strategies and tactics for liberation from North American racist oppression were transformed. Frederick Douglass, who had opposed Henry Highland Garnett's call for insurrection in 1843, by the 1850s began to believe that liberation could only be obtained by resorting to violence.

The other side of the coin was the resistance of the slaves themselves, ranging from the Denmark Vesey conspiracy of 1822 to the Nat Turner rebellion of 1831, and the resistance exemplified by thousands of runaway slaves. Such resistance ultimately inspired John Brown's bold assault on Harpers Ferry in 1859.

The tradition of the field Negro revolt was expressed by slave rebellions and runaway slaves. Those slaves who escaped slavery often formed alliances with the anticolonial Native Americans' resistance movements and fought to maintain their autonomy and independence. Later the tradition of the field Negro revolt was manifest in the emigration movement (which also included many elite Blacks) and a massive populist movement, consisting of both Black and White farmers.

During Reconstruction Blacks helped establish democratic government, free public education, progressive social legislation, and engaged in populist collaboration with White farmers on an unprecedented scale. Against this democratic insurgency, the southern ruling class used violence and fraud to bring Reconstruction to a halt in state after state. For Blacks a state of terror existed in the South with lynchings, chain gangs, segregation, debt peonage, and massive disenfranchisement.

This was the context within which Booker T. Washington came to prominence espousing a strategy which did not appear threatening to the White power structure. Washington counseled Blacks to learn the value of manual labor, hard work and thrift, and to practice the Christian virtues of being clean and quiet. These values rather than empty rhetoric and flashy protest would enable Blacks to win acceptance. Although Washington's strategy would be called a comprador strategy by the terms that came to be used in the middle twentieth century, his strategy was essentially a nationalist one.

In 1905 W. E. B. Du Bois and William Monroe Trotter formed the Niagara Movement, an all-Black organization which focused on the legal redress of grievances in stark contrast to the accomodationist program of Booker T. Washington. Despite the failure of the talented tenth radicals, it prefigured the approach of the National Association for the Advancement of Colored People (NAACP) which was founded in 1909.

In the period from 1910 to 1920 Blacks migrated in increasingly large number to northern cities to take jobs in industry. During the summer of 1919 there was a total of twenty-five race riots stemming from economic insecurity over a shortage of jobs, and competition between Blacks and Whites for housing and recreational facilities. The context for the ferment of this period was the return of the soldiers from World War I, including Black soldiers who had gained a new international sense from their participation in the war. For people of African descent the war experience disabused them of the notion of European cultural supremacy. The war also stimulated revolutions against imperialism and colonial domination, which inspired the Black populations in the United States and the West Indies, as it did other subjugated people.

The demographic consequences of the great Black migration are also important considerations. The concentration of Black people in urban areas led to the enrichment and elaboration of Black culture. This concentration also led to the development of dense networks of association which supported the lives of these new urban dwellers. In contrast to approaches which emphasize the significance of the rural experience in the Black Belt South, it was the process of urbanization and proletarianization which facilitated the elaboration of the national factor in the African American experience.

This was the context for the rise of the New Negro radicals manifested in the Garvey movement, the Harlem Renaissance, the Messenger Group, and the African Blood Brotherhood. Within the White Left there were important differences on the "Negro Question." The socialists viewed Black people as a part of the working class, who were sorely oppressed by racism, but argued that the fight for socialism would eliminate the basis of racism, which was a capitalist strategy to divide and conquer the working class. The Socialist Party was said to be the party of the entire working class, not for any special part of the working class. W. E. B. Du Bois and Hubert Harrison were Black notables in the Socialist Party (for a short time), but the Black membership of the Socialist Party was negligible.

The Communist international on the other hand argued that oppressed nations (including Negroes in the United States) should have the right of self-determination. The African Blood Brotherhood was instrumental in articulating this position within the Communist International, and began to work within the United States with the CPUSA. Some of the top leadership of the African Blood Brotherhood joined the CPUSA during the 1920s since they agreed overall with the Comintern's line about the imminence of the world socialist revolution. ABB leaders, Cyril Briggs and Richard Moore, became key leaders of the CPUSA, enabling it to play an important role in the fight for racial equality. But Briggs and Moore were eventually purged from the party for nationalist deviations. Despite their theoretical support for the right of self-determination of the Negro Nation, in practice the CPUSA was quick to attack Black militants as nationalists.

During the 1930s Du Bois called for the exploitation of certain forms of self-segregation in the economic and educational spheres to bolster Blacks in the face of desperate economic times. These calls, reminiscent of the antebellum nationalists, led to conflict with NAACP officials. Du Bois was asked to leave the NAACP in 1934. During this "Black nationalist" phase Du Bois articulated the most sophisticated understanding of world capitalism even till this day.[14] Du Bois anticipated a world-systems theory which emerged out of the work of Third World intellectuals (like Samir Amin and Anouar Abdel-Malek) and Western intellectuals who worked in the Third World (Andre Gunder Frank, Immanuel Wallerstein, and Giovanni Arrighi).

During the 1930s the Nation of Islam emerged out of the remnants of the Garvey movement and Noble Drew Ali's Moorish American Science Temple. During this same period Mussolini's troops marched into Ethiopia, generating a massive resistance to the intervention among African Americans and people of African descent in the Caribbean and South America. This period saw the rise of various "Don't Buy Where You Can't Work" campaigns throughout the urban North, precursors to the 1960s' demand for community control.

A. Philip Randolph's threat of a March on Washington led Roosevelt to establish the Fair Employment Practices Committee and to bar discrimination in defense industries and federal bureaucracies. Randolph, a partisan of the Socialist Party and fiercely antinationalist, believed it was necessary to organize through mechanisms that were national in form. Thus both the Brotherhood of Sleeping Car Porters and the March on Washington Movement were all-Black formations. The National Negro Congress was an even more formidable arena for articulating strategies of Black liberation.

But the Black Freedom Struggle suffered grievously after this period because of the removal of Paul Robeson and W. E. B. Du Bois from the national scene. The concerted attack on the two most outstanding radicals in the Black Freedom Struggle undermined the increasingly radical nature of the grassroots Black social struggles since there ceased to be any leader of national significance who championed the cause of African liberation and socialism.

Blacks returned from World War II more determined than ever to end racism in the United States. They had clashed with White GI's at bases around the world and within the United States. Although the United States emerged from World War II as the most powerful nation in the world, the existence of a powerful antagonist (the former Soviet Union), who was quick to point out the injustices suffered by Blacks, created a conjuncture which was favorable to Black rebellion.

The civil rights movement was the first phase of this rebellion. De jure segregation crumbled under the assault of the civil rights movement. However de facto segregation in the North proved to be much stronger. Although Malcolm X had been able to mobilize many Blacks in the northern ghettos into the Nation of Islam, as he moved closer to the civil rights movement, and to the radical anticolonial movements in Africa and the Third World he lost favor within the leadership of the Nation of Islam who were now too comfortable with their new level of wealth to rock the boat, but were also manipulated against Malcolm by the FBI who feared the rise of a Messiah who could unify the militant elements within the Black community. But this process was already underway when Malcolm was killed. The young militants of the Student Nonviolent Coordinating Committee (SNCC), the Congress of Racial Equality (CORE), and the Revolutionary Action Movement (RAM) articulated the grievances of the rebellious masses of the inner city into a call for Black Power, and attempted to carry out the kind of strategy which was in the process of development when Malcolm was killed. While Martin Luther King Jr. was not a part of the Black nationalist camp, he too had been pulled into the revolutionary maelstrom of the period, leading to appeals for the death of this apostle of peace from the leadership of the FBI.

While SNCC and RAM were the first centers of radical Black Power, they were undermined by the crisis of the civil rights movement, and the repression of its most radical organizations. But the times called for moving beyond the stalemate of the civil rights movement to new centers of struggle as the mantle of radical Black Power passed to the Black Panther Party and the League of Revolutionary Black Workers.

The Black Panther Party spoke directly to the mentality of inner-city Black youth, but developed the capacity to speak across the racial divide to working-class people and intellectuals from many different ethnic and racial groups. They developed the idea of a rainbow coalition from the ground up, and inspired organizations such as the (Puerto Rican) Young Lords Organization in Chicago and Young Lords Party in New York City; the (Chicano) Brown Berets in Chicago, Texas, and California; the (poor White) Young Crusaders; and the (Asian) I Wor Kuen and the Asian Study Group (later the Workers Viewpoint Organization) in California and New York.

FBI director J. Edgar Hoover argued that the Black Panther Party was the greatest threat to the national security since the civil war, and devoted more resources on destroying the party than it did on fighting organized crime. The FBI's declaration of war against the BPP decimated the young organization before it could become deeply rooted among the communities in which they existed.

Newton cautioned against an overreliance of a military strategy. He did not think they were ready for a military stance against the state. They were a political organization, and their primary responsibility was to unite with the people, so that they could lead a protracted struggle for a democratic, just, and egalitarian society. Newton's grasp of the global scope of the relations of rule of the capitalist world exceeded that of any other North American political leader. He was thus able to articulate the international nature of the struggle against it in a manner that was far removed from the obligatory language of internationalism of the world Left. This led him to question the strategy of seeking state power which had been the dominant strategy of antisystemic movements for 150 years.

But the organization was destroyed by the state which took advantage of the organization's inexperience, youth, and mistakes. The organizations which emerged in the wake of the demise of the Black Panther Party drew several lessons from the party's demise. They thought that a more disciplined form of organization was needed and a more coherent ideology was in order. They thus turned in large numbers to the formation of Marxist–Leninist Parties which used the organizational form of democratic centralism. The major African American organizations which were involved in this movement have yet to be the subject of a systematic scholarly inquiry. Amiri Baraka's Congress of African People became the Revolutionary Communist League, and eventually united with (the Asian) I Wor Kuen, and (the Chicano) August Twenty-ninth Movement to form the U.S. League for Revolutionary Struggle. The Youth Organization for Black Unity, People's College, Malcolm X Liberation University, the Lynn Euson Institute, and the Marxist–Leninist Collectives of San Francisco united to form the Revolutionary Workers League, which eventually united with the remnants of the Young Lords Party to form the Revolutionary Wing, and later with the (the Asian) Workers Viewpoint Organization to form the Communist Workers Party. Much of the membership of the League of Revolutionary Black Workers joined the Black Workers Congress, others joined the Communist League, which later became the Communist Labor Party. Some of the most powerful Black radical leaders such as Max Stanford of the Revolutionary Action Movement became associated with the African Peoples Party, some of whose members then spun off into the Black Workers for Justice.

Some of the organizations who came out of this period retained their revolutionary nationalist orientation: Kwame Ture's (formerly Stokeley Carmichael) All-African People's Revolutionary Party; the African People's Socialist Party; and the New Republic of Africa. Some of the important new organizations in this tradition include the New African People's Organization, and the New York City–based December 12th Coalition.

The revolutionary nationalist organizations have proven to be more durable, and have come to public attention in some crisis situations. The African Peoples Socialist Party gave leadership to the People's Democratic Uhuru Movement in the rebellion against police repression in St. Petersburg, Florida. In New York City the hip-hop group Dead Prez have affiliated with the Uhuru Movement. The December 12th Movement has organized civil disruptions in response to acts of official or White mob racial violence in New York City. They have continued to be highly visible in the Black Freedom Struggle in New York, and some of its members have connections with a community center in Brooklyn called Sista's Place.

Most of the high-profile individuals and organizations with whom the public has some knowledge represent the more moderate and mainstream segments of the movement. Many of the radicals now largely work within these movements, but not on their own terms. The most urgent task that the radicals face, who are now attempting to organize on their own terms to discuss the way forward, is to develop a means of working among the broad masses of the people, helping to form grassroots initiatives, proposing means of addressing the larger issues, and addressing the need for radical solutions in a manner which makes sense to the masses of people in our inner cities.

Conservative Black nationalism is an expression of the competition within the existing system. Yet it should be clear that such a movement is legitimate in its own right, as much as any other nationalist movement, or attempt to use ethnic politics to bolster a group's position within the status quo.

At this time the Nation of Islam is undergoing somewhat of a fissure with the expulsion of Khallid Abdul Muhammad who did not wish to play the conservative role, but a much more provocative role. While Khallid Muhammad regularly declared Minister Farrakhan to be his spiritual father there could not be more differences in their tactics. While there is little indication that there is substantive differences between the two men, Muhammad serves the White establishment's purpose by posturing as a revolutionary with a frighteningly *reactionary* line. Khallid Abdul Muhammad's politics are entirely different from the politics of Malcolm X who he claims to respect and admire, and the Black Panther Party of Huey P. Newton, Bobby Seale, Elaine Brown, Fred Hampton, and Alprentice Bunchy Carter, the descendants of which he fraudulently claims to lead.

Should the revolutionaries who truly follow the tradition of Malcolm X and the Black Panther Party muster enough strength to come to the fore, they will most certainly be confronted with the opposition of these two representatives of conservative Black Nationalism. But the mainstreaming of these characters is designed precisely to steal the thunder of the revolutionaries, and to continue the marginalization of a force who could potentially bring coherence to the dispossessed and disenchanted masses of North America. These revolutionary forces, however, are divided and weak.

The emergence of the Black Radical Congress in 1997–1998 indicated a revitalization of the radical/revolutionary tradition within African American politics. This is a quite promising development despite the difficulties in overcoming some of the sectarianism which has long plagued the Black liberation movement.

Despite the marginalization of the Black radical tradition during the post-1970s' counterrevolution, some organizations continued to operate and show signs of increasing strength in the last few years. The African People's Socialist Party under the leadership of Omali Yeshitela survived the counterrevolution and moved its national headquarters back to the site of its founding in St. Petersburg, Florida. In the 1990s the APSP organized the National People's Democratic Uhuru Movement which creatively developed popular institutions in the cities around the country where they have a presence. In

1996 they provided important leadership within the Black community of St. Petersburg, Florida, during and after a rebellion against police repression and murder. When the police and the city administration moved to preempt any response to the murder by rounding up members of the Uhuru Movement, the organization was defended by the community using insurrectionary means. This is an example of a revolutionary nationalist organization with deep roots within their local community, who promote a democratic, egalitarian, and emancipatory approach to the problems of the Black inner city. The Uhuru Movement in St. Petersburg is clearly a model of Black community empowerment worthy of further study and emulation.[15]

The efforts to consolidate the new Black Panthers into a national movement called The New Panther Vanguard Movement is another very promising sign of the revitalization of the revolutionary approach within Black nationalism. This effort is particularly promising in my view because it represents a consolidation of local efforts, by people who have roots within their local communities, rather than building a movement from the top down. While some of the locals lack the sophistication of the original Black Panther Party led by Huey P. Newton, Bobby Seale, Elaine Brown, David Hilliard, Erika Huggins, Bunchy Carter, Fred Hampton, Kathleen Cleaver, Geronimo Pratt, Dhoruba bin Wahaad and others, the construction of a national organization seems to be a promising step in that direction.[16]

The New York City–based December 12th Movement is capable of bold organizational forays that disrupt the business-as-usual oppressiveness of the city's political and economic elite, and the large legions of people hustling to get their own piece of the pie. This large intermediate strata, along with an exclusive upper-working-class strata (dominated by males from the White ethnic groups) is the base of a quite reactionary, narrow, and self-centered political vision within New York City, which is racist to the core. This hard-core racism is the basis for ultranationalist positions among the besieged communities who are the targets of this racism. On the other hand, the large number of working people from every corner of the globe present a mosaic of proletarian cultures. But the very diversity of this group means that the core proletarian groups (Black and Latino) must be exceptionally open, flexible, and outreaching in their approach. The leadership must themselves be both proletarian and cosmopolitan. Ultra nationalism and dogmatism is essentially isolating for building beyond one's own community, and is usually representative of the bourgeois aspirations of the ethnic petty bourgeoisie. This is precisely the kind of political culture which presents a milieu for opportunist hustlers like Khallid Abdul Muhammad to push narrow self-serving agendas, thinly disguised behind a fusillade of revolutionary-sounding rhetoric, more intended to serve the political purposes of the elite than building a serious revolutionary movement among the African American people, or the African people more broadly.

This is not to say that the ethnic petite bourgeoisie are the main barrier to the aspirations of the lower-working-class ethnic populations of the United States. This ethnic petite bourgeoisie have as much right to their bourgeois aspirations as anyone else. It is important that we understand just what these aspirations are, so that confusion is not created by the conflating of the grievances of the different strata of the oppressed ethnic strata.

But radical Black nationalism is essentially an antisystemic movement pressing for the unity of all the oppressed and exploited within the United States to come together for an egalitarian route out of the collapse of capitalism. Thus we must beware of any type of knee-jerk, antinationalist positions for within the social movements of the United States these have almost always (but not always) served reactionary purposes, moving progressive movements and people to the Right away from the most rebellious and potentially revolutionary constituencies.

NOTES

Portions of this chapter were originally published in *We Are Not What We Seem: Black Nationalism and Class Struggle in the American Century*, by Rod Bush, New York: New York University Press, 1999. Reprinted by permission of the New York University Press.

1. See William Julius Wilson, *The Declining Significance of Race: Blacks and Changing American Institutions* (Chicago: University of Chicago Press, 1978); and William Julius Wilson, *The Truly Disadvantaged: The Inner City, the Underclass, and Public Policy* (Chicago: University of Chicago Press, 1987).

2. Thus Jack Kemp's praise of Minister Louis Farrakhan makes perfect sense. For an elaboration of this theme, see Robin D. G. Kelley, "The Crisis: Is Self-Help the Capitalism of Fools?" *Village Voice Literary Supplement* (March 6–11, 1996); Adolph Reed Jr., "Behind the Farrakhan Show," *The Progressive* 58 (4) (April 1994): 16–17; Adolph Reed Jr., "Ebony and Ivory Fascists," *The Progressive* 60 (4) (April 1996): 20–22; and Wahneema Lubiano, "Black Nationalism and Black Common Sense: Policing Ourselves and Others," in *The House That Race Built: Black Americans, U.S. Terrain*, ed. Wahneema Lubiano (New York: Pantheon, 1997).

3. The complicity between the state and conservative nationalists in the murder of Malcolm X has been alluded to, but too much emphasis has been placed on attempts to disrupt the Black liberation movement by fishing in troubled waters, and too little on the direction of the disruption, that the state invariably sides with the more conservative elements. For a discussion of this issue, see Haki Madhubuti, "The Farrakhan Factor: The Question That Will Not Go Away," in *Claiming Earth: Race, Rage, Rape, Redemption: Blacks Seeking a Culture of Enlightened Empowerment*, ed. Haki Madhubuti (Chicago: Third World Press, 1994).

4. See Cornel West's critique of Black Marxists in *Prophesy Deliverance! An Afro-American Revolutionary Christianity* (Philadelphia: Westminster, 1982), and

his critique of Black Nationalists in *Race Matters* (Boston: Beacon, 1993). However, if he is to take his choice of nationalists, it is Elijah Muhammad over Malcolm X. See his contribution to Joe Wood, ed., *Malcolm X in Our Own Image* (New York: St. Martin's, 1992).

5. See Immanuel Wallerstein, *Historical Capitalism* (London: Verso, 1983); and Immanuel Wallerstein, "The Ideological Tensions of Capitalism: Universalism vs. Racism and Sexism," in *Race, Nation, Class: Ambiguous Identities*, ed. Étienne Balibar and Immanuel Wallerstein (New York: Verso, 1991).

6. John D. Nagle, *Introduction to Comparative Politics: Political System Performance in Three Worlds* (Chicago: Nelson-Hall, 1985), 15.

7. E. K. Hunt, *Property and Prophets: The Evolution of Economic Institutions and Ideologies*, 4th ed. (New York: Harper and Row, 1981), 40–41.

8. Quoted in Robert Tucker, *The Marx–Engels Reader* (New York: Norton, 1972), 287.

9. Nagle, *Introduction to Comparative Politics*, 17.

10. I recall my days at Howard University in the early 1960s as a working-class student in what was at the time considered to be the bastion of the Black bourgeoisie. It was a standing joke among many of the students that "some of us just aren't ready."

11. Among African Americans, Vernon Jordan, Jesse Jackson, Clarence Thomas, and Colin Powell may be considered in this category.

12. See Robin D. G. Kelley, "People in Me," *Colorlines* 1 (3) (winter 1999): 5–7.

13. For a detailed review of the split within the Nation of Islam, see Rod Bush, *We Are Not What We Seem: Black Nationalism and Class Struggle in the American Century* (New York: New York University Press, 1999).

14. See especially W. E. B. Du Bois, *Black Reconstruction in America 1860–1880* (New York: Atheneum, 1970).

15. I am aware that some individuals and organizations on the Left consider the African People's Socialist Party to be sectarian. This is a complicated issue, but sectarianism is rampant throughout the progressive movement. However, attitudes toward the APSP and other nationalist organizations are often affected by the widespread antinationalist sentiment that exists within the White Left, attitudes which reflect both the racism of the wider society and the often unexamined assumption that the White Left has the right of ideological tutelage. This idea is often shared by Black militants who work within largely White Left organizations and those who seek to ally with them. The African Blood Brotherhood who argued for the necessity of Black leadership ran into a similar problem in its relation with the CPUSA. This is something quite a bit more complicated than the idea that these militants are selling out the Black community.

16. A recent issue of the Black Panther International News Service was critical of some aspects of the New Black Panther Party actions in Jasper, Texas, clarifying that they were not responsible for the actions there, particularly of the narrow nationalist statements made by Khallid Abdul Muhammad. Khallid Abdul Muhammad of course is closer to his own roots in Texas, in contrast to his actions in Harlem. A member of the New York City chapter told me that they had a meeting with Khallid Abdul Muhammad and rebuked him for giving the impression that he was in the leadership of the New Panther Vanguard, when in reality his alliance was with the Dallas, Texas, New Black Panther Party.

REFERENCES

African People's Socialist Party. "Apartheid Law! Police Tyranny! What is the Weed and Seed Program." *The Burning Spear* (September–October 1997): 12–13.

Amin, Samir. *Class and Nation.* New York: Monthly Review, 1980.

Balibar, Étienne, and Immanuel Wallerstein. *Race, Nation, Class: Ambiguous Identities.* New York: Verso, 1991.

Brath, Elombe. Telephone interview with the author, October 1995.

Bush, Rod. *We Are Not What We Seem: Black Nationalism and Class Struggle in the American Century.* New York: New York University Press, 1999.

Carmichael, Stokeley, and Charles Hamilton. *Black Power: The Politics of Liberation in America.* New York: Random House, 1967.

Davis, Horace. *Toward a Marxist Theory of Nationalism.* New York: Monthly Review, 1978.

Drake, St. Clair. *The Redemption of Africa and Black Religion.* Chicago: Third World Press, 1970.

Du Bois, W. E. B. *Black Reconstruction in America 1860–1880.* New York: Atheneum, 1979.

———. *Dusk of Dawn: An Essay toward the Autobiography of a Race Concept.* New York: Schocken, 1970.

———. "Marxism and the Negro Problem." In *Voices of a Black Nation: Political Journalism in the Harlem Renaissance*, ed. Theodore Vincent. San Francisco: Ramparts, 1973.

Fanon, Frantz. *The Wretched of the Earth.* Trans. Constance Farrington. New York: Grove, 1966.

Hunt, E. K. *Property and Prophets: The Evolution of Economic Institutions and Ideologies.* 4th ed. New York: Harper and Row, 1981.

Kelley, Robin D. G. "The Crisis: Is Self-Help the Capitalism of Fools?" *Village Voice Literary Supplement* (March 6–11, 1996).

———. "People in Me." *Colorlines* 1 (3) (winter 1999): 5–7.

———. *Yo' Mama's Disfunktional: Fighting the Culture Wars in Urban America.* Boston: Beacon, 1997.

Locke, John. *A Second Treatise of Government.* New York: Bobbs-Merrill, 1952.

Lubiano, Wahneema. "Black Nationalism and Black Common Sense: Policing Ourselves and Others." In *The House That Race Built: Black Americans, U.S. Terrain*, ed. Wahneema Lubiano. New York: Pantheon, 1997.

Madhubuti, Haki. "The Farrakhan Factor: The Question That Will Not Go Away." In *Claiming Earth: Race, Rage, Rape, Redemption: Blacks Seeking a Culture of Enlightened Empowerment*, ed. Haki Madhubuti. Chicago: Third World Press, 1994.

Malcolm X. *The End of White World Supremacy: Four Speeches by Malcolm X.* New York: Merlin House, 1971.

Mao Tse-Tung. "Oppose Racial Discrimination by U.S. Imperialism." In *The Political Thought of Mao Tse-Tung*, ed. Stuart Schram. New York: Praeger, 1969.

Moses, Wilson Jeremiah. *The Golden Age of Black Nationalism: 1850–1925.* New York: Oxford University Press, 1978.

Muhammad, David. Presentation at St. John's University, Black Solidarity Day, November 9, 1998.

Nagle, John D. *Introduction to Comparative Politics: Political System Performance in Three Worlds*. Chicago: Nelson-Hall, 1985.

New Panther Vanguard Movement. "Editorial: Jasper and the New Black Panther Party." *The Black Panther International News Service* 1 (5) (fall 1998): 3.

Raboteau, Albert. *Slave Religion: The "Invisible Institution" in the Antebellum South*. New York: Oxford University Press, 1978.

Reed, Adolph, Jr. "The Allure of Malcolm X and the Changing Character of Black Politics." In *Malcolm X in Our Own Image*, ed. Joe Wood. New York: St. Martin's, 1992.

———. "Behind the Farrakhan Show." *The Progressive* 58 (4) (April 1994): 16–17.

———. "Ebony and Ivory Fascists." *The Progressive* 60 (4) (April 1996): 20–22.

Robinson, Cedric. *Black Marxism: The Making of the Black Radical Tradition*. London: Zed Press, 1983.

———. *Black Movements in America*. New York: Routledge, 1997.

Sales, William W., Jr. *From Civil Rights to Black Liberation: Malcolm X and the Organization of Afro-American Unity*. Boston: South End, 1994.

Sleeper, Jim. *The Closest of Strangers: Liberalism and the Politics of Race in New York City*. New York: Norton, 1990.

Stuckey, P. Sterling. "History of the Black Peoples of America." In *The World Encyclopedia of Black People*. Vol. 1. St. Clair Shores, Mich.: Scholarly Press, 1975.

———. *The Ideological Origins of Black Nationalism*. Boston: Beacon, 1972.

———. *Slave Culture: Nationalist Theory and the Foundations of Black America*. New York: Oxford University Press, 1987.

Tucker, Robert. *The Marx–Engels Reader*. New York: Norton, 1972.

Wallerstein, Immanuel. *After Liberalism*. New York: The New Press, 1995.

———. "Antisystemic Movements: History and Dilemmas." In *Transforming the Revolution: Social Movements in the World System*, ed. Samir Amin et al. New York: Monthly Review, 1991.

———. *Historical Capitalism*. London: Verso, 1983.

———. "The Ideological Tensions of Capitalism: Universalism vs. Racism and Sexism." In *Race, Nation, Class: Ambiguous Identities*, ed. Étienne Balibar and Immanuel Wallerstein. New York: Verso, 1991.

———. "1968, Revolution in the World-System: Theses and Queries." In *Geopolitics and Geoculture: Essays on the Changing World-System*. New York: Cambridge University Press, 1991.

West, Cornel. "Malcolm X and Black Rage." In *Malcolm X in Our Own Image*, ed. Joe Wood. New York: St. Martin's, 1992.

———. "Nihilism in Black America: A Danger That Corrodes from Within." *Dissent* (spring 1991): 221–226.

———. *Prophesy Deliverance! An Afro-American Revolutionary Christianity*. Philadelphia: Westminster, 1982.

———. *Race Matters*. Boston: Beacon, 1993.

Wilmore, Gayraud. *Black Religion and Black Radicalism: An Interpretation of the Religious History of Afro-American People*. Maryknoll, N.Y.: Orbis, 1983.

Wilson, William J. *The Declining Significance of Race: Blacks and Changing American Institutions*. Chicago: University of Chicago Press, 1978.

———. *The Truly Disadvantaged: The Inner City, the Underclass, and Public Policy*. Chicago: University of Chicago Press, 1987.

Wood, Joe, ed. *Malcolm X in Our Own Image*. New York: St. Martin's, 1992.

10

Commodification and Existence in African American Communities

Paget Henry

One of the consequences of the rise of "the new cultural politics of difference"[1] in the 1980s has been a fragmenting of counterhegemonic discourses along fault lines such as race, gender, class, and other liminal or phobogenic signifiers of difference. On the one hand, the splintering of the anticapitalist unity that had previously connected them has made more audible the voices of groups that had been suppressed or silenced. On the other hand, this multiplying of differences has generated a deep mistrust of all unifying or umbrella concepts that could serve as rallying points. This rejection of universalizing general concepts of domination in the interest of identifying specific ones has created problems of communication, solidarity, and alliance formation.

Given these praxis-related problems, it is not surprising that scholars have been proposing new concepts that address these concerns without losing the greater audibility that has come with the turn to difference. Thus, Sylvia Wynter proposes the concept of liminality as a "transcultural" construct[2] that is capable of making a contribution here. I would like to propose the concept of commodification as another as it cuts across the modern experiences of many different groups. Using the case of African American communities, I will show its usefulness for establishing links between issues of class, race, and culture.

In this chapter, I examine the impact of modern processes of commodification on the economic and cultural lives of Black communities. In particular, I focus on the socioeconomic and existential consequences of this process of modern sociocultural reorganization. I argue that the process of commodification in Black America has followed a distinct trajectory because of the ways in which it has been racially inscribed. I trace the complex economic and cultural impact of this racializing of commodity production over time. In doing so, I show that although the commodification of

African American labor, culture, and material goods brought an excessive share of dehumanization and cultural alienation, it did not bring the material wealth it produced for White America. This difference in outcome I link to the way in which the process of commodification has been raced in the case of African Americans. In the end, this outcome legitimates the claim regarding the usefulness of the concept of commodification to establish bridges between issues of class, race, and culture.

COMMODIFICATION: AN OVERVIEW

Communities are bounded spaces in which a self-identified group of human beings realize a wide range of material and ideal interests through shared sets of intricate and multidimensional interactive practices. Communities may be subnational, national, or supranational in scope. The multidimensional nature of communal interactions extend from the spiritual and religious, through the imaginary and aesthetic, to the political and economic.

Modern societies, particularly their capitalist variants, have been particularly hard on the structures of communities. This tension between community and capitalist modernity has been well established in the sociological literature that accompanied the rise of capitalism in western Europe. Ferdinand Töennies characterized this tension by contrasting gemeinschaft and gesellschaft.[3] Émile Durkheim attempted to capture it in the contrast between mechanically and organically integrated societies.[4] Karl Marx thematized this tension through his concept of commodification,[5] while Max Weber made his attempt through the concept of rationalization.[6] Today, Jürgen Habermas has reformulated these earlier attempts as an opposition between communicative rationality and technocratic rationality.[7]

What these formulations all share is a concern over the corrosive effects of the marriage between technology and commodity production on the norms, ideals, and interactive practices that are necessary to sustain communities. These effects of technocratic commodity production disrupt the normative foundations and interactive practices of communities in two ways. First, they carry within them a tendency to impose the commodity form not just on objects of material production, but also on those of cultural production. This commodification of culture transforms it profoundly, and reduces its capacities to delegitimate capitalist practices. Second, because it depends on science, technocratic commodification encourages the institutionalization of the sciences as the dominant discourses of the cultural system. With this hegemonic status, the cognitive claims of the nonscientific discourses are correspondingly devalued, along with their abilities to establish ideals, legitimate norms, and frame interactive practices. I want to examine each of these separately.

The process of capitalist commodification has been given its classic description by Marx. In *Capital*, he shows that the wealth of capitalist societies exist in the form of "an immense accumulation of commodities"[8] that are capable of being exchanged. For Marx, a commodity is a useful object that has been inscribed in a system of signification. This inclusion assigns it an "exchange-value" and hence the possibility of circulating within the system of exchange made possible by the similar inscription of other objects that have "use-value." In the capitalist mode of production, this system of signification is an instrumental discourse of abstract, quantified labor whose carefully fixed signifiers and relations of equivalence make possible the incorporation of use-values into systems of exchange. Once inscribed in this laborist discourse, the specific qualities and prior values that marked the object cease to be its primary signifiers. Whatever the discourse in which this object was previously inscribed, it is displaced and ceases to be the primary determinant of the object's meaning. Space must be made in the discursive economy of the would-be commodity for this laborist discourse. In other words, to circulate through the exchange networks of capitalist markets, the primary signifier of a use-value must be its price. Marx saw this numerical symbol as the quantitative indicator of the socially efficient amount of necessary labor time that should be devoted to the production of this commodity.

The aim of this discursive reinscription of use-values is not the production of a book or some other form of semiolinguistic production. On the contrary, the goal of these textual reallocations is the profitable production and circulation of material commodities through institutions of private property. The covers of these pages have been the walls of factories, which imposed competitive and technocratic constraints on the semiotic play usually allowed in books or in prior modes of discursive inscription. In other words, the commodity form imposes a systemic logic on the use-values incorporated into it. This logic disrupts the prior inscriptions of the object whether political, aesthetic, or spiritual. Hence the potential in commodity production for corroding the values and discourses that legitimate community structures.

Complementing these effects of commodity production are its complex feedback relations with science and technology. In these relationships, science and technology serve as powerful discursive aids to increasing both the innovative nature and the efficiency of commodity production. In return, research efforts in science and technology are ably supported with some of the profits generated by commodity production. Consequently, this is a mutually reinforcing relationship that contributes greatly to the institutionalizing of the sciences and technology as hegemonic discourses. This is the process of rationalization that Weber analyzes so carefully. Like the discourse of the commodity, those of science and technology impose their own distinct instrumental forms on the objects they explain, and incorporate them into logics of their own. This incorporation results in a radical transformation of the object.

The latter is reconstructed within a different transcendental horizon. As Habermas shows, this is an empirical, instrumental horizon in which objects are constructed from the point of view of an interest in their technical manipulation and control.[9]

Habermas also suggests that the categories of this transcendental horizon produce two effects that are related to its tendency to negate or eclipse alternative categories and conceptual constructions arising from the transcendental horizons of nonscientific discourses that are not interested in technical control. First, these alternative categories and concepts are systematically devalued and the cognitive claims based on them categorically rejected. The historic battle between science and religion in the West is a good case in point. Second is the tendency to delinguistify the objects that are incorporated into scientific and technical discourses. According to Habermas, our everyday experiences of objects are profoundly shaped by their inscription in language. The latter imposes a dialogical form on them, which also embeds them in a system of communicative rationality. These dialogical and communicative structures are important foundations of the interactive practices of communities. The instrumental categories of science and technology can erode these linguistic foundations because the logics into which they incorporate objects are usually of a monological—that is, quantitative, deductive, or inductive—nature rather than a dialogical one. Added to the corrosive powers of the dynamics of commodity production, we can begin to see why this marriage has been such a threat to the norms, ideals, and interactive practices of communities.

Ever since its inception, this system of commodity production has been characterized by an expansionary logic, pushing it to incorporate new areas of human activity both at home and abroad. Thus, it should come as no surprise that this system of production and exchange did not stop with the incorporation of material goods. Particularly in the second half of the twentieth century, capitalist firms have moved aggressively to incorporate cultural creation into the sphere of commodity production. This industrialization of cultural practices becomes feasible as technology makes the mechanical reproduction and dissemination of cultural and informational products possible. As these technologies have become available, more and more cultural artifacts are being mechanically reproduced as commodities. From newspapers, magazines, and books to music, acting, and most recently computerized information, we can see this progressive incorporation of culture into the sphere of commodity production.

Again, what is important for us here is the impact of the superimposing of the commodity form along with its competitive and technocratic logics on the discursive processes that generate cultural and aesthetic value. A clash comparable to that between use-value and exchange-value ensues, radically transforming the power and practices of cultural discourses to create and legitimate realities. Thus, it is exchange-value that allows the process of commodification to establish links between cultural and economic productions. Habermas describes this clash between cultural and technocratic value as the colonization of the life-world by systems of instrumental action.[10] This technoscientific colonization has dramatically increased the differentiating and autonomizing of discourses into specialties that must deal in some way with the hegemonic status of the sciences. The result has been a progressive fragmenting and abstracting of experience whose dispersions and diffractions are currently being viewed through the prism of language, the latest discourse to differentiate and autonomize itself. This could very well be the key to the phenomenon of postmodernism. Hence Fredric Jameson's attempt to explain it in terms of the cultural logic of late capitalism.[11]

COMMODIFICATION RACIALIZATION AND CULTURAL HYBRIDIZATION

So far, my examination of the commodity discourse of Western capitalism has shown that it is marked by strong exclusionary and recoding practices that have given rise to oppositional and corrosive relations with a wide variety of cultural practices that have been vital for community life. However, to grasp the full impact of this discourse on African American communities, we need to look at some additional ambivalences and exclusionary practices not mentioned so far. Unlike those discussed, these additional ones become much clearer when I focus on the global impact of this commodity discourse, and not just its impact on the societies of the West. These additional ramifications are particularly clear in territories colonized by the West. These territories were in many ways "the other" of the West, and hence were seen and treated differently.

In the colonies of the capitalist periphery, the primary discursive allies of commodification were not science and technology but processes of racial inscription and cultural colonization. In other words, the primary cultural changes accompanying peripheral commodification were not processes of rationalization and scientization as Weber and Habermas describe in the case of the West. On the contrary, their places were taken by processes racialization and cultural hybridization that were systematically linked to the legitimacy needs of the repressive conditions under which labor and colonial rule were secured in the peripheral areas.

Racialization was a radical form of dehumanization that was distinct from the dehumanizing tendencies of commodity and technocratic discourses. Racialization dehumanizes through processes of biological inscription that radically detaches identities from cultural meanings and practices. Identity is confined largely to the body or aspects of it. Thus, Africans ceased being

Akan, Yoruba, or Igbo and became Blacks. The Chinese became Yellow, Native Americans and Native Caribbeans became Red, while the people of India became Brown. Confronting these racialized groups, Europeans became White. These racial inscriptions were then linked to Western origin narratives, stories of conquest, and civilizing missions and so developed into fullblown legitimating ideologies. It was in this context that Faust, hero of development in the West, became Prospero in the periphery.

Accompanying these racial transformations in identity were processes of cultural hybridization. These resulted from the control that colonial elites had to exercise over indigenous cultural systems if they were to resolve their legitimacy problems. Thus, indigenous practices that delegitimated the colonial order or legitimated the precolonial order had to be suppressed. Furthermore, hierarchical relations were established between the discourses of one cultural system and those of the other. Thus, the result was not the colonization of the peripheral life-world by systems of scientific and instrumental action; rather, it was the colonization of one life-world by another. This resulted in asymmetrical processes of semiosemantic borrowing, mixing, and resisting in which subordinate cultures were more profoundly transformed than the hegemonic ones. The two cultures are locked in what Rex Nettleford calls "a battle for space."[12] This was the structure of domination that gave rise to processes of hybridization that eventually creolized the identity of many peripheral societies as in the cases of the Caribbean and Black America.

These processes of racialization and cultural hybridization, along with those of commodification and technocratic rationalization are vital for understanding both the modern identity of African Americans and the chaos that is threatening their communities. Indeed, to grasp these forces threatening African American communities it is better to view the latter as parts of the periphery rather than of the center of American capitalism. Thus, the economies of these communities have been for the most part dependent, "monocrop" economies that, like the external colonies, are still trying to industrialize themselves and find a stable place in the world economy. In the domain of ego-genesis or self-production, African American communities are marked by self-formative processes that result in racially distinct oppositional tendencies that W. E. B. Du Bois labels double consciousness.[13] E. Franklin Frazier sees the racialization of the African American self-formative process as producing inferiority complexes that required compensatory projects of recognition.[14] One of these was the Black bourgeois practice of exaggerating the significance of its entrepreneurial activities. Both of these characterizations are similar to Frantz Fanon's portrait of the racialized Afro-Caribbean identity.[15] Thus, my primary task in the remainder of this chapter is to examine the impact of this raced process of commodification and related processes of cultural hybridization on the productive and self-formative domains of African American communities.

AFRICAN AMERICANS RACIALIZATION AND COMMODIFICATION

The intricate and multidimensional webs of interactive practices that characterize Black communities, whether in Brazil, the Caribbean, or the United States have deep roots in Africa.

Indeed, it is the modernization and commodification of African communal structures within the African American context that is my primary concern here. From these African beginnings, African Americans inherited a strong sense of community. Both the personal and collective identities that helped to define African American communities were systematically linked to spiritual discourses that thematized the problems of human self-formation in terms of the ego's relationship to its unconscious ground. This originary ground was conceptualized polytheistically as a pantheon of gods and goddesses who were actively involved in the process of human self-formation and were therefore capable of determining the fate of an individual or group. In other words, early African American identities were inscribed in mythic and religious discourses of fate and destiny, which also provided the discursive legitimization for communal norms and interactive practices. The rise of modern African American identities and community structures in response to processes of commodification, cultural hybridization, and racialization must be traced against this African background.

As noted earlier, Western capitalism has always been an international system of production that requires peripheral areas to supplement the activities in its imperial centers. The commodification and racialization of African Americans cannot be separated from these imperial projects of Western capitalism. Indeed, the African American experience, like that of South Africa, was a case of double colonization—external and internal. This colonial experience linked the process of commodification to those of racial and class domination in such a way that African American patterns of class/race exclusion from the larger American community would be different from that of all other ethnic groups.

As British imperial possessions, the American colonies had their peripheral functions to perform—the supplying of agricultural goods. Thus, the southern colonies in particular emerged as important agricultural peripheries, producing tobacco and cotton for export to Britain. The Caribbean colonies were doing the same with sugar. The modern commodification of African existence begins with the purchasing of Africans as slaves to work on these "New World" plantations. This forced commodification of African labor in these systems of plantation production would lock the train of Black modernity along an oppressive track whose major stops have been sharecropping, persistent poverty, economic underdevelopment, racial exclusion, and ghettoization.

The commodification of African American existence began not with the commodification of goods, but with the previous imposition of the commodity form on the labor of this group. Inscribed in this way, African Americans were instrumentalized, dehumanized, and traded on auction blocks and in labor markets. Like the experience of Africans on Caribbean plantations, this was not the standard imposition of the commodity form on units of labor power. As C. L. R. James suggests, this imposition was the work of a capitalist like Herman Melville's Captain Ahab or William Shakespeare's Prospero, who inhabited racialized commodity worlds.[16] Hence the emergence of race as a fellow traveler on the train of African American modernity.

This grafting of race onto the commodity form, this integrating of racial and commodity discourses is extremely important for any analysis of the nature of economic life in modern African American communities. It introduced a distinct set of dynamics into African American economic life that both reinforced and contradicted the accumulative and extractive logics of commodity discourses. As Fanon points out, racial domination strives to maximize the othering and excluding of its subjugated group, and not the extracting of surplus labor time as in the case of class domination. The logic of racial domination is realized in apartheid, that of commodity production in capital accumulation. Consequently, the racialization of African Americans introduced an exclusionary dynamic that did not follow directly from their commodification.

These exclusionary tendencies have left their mark on all of the major institutions of modern African American communities. These institutions all have a double aspect much like the double consciousness of which Du Bois speaks. On the one hand, these institutions had to reproduce Black labor power for White-owned plantation economies. In this limited function, they were a part of the larger White society. On the other hand, those reproductive activities had to be carried out in Black communities that were racially separated from White ones. For example, African American women were indispensable sources of labor in the reproduction of White families, while their own reproduction took place in racially separated communities. Similar patterns of separation and segregation mark the religious, educational, and economic lives of American Blacks. These separations demanded by the logic of racial inscription, manifested themselves residentially and normatively, but most profoundly at the categorical level of the difference in value between White and Black lives.

These dualist tendencies toward parallel but separate institutions in American society have been widely recognized by scholars of Black life. Thus, in spite of being Christian, the separation between Black and White churches is well established in the scholarly literature. The same has been true for colleges and universities. In the professions, whether law, engineering, sociology, or political science, we can observe tendencies to form separate professional associations as a result of processes of racialization and racial exclusion.

However, in the study of the economies of African American communities, the institutional dualism produced by racialization tends to be overlooked. Unlike studies of Black churches or Black colleges, most studies of Black economic life do not assume a racially separated economy whose leading sectors, rates of growth, patterns of ownership and investment, wage structures, and balance of "imports" and "exports" are systematically linked to the quality of economic life in Black communities. In the case of Frazier, this economy was dismissed because it was at the center of the "make-believe" world through which the Black bourgeoisie dealt with its inferiority complex.[17] Among Black Marxists such as James Boggs it was rejected for development strategies based on social ownership and control by the Black community.[18] More often than not, these studies tend to assume the existence of one economy—a national but White economy from which Blacks are excluded. The persistent poverty of African American communities is assumed to follow from this exclusion. The value of this claim is well established in the literature. Thus, my aim here is not to contest the importance of job discrimination, rather, it is to suggest that an exclusive focus on job discrimination often makes invisible the other half of the dual set of economic institutions demanded by racialization. In other words, is there a set of Black economic institutions that are the equivalent of the Black church or Black colleges and hence should be treated with the same importance? I argue for an affirmative answer to this question. Furthermore, I suggest that the structural transformation of these economic institutions must be a part of any comprehensive program for change.

COMMODIFICATION AND THE
POLITICAL ECONOMY OF BLACK AMERICA

One of the distinguishing marks of the process of commodification in peripheral areas has been the very high level of violence that accompanied the rise of their modern political economies. Organized violence has been an integral part not only of the formation of these political economies, but also of their day-to-day functioning. In addition to the class violence associated with the extraction of surplus labor, the constitutive violence of peripheral economies was also racial and political as racial groups had to be subordinated and local sovereignties displaced. The mobilizing of this violence was also used to impose a number of institutional constraints that severely limited the capacities of peripheral economies to diversify, innovate, expand, and hence accumulate capital. Thus, imperial Britain, through the Board of Trade, imposed a large number of restrictions on the economic activities of the American colonies that became important factors in their anticolonial revolt.

In corresponding ways, the racialization of African Americans within the imperially restricted contours of the American colonial and postcolonial economies produced a racially restricted set of economic institutions that crippled African American capacities for growth and accumulation. As noted earlier, the commodification of African American economies begin not with goods, but with the imposition of the commodity form on African American labor power. Thus, it should come as no surprise that the dominant output shaping the structure of early African American economies was the forced expenditure of its labor power on White-owned plantations, in exchange for the barest of reproductive needs. Supplying these plantation demands for labor became the foundational and major activity of Black economies. Labor was their major "export" and their "leading sector." Reproducing the bodies that were the carriers of this labor power consumed the major allocations of already meager resources in these economies. In short, the production of this commodity laid the foundations for the labor-exporting nature of African American economies.

The structural impact of the dynamics of this labor-exporting activity goes a long way in explaining many of the distinguishing features of African American economies. First, like so many other peripheral economies, this was a narrowly specialized economy that approximated the condition of being a "monocrop" economy. Given the proportion of its labor resources that were allocated to plantation production, all other economic activities undertaken could only be done on a small scale. Thus, whether it was the cultivating of slave plots, doing odd jobs, or plantation production among free African Americans, these could not develop into major sectors of these economies. In short, the patterns of resource allocation constituted major obstacles to innovation and diversification into alternative areas of production. Hence the persistence of labor exporting as the monocrop of these economies.

Second, this near exclusive practice of exporting labor to White plantations gave rise to patterns of dependence on external demand that persist into the present. The monopsonistic hold of the plantation separated processes of supply and demand within African American economies, creating disequilibria that inhibited internally driven growth. The major demands to which the production of supplies of labor was directed were located outside of African American communities. Thus, economic production was progressively separated from demands generated within African American communities and over which they could have exercised some measure of control. Consequently, the growth of production in response to one set of economic demands generated within African American communities did not stimulate production in other areas of these economies. These kinds of linkage effects are the basic building blocks of economic growth. However, these were effectively inhibited by the near exclusive orientation of Black supplies of labor to the demands of White plantations. This separation of Black supply from Black demand could only mean Black economic dependence on White demand. If these economies were not racially separated, this would not necessarily have been a major problem as some of the profits generated from this use of Black labor would be reinvested in African American communities.

Third, as African American economies began as slave economies, they were systems of production in which workers were not paid wages but given in exchange for their labor the barest measure of their reproductive needs. This particular mode of labor exchange meant that these economies were underfinanced and therefore could develop only the most rudimentary financial institutions. Under these conditions, accumulating capital was a rare occurrence. When it did occur, it was among a small number of free African Americans. In other cases, the African American invested first not in a business venture but in his or her own freedom or that of a relative. Thus, the possibilities for growth driven by repeated cycles of accumulation and investment were effectively blocked in these economies.

From these structural features, we can conclude that the first African American economies were externally dependent labor exporting economies, with strong tendencies toward stagnation, and virtually no capacity for accumulation, diversification, and growth. These features cannot be separated from the double existence of these economies. What was distinctive about this existence was its location in racialized economic spaces, where racially coded patterns of supply and demand blocked possibilities for accumulation by African Americans on either side of this double economic life. Under these conditions, commodification did not produce wealth, but previously undreamt levels of immiseration that dramatically increased the coefficient of adversity in Black existence.

POSTSLAVERY AFRICAN AMERICAN ECONOMIES

The next major phase in the economic formation of Black America was the introduction of wage labor at the start of the postslavery period. This period also saw the urbanization and national dispersal of African American communities, as Blacks began leaving the South in large numbers. The responses of African Americans to these developments produced two important changes in their economic life: one was rural and the other was urban. The rural shift was an attempt to convert the practice of exporting plantation labor into one of independent farming. However, this was blocked by lack of access to both finance and land. What resulted instead was a system of sharecropping in which most of the labor expended by rural African Americans continued to be "exports" to White plantation economies. The major difference with the slave system was that African American workers did get to keep a small portion of the surplus produced. However, the size was such that workers were constantly in debt to meet basic reproductive needs. These sharecropping economies were also located in racialized spaces that were similar to those of the slave economies. Hence the continuation of Black immiseration.

The urban transformation was the result of Black migration out of the South to urban areas of the North and West to fill industrial demands for labor in these sections of the country. Although demanding a different type of labor, this shift did not constitute a major break with the old pattern of labor exporting. This activity remained the dominant sector of these urban Black economies. Here, African American economies were exporting labor not to plantations but to White-owned industrial factories that were located outside of Black communities and whose profits would not be reinvested in their economies.

In spite of this continuing dependence on White demand for labor, John Sibley Butler shows that the urban transformations of the postslavery period included the first major attempt by a racial or ethnic minority in the United States to develop an enclave economy as a strategy of development.[19] As many studies have shown, the initial arrival of Blacks in the North was not met by their immediate economic and social isolation. Their economic activities were not forcefully confined to highly racialized spaces. Taking advantage of this more open economic environment, African Americans began using their savings to open small businesses. This turn to entrepreneurial activity was encouraged nationally by Booker T. Washington's National Negro Business League and organizations such as the National Negro Press Association and the National Negro Insurance Association. As Frazier points out, these organizations as well as earlier groups of Black entrepreneurs emphasized values of piety, thrift, and profit making in the "bourgeois spirit represented by Benjamin Franklin."[20] Between 1867 and 1917, the number of African American enterprises increased from 4,000 to 50,000. These were service-oriented enterprises—restaurant owners, caterers, grocers, barbers, and undertakers—some of which served an exclusively Black clientele, while others had both White and Black clients. In addition to these types of enterprises, the postslavery period also saw the rise of Black banks, insurance companies, and mutual aid societies, giving rise to an emergent financial sector and a tradition of saving for investment.

With these types of entrepreneurial undertakings and basic savings and credit institutions in place, the stage was set for the growth of a classic American ethnic enclave economy in which entrepreneurship played a key role in the generating of income and wealth. All that was needed was a continuing increase in outside patronage of these enterprises that were also rooted in the economic demands of Black communities. This combination of internal and external patronage is necessary for the volume of demand required to make these enterprises profitable. In other words, these enclave economies needed to produce "Little Africas" where people of African and non-African descent would shop and eat as they would in Little Italy or Chinatown. However, as is well known, this did not occur. Instead of enclave economies and Little Africas, there emerged ghetto economies. Between 1900 and 1940, the more open economic spaces of the North were systematically racialized and closed as the number of African Americans migrating from the South increased. The new policies of racial ordering were based on the spatial confinement of the residences of African Americans, out of which came the ghettos of many northern cities. The ghettoizing of African Americans represented a new form of racialization that emerged out of explosions of White violence in the race riots that marked the first two decades of the twentieth century. As Douglas Massey and Nancy Denton show, this violence was followed by a series of real estate and other economic practices that institutionalized the forced retreat of Blacks from White areas.[21] They also point to the importance of neighborhood improvement associations, the Homeowners Loan Corporation, and the Federal Housing Administration in these projects of ghettoizing African Americans. Ghettos in urban areas like New York, Chicago, and Washington were Black cities within White ones. As complex urban structures, they contained Black economies that ran parallel to the White ones outside of the invisible walls of the ghetto.

The difference between these ghetto economies and enclave economies is the extent to which the racialized spaces of the former cut them off from external patronage. Ghetto economies do not exist in open socioeconomic spaces where customers can be attracted by types of incentives and forms of advertising. On the contrary, they exist in racialized spaces that are to be avoided. This cutting off of external patronage is in my view a major factor in the failure of the African American experiment in enclave development. Also important in this regard was the high level of White ownership of the real estate and retail sectors, the two most lucrative areas of Black urban economies. This pattern of external ownership of key sectors mirrored that of many peripheral economies. In addition to these factors, Frazier identifies two other factors affecting the failure of Black enterprises. The first is what he describes as the "sociological fact that the Negro lacks a business tradition, or the experience of a people who, over generations, have engaged in buying and selling."[22] The second is the already noted psychoexistential fact of the unrealistic compensatory inflatings of its activities by the Black bourgeoisie in response to its inferiority complex. These four factors are all connected and can be brought together to provide a more comprehensive explanation.

The failure of the ethnic enclave experiment meant that entrepreneurship and Black business would not constitute an alternative to the exporting of labor and that African American economies would continue to be dependent on external White demands for labor as primary sources of income generation.

However, the composition of these labor exports continued to change with urbanization, thereby developing a small elite of professionals—craftsmen, doctors, lawyers, entertainers, professors, and clerks—in addition to industrial workers. This is the factor that leads Frazier to make the claim that the economic basis of the Black middle class was its professional fraction and not its entrepreneurs.

AFRICAN AMERICAN ECONOMIES AND THE NEOLIBERAL TURN

The failure of the postslavery enclave strategy did not end African American attempts at economic transformation. The onset of the depression and the rise of the New Deal brought important shifts in the political economic outlook of African Americans. The historic ties to the Republican Party and the belief in the small business strategy were replaced by new ties with the Democratic Party and a turn to the agency of the state for the initiatives and programs that would transform Black economies. However, it took the civil rights movement and urban uprisings of the 1960s and 1970s for this shift to bear some real fruit. These were the policies of desegregation, affirmative action, job training, and loans to small business. The latter two were essentially emergency measures that did not address in a comprehensive way the complex set of factors blocking Black economic growth.

The job training programs only reinforced the labor exporting tendencies. The loan policies of the Small Business Administration addressed the credit needs of Black businesses but left their problems with external ownership and racially restricted markets unaddressed. The failure of these state-led policies meant that the train of Black economic development was not dislodged from its ghettoized labor exporting tracks. Thus, in spite of the dynamism of this period which saw the rise of Black mayors in a number of cities, the economic results were disappointing.

Since the early 1980s, the liberal ideologies that justified the previously mentioned state policies have been replaced by neoliberal ones of a more conservative nature. The latter tend to emphasize the market and private-sector initiative in economic development. However, in this case the private initiatives being privileged by the state are those of the big corporations. Consequently, the neoliberal turn has essentially been about corporate restructuring in the face of growing competition from abroad. On the home front, this restructuring has emphasized such changes as the replacement of the liberal state by a conservative corporate state, reducing state regulation of capital including affirmative action procedures, making capital more mobile internationally, supporting it with supply side incentives from the state, and weakening both unions and the enforcement of labor legislation. Within the framework of this new political economy, American corporations have been able to restructure themselves. Through mergers and acquisitions they have gotten larger; and through massive layoffs, wage cuts, new technologies, and reductions of benefits, they have been able to cut labor costs. The result has been a period of intense competition, hypercommodification, and soaring profits that has led some to see an emergence of a "winner-take-all society."[23]

In this new era of economic Darwinism and hypercommodification, it should come as no surprise that the specific economic problems of Black communities have basically been ignored. A small number of African Americans have been able to share in this boon through the sale of more technical labor or through investments in a very bullish stock market. This has expanded the size of the Black middle class but has not affected the residential segregation or the economic disequilibria of Black communities that continues to inhibit their capacities for generating wealth. Consequently, from this neoliberal period we can only expect contradictory results: an increase in "the gross domestic product" of Black economies most of which will be absorbed by two groups: first, a small number of Black millionaires who make their money in entertaining, sports, or the stock market; and second, a growing but still small middle class whose professional labors will continue to increase in value in White labor markets. Left out will be a working class whose skills are declining in value, and a growing underclass that has been outside of any of these economies, Black or White. The fate of these discarded individuals will have to await a new economic upsurge that will be able to mobilize some of the capital from this round of Black accumulation.

COMMODIFICATION CULTURE AND BLACK EXISTENCE

More often than not, analyses of African American culture have been separated from the kind of economic analysis carried out in the previous section of this chapter. However, there is no need to repeat that practice here, as one of the advantages of the concept of commodification is that it allows us to bring together cultural and economic analyses. We are able to do this because it allows us to grasp both cultural meanings and economic use-values from the point of view of their modern inscription in a discourse of profit-oriented production. The disadvantage is that it exposes us to dangers of economic reduction, which I will do my best to avoid.

Particularly in the case of African Americans and other peoples of African descent, this continuity between the commodification of material goods and nonmaterial cultural practices is easy to observe. It becomes quite clear if we again make our starting point the commodification of African American labor in the contexts of the plantation and industrial economies of America. Translated from abstracted economic systems into the lived experiences of everyday African American men and women, this history of African American labor in commodity form issues into a complex oppositional discourse. In its complexity, this discourse echoes not only many of the politico-existential themes of alienation, loss, and rebellion of Marx's *Economic and Philosophical Manuscripts*, but also racial themes that reflect the distinctness of the African American experience. These experiences of negation as slave and wage laborers and the counterattempts at negating these negations became important creative bases from which African Americans would redefine themselves, transform their African cultural heritage, and attempt to establish a place for themselves in America.

Unlike the negations of self produced by the imposition of the commodity form, the negations or experiences of not being able to be that traditional African cultures addressed were primarily spiritual in origin. These were cultures that prioritized the spiritual foundations of existence and saw the latter's existential significance in the ways in which they supported, regulated, or negated the activities and choices of the human ego. As noted earlier, the spiritual dimensions of existence were discursively represented as gods, goddesses, and ancestors who were actively involved in the making and day-to-day functioning of individual human selves. They rewarded the moves and choices they perceived to be good and vetoed those they thought to be bad. Vetoing took the form of sickness, paralysis of will, weakening of motivation, and social failure—negations that left the ego open to experiences of not being able to be, and hence to anxieties over its spiritual fate. Thus, the affirmation of our choices for ourselves and the realization of personal goals were always subject to these types of spiritual negations. Not surprisingly, these were the negations of human self-affirmation that traditional African cultures were skilled at resolving.

With the commodification of African American labor on the plantations of the American South, self-affirmation encountered new forms of negation that the African heritage had not directly addressed. These new modes of not being able to be stemmed directly from obstacles that commodification placed in the way of African American attempts at fashioning and realizing positive images of themselves. This estrangement from posited images of self could be very easily thematized by the discourse on alienation that Marx outlines in the *Economic and Philosophical Manuscripts*, in which the existential dimensions of the modern commodification of labor are very clearly laid out.

In addition to these class-based negations that followed directly from the process of commodification, African Americans also had to deal with negations that were more directly related to the racialization of their identities. To the negations of the commodity form, racialization added the negative status of being inferior because one was Black. This status was embodied in the stereotypical figure of "the nigger." Racialization "niggerized" the identity of African Americans and in so doing radically devalued their humanity in ways and on criteria that were different from the devaluations produced by commodification. Thus, to affirm oneself as a nigger was in effect to negate oneself. Consequently, positive self-affirmation required overcoming, getting around, or negating this stereotype that was deeply entrenched in White America.

The consequences of this racialization of the African American identity are well known and have been extensively discussed. For example, Du Bois sees it as producing a fundamental division in the existence of African Americans that he refers to as double consciousness. The double nature of this divided consciousness is its "sense of always looking at one's self through the eyes of others, of measuring one's soul by the tape of a world that looks on in amused contempt and pity."[24] The anguish of this double consciousness derives from its embeddedness in the binary Black/American, which cannot be resolved as long as America continues to mean White America. This is the source of the restlessness of which Du Bois speaks—the restlessness of "an American, a Negro; two souls, two thoughts, two unreconciled strivings; two warring ideals in one dark body, whose dogged strength alone keeps it from being torn asunder."[25]

A similar set of images emerges from Fanon's analysis of the existential consequences of racialization, or what he refers to as the epidermalization of Black identity. In Fanon's view, positive affirmation of self in the face of niggerization often took the inauthentic paths of wearing White masks. Hence his suggestion that racialization produced an "existential deviation" in the lives of African Americans and Afro-Caribbeans. This deviation is quite similar to Frazier's inferiority complex. As in the case of Du Bois, Fanon's deviation is accompanied by a restless anguish that can be linked to the tensions of the Black–White binary that frame the White masks and the Black identities they must conceal.

More recently, Lewis Gordon has picked up and carried forward this theme of the existential implications of racialization. In particular, he stresses the anti-Black nature of the world created by the West, the strategies of bad faith by which this racist world is maintained, and the tendencies to revolt that it has produced in African Americans. For example, in regard to the first of these three points, Gordon makes the very pointed claim: "for many black people, when the question of their blackness is raised, there is but one challenge from which all others follow. It usually takes the form of another question: what is to be done in a world of nearly a universal sense of superiority to, if not universal hatred of, black folk?"[26] Gordon then goes on to suggest that "it is this question that animates a great deal of the theoretical dimension of black intellectual productions."[27]

In sum, the existential consequences of both commodification and racialization for African Americans were new negations of self that had to be negated or superseded; negations that established socioeconomic and racial blocks along African American paths to social well being. In the language of Fanon, these negations produced existential deviations in the lives of African Americans that required a different set of discursive practices than those inherited from Africa.

According to Frazier, this transformation of the African heritage gave rise to two distinct cultural traditions within Black America: "the genteel tradition of a small group of mulattos who assimilated the morals and manners of the slaveholding aristocracy; and the other, culture of the black folk who gave the world the spirituals."[28] The genteel tradition developed primarily among the mulattos of Charleston and New Orleans and then moved to other cities. However, with the ending of slavery and the rise of professional middle classes in African American communities, the social privileges that sustained the distinctness and leadership of this class quickly eroded, resulting in its demise. With this change in class leadership, the genteel culture of the mulattos gave way to a more consumer-oriented culture at the center of which was money and its related processes of commodification.

The Black folk tradition was the culture produced by the masses of African Americans. It emerged in the rural communities of the South, particularly in the cotton belt. Thus, it was linked to the plantation and the system of sharecropping. At the center of this culture was the Black church. Frazier suggests that it was in the church that African Americans had found a meaning for their existence, which had been so profoundly problematized by the new negations associated with racialization and commodification. It was "in the church that the Negro Spirituals or religious folk songs, were born."[29] These spirituals were some of the more important original creations of African Americans in response to the new challenges in their changed existential situation. Consequently, they were important steps in the birth of African American culture. For Frazier, "the spirituals reflected, on the whole the philosophy of the Negro folk. This philosophy represented an attitude of resignation in the face of a hard fate—the struggle to make a living and realize himself in a world dominated by the white man."[30] Here, the existential themes in Frazier's analysis are quite explicit.

Just as urbanization and migration out of the South destroyed the genteel tradition, so in Frazier's view it destroyed the Black folk tradition. Cut off from its roots in the rural South, the Black folk tradition became a secular parody of the original that African Americans were abandoning for the more scientistic and nonfolk culture of Euro-America. In this declining secular incarnation, the spirituals became the blues and storefront churches became neofolk attempts to cling to the religious traditions of the past. The religion of urban African Americans was thus a crisis-ridden attempt to adapt rural solutions to urban negations of self that were more deeply secular in their origins. Consequently, without greater access to urban resources, the urban Black American is likely to be more open to experiences of nonbeing as his or her declining cultural resources are less able to cover rising existential deficits. This I think is a deeper sense in which Cornel West's discussion of rising levels of nihilism in Black communities should be read, and not in terms of discourses of family pathology.

Although a little over forty years have passed since Frazier wrote *The Black Bourgeoisie*, we are still moved by the power of his analysis and the continuing relevance of so many of his insights. But in spite of these lasting contributions, we must raise the question of the accuracy of Frazier's account of the modernization of African American culture in the light of the civil rights movement and the current neoliberal turn.

With regard to this issue, three important points can be made. The first concerns Frazier's acculturative approach to problems of modernization. His approach to the modernization of African American culture is strongly influenced by the culture contact theory of Robert Park. Drawing on this theory, Frazier identifies six broad areas of "race and culture contact"[31] that emerge from the global expansion of western Europe: the United States, Latin America, the Caribbean, Africa, Australia/New Zealand, and the "older civilizations of Asia." Frazier then uses the concept of acculturation to theorize the cultural changes that resulted from these contacts. In particular, he links the degree of acculturation to the density and hierarchical nature of intergroup contacts. With regard to variations in degrees of acculturation, Frazier sees the highest levels of acculturation as being represented by the African cultures of the New World, while the lowest were represented by the Asian civilizations. The latter, in spite of significant borrowing, particularly in the areas of science and technology, have been able to keep their basic cultural patterns intact. By contrast, the modernization of African cultures, particularly the African American culture, has taken place at the price of a radical uprooting of basic patterns. In other words, African cultures were seen as fragile, premodern formations that were unable to withstand the contact with modern European culture. Hence Frazier's well-known position on the absence of African survival in African American culture. With these African erasures, the modernization of African American culture essentially meant its Westernization.

The problem with this approach is that the concept of acculturation is a very value-laden one. It carries within it a strong bias that assumes the ability of hegemonic cultures to completely absorb or erase subordinate cultures after only partial conquests of the latter. Frazier makes use of this assumed ability of Western cultures too loosely. Thus, the data he often presents provides solid support for a thesis of partial destruction but not the total elimination that he wants to claim. This claim only becomes reasonable if to the evidence of partial destruction one adds the assumption that the West will complete the job.

A less-value laden concept for representing the cultural changes in Frazier's contact situations is that of hybridization, which I have already discussed. I noted that it rests on the assumption that when cultures are in contact there are complex processes of borrowing, mixing, and resisting and attempts at suppression. Consequently, the use of this concept requires microanalyses of specific cultural forms and practices to assess historical trends in the battle for space between the cultures. In other words, when using this concept we cannot assume that we know in advance the outcomes of these battles.

Looking at African American cultures through the lens of hybridization, it becomes easier to raise and answer specific questions about the ways in which African Americans have been resisting, yielding, borrowing, and adapting to their contacts with the West. From this perspective, Frazier seems to have underestimated the extent to which the African heritage continues to influence the lives of African Americans. His position on acculturation is not consistent with the claim that the spirituals and Black religion are paradigmatic cases of the originality of the folk tradition. Both of these are clearly hybrid formations whose African and European elements can be recognized. The revival of African nationalism and Pan-Africanism in the 1960s is just one other indicator of this persisting influence. Another has been the continuing influence of Africa on African American scholarship, one example of which would be the Afrocentrism of Molefi Asante, Malauna Karenga, and Marimba Ani. These all point to the survival of a distinct African American culture in which African elements are still struggling for space.

The second difficulty in Frazier's account of the modernization of African American culture is that it does not directly address the degrees of rationalization that specific discourses of African American culture have experienced as compared to their European American counterparts. As noted earlier, modern commodity production is inseparable from its complex feedback relations with science and technology. These mutually reinforcing relations have helped to institutionalize the sciences in European American culture. This institutionalization of the sciences has succeeded in establishing a normative position for them in European American academies, forcing nonscientific disciplines to evaluate and transform their practices in the light of the achievements of the sciences. Although this process of scientific rationalization has been basic to the modernization of many cultures, there are significant variations in the extent to which it has occurred and the conditions under which it takes place.

As in the case of cultural hybridization, the extent of discursive rationalization has to be examined on a case-by-case basis. Here, too, there is a battle for space as nonscientific discourses resist their "colonization" by the hegemonic sciences. The discursive compromises that result from these struggles differ significantly and make for important differences between modern cultures. Thus, we cannot follow Frazier and assume that "as a result of contacts with the public school, the children of the folk have sloughed off the folk beliefs of their parents and learned the secular, scientific techniques of survival in the urban environment."[32] This is a problematic generalization from contact theory that assumes the power of science to erase the folk tradition rather than develop it.

However, if we pose directly the question of the developmental or nondevelopmental impact of scientific rationalization on the discourses of African American culture, a very different picture emerges. Some practices have remained largely unchanged, some have been dramatically secularized, and some have been reinforced. The resulting discursive compromises and related degrees of scientific rationalization are quite different from those of Euro-America. This would follow from weaker scientific ties with the considerably less significant entrepreneurial establishment in Black communities that Frazier emphasizes. Consequently, any equivalence in scientific outlook can only go so deep. As we move beyond the levels of classroom learning and the consuming of technologically produced commodities, very significant differences begin to emerge. However, these differences do not support the view of the scientific erasure of the Black folk tradition; rather they point to the existence of a dominated but living Creole culture making its own resistances and accommodations to the growth and current hegemony of the sciences.

My third point is that the process of Black cultural commodification is also marked by patterns of difference that are quite similar to those of the process of rationalization. In African American communities, processes of cultural commodification have moved along the tracks of the labor exported to various markets in the European American culture industry. The African American cultural system has continued to produce athletes, musicians, singers, actors, and other artists and entertainers who are absorbed by the culture industries of the European American economy. It is primarily, though not exclusively, through the capital and technology of these industries that the commodification of African American culture has taken place. Thus, Frazier is right in stressing the extent to which the rise of a professional Black bourgeoisie has increased the commodification of African American culture. These factors have been responsible for important areas of convergence or overlap between the commodified areas of both African and European American cultures.

For example, both have had their cultural products inscribed in what Wolfgang Haug calls "commodity aesthetics." This aesthetic he traces to its roots in the contradiction between use-value and exchange-value. From the standpoint of use-value, exchange-value is a means to acquiring a useful object. From the standpoint of exchange-value, "use-value is only the bait" to entice the buyer.[33] This baiting leads to a great concern over the appearance of use-values. For Haug, the key to commodity aesthetics is the extent to which this concern leads to a separating of the sensual appearance of the commodity from the conception of its use-value. This separation establishes the basis for aesthetic illusions on or around the body of the commodity that can be created by the "technology of sensuality."[34]

These dynamics of commodity aesthetics operate in both African and European American cultures as a result of their penetration by the culture industries. But here again, we must be careful in our reading of these points of convergence. First, in spite of its well recognized corrosive powers, we cannot assume that commodification will exhaust the Black folk tradition beyond the point of self-renewal. Again, this is a battle for space whose outcomes we cannot determine in advance. The history of Black music is almost synonymous with this battle against the encroaching powers of commodification, with different periods producing very different compromises with corporate forces. Second, in spite of sharing such battles with European American cultural producers, the entrepreneurial factor also emerges here as an important point of difference in the commodification processes of European American and African American cultures. Black culture industries have been among the most successful of Black enterprises. However, these have for the most part been forced to operate in the racialized markets and economic spaces of the ghetto economy. The success of many of these industries is linked to the fact that their products have been able to reach wider markets without these non-Black patrons having to enter Black communities. Consequently, Black cultural labor is commodified in White culture industries but the reverse is still a rare occurrence. In short, the commodification of Black culture points to a distinct trajectory that cannot be separated from the larger history of Black commodification and the actual patterns of growth and contraction in the discourses and practices of African American culture.

If valid, these three points should remove us from Frazier's view of African American culture as a folk formation whose modernization has cost it its distinct identity. At the same time, they allow us to see African American culture as a distinct Creole formation that is in the throes of a difficult transition from a folk culture to a highbrow but commodified version of itself. Because of the hybrid nature of the folk heritage and the different existential challenges to which it must respond, this culture will continue to be marked by African and racial elements that will set it apart from European American culture. However, its European American heritage and its commodification by the European American culture industry will make this highbrow version an industrialized one with important areas of overlap with its European American counterpart. The future of this still incomplete project must always remain open. Given its record of struggle and survival, if we are to lean in one direction it should be the direction of success.

However, this stand should not be taken to mean that success is at hand. On the contrary, the current neoliberal turn with its dramatic intensification of processes of material and cultural commodification is likely to be a particularly difficult one for the growth of African American culture. We can expect deeper invasions by European American culture industries into the various sectors of the African American cultural system. This should bring with it significant increases in the grip of commodity aesthetics on African American cultural production. As a result, fortunes will be made that will transform both the economic and cultural life of African American communities. However, given the concern of commodity aesthetics with the surface of use-values—their brand names, packaging, advertising, and so on—the competition between products in the sphere of circulation becomes a "competition of impressions."[35] Rather than depth, this is an aesthetic that places great emphasis on "techniques designed to impress."[36] The ascendancy of such a discourse can only occur at the cost of depth and the quality of the aesthetic value produced. Thus, rather than increasing the existential depth or the cosmogonic breadth of African American cultural production, this period is likely to see a contracting of these dimensions. In other words, there are still many more mountains to climb before the highbrow transformation of the African American folk tradition will be complete.

CONCLUSION

If the African American case is instructive, it suggests that all groups with marks of liminal difference will have their own distinct encounters with the various dimensions of the commodification process. Experiences of self-negation, cultural erosion, and economic development or underdevelopment will be particular and distinct. However, it also suggests that the liminalizing of commodification processes, whether through race, gender, or ethnicity will steer them in directions that are disadvantageous for these groups. Consequently, their negatively marked identities are linked to the workings of a capitalist system of commodity production. Who they are and what they can or cannot be is determined in large part by the workings of this system. Hence the need for these groups to be very aware of the impact of such systems of production on both their material and human prospects. Herein lies the potential of the concept of commodification for building bridges between the struggles of various communities that have been liminally marked as different.

NOTES

1. Cornel West, *Keeping Faith: Philosophy and Race in America* (New York: Routledge, 1993), 3.

2. Sylvia Wynter, "Is Development a Purely Empirical Concept or Also Teleological?" in *The Prospect for Recovery and Sustainable Development in Africa*, ed. A. Y. Yansane (Westport, Conn.: Greenwood, 1996), 326.

3. Ferdinand Töennies, *Community and Society* (New Brunswick, N.J.: Transaction, 1988).

4. Émile Durkheim, *The Division of Labor in Society* (New York: The Free Press, 1968), 70–146.

5. Karl Marx, "The Economic and Philosophical Manuscripts," in *Marx's Concept of Man*, ed. Erick Fromm (New York: Frederick Ungar, 1966), 93–118.

6. Max Weber, *The Protestant Ethic and the Spirit of Capitalism* (New York: Scribner's, 1976), 13–31.

7. Jürgen Habermas, *The Theory of Communicative Action*, vol. 2 (Boston: Beacon, 1989), 153–197.

8. Karl Marx, *Capital*, vol. 1 (New York: International, 1967), 25.

9. Jürgen Habermas, *Knowledge and Human Interests* (Boston: Beacon, 1971), 301–317.

10. Habermas, *Theory of Communicative Action*, 2:325.

11. Fredric Jameson, *Postmodernism or the Cultural Logic of Late Capitalism* (Durham, N.C.: Duke University Press, 1991).

12. Rex Nettleford, *Inward Stretch Outward Reach* (London: Macmillan, 1993), 80.

13. W. E. B. Du Bois, *The Souls of Black Folks* (Greenwich, Conn.: Fawcett, 1961), 16.

14. E. Franklin Frazier, *The Black Bourgeoisie* (New York: The Free Press, 1965), 130–149.

15. Frantz Fanon, *Black Skin, White Masks*, trans. Charles Lamm Markmann (New York: Grove, 1967), 141–209.

16. C. L. R. James, *Mariners Renegades and Castaways* (London: Allison and Busby, 1985), 11–39.

17. Frazier, *Black Bourgeoisie*, 153.

18. James Boggs, *Racism and the Class Struggle* (New York: Monthly Review, 1970), 144.

19. John Sibley Butler, *Entrepreneurship and Self-Help among Black Americans* (Albany: SUNY Press, 1991), 143–164.

20. Frazier, *Black Bourgeoisie*, 34.

21. Douglas Massey and Nancy Denton, *American Apartheid* (Cambridge, Mass.: Harvard University Press, 1993), 26–59.

22. Frazier, *Black Bourgeoisie*, 165.

23. Robert Frank and Phillip Cook, *The Winner-Take-All Society* (New York: Penguin, 1996).

24. Du Bois, *Souls of Black Folk*, 16–17.

25. Du Bois, *Souls of Black Folk*, 17.

26. Lewis Gordon, "Introduction: Black Existential Philosophy," in *Existence in Black*, ed. Lewis Gordon (New York: Routledge, 1997), 1.

27. Gordon, "Introduction."

28. Frazier, *Black Bourgeoisie*, 113.

29. Frazier, *Black Bourgeoisie*, 117.

30. Frazier, *Black Bourgeoisie*, 118.

31. E. Franklin Frazier, *Race and Culture Contact in the Modern World* (Boston: Beacon, 1970), 11.

32. Frazier, *Black Bourgeoisie*, 119.

33. Wolfgang Haug, *Critique of Commodity Aesthetics* (Minneapolis: University of Minnesota Press, 1986), 15.

34. Haug, *Critique of Commodity Aesthetics*, 17.

35. Haug, *Critique of Commodity Aesthetics*, 34.

36. Haug, *Critique of Commodity Aesthetics*, 34.

IV

LIBERALISM, POSTMODERNISM, AND THE QUEST FOR COMMUNITY

11

Black Philosophy
As a Challenge to Liberalism

Eddy Souffrant

INTRODUCTION

The discussion that follows critiques individuality as the fundamental constituent of liberalism. I argue that if indeed individuality is the fundamental constituent of the theory, liberalism is at worst unsympathetic to groups and at best relegates group membership to a secondary role. I use Black philosophy to show how skillful thinkers of the theory of liberalism have attempted to recover the latter's reputation.

Critics of liberalism offer that liberalism would lead to an antagonism of groups whereas the supporters of the theory attempt to expand its basic constituents. The debate about multiculturalism is a case in point about whether all groups can be afforded equal respect in a liberal society. Charles Taylor argues that liberalism is essentially a theory of recognition, and that the multiculturalist movement is but the most recent example of the liberal emphasis on individual expression and its recognition. I argue that the strategy for recognition provided within liberalism is only a partially complete strategy. Recognition within the liberal tradition does not assess the full contribution of group membership to the development of individuality.

Liberalists are aware of the deficiency of the theory and have attempted to patch it. But the different patchworks to recover liberalism in light of the recent debates on multiculturalism are unnecessary if one looks at some portions of the liberal works of John Dewey.[1] I argue that if properly understood Dewey's work answers quite satisfactorily the demands of multiculturalism and in the end makes multiculturalism obsolete. Dewey, however, does not answer satisfactorily the contemporary problem of transcultural, transcommunal participation or appurtenance.

GROUP MEMBERSHIP AND PARTICIPATION

Hilary Putnam and Ruth Anna Putnam,[2] while speaking of democratic education and pluralism in American society, suggest that

> [t]he aim , . . . [of culturally diverse curriculum] is to prepare the future citizens of a pluralistic society. A pluralistic society . . . is a society in which members of each group respect the cultures and values of other groups. Respect, unlike mere tolerance, requires some knowledge of the other culture; one cannot respect what one does not know at all. Obviously, in as plural a society as ours, . . . [o]ne would hope that everyone would have some non-superficial knowledge of the history, tradition, art, or literature of at least one group not his or her own.[3]

And later, they remind us that

> [w]e belong, each of us, to more than one community; yet all of us belong to the large community called the United States of America. It is important, . . . that there be many shared interests within that large community; it is also important that that large community engage in fruitful interaction with the smaller communities within it and that those smaller communities interact cooperatively with one another. In fact, unless these latter interactions take place, the large community will be unable to develop sufficiently strong bonds of shared interests.[4]

As Putnam and Putnam emphasize the role of a multicultural curriculum in American society, they reveal a tendency in the multiculturalism debate to conflate issues of culture and ethnic community with those of the political. The community called the United States of America is foremost a political environment, a political community. Political communities, distinguished from ethnic or cultural communities, tend to be whole and self-contained, whereas ethnic communities as we face them in this contemporary world are by definition transnational or supranational. And while Putnam and Putnam have correctly identified the shift taking place in American society, where indeed a multitude of communities are demanding an acknowledgment from others within the larger and shared community, to try to accommodate that transformation, they do not consider the transnational or supranational implications of the presence of ethnic and cultural communities.

The Putnams argue for the importance of inclusion in American democracy and believe correctly, in my view, that the integrative aspect of the American community is achieved by way of the knowledge of the "Other." As one of the most visible of "Other" groups, immigrants have always challenged the strength of the principles of liberal democracies here and abroad. They have tested those democracies' will to inclusion.

The American liberal democratic society is a peculiar democracy in that it has cultivated within its borders immigrants of a sort, excluded groups, who by virtue of their contributions to the sociocultural and socioeconomic viability of the country should not be excluded. To emphasize the point, I would like to introduce a categorization that groups on the one hand indigenous immigrants and on the other hand national immigrants. The former group is composed primarily of individuals that share similar territorial, sociopolitical space with other citizens of a nation-state but are, or have been, nevertheless excluded from complete participation in the sociopolitical life of the political environment even if they had wished to take part in that life. Many groups at some point or other in American liberal democracy fit that category, for example, Native Americans, African Americans, women, gays and lesbians, the mentally and physically challenged, and so on. Reasserting the civil rights of these individuals is one of the many movements that have tried to carve a securely protected place in the traditional structures of the society for the members of these groups.

Many of these indigenous immigrants have been active in helping restore those protective rights to inclusion and participation. The African American experience and the ensuing philosophies based on that experience reflect this active attempt at inclusion in a traditionally exclusionary American liberal democracy. The works of Booker T. Washington and W. E. B. Du Bois help explain why the African American group qualifies as Other. Its experience with the institution of slavery and its legacy has alienated it both as a viable member of the society and as a participant in the sociopolitical life of American society. That as a group the slaves were contributors to the economic life of the society does not in any way diminish my claim of their subsequent alienation from American political life anymore than we need accept that a car or a tilling machine or a donkey is worthy of social and political participation. I maintain here that the inherent exclusionary component of liberalism in its American interpretation of sociopolitical alienation constitutes the canvass against which the works of Washington and Du Bois gain significance as crucial arguments for inclusion in American society.

I contrast these political aliens, these indigenous political immigrants and traditionally excluded persons with national immigrants. Members of this latter group are individuals who are, per force of culture, birth, and place of origin, marked as outsiders of the sociopolitical environment. Citizenship, which is one of the many ways to undermine exclusion, presumably immunizes this type of immigrant from the ills of socioeconomic alienation. Political representation by way of group association is another way to guarantee participation in the political life of the adopted nation-state. As strategies, the argued recognition, citizenship, and political representation are but three of the mechanisms initiated by excluded members of the contemporary American liberal democracy.

Risking redundancy, the works[5] of Du Bois and Washington are indeed significant. But by their very import, these works have also helped cultivate a neglect of another aspect of exclusion: national immigration. National immigration perhaps better referred to here as transnational migration is in my view a novel challenge, a criticism of traditional liberal democracies.

PLURALISM AND THE CALL FOR INCLUSION

Washington in his explicit rejection of the link with Africa[6] concerns himself with the presence of peoples of African descent within the borders of the United States. Du Bois—although aware of the significance of Africa as both a source of culture, identity for in the least, persons of African descent, and an impetus for contribution to American society[7]—does not speak of the transit between adopted and original homelands by peoples of dual nationality or culture. His Pan-Africanism fueled a criticism of the American society in which he lived and worked.

Both Du Bois and Washington, perhaps as a result of the institutions against which they were struggling within American society, interpret inclusion in American society as either a necessary rejection of one's original culture and homeland or an acceptance of their contemporary American society.[8] I will not take this tendency exhibited in Washington's and Du Bois's works as a significant criticism of their views. For it might be corroborated that immigrants, with very few exceptions, in point of fact felt by force of international politics or economics to rid themselves of their initial cultural habits and respective homelands.

For a long time, this severance with the past spoke to the experience of a number of new Americans fleeing persecutions of all sorts. These variedly persecuted individuals, some from Europe, some from Africa, and some from Asia, were in effect being forced to cut ties with their homeland and to strongly plant themselves in their new found home and nation-state.

Successful integration and inclusion in American society in the nineteenth and twentieth centuries depended in large part on one's ability to quickly assert oneself in this new homeland. Enterprise, industry, and individual expression of creativity were valued tools with which to deal with the new environment and these instruments were consistent with the basic tenet of American liberal democracy, that is, that the individual is free to pursue his goals.

The new wave of immigrants is shedding light on a shift in the traditional American experience. The politically persecuted continue to be welcomed in the American sociopolitical environment. The bulk of new immigrants are economic refugees with strong social and cultural ties to their initial homeland. These new immigrants cannot successfully shed their group appurtenance. To echo the quoted thoughts of Putnam and Putnam, the new immigrant is a member of a group and is markedly so. Her language, her mannerism, and her experiences to the New World speak to this point. She is also a member of a family. Were she to opt, in the interest of the individualism of traditional liberal democracy, for a rejection of these memberships, she would nevertheless have to contend more or less temporarily with her categorization by the new found land as Other and alien.

The new immigrant is Other and alien in at least two simple senses. She is new to the adopted cultural space and short of some institutional efforts to incorporate her within the new sociopolitical environment, and she will endeavor lest she perishes to be a contributing component of the adopted land. In this first sense, the motivation to uproot herself from a familiar environment precludes idlesse even in an unfamiliar territory. So the new immigrant in this first sense is aware by force of unfamiliarity with her Other.

The second sense of Otherness follows from the first, for as edifices are erected to acculturate her in the new environment, the sociopolitical forces of the society acknowledge her Otherness. But of course, when the sociopolitical environment does not provide the means for such acculturation, it makes a show of a presumption of sociopolitical homogeneity that denies the significance of the immigrant's contributions while simultaneously asserting her alienage. The point of fact is that regardless of structural amenities for appropriate inclusion, the immigrant is present and is a part of our sociopolitical and socioeconomic environment. Denying that presence indeed is a categorization of her as Other and alien.

The struggle for inclusion is not new to, nor is it typically inconsistent with liberal democracy. The significance of the contribution brought forth by the presence of the new immigrants is that liberal democracy is being challenged to take groups and group membership, in lieu of group representation, seriously.

BLACK PHILOSOPHY AND GROUP RELEVANCE

In the American tradition, the struggle for inclusion is illustrated in the political demands and works of a number of African Americans and other excluded Americans. In its African American version, the challenge to American liberal democracy voiced by Washington and others has highlighted an emphasis on the best means of inclusion for African Americans. One may or may not agree with Washington's assessment[9] that slavery impacted negatively both the Blacks and Whites of American society, but it is significant to notice that for him, one's way "up from slavery" (borrowing his phrase) is by individual enterprise. Contrast his view with another plea for inclusion by Du Bois. In his "The Souls of Black Folk,"[10] Du Bois suggests that Washington's analysis is incomplete. And that contrary to Washington's offer, slavery whether by design or accident benefitted Whites in a society that imposed an awareness of race that when coupled with institutional support (e.g., slavery) distinguished

Blacks from Whites, and Blacks from other Blacks. This observation of separation motivates Du Bois's attempted solution to the American problem of
race-prejudice and its legacy. And for Du Bois, acceptance and inclusion in
American society is achieved as one determines one's cultural contribution.
Furthermore, one gathers that Du Bois's motivation to identify a specifically
African American cultural contribution is also to solve the problem of Blacks'
"double consciousness," a pathology in the context of slavery and oppression
that prevented them from developing a sense of self, independent of the distorted vision of themselves by the Other, the oppressor or the structurally
powerful.

The examples of Du Bois and Washington suggest that the struggle for inclusion, whether of the old immigrants or of traditionally marginalized members of the society, has been accommodated by American liberal democracy.
The accommodation, however, when successful, is such in large part when
the groups that are "let in" have adopted, or do share, some of the fundamental values of liberal democracy. This observation suggests to me that liberal democracy has thrived on presumptions of an atavistic individualism
and of a shared, roughly similar culture.

The old immigrants that have helped shape the recorded history of the
United States shared the ideals of eighteenth- and nineteenth-century Europe. The marginal groups and transplanted individuals used as slaves or
workers in the United States shared or came to partake in as similar a vision
of American democracy and society as did the traditional members of the society. Assimilation in American society meant that the marginal groups ad-
justed to the dictates of individualism or representative democracy.

I have thus far proposed that two African American thinkers, and to a certain extent the debates about the presence of Africans, among others, in the
United States have emphasized until recently one or the other of the previously mentioned aspects of assimilation. The adoption in one form or another of the tenets of liberalism and representative democracy made the transition from outsider to participating alien relatively easy.

The new immigrants with their continued allegiance and transnational
contacts to an original homeland are offering a change in the American fab-
ric that I articulate through the following challenge to American democracy:
How does one maintain allegiance in one form or another to his or her original homeland while actively participating in the American socioeconomic,
and per force, political viability of the country without penalty?

The evidence thus far seems to suggest that the penalty is inevitable. For
one's contribution in American society is not remunerated in political currency. The new immigrant is required to uphold an antiquated or Cold War
comportment of complete uprooting from or rejection of the original homeland. At least three facts ask for a different attitude vis-à-vis contemporary
migration: (1) we are no longer in the era of the East–West confrontation, so

the political justification for a complete, unnatural break with place(s) of origin is not any longer as convincing as it might have been in an earlier time; (2) progress in current technology makes it less attractive for the displaced individual and his or her family (whatever the reason for the displacement) to remain estranged from the culture of origin; and (3) is what I call a requirement of reciprocity. The host countries to which the new immigrants migrate have for the most part a favorable relationship with the immigrants' home countries. The economic or political reasons that have motivated the migration are linked in some way to the host country even if at no other level but the diplomatic one.

Consider the recent events in Haiti (e.g., the Aristide restoration) and the history of its relationship with the United States. Consider the history of France and Algeria, Tunisia, or Morocco. Consider England or Holland and Shell Oil in Nigeria. Consider the history of the relationship of Indonesia with Australia or Japan. The events that have taken place in the countries of Haiti, Algeria, Nigeria, and so on that compel disadvantaged members of those countries to move to a new land are all linked to policies or lack thereof of the older, richer, militarily more powerful member(s) of the given conjunctions.

In short, migration is tightly linked to the international relations of at least two political environments, the country whence the migrants come and toward which they move. I propose a collective responsibility that would yield a mode of interaction whereby these migrants could stay in the homeland and when that option is not available and they migrate to a country like the United States, that at the very least they be granted full "plural membership."[11] Where this international argument does not convince the reader, one could marshal an alternative reciprocity argument that links the actual contribution of the immigrants in the new homeland with their transnationality. Again, plural membership could be assigned on the basis of the contribution of these immigrants to the economic, social, and cultural viability of the host country. Clearly, the immigrants' contribution is, in an ironic twist, supportive of the very political institutions that reject the immigrants full participation but accept a participation that is only associative and representative within the boundaries of the new host land.

Relying again on the contemporary movements of persons, it seems to me that a radical uprooting is unlikely. And since complete displacement of persons from either a home country or culture is neither attractive nor appropriate to the times, the test for global liberal democracies will be their ability to properly accommodate the new immigrants. Can liberal democracy adapt to the change and answer to the new reality?

It will be the task of social scientists and thinkers to delineate not only the constituents of that change, but also the way in which it will be incorporated into the new American democracy. My modest contribution here consists in offering the following: It is important to take seriously a person's group

membership and not simply his or her "political"/representational association. Traditional liberalism—even with its contemporary alterations—has not
satisfactorily included the new immigrant, for she is still being asked à la
Aristotle that her political representation and participation be based on a
conception of citizenry that is antagonistic to the contemporary international
reality.

MULTICULTURALISM TO EXPAND LIBERALISM

Multiculturalism is a conceptual alternative to traditional liberalism as the latter was previously exhibited. On the one hand, in liberalism the individual
creates her social and political environment. And she creates the environment that best suits her atomistic vision. She presumes the public to be antagonistic to her goal, hence she holds dearly to a principle of noninterfer-
ence because her genius is self-realized and primordial for a thriving and
civilized society. Furthermore, she demands that when infringement occurs
against her will that the infringement be justifiable.

In multiculturalism, on the other hand, the individual is and understands
that she is, fundamentally, who she is only as a result of her belongingness,
her membership in a multitude of cultures. For example, she understands
fully that she is born of a particular lineage, that she is a woman, that she is
classified as a member of a particular ethnic group, that she is a professional,
a mother, a loving partner, and so on.[12] And she believes that these attributes
are constitutive and formative of her personhood. In short, the person in the
multicultural schema is aware that she is from a particular culture and that
she also belongs by classification or choice to numerous other cultures.

Notice that the multiculturalist might very well agree with the liberalist in
what constitutes interference. And she might demand that the same limits advocated by the liberalist be elements of her own multicultural sociopolitical
environment. Her point, however, is that the liberalist does not speak of the
sources of personhood. The liberalist, in the multicultural thinker's mind,[13] is
trained to shed his multicultural foundation. The ideal mature person in liberalism is trained to view himself independently, outside or without a community of persons. The mature liberal person is fundamentally alone with his
ingenuity.

And it is not at all by accident that the liberal is fond of clubs. In his search
for significant membership, he becomes a club member, he forms a class of like
minds and training. Notice that exclusionary associations are indeed a trade-
mark of contemporary liberal societies.[14] And the membership in these associations speaks to a dual need of the liberalist. Club membership is believed to
help solve both the problem of isolation and exclusion (which are of particular
theoretical interest to the liberal and his critics) and the necessity of social mem-

bership. I submit, however, that simple aggregatory membership is a substitute and an attempt to recover developmental and cultural belongingness.

The multiculturalist, contrary to the liberalist, acknowledges the value of developmental environments. She realizes that cultural membership is in reality constitutive of the complete person. The alternative proposed to her in this section however, is by no means the only response to the assault of the liberal atomist.

CHARLES TAYLOR'S RECOVERY OF LIBERALISM

As J. S. Mill has proposed in "On Liberty," the sign of a lively and thriving society is in its nurturing of individuality. An expression of individuality is valuable to the extent that the mature person expresses her genius. The ingenious individual in the liberal society shares her unique gift with her fellow citizens. This detour into the productive component of liberalism would seem to strengthen my stand that liberalism is fully antagonistic to nurturing, developmental, and formative environments, the very emphasis of multiculturalist movements. Charles Taylor provides a recovery of liberalism and he appears to incorporate the needs of multiculturalism into the fundamentals of liberalism. Let me examine his success!

The individual given the conception of liberalism mentioned earlier produces that which is consistent with her peculiarities. Given this summary of the view, one need go no further, it seems to me, to realize that the liberal society is fundamentally one of passive or unforced exchange and that its exchange is of the products of the individual's genius. And for this activity to take place one needs an appropriately unobtrusive environment in order to express that genius.

Crawford Brough Macpherson[15] argues that liberalism is discredited given the injustice of property acquisition. The question given Macpherson's analysis is whether we ought to jettison the theory altogether. Short of a dialogue concerning whether Macpherson's analysis makes a show of a lack of understanding of the theory or not, we might do well if we seek to consider liberalism's relevance vis-à-vis contemporary issues to consider whether liberalism can accommodate persons of multiple cultures. Taylor agrees that the problem of liberalism cannot be solved by a deeper understanding of the requirements of the theory. Rather, for him, adapting the theory to the needs of human beings in the contemporary period is a more appropriate route than searching for hidden messages lodged in the entrails of the theory. He proposes a conception of the crucial component of human beings that starts the examination of whether liberalism is a suitable theory for our times and for the issue of multiculturalism. For him:

> This crucial feature of human life is its fundamentally *dialogical character*. We become full human agents, capable of understanding ourselves, and hence of

defining our identity, through our acquisition of rich human languages of expression. . . . But we learn these modes of expression through exchanges with others. People do not acquire the languages needed for self-definition on their own. . . . The genesis of the Human mind is in this sense not monological, not something each person accomplishes on his or her own, but dialogical.[16]

Taylor believes that this essential feature of being human transforms the type of relationship that individual members of a society cultivate. One is no longer, given the traditional conception of liberalism, required to simply leave others alone to express themselves. According to Taylor's "dialogical" interpretation of the human being, one's demand on government or the powers at large are different. One may require of government that it affords equal recognition to everyone's expression. And Taylor understands that equal recognition reinforces a democratic society because

[e]qual recognition is not just the appropriate mode of a healthy democratic society. Its refusal can inflict damage on those who are denied it, according to a widespread modern view, as I indicated at the outset. The projection of an inferior or demeaning image on another can actually distort and oppress, to the extent that the image is internalized. Not only contemporary feminism but also race relations and discussions of multiculturalism are undergirded by the premise that the withholding of recognition can be a form of oppression.[17]

For Taylor, recognition has generally taken two forms in the public arena. Traditional liberalism has emphasized a first type of recognition expressed primarily in the politics of equal citizenship. According to that version of recognition, government or the public institutions proceed to make everyone equal by establishing individual rights and immunities. Taylor contrasts the traditional liberal interpretation of recognition, that is, the recognition expressed in the politics of equal citizenship with the politics of difference. In the latter version, recognition requires an emphasis on the distinct identity of individuals and/or groups that have been glossed over, abused, and to a certain extent neglected by the dominant culture. Notice that these two interpretations of the criterion of recognition are related, and for Taylor the politics of difference is an extension of the politics of human dignity.

It might not be clear how the politics of recognition, the more encompassing conception of the two aforementioned politics, might be related to the project of multiculturalism. Taylor seeks to develop that relationship and considers a general criticism usually brought against traditional liberalism. He articulates that criticism in the following way: "The charge leveled by most radical forms of the politics of difference is that 'blind' liberalism [is itself] the reflection of particular cultures. And the worrying thought is that bias might not just be a contingent weakness of all hitherto proposed theories, that the very idea of such a liberalism may be a kind of pragmatic contradiction, a particularism masquerading as the universal."[18]

If this criticism is warranted, the problem of multiculturalism is shifted from one where particular cultures are not recognized to one where a specific type of culture is camouflaged in the cloak of liberalism, thus eliminating any pretense of objectivity or universalism. So one would understand why Taylor is concerned about not "throwing away the baby with the bath water." The issue of concern is really not, as far as Taylor is concerned, the issue of the relevance of liberalism. For him, liberalism is fresh, relevant, and resourceful. The criticism if sound, is of perhaps the masqueraded culture and perhaps to its claim of universalism. And if Taylor is right, the issue being contested is one of the valuation of cultures, of whether a particular culture might be used as the standard for all others. Taylor admits that liberalism in its foundation does not purport to be culturally neutral. In his expression of a version of multiculturalism, namely, its international aspect, he states:

> Liberalism is not a possible meeting ground for all cultures, but is the political expression of one range of cultures, and quite incompatible with other ranges. Moreover, as many Muslims are well aware, Western Liberalism is not so much an expression of the secular, postreligious outlook that happens to be popular among liberal *intellectuals* as a more organic outgrowth of Christianity—at least as seen from the alternative vantage point of Islam. . . .
>
> All this is to say that liberalism can't and shouldn't claim complete cultural neutrality. Liberalism is also a fighting creed. The hospitable variant I espouse, as well as the most rigid forms, has to draw the line. There will be variations when it comes to the schedule of rights, but not where incitement to assassination is concerned. But this should not be seen as a contradiction.[19]

Taylor's point is that given the history of liberalism, it values a particular culture: Western culture. Furthermore, he suggests that acknowledging this culture does not require a denigration or a denial of the relevance of other cultures. So to the extent that individuals are fundamentally dialogical and that their interactions with others is essential to their humanity, a denial of that interaction or a denial of the propitious environment for that interaction to take place is an affront to the individual human being in need of that nurturing environment.

But to say that liberalism means to recognize that a nurturing environment is essential to one's survival as a human being is not to say that all nurturing environments have equal worth. So for Taylor, affording equal respect to a person's culture is not in any way a determination that all cultures are of equal worth. So he thinks that the multicultural debate is sometimes framed as one where equal value of cultures is demanded.

And if it is presumed that education is one of the primary means by which to maintain and disseminate culture, the demand for the recognition of all cultures is a request for the equal value of all acculturation institutions.

With this as the very fundament that multiculturalists advocate, it is not surprising that, when the demands for recognition are made in the area of education, the proposition asks for greater recognition for women and people of "non-Europeans races and cultures." Furthermore, Taylor contends that even if it were true that liberalism as exhibited in recent sociopolitical settings is hegemonic in character, the politics of recognition necessarily should accommodate curricula that would alter the hegemonic trends. However, the politics of recognition does not support the presumption that all cultures are owed equal respect. Such a presumption would preclude any determination of whether indeed the cultures in question would have made equally important contributions to human beings. Using these contributions as standards for the evaluation of cultures, the claim of equal worth is unwarranted until further evaluation.

Taylor's advocacy of multiculturalism does not support claims of the equal worth of cultures. He argues that the demand for equal worth could be interpreted as a consideration that each culture is equally worthy of consideration vis-à-vis its contribution to humanity. And since equal worth is to be determined once the actual contribution has been registered, multiculturalism would be a goal sought but not yet achieved. In this sense, multiculturalism might be a prescriptive concept: "There is perhaps after all a moral issue here. We only need a sense of our own limited part in the whole human story to accept the presumption [of multiculturalism]. It is only arrogance, or some analogous moral failing, that can deprive us of this. But what the presumption requires of us is not peremptory and inauthentic judgments of equal value, but a willingness to be open to comparative cultural study."[20] In the end, it might be said that Taylor has modified liberalism. Indeed, one might suggest that before his appeal to an openness to "comparative cultural study," Taylor has acquiesced to the accusations that liberalism would deny recognition and perhaps worth to particular cultures, specifically those not consistent with the historically Western tradition.

In a manner reminiscent of the African American struggle exhibited by the writers mentioned earlier, and even in some of its most recent expressions,[21] liberalism is locked within a political, and now given Taylor's elucidation, a geopolitical territory. Thus, liberalism continues the trend first remarked on with the presence of African Americans within American territory. The attempted recovery of liberalism from its silence on formative groups therefore would appear to have failed, but for the alternative that Dewey's work on education in a liberal democratic society proposes, even if an account of transnationalism is absent from it.

DEWEY, EDUCATION, AND DEMOCRACY

Dewey's primary concern in his essays on democracy and education[22] is to strengthen the relationship between those two very concepts. In my understanding, Dewey identifies democracy as a natural process resulting from both increased individualization and, broadly speaking, economic factors. As a natural state of affairs, democracy is vulnerable to numerous negative forces. So, to prevent the passing of democracy, he devises a theoretical instrument that would help nurture the liberating state of affairs found in democracy, which in turn is strengthened by the proper use of education. Dewey assigns a more liberating role to education and asserts that:

> It is not enough to see to it that education is not actively used as an instrument to make easier the exploitation of one class by another. School facilities must be secured of such amplitude and efficiency as will in fact and not simply in name discount the effects of economic inequalities, and secure to all the wards of the nation equality of equipment for their future careers. Accomplishment of this end demands not only adequate administrative provision of school facilities, and such supplementation of family resources as will enable youth to take advantage of them, but also such modifications of traditional ideals of culture, traditional subject of study and traditional methods of teaching and discipline as will retain all the youth under educational influences until they are equipped to be masters of their own economic and social careers. The ideal may seem remote of execution, but the democratic ideal of education is a farcical yet tragic delusion except as the ideal more and more dominates our public system of education.[23]

For Dewey, education is not an instrument to maintain a particular system of subordination, and as such, it is antagonistic to the hegemonic liberalism that expresses itself in domestic or international fora. In addition, Dewey's historical account of education is progressive as it highlights the history, role, and development of education.

With Dewey's analysis, one comes away with the view that education was instrumental in the stratification of society as it subordinated individual expression to ideals of class and state. Those ideals are antagonistic to Dewey's conception of the appropriate interaction of individuals within social boundaries. He argues that recent social and political events have changed the interaction between individuals, and again here it is the interaction within a particular sociopolitical boundary. Consequently, the purpose of education must change to adapt to the times since generally its aim is to nurture the natural forces of history.

The times have witnessed the emergence of a democracy that has helped eliminate the antagonism between the individual and the state. But for Dewey, democracy is not strictly a form of government, it is also a social mode of being:

> A democracy is more than a form of government; it is primarily a mode of associated living, of conjoint communicated experience. The extension in space of the number of individuals who participate in an interest so that each has to refer his own action to that of others, and to consider the action of others to give

point and direction to his own, is equivalent to the breaking down of those barriers of class, race, and national territory which kept men from perceiving the
full import of their activity.[24]

With the immediate relevance of the quotation to us as multiculturalists, it is
also important to grasp the interpretation of democracy proposed here.
Dewey wants to distinguish his contribution from that advanced by those
termed "hypothetical naturalists." These are theorists who hypothesized a
state of nature and who have determined the kinds of government or social
institutions that would be appropriate to maintain an ideal conception of a
thriving individual. In contrast to these individuals, Dewey determines that
the interaction between specific instantiations of these three elements—"nature," "institutions," and "individuals"—has given way to democracy. That is
to say the common interests and capacities of individuals are not the result
of hypotheses but are instead the results of actual economic and migratory
developments on the one hand, and, on the other, increased individualization and common interests. Such forces of history diminish the "distance" between peoples.

In the diminution of that distance is found two constituent characteristics
of democratic society. For Dewey, the democratic society is one where
shared common interests are replaced by mutual interest. Mutual interest is
a source of moral control. For the individual, mutual interest limits the extent
of his or her actions. Mutual interest is a practical moral standard. It guides
the individual's actions.

Dewey is also aware of the significance of groups. He holds that in a democratic society, the interaction between groups is more fluid, and as a result
of the fluidity of interactions, habits change because of the "continuous readjustment through meeting the new situations produced by varied inter-
course."[25] In Dewey's version of a liberal democratic society, that society
does not require the modification suggested by multiculturalism. Rather, it
meets the challenge head on by suggesting that the problem of exclusion
elucidated by multiculturalism is not a problem of democracy but instead is
a problem of attempted hegemony. In other words, it is the problem of antagonistic forces in the natural progress toward democracy.

Dewey would indeed look on the contemporary period and think that the
calls of multiculturalism are reflective of a failure of the members of the society to heed his suggestion that we deliberate. He argues that in order to
maintain a thriving atmosphere of democracy, deliberation is required. For
him to deliberate is to engage in the "free interchange of the varying modes
of life-experiences."[26] Deliberation is useful only when it has been assessed
appropriately what the contemporary state of affairs is and when that state
of affairs is deemed appropriate enough to be maintained. While the multiculturalists wish for a free exchange of varying modes of life, they have not

sustained a progressive democratic movement because in their case deliberation was not undertaken. In the multiculturalism debate, we have ended up therefore, in Dewey's words, with a society of individuals with divergent interests and sterile habits—the very ideal of traditional liberalism.[27]

CONCLUSION

My discussion about Putnam and Putnam, Washington, Du Bois, Taylor, and Dewey ends with the very question that motivated it: What is to be done then when progressively democratic societies purportedly maintain rigid barriers between groups and individuals? A quick answer would be "let's deliberate." Or, perhaps, in the manner of Putnam and Putnam one might opt to familiarize oneself with a different culture. Both solutions, however, presume a shared political space, a shared political culture whose members have adopted the dicta of associative living. The new immigrant, the new resident alien, the new Other has allegiances to more than one political god. To this transnational reality, none of the figures examined in this chapter other than Dewey seem to offer a viable alternative to liberalism's adherence to productive individualism and associative representation. In my perspective, this failure of liberal democracy is not fatal, but it is informative and instructive. Also, we are led to believe that some solutions to the problem of exclusion might be found.

Helped by the philosophies of persons lodged in the darkness of American democracy, for example, Washington and Du Bois, and by persons concerned with the thriving forces of democracy, for example, Putnam and Putnam and Dewey, I hope to have shown that the legacy begun by these individuals must continue despite the current lack of a propitious environment. Dewey reminds us that education breaks down the barriers of national boundaries, class, and race in the manner that democracy, "associated living," and shared interest break down the barriers of individualism and hegemonic tendencies.

Dewey appears to propose at least one answer to the hegemonic exclusion in American liberal democracy. His notion of deliberation, which also shapes Black philosophy's conception of democracy, is one that emphasizes group appurtenance rather than the dominance of an atomistic individualism. Black philosophy was instrumental in this chapter in pointing to an exclusion that sheds light on a distinction between indigenous and transnational immigrants. Although the transnational immigrant challenge has not been explored here, it is my hope that Black philosophy's heuristic value has been displayed. Black philosophy has challenged traditional liberalism to account for group appurtenance. However, I am hopeful that the contribution of my inquiry is also found ultimately in its display of the potential flexibility

of a conception of democracy that neither the liberal nor the ethnic visions
have properly considered.

In an increasingly global environment, forced, singular, and hegemonic
political identity cannot be the primary requirement of a truly democratic environment. The starting point for ensuring the viability of such an environment in the face of global realities necessitates the guarantee of a space
where different modes of living would be experienced. The surge of new
contemporary immigrants is the first sign for the need of such a convivial setting. A conception of global democracy as an environment where the new
immigrant's identity can thrive would be consistent with Dewey's own of-
ferings. Furthermore, it would be an attractive solution to transnationality
given my argument that both liberalism and multiculturalism have failed to
address the issues of the contemporary reality of citizenry. The transnational
or transcultural environment is not yet realized, although its members and
inhabitants are present. It goes without saying that our first steps would be
an appropriate formulation of transnational identity and plural citizenship.

NOTES

1. This chapter was influenced by John Dewey, *Democracy and Education: An
Introduction to the Philosophy of Education* (New York: Macmillan, 1916).
2. Hilary Putnam and Ruth Anna Putnam, "Education for Democracy," *Educational Theory* 43 (4) (fall 1993).
3. Putnam and Putnam, "Education for Democracy," 373–374.
4. Putnam and Putnam, "Education for Democracy," 375–376.
5. See John Hope Franklin, ed., *Three Negro Classics* (New York: Avon, 1965). The
implicit criticism of liberalism by W. E. B. Du Bois and Booker T. Washington are
drawn from Franklin's text where Du Bois's "The Souls of Black Folk" and Washington's "Up from Slavery" are reprinted.
6. See Booker T. Washington, "Up from Slavery," in *Three Negro Classics*, ed. John
Hope Franklin (New York: Avon, 1965).
7. In the third chapter of "The Souls of Black Folk," Du Bois refers to his knowledge of the relevance of peoples of African descent to the international/global community but he reiterates his concern about the plight of Blacks and focuses primarily
on the healing or eradication of the scars of American slavery. See W. E. B. Du Bois,
"The Souls of Black Folk," in *Three Negro Classics*, ed. John Hope Franklin (New
York: Avon, 1965).
8. Cf. Washington, "Up from Slavery," where Washington, by sheer will or ignorance of the facts of his birth, severs any ties with an African and lodges himself firmly
in American soil, slavery, and its institutions. Likewise, Du Bois, despite his adherence to the international import of Africa, concerns himself strictly with the plight of
folks of African descent in the United States of America. While both are concerned
about the American experience of peoples of African descent, I believe that Washington's negation of a link beyond American borders contrasts well with Du Bois's

very insistence on the connection of the various international African struggles against oppression.

9. Washington, "Up from Slavery."

10. See Du Bois, "Souls of Black Folk."

11. In another context, Tahar Ben Jelloun speaks of the way that such attempts could be made. He explains how France and Morocco could develop a mutually respectful relationship that would help integrate members of the Moroccan community in France without racism on the one hand and alleviate the need for exploitative immigration on the other hand. See Tahar Ben Jelloun, *Hospitalité française* (Paris: Seuil, 1984).

12. For a conception of a multicultural society, see Putnam and Putnam, "Education for Democracy."

13. For an example of the multiculturalist, see Putnam and Putnam, "Education for Democracy." Pay particular attention to the contrast they draw between their work and that of Arthur Schlesinger.

14. One could argue that the increasingly transient population of the world has no choice but to indulge in loosely formed associations. And, furthermore, that it is increasingly the case that basic communities are no longer available. The atomistic or rather the liberal individual is becoming more and more a reality. To this perceived reality, I should like to offer the recent debates in immigration studies concerning transnationalism. My understanding of transnationalism suggests that contemporary immigrants are no longer as prone as traditional immigrants to sever all ties with the motherland. In fact, with advances in technology they are strengthening those ties and relationships by their frequent trips and communications with members in the home countries. So to answer the would-be critic of multiculturalism, I would offer that recent movements in immigration are pointing strongly in the direction of multicultural societies.

15. Crawford Brough Macpherson, *The Real World of Democracy* (Oxford: Clarendon, 1966).

16. Charles Taylor, *Multiculturalism and the Politics of Recognition* (Princeton, N.J.: Princeton University Press, 1992), 32.

17. Taylor, *Multiculturalism*, 36.

18. Taylor, *Multiculturalism*, 44.

19. Taylor, *Multiculturalism*, 62.

20. Taylor, *Multiculturalism*, 73.

21. See Bernard R. Boxill, *Blacks and Social Justice* (Totowa, N.J.: Rowman and Allanheld, 1984). Boxill provides among others some contemporary representations of Washington's and Du Bois's views, but he primarily reinforces my point that the struggle for inclusion and the criticism of some aspects of liberal democracy are bordered by the political territory of the United States of America. Taylor echoes the same emphasis even if in this instance he casts his nets wider and encompasses the Western tradition. The recognition that he believes liberalism affords is one that gives precedence to a political tradition. And when speaking of the immigrants, we remember that they are asked to take in a society at a price above and beyond the price of transplantation. They are asked to let go of their culture, homeland, and citizenship to adopt a Canadian, French, or American tradition, and now, as demonstrated in Taylor's work, they are told to acknowledge the preeminence of one of a number

of global traditions: the Western tradition. Displacement continues to be the mark of liberalism despite Taylor's efforts.

22. John Dewey, *Democracy and Education* (New York: The Free Press, 1966).

23. Dewey, *Democracy and Education*, 98.

24. Dewey, *Democracy and Education*, 87.

25. Dewey, *Democracy and Education*, 86–87.

26. Dewey, *Democracy and Education*, 84.

27. Dewey, *Democracy and Education*, 84.

12

Democracy, Transitional Justice, and Postcolonial African Communities

George Carew

Since independence, the problems of justice and fair play have been hotly debated issues in ethnic politics. The diverse populations of most African states have not all enjoyed to the same degree the benefits and opportunities their respective states have to offer, despite the official pronouncement on the part of the leadership to treat all their citizens alike. In this connection, Western democracies, which are based on unified homogeneous models, have served as points of reference. Recently, however, it is the debate in the United States and Canada on social justice in plural societies that has caught the attention of social theorists and human rights activists. These issues are of interest not only to plural societies such as the Untied States and Canada, but also to the emerging democracies of Africa, eastern Europe, and Asia.

The task of this chapter is to show that the fundamental difference between the United States and Canada and the newly independent states of Africa is that the latter are still undergoing a process of democratic transition, which requires not only a political, but also a moral transformation from an unjust to a just social order.

I argue mainly from a social constructivist perspective of racial/ethnic identity. That is, the idea that racial and ethnic identities are not natural or given but socially constructed. I show first that creating moral ethnicity requires a shift from essentialized social relations to relations governed by moral rules. The role of justice in this transitional process will help us overcome the obstacles to the development of moral ethnicity. Second, I argue that this project entails a limited justification of preferential policies because how we get from where we were, with extensive social cultural domination and economic inequality, to a social order that guarantees real freedom for all would require preferential treatment for all those who need help to develop their moral personality.

Let me begin by explaining why I do not approach the issue in the familiar manner of determining legitimate claims by appealing to a retributive model of justice or to some approximate model grounded in the principle of nondiscrimination. Most arguments that appeal to social justice have one serious defect, namely, they tend to focus exclusively on distributive issues, that is, on how wealth, offices, resources, and status are distributed or redistributed in society. The reason why this is an inadequate response to the problem of undeserved inequality is that these periodic redistributions do not eliminate the root cause of the problem. Taking from those who have to give to the disadvantaged does not have the effect of eliminating class distinctions or other forms of social domination.[1] As long as there are obstacles in the path of the oppressed, which deny them equal access to resources, the redistribution of income and so on will provide only temporary relief rather than a lasting solution to the problem of oppression and domination. What I am proposing then is a commitment not only to justice, but also to freedom. A just society in my view is also a free society in which individuals are self-regulating and uncoerced.[2]

CONSTRUCTING A DEMOCRATIC COMMUNITY

The position I have advanced so far presupposes a particular conception of political community. It is a vision of political life as combining human freedom with social justice or a concern for the common good. It will be useful to state this theory at this time because it will provide the ongoing instrument of my defense of transitional justice. The starting point of a social theory is usually a conception of human nature, including an account of basic human needs and capacities, such as the ability to reason and to cooperate with others in the pursuit of a common good. From these accounts, we are able to deduce the general principles or virtues. On the basis of these principles, we can then design institutions and regulate social practices.

Human beings are, generally speaking, affected by "natural" and social forces, which condition their lives. Natural forces such as earthquakes, hurricanes, and tornadoes are events over which we have little or no control and for the most part leave us with a feeling of helplessness. Social forces, unlike natural forces, are the result of human convention. This means that we have the capacity to reshape or refashion our social order if we choose to do so.

When faced with a social order that is hostile to the freedom and well being of human beings, the individual, rational, communicative animal has a moral duty to assist in the creation of a human and moral world. Indeed, it will not only be incompatible with human nature for it not to do so; it will also be suicidal. The capacity for moral autonomy is what distinguishes humans from animals. This is what makes it possible for us to create a harmonious social order that permits us to pursue our desires and interests. Politics is the means by which we can attain the goal of social harmony. Through rational and peaceful discussions we are able to establish rules and procedures that would subsequently guide us in reconciling group differences. Thus, to ignore exercising our capacity for moral autonomy amounts to cultural suicide, and that is to say, either we may very well accept to live in a world that others have created for us and that serves their purpose rather than ours or in the extreme case we may continue to live under the primitive conditions of the so-called state of nature that is completely unregulated by laws.

This is the reason why social orders in which social relations are essentialized are considered dehumanizing, because they constitute identities that are defective and deficient in moral autonomy. It would require the moralization of social relations to create the type of personalities capable of cooperating with others for the common good.

As such, the ideal of collective freedom rests on the universal desire on the part of human beings to create a human and moral world, free of the social obstacles that tend to imprison the minds of people, rendering them helpless and incapable of exercising moral agency.

The ideal of collective freedom faces a formidable challenge in plural societies including groups that are culturally, religiously, and ethnically distinct.[3] How do we establish a basis for collective self-determination among groups that are so diverse?

From the perspective of a social order in which values and preferences are determined by social processes, cultural diversity might present a problem only if social relations are not already governed by moral rules. A social order that is grounded in widespread ignorance and delusions clearly lacks the resources for the individuals or even members of groups to step up and collectively determine their goals. What is required in this case is the moralization of the social order in order to transform essentialized and denigrated identities that are the victims of delusions into morally autonomous persons. Once social relations are based on moral rules, it will be possible to establish shared values that all can endorse.[4]

To achieve greater clarity on the uniqueness of this ideal, I contrast it with a competing ideal, namely, liberal individualism. Liberal individualism is skeptical of the ideal of collective self-determination as the realm of freedom. The basis of liberal skepticism is to be found in the inherent threat collective self-determination poses to individual autonomy. But theorists of collective self-determination have argued that, far from endangering autonomy, collective self-determination presupposes it. I will elaborate.

Liberal critics of collective self-determination take the view that collective freedom implies participatory politics, in which case dissenting minorities might have their preferences overridden. What this shows is that there is no protection for individual autonomy. Theorists of collective freedom have rejected this version on the grounds that it is a version of collective freedom that is derived from rights-liberalism. The notion of collective freedom rooted in social constructivism has built-in safeguards to prevent the corrosion of individual autonomy. The differences between the two views on collective freedom are clearly differences in perspectives with far reaching ontological and epistemological implications. It is useful to explore these implications as they certainly have a bearing on the autonomy question.

Let me consider, for example, liberal individualism. The starting point is that people must be viewed as individuals rather than as members of groups. This is because on the abstract unified model, which underlies liberal individualism, group difference and other particularities are excluded because they are deemed to be politically and socially insignificant. What is important here is what people share in common. This will constitute the basis for treating everyone the same way. Differences such as cultural, religious, and ethnic aspects should be privatized and kept away from the public sphere.

Liberal critics have objected to this form of theorizing on several grounds.[5] The core objection and possible source of all the other objections is that the abstract conception of agency is grounded in a false ontology. It views individual identities as well formed and fixed. This does not reflect the fact that individual identities are socially constructed, in which case our very preferences and values, which on the liberal model are reflective of autonomous choices, will now be considered dependent on social processes.

A number of objections flow from the detachment of abstract agency from the historical and situated experiences of individuals: It has been objected that liberal discourse is a totalizing discourse that excludes opposing voices. Because the liberal framework recognizes individuals, not groups, it obscures the fact that dominant groups might tend to offer their own unique group experiences as the norm, thereby requiring members of subordinate groups to adopt their standard as the basis of excellence. Another objection that builds on this criticizes this assimilative ideal of liberalism for promoting the monopolization by a dominant group of the means of information and communication. The dominant group needs the control of these institutions to reinforce its ideology. Without an ideological base, a despotic system will have to rely on naked force for its survival. In short, this version of liberalism rests on a rejection of difference. Subsequently, it cannot account for group diversity in a democratic order.

In contrast, the constructivist approach addresses the failure of rights-liberalism to situate the moral agent within the social processes that would partly shape his or her identity. Once this is done, a different view of the relationship between individual and collective autonomy or freedom emerges.

In order to reshape a social order that is hostile to human existence, we need collective action. Indeed, one person, acting alone, could not alter a social order. This can be achieved only through the cooperative effort of autonomous individuals. For only people with a sense of freedom would share the vision of politics as a sphere where their actions are free and uncoerced, and therefore would feel the urge to combine their efforts with people of similar dispositions to bring about the desired state. The very idea of collective self-determination presupposes individual autonomy.[6]

The liberal critic, however, has not yet been completely answered. To say that individual autonomy is presupposed in collective self-determination does not clarify the problem of why minority preferences should be overridden. On what grounds are minority preferences overridden? Is there any protection against the tyranny of the majority? To answer the question, we must turn to the notion of political community employed here because it implies a distinctive rhetorical structure.

The rhetorical structure of political discourse entailed in the process of collective self-determination is not based on intuiting a fact, but on the intersubjective agreements of citizens. There are important differences between the two approaches. Although both are committed to giving equal consideration to every interest, they differ in one important regard: while the liberal conception treats individual preferences as complete and fixed, the deliberative conception views preferences as shifting.[7] Again, these differences reflect a deeper disagreement. Whereas liberalism takes the view that the individual cannot be mistaken about his or her interest and that he or she is the sole judge of what is best for him or her, deliberative democracy adopts the position that the individual can be persuaded to alter his or her preferences. There are times when we do not have all the facts and as we learn more from our discussion with others, we discover our mistakes and thereby amend our initial preferences. Thus, while it does not make sense to give reasons for preferences that are fixed, the giving of reasons is crucial to deliberative democracy.

Deliberation, however, is not simply a matter of giving reasons. Reasons are only acceptable when they reflect background conditions, which set limits to what can count as a reasonable explanation. The background conception of citizens as moral agents is the basic concept from which a number of principles are derived. From the commitment to moral equality quickly flows the obligation to protect the uncoerced agreement of others, which is to say that it follows from the fact that people are free and equal, that no one should be arbitrarily subjected to the will of another, and that there is a duty to respect the preferences of others.[8] The mutual reciprocity that exists between individuals obligates us to respect the rights of persons even when we disagree with their views.

With the description of the background conditions that provide a framework for deciding reasons that are acceptable, I may now return to the question the liberal critic posed: How is individual autonomy secured in the process of preference formation? I have argued that the process of deliberation, which includes the giving of reasons in support of one's preferences, has built-in safeguards to prevent the possible corrosion of individual autonomy. The background conditions set limits not only to what is admissible, but also to what is inadmissible. This way it protects the private sphere of individuality. For example, a preference to dominate others, which is in violation of the principle of individual autonomy, would automatically be expunged. In ensuring that social relations are governed by moral rules rather than by a bargaining process, deliberative discourse actually offers the best guarantee against the corrosion of individual autonomy.[9]

On the basis of this conception of political community, I now proceed to tackle the problem of politicized ethnicity. The politicization of ethnic identities in Africa deserve scrutiny on account of the dominant role these identities have played in undermining the process of democratic transition. When one takes into account that competitive ethnopolitical identities are oppositional constructs, it becomes clear why it will be difficult for individuals to step up in order to utilize democratic resources for building broad coalitions or for resolving differences. What should we do to resolve the tension between ethnic and political identities? Are ethnic identities compatible with democratic identities? I argue that democracy is compatible with only one form of ethnic relations, namely, social relations based on moral principles.

MORAL ETHNICITY

The quest for moral ethnicity is grounded in the theory of the moral transformation of the social order. How and in what way can we democratize a social order in which ethnic social relations are essentialized? The answer, I submit, lies in moral ethnicity,[10] that is, that reified identities must be made to regain moral autonomy. Consider, for example, groups in social hierarchies engaged in a sort of dissonance-reducing strategy. That is to say the attitudes of both beneficiaries and victims of existing injustice condone the system of domination. While on the one hand beneficiaries might look on the system as just, thereby blaming the victims of oppression for their miserable plight, on the other hand the victims themselves might view their situation as deserved. When both beneficiaries and victims view the phenomenon of oppression in this way, it is an obstacle not only to the recognition of social injustice, but also to the exercise of moral agency. And this would make any effort at remedying the situation through rational discussion a practical impossibility. Victims of delusions are neither autonomous nor rational. Because they are not rational, they cannot engage in any kind of meaningful discussion where people are expected to learn from their mistakes. Also, the fact that moral agency is extinguished means that victims are already reconciled to their fate. Therefore, it is important that people be cured first of their delusions and ignorance before they are encouraged to step up and utilize the deliberative process.[11]

A transitional stage is anticipated. That is to say, the passage from social orders with essentialized social relations to political communities governed by moral rules implies a bridge or connecting link. However, the question of how to address nonideal conditions poses a real dilemma. On the one hand, if we apply the rules that are obtained in the ideal order, we presuppose the existence of moral agents, which is clearly not the case in essentialized settings where nonideal conditions lack resources for the exercise of moral agency. On the other hand, if we fail to utilize moral principles, we simply reinforce existing despotic conditions. One way to overcome this dilemma is to temporarily relax the rules of procedural fairness in order to secure the proper conditions for moral transformation. Justice demands that all structures of oppression—social, cultural, economic, and political—be removed as a precondition for the implementation of the rules of procedural fairness. But what exactly are these transitional rules? What is the basis of their justification? It is to this that I must now turn.

TRANSITIONAL JUSTICE

Justice in a free society requires that citizens be treated equally. But how do you treat people equally in the face of persistent racism or ethnic discrimination? Will justice have been achieved in the claim that people are being treated equally without any effort to remove the harm/injuries (e.g., social and psychological harm) they have suffered largely on account of their ethnic or racial background? The answer to such a question would depend on the version of liberalism articulated. Liberal theorists have different views on freedom and equality. Most of these accounts, however, are critically flawed.

In this chapter, I examine one view of liberalism, show why it is flawed, and suggest an alternative view that overcomes the problem. I argue that the liberal view that only individuals count ignores the fact that group membership and shared cultural practices are important to individuals and are instrumental in shaping individual values and personalities. Thus, when people are discriminated against by having an identity assigned to them, which has nothing to do with their achievements as individuals, the situation can be remedied only if those obstacles that make it impossible to treat people as equals are first removed. I approach this issue by contrasting two views on equal treatment.

TWO PERSPECTIVES ON THE
PRINCIPLE OF EQUAL CONSIDERATIONS

Concerning one interpretation of the liberal view of treating people equally, we are asked to give equal weight to everybody's interest. This idea rests on the normative principle of nondiscrimination. Liberals have considered this a core principle. Stated simply, it affirms that since persons are moral equals, no one ought to be discriminated against on irrelevant grounds. For example, the race, color, and/or ethnicity of individuals are not attributes for which they can be held responsible. They should not therefore be discriminated against for "owning" them. Justice demands that people be accountable only for choices they have made or for actions they could have prevented.[12]

This view has intuitive appeal, but it evaporates when applied to problematic cases. For instance, how would this principle address the issue of compensating victims of ethnic hatred or injustice? The retributive model of justice that is derived from the core principle is clearly not helpful in such cases.[13] The model is too limited to address such issues. It requires us to identify the real victims of ethnic justice and those who perpetrated the crime. This is difficult to achieve when both beneficiaries and victims of ethnic domination view their system as just. An individual who is disabled in this system may very well believe that his or her disability was deserved. Even if he or she chooses not to believe that he or she is to blame, the laws and those in authority would insist on holding him or her responsible for his or her plight. As long as the beneficiaries of an oppressive order do not recognize that their system is unjust or that they share the same responsibility for the oppressive conditions, it will be difficult to proceed with any meaningful reforms.[14] An alternative approach that aims at giving people with disabilities the necessary support to ensure their competitiveness raises more questions than it answers, since affirmative action policies lead to discrimination. If we say that ethnic discrimination is wrong because it treats people unfairly, then reverse discrimination must also be wrong because it involves taking benefits away from those who have earned them to give to the less deserving members of the community.[15]

The fundamental weakness in the preceding arguments is that they presuppose the principle of nondiscrimination to be the basic, normative principle. This makes color-blind policies, that is, policies that are based on merit, the sole basis for dealing with social justice issues. But as Amy Gutmann observes, the core, normative principle is the principle of fairness, not the nondiscrimination principle.[16] Which is to say that the principle of nondiscrimination is derived from the fairness principle, and not the other way around. The concept of fairness is basic in that we generally say that it is fair to give equal consideration to people's interests. But does this mean that the notion of fairness applies only to cases where we treat people the same way? Consider those cases where overlooking obstacles to the realization of individual goals will do grave injustice or harm. Will fairness require that we treat each case on its merit rather than by a general rule that applies equally to all cases? It is a matter of equity or fairness that people's real needs not be ignored even when we aim to treat them equally. For example, consider victims of ethnic discrimination who may require disproportionately more resources for their moral development than beneficiaries. If we choose to treat both victims and beneficiaries equally, that is in the same way, we overlook the fact that the volume of assistance that they may each require would be substantially different. It will then be unfair to give them equal shares. The right thing to do in such cases is to give each person what he or she requires for his or her moral development.

Compared to the fairness principle, the principle of nondiscrimination has a limited application. That is, it applies only to cases where it makes sense to treat people the same way. By way of contrast, the fairness principle takes into account both when it is necessary to treat people differently and when you need to treat them in the same way. This suggests that the fairness principle, unlike the principle of nondiscrimination, is not abstract but rather grounded in the historical and situated experiences of individuals.

The fact that the principle of fairness rather than the principle of nondiscrimination is the core principle has shifted the color-blind/color-conscious controversy in an entirely new direction.[17] When the principle of nondiscrimination was conceived as the core principle, color-blind and color-conscious policies were contradictory. The principle of nondiscrimination has no room for the recognition of difference. From the standpoint of fairness, however, color-blind and color-conscious policies will feature not as conflicting but rather as supplementary. That is to say, color-conscious policies would be required to move us in the direction of a society with opportunity for all. Once this goal is achieved, color-conscious policies will fade away to be replaced by color-blind policies. Color-blind policies are deemed useful where there are no impediments in the way of treating people as equals. Once we adopt this expansive notion of the fairness principle, we are able to overcome the incoherence of color-conscious policies.

In sum, the liberal notion of equal consideration ignores issues that produce extensive sociocultural and economic inequalities. In contrast, the expansive notion of fairness, which presupposes historical and particularistic conditions, probes the causes that have institutionalized inequalities. It is this expansive notion of fairness that is entailed in the notion of transitional justice. For example, it may not be unfair to treat victims differently from beneficiaries of an unjust social order if it is demonstrated that as a result of a long period of subjugation and economic exploitation they require more resources to support their moral transformation. Color-conscious policies should thus be viewed as creating the necessary conditions, which include moral autonomy and the material and social conditions, for the activation of the deliberative process. Thereafter, we should apply color-blind policies to realign individual and group interests with the common good.

I now want to apply these theories to postcolonial societies. For analytical purposes, I distinguish between two distinct categories of ethnic relations.[18] The first consists of ethnic relations that are based on essentialist perceptions. Essentialist perceptions are based on real or imaginary fears that other cultural groups are a threat to the physical, cultural, and social survival of one's group. Ethnic violence and hatred are the normal outcomes of such fears. The second category consists of ethnic relations that are based on pragmatic group perceptions. In the case of pragmatic group perceptions, people are not threatened by the existence of other cultural groups. Rather, they view other groups as competitors for the scarce resources and limited offices in the state. Based on these distinctions, we need not view all forms of group domination as defined by essentialism. Group essentialism is simply one out of a range of oppressive group conditions. Thus, the absence of essentialist conditions in intergroup relations would not necessarily mean the absence of domination. If my aim is to rid society of all forms of social domination, rather than just essentialist ones, the investigation of pragmatic perception as a possible source of powerlessness resulting from economic exploitation should feature in my analysis.

The postcolonial states that are classified as essentialist are Burundi, Rwanda, and South Africa. The majority of African states, however, are in the pragmatic group category. I want to discuss Nigeria as a paradigmatic case of the latter. First, however, let me now discuss states that exemplify essentialist perception.

When we consider the cases of Burundi, Rwanda, and South Africa, we discover that they share a defining feature, namely, that they are social hierarchies built on ethnicity or race. The Tutsi in Burundi and Rwanda[19] and the Whites in South Africa[20] operated oppressive systems that harmed and curtailed the freedom of many of their citizens. The transition to democracy did not appear to have resolved the ethnic antagonism between Hutus and Tutsis. Democracy paradoxically had lifted the lid that kept these groups in check for centuries. These deep distrusts that exist between these groups have simply paralyzed any meaningful effort to get them to resolve their differences amicably. There is no evidence that Burundi and Rwanda adopted policies aimed at resolving their ethnic crises. They relied instead on political and constitutional measures to mediate their ethnic differences. This was a mistake because there was clearly a need for programs such as a preferential policy to assist both victims and beneficiaries to overcome the moral crises that had engulfed their respective countries. South Africa for its part adopted social policies aimed at overcoming racial and ethnic animosity. I want to examine its approach carefully, show why it is flawed, and suggest one way it should have been approached.

In the case of South Africa, democratic resources have been utilized to mediate these racial differences. But I argue that its policies of racial harmony are very much the same policies as in the United States. There are two reasons why they will not work in South Africa. First, affirmative action will benefit the middle class and those able to compete or to take advantage of the limited opportunities for self-advancement. But it will offer little by way of relief to the poor, illiterate masses who have been marginalized by apartheid. When the African National Congress formed the government, the party hierarchy moved to the rich, White suburbs, leaving the poor, Black ghettos behind. And as more middle-class blacks are absorbed into the once exclusive White business circles, the gulf between wealthy and poor Blacks will become bigger. It remains to be seen to what extent, if any, this emphasis on class alliance might promote racial harmony. However, even if South Africa succeeds in transforming a racial struggle into a class struggle, it would still have failed to overcome the problem of social oppression.

The second reason finds that the concern with distributive issues tends to downplay questions of production. The question we must ask is whether redistributing income from those who own productive assets to those who do not will eradicate class exploitation and other forms of oppression? As long as the White minority remains in sole possession of the productive assets of South Africa, no amount of redistribution would eliminate social domination in racial relations in South Africa. While it is true that few Blacks would be absorbed into the system, the majority will remain marginalized.

So we can argue that there are two reasons why preferential policies and set asides are necessary in states dominated by essentialist perceptions. First, preferential policies and quotas would be useful in the eradication of negative stereotypes. By creating role models for oppressed and disadvantaged groups in Burundi, Rwanda, and South Africa, such policies would dispel the myth about a particular group's ability to hold and excel in highly valued jobs. Also, group members of the stigmatized community would have a favorable and positive image of themselves. They would now realize that it is possible to set their goals higher and to work for their realization.

Second, preferential policies may be required to democratize the decision-making process. In social hierarchies, the major institutions, that is, economic, governmental, and bureaucratic, are usually dominated by oppressive groups whose values and interests determine not only the standard and qualification of officeholders, but also the value and significance attached to certain offices. What this creates is a racialized (as in South Africa) or ethnicized (as in Rwanda and Burundi) division of labor in which the unattractive jobs or demeaning functions are reserved for stigmatized groups. Once the decision-making process in all these institutions is democratized, despised groups in these states would certainly reject negative characterizations that had been invented to subjugate them. They would only agree to a distributive scheme that is fair to everyone.

I now turn to the issue of ethnic relations in Nigeria. I have characterized Nigeria's ethnicity as having pragmatic perceptions. In other words, although there is no underlying group hatred that prevents them from stepping up to utilize democratic resources to resolve conflicts or to forge new alliances for the purpose of promoting their mutual interests, they are nevertheless not free of social domination. The point of my argument is simply that ethnic minorities in these states are at a disadvantage in ethnic competition and it does not appear that the democratic process had devoted adequate resources to prevent the oppression and exploitation of these vulnerable groups. Since larger ethnic groups usually have numerical advantage in majoritarian democracy, this can be used to deny minorities access to the public, thus making interethnic competition inherently exploitative and unjust.

Consider the case of Nigeria with well over 100 ethnic groups.[21] Only three main ethnic groups, Hausas, Yorubas, and Ibos, have dominated the political process. The minor ethnic groups are at the periphery of Nigerian politics in the sense that their influence is limited to the local scene. For these groups to access the political center means that they would have to ally themselves to one of the three main ethnic groups in the center: Yorubas, Hausas, and Ibos. Given the fact of their minority status, these groups usually have a weak bargaining power, which means in effect that they must accommodate themselves to the wishes and interests of the dominant groups.

It is worth noting that political theorists have always advocated coalition-building politics as the answer to ethnic antagonism. But coalition-building politics is a technical definition with scientific rather than moral interest. It does not focus on the moral significance of group exploitation. We cannot get answers to the question: Why is ethnic bargaining unfair? And yet this is precisely what we need to answer to satisfy ourselves that a state is just. It is only fair that citizens are not denied equal access to resources and opportunities on account of their race/ethnicity. Again, what is needed is that each group be allowed to participate in the decision-making process not in the form of bargaining, but in seeking remedies and reaching agreements that would be fair to all. It is this expression of collective will that Nigeria must yet attain in order to forge a democratic community.

CONCLUSION

I have argued that when ethnic relations are characterized by domination, they raise a serious question about social justice, namely, that some people might have been denied equal opportunities on account of their ethnicity or race. The corrective to this unjust state, I have argued, does not lie in pursuing an ideal order in which this situation is remedied by reinstating the principle of equal treatment. Rather, the corrective lies in realizing that a system of domination exists and must be eliminated prior to the transition to an ideal and just order. It is therefore necessary that preferential treatment be given those who require additional resources to regain their moral autonomy and to overcome powerlessness and marginalization.

NOTES

I am grateful to G. B. Madison for reading an earlier draft of this chapter. This chapter was also delivered at the Fifteenth International Social Philosophy Conference sponsored by the North American Society for Social Philosophy, Massachusetts College of the Liberal Arts, North Adams, Massachusetts, August 7–9, 1998.

1. For a documented study of the problems that face social theorists who define justice in distributive terms, see Iris M. Young, *Justice and the Politics of Difference* (Princeton, N.J.: Princeton University Press, 1990), 16–22. In Young's view, distributively oriented theories tend to obscure the institutional context that determines material distributions.

2. A political community that rests on the ideal of collective freedom is opposed to the liberal view that essentializes the rights of the individual. On the latter view, the individual is unfree only when he or she is prevented from exercising his or her rights. This means that people who are not entitled to certain rights cannot claim to be unfree even when it is apparent that the nature of their oppression is due to the fact that they are being denied these rights. The ideal of collective freedom rejects the vision of society as the network of private needs and interests. It proposes, instead, a vision of political life with a genuine concern for the "common good." It is a vision that must be articulated less on a deontological basis than on poststructuralist terms.

3. See J. Donald Moon, *Constructing Community* (Princeton, N.J.: Princeton University Press, 1973), 35.

4. Once people acquire autonomy and individuality that are presupposed in a moral community, we can expect that they will encourage the development of policies and institutions that provide ways of reaching agreement. This is compatible with the existence of a plurality of goods.

5. Young, *Justice and the Politics of Difference*, chapter 4.

6. Moon, *Constructing Community*, chapter 2.

7. In this regard, liberal critics reject the view that there are moral objective facts out there for the individual to "discover."

8. See John Locke, *Two Treatises of Government*, ed. Peter Laslett (Cambridge: Cambridge University Press, 1992).

9. As G. B. Madison observes, "from the point of view of Communicative rationality, only these agreements are agreements in the proper sense of the term that are rational or reasonable and the test for this is universalizable. This does not mean that for an agreement to be rational, it must be shared to be rational, it must be shared by everyone, that it be universally accepted in point of fact. An agreement reached by a majority will be universalized, and thus rational, if the advantages it confers and the

obligations it imposes concern as much the majority as they do the dissenting minority." See G. B. Madison, *The Logic of Liberty* (Westport, Conn.: Greenwood, 1986), 224.

10. Alternative approaches have either denied the existence of ethnicity or minimized its significance by accusing politicians of exploiting such sentiments for selfish political reasons. The underlying view here is that ethnicity is a primordial sentiment that fades away with modernization. As such, we can eliminate ethnicity through economic reforms. Against these views, I argue that a deeper understanding of the problem indicates the prior need of moral transformation as an indispensable precondition for political and economic development. See Harvey Glickman, ed., *Ethnic Conflict and Democratization in Africa* (Atlanta, Ga.: African Studies Association Press, 1995).

11. Victims of brain washing are irrational in the sense that they are incapable of taking an unbiased view of an opposing perspective. They may as a result be incapable of rectifying their errors, which is to say that they make learning impossible. For a brilliant treatment of this problem, see Cass R. Sunstein, "Democracy and Shifting Preferences," in *The Idea of Democracy*, ed. David Copp et al. (Cambridge: Cambridge University Press, 1993), 196–230.

12. For a collection of excellent articles, see Marshall Cohen et al., eds., *Equality and Preferential Treatment* (Princeton, N.J.: Princeton University Press, 1977).

13. For an interesting discussion of the complexity of this problem, particularly in ancient wrongs and modern rights, see George Sher, *Approximate Justice* (Lanham, Md.: Rowman & Littlefield, 1997), especially chapter 1.

14. See Iris M. Young, "Displacing the Distributive Paradigm," in *Justice and the Politics of Difference* (Princeton, N.J.: Princeton University Press, 1990), chapter 1.

15. Theorists who advocate color-blind policies view them not only as fairness issues, but also as a factual solution to the underlying problem that is economic. Class preferences should replace race preferences because economic injustice is at the root of racism. This view is simply false, because while economic policies are useful in raising the standard of living of the oppressed , they are certainly not sufficient to address racial injustice.

16. K. Anthony Appiah and Amy Gutmann, *Color Conscious: The Politcal Morality of Race* (Princeton, N.J.: Princeton University Press, 1996), 109.

17. The emphasis it would seem has shifted from a commitment on an equal footing to the recognition that racism should be eradicated at all cost.

18. Donald Rothchild makes this useful distinction in his "Hegemonial Exchanges: An Alternative Model for Managing Conflicts in Middle Africa," in *Ethnicity, Politics, and Development*, ed. Dennis Thompson and Dov Ronen (Boulder, Colo.: Lynne Rienner, 1986).

19. See Thomas Laely, "Peasants, Local Communities and Central Power in Burundi," *Journal of Modern African Studies* (Cambridge), 35 (4) (1997): 695–716; see also M. Catherine Newbury, "Ethnicity in Rwanda: The Case of Kinyaga," *Africa* (London), 48 (1) (1978): 17–29.

20. See Kanya Adam, "The Politics Redress," *South African Style Affair, the Journal of Modern African Studies* 35 (2) (1997): 231–249.

21. Brian Smith, "Federal–State Relations in Nigeria," *African Affairs* 80 (July 1981): 355–378 see also Ali D. Yahaya, "The Creation of States," in *Soldiers and Oil: The Political Transformation of Nigeria*, ed. Keith Panter-Briek (London: Frank Cass, 1978), 201–223.

13

Community: What Type of Entity and What Type of Moral Commitment?

Leonard Harris

Communities are forms of association. Thinking of communities as disconnected aggregates or ontological entities, I venture, is misleading. Conceiving of communities as complicated, interlaced populations and dropping the language of the absolute "Other" recommends defensible moral commitments and explanations. I discuss how moral commitments are influenced by the way we explain and conceive communities.

Which moral commitment is more compelling: fighting for the liberation of a raciated ethnicity (race/ethnic enclave communities) or fighting for the liberation of the working class? If the liberation of the working class will end racism and racial liberation is the highest priority, then fighting for the liberation of the working class has a strong moral appeal. On this view, the exploiting classes, including Black members of such classes, would not be considered a group for which liberation is designed. However, if class liberation will not end racism across lines of class as predicted, then the moral appeal to fight for the liberation of the working class is less compelling.

If racism will end with the success of race or ethnic enclave economies, then a moral commitment to a raciated ethnic group uplift outweighs appeals to class liberation. The ending of racism on this view means that Black members of exploiting classes can sustain their class status but would no longer suffer racial discrimination or insults. In addition, if racial or ethnic identities are considered an abiding source of pride, self-worth, and self-confidence, then high moral commitment to a racial group is quite reasonable. Under the condition of racial slavery, for example, every Black person had a good reason to only focus on Black abolition. However, if a prediction of racism ending with the success of racial enclave economies in a modern capitalist world is false and the highest priority is racial liberation, then the moral appeal of romantic racialism is less than compelling.

The moral commitments we should accept for the purpose of class or racial/ethnic liberation are heavily influenced by the efficacy of our predictions—predictions that depend on the saliency placed on race and class as causal variables. The usual way of thinking about moral commitments, I believe, is often confused because the crucial role of explanatory prediction is undervalued and because conceiving of communities as ontological entities, entities in a world of Manichean "Others," lends itself to untenable moral positions.

Raciated ethnicities and classes are, I suggest, fundamentally two different kinds of entities and merit certain important distinct considerations when deciding on appropriate moral commitments—especially commitments to communities that entail strata of both race and class divisions.

The term "raciated ethnicity," which best describes African Americans, collapses the distinction between race and ethnicity.[1] A raciated ethnicity is to be understood as a social construction. "The term 'social race' is used because these groups or categories [e.g., Negroes in America, mulattos in Brazil, and mestizos in Mexico] are socially, not biologically, defined in all of our American societies, although the terms by which they are labeled may have originally referred to biological characteristics."[2] Actual biological categories have little to do with the way social races are defined. Actual ancestry and appearance are normally manipulated, for example, one drop of sub-Saharan African blood makes someone Black in the United States rather than 51 percent; White women almost never announce they are related to Black women by virtue of often sharing the same paternal great-grandfather. Even if there are no integrative structures between Blacks in the United States and Blacks in Brazil, the world of racial identity is imposed. Race can refer to a category of individuals with socially ascribed properties. The integrative structures of family, business, religion, language, class, or geographical ties help shape ethnic traits; categorization as a race forms one such trait. A raciated ethnicity, however, is not the same kind of entity as a class.

Classes always share types of assets, skills, income, and ownership patterns as integrative structures. Classes invariably divide societies, and may be conceived as divided into upper, lower, and middle; divided in terms of proletariat, working, petty bourgeois, bourgeoisie, ruling, and capitalist class; or divided in status definitive terms such as managerial, service, wage-earning, salaried, property-owning, and business class. Each of these modes of describing a "class" rests on background assumptions about the nature of humans, explicitly or implicitly. A few of these ways will be discussed later in this chapter.

Liberals tend to think of persons as individual actors, subject to the whims of fate or evolution and likely to fall into one of three rather arbitrary divisions of upper, middle, or lower class. Liberals are likely to describe relations in terms of "interactions" between individuals or loose-fitting groups and view development as flowing in tendentious progress or mysteriously ordained development. The existence of classes tends to be considered relatively stable with, at best, changes in the future world where the least well off may improve their lowly condition, while class divisions remain. Class membership is usually considered achieved by the force of character, luck, heritage, or some set of personal traits. Aristotle, Thorstein Veblen, and Robert K. Merton, for example, thought in terms similar to the description of the upper, middle, and lower classes.

For Karl Marx, it is the arrangement of competing economic interests, labor, and the means of production that are the primary sources of value. Persons are driven by material condition and as producers within defined circumstances, those circumstances shape what they tend to think and how they tend to act. The existence and ownership of private property determines, more than any other variable, inequalities of income, status, and privilege. Class conflicts tend toward teleology of universal human liberation. Classes are objectively defined; independent of how individuals define themselves, they fit into a class according to their relationship to production. For Marxists, such as E. O. Wright or David Harvey, liberation is a matter of the ending of class conflict, thereby making possible the existence of freely producing agents unfettered by harmful and unnecessary national, racial, ethnic, and gender divisions.

For Max Weber and Émile Durkheim, persons are driven by a psychosocial desire for status, for a sense of being worthy, and to be owners of the symbols and sources of power. The hoarding of opportunities and transferring of privileges to a select group are some of the main causes of inequalities such as income and ownership. Class membership is defined by social perceptions and market positions (e.g., occupation and the degree of deference or privilege enjoyed). Status is the source of privilege. Thus, a eunuch may be rich but he is always without the status of an aristocrat, even if the aristocrat is poor, destitute, and stupid. At best, the least well off may gain status markers or status markers associated with the least well off may become less offensive. The probable course of life is shaped by a variety of structures, for example, rules, formalized behaviors, laws, and methods of controlling life choices. The classes that exist might change for Weber, but classes as such are endemic to our being. Managerial, industrial worker, peasant, or some other form of segmented market descriptions may be used. However, no one class is driven to ensure universal human liberation. Whether character traits, modes of production, or structures conjoined with sociopsychological natures, classes in the previous examples are understood in terms of market segments corresponding to kinds, more or less permanently segregated and causing behavior across lines of national origin, ethnic identity, racial composition, or geographic location.

Raciated ethnicities share properties like skin color, language, and tastes (aggregated traits) as integrative structures. They also share, in a very uneven fashion, common experiences and status that help form group behaviors and allegiances. The core culture of African Americans, for example, includes Christian churches of the Protestant or Baptist sort, deep race consciousness especially of vicious exclusion, family structures ravaged by slavery, limited asset inheritances, and expressive cultural forms of dance or songs and Africa, especially Anglophone West Africa, which is seen as the ancestral home. There are institutions that enliven and sustain these relationships. But it is false that Blacks not bound to the core culture or not sharing its traits are inauthentic and necessarily lacking in self-respect.

A raciated ethnicity is composed of relational variables. Members of a raciated ethnicity, for example, biologically reproduce one another. That is, they intermarry, with the parents passing their assets on to their progeny. Approximately 93 percent of all Black and White Americans marry within their race; Asians, especially Japanese American women, are highly likely to marry outside their ethnicity. "Hispanic American," for example, is a census category that includes any number of races; it is a language formation that binds and is a marker or other binding trait such as religion and heritage. In another example, the majority of Blacks outside of Africa are bound together by Portuguese and a South American experience (Black Americans are not representative, linguistically or culturally, of Blacks outside of sub-Saharan Africa, although they are collectively the wealthiest and thereby dominate media presentations internationally). Thus, some populations are relatively stable breeding groups and others are in radical transition, but all are highly likely to change marital patterns. What sanctions and rewards incline persons to form long-term commitments and parental habits?

Heritage is a proxy for ethnicity and, in a racist society, a proxy for race.

Raciated ethnicities have a stake in maintaining their ethnicity, if not their race.[3] Persons of the same social kind tend to trust one another. Every survey on trust tells us that Whites distrust Blacks more than they distrust other Whites or Asians. Blacks, given a history of suffering from racists stereotypes, do not trust one another as much as Whites trust other Whites. Blacks, however, receive far greater respect and recognition from other Blacks, while Whites tend to deny Blacks high regard and privileges.

The most important ties we have are those that bind wife and husband, father and mother, siblings, cousins, aunts, uncles, lovers, and friends; that bind us to sources of sustenance, including jobs, retirement benefits, and health care resources; that bind us to the physical neighborhoods wherein we feel comfortable and to the people who share, even if imagined, similar experiences; that bind us to the people we share our vacation time with and when depressed, our deepest fears. All of these ties shape communities. Such relations are often discussed in terms of "community." Our first responsibilities and thereby moral commitments are to those that constitute this day-to-day world. Yet, status, class, and race markers complicate these very real day-to-day relations. One way to understand the distinction I am describing is to think that a raciated ethnicity is a category like male/female, Christian/Muslim, or citizen/foreigner, and continua such as rich/poor, ruling class/working class, and so on bifurcate this category.[4] We often gain a sense of self-worth from embedded identities and feel deeply humiliated or insulted when the group or one of its members is treated with disdain. Yet, I believe, it is the complexity of categories and continua that shape outcomes. However, believing in the universal salience of race as a categorical or continua variable is deeply misguided.[5]

Racism, I believe, is a way of killing by viciously robbing the assets of one population for the benefit of another. Differential accumulation of assets and opportunities are compounded, recurring exponentially over generations and thereby perpetuating radical categorical differences. However, contrary to Derrick A. Bell, I do not believe that raciated entities are permanently constructed in their current form. Even if they are, they do not, contrary to romantic racialists, constitute stable ontologies reflective of human natures or historically causing, invariably, arrangements of human life across stratifications, classes, categories, and status.[6]

One way to see why races are not stable ontological entities with the type of forceful integrative structures as classes is by considering moral conflicts that entail competing conceptions of the Black community. The goal of the following example is to suggest that it is possible to have a moral commitment to the Black community (as a collection of core associations)—which is a commitment of a certain kind—and a commitment to the working class. The latter commitment conflicts with a community commitment in cases where there is a conflict between "workers" (inclusive of White workers) and Blacks who are not members of the working class. Although the Black bourgeoisie or managerial class has never been large enough to matter much, it has been large enough to generate conflicts with those that have a commitment to the working class or to a romantic racialist definition of the "Black community" (i.e., biological or socially defined races forming closed historical kinds within which emotional and material goods should be developed). I limit the discussion to romantic racialist and socialist, bourgeoisie or not, in the following discussion.

Edward W. Blyden understands the world in terms of ethnic kinds (African, European, and Asian) coterminous with racial kinds (Negroid, Caucasian, and Asiatic) and numerous subgroups of races.[7] Blyden, however, has a singularly similar understanding of human nature as his fellow romantic racialists: all persons are fundamentally driven to constitute separate racial kinds and form civilizations corresponding to those kinds. "Communities" for Blyden are always raciated. Analogously, Johannes G. Herder as well as Herbert Spencer cut up the world in similar ways—biology, nature, and consciousness cause behaviors according to racial and ethnic kinds.

Blyden uses a sort of interactionalist account (races need their own nations so they can have equitable interactions with each other). He is dedicated to a raciated ethnicity (African Negroes in his case) and is simultaneously a socialist (dedication to the uplift of the working class and equitable distributions of social goods). The reason that he can hold dual commitments is that the two entities are fundamentally different kinds. However, Blyden also believes that an authentic Negro would be motivated by unique African traits (such as communal, deeply religious, expressive, and so on), that Blacks formed an ontological entity, and that anyone who does not agree with him is existentially inauthentic. Such general traits, however, provide no certain direction about whether to support workers against capitalism, whether to believe that class differences are inevitable, or whether managerial classes have the best interest of the least well off at heart. Blyden has no way of neatly deciding about class conflicts within each racial or national kind, nor does he have a way of arguing for class unity across lines of national kinds. Thus, to the extent that Blyden believes in the universal salience of race, his moral commitments are so tied and there is no way for him to be committed to a socialism that crosses ethnic and racial boundaries.

Marcus Garvey's Universal Negro Improvement Association (UNIA), the largest nationalist movement in the history of African Americans; W. E. B. Du Bois's National Association for the Advancement of Colored Peoples, the nascent organization that promoted legal changes to segregation as well as nonviolent direct action protests and directed boycotts; and Hubert Henry Harrison's Socialist Party, a party that exemplified the largest allegiance of African Americans to socialism—all vied for the loyalty of African Americans. The road to liberation from racism, they believed, was dependent on their approach. Moral commitment was demanded by each group and opposing approaches were decried as fundamentally harmful and indicative of approaches that created self-deprecation or inclined persons to be self-deprecators.

The tremendous migration of African Americans from declining agricultural and rural locations to the growing industrial and urban centers in the early twentieth century provided a new material situation. Increased incomes and effective mass communications enhanced the process of ethnogenesis. Progressively, African Americans saw themselves as a race and an ethnic group distinct from and oppressed by other groups. Kansas City, Chicago, Cleveland, Philadelphia, and New York became not only important industrial centers employing African Americans, but also cultural centers where previously itinerant musicians, artists, and journalists could find regular employment and maintain stable families. American slavery had already accomplished the destruction of nearly all native African religions and thus African Americans were a homogenous religious population. At most, there were competing denominations and subpractices that were African survivals or new adaptations, but no specific gods or coherent faiths of the Mende, Fulani, or Asante. Even voodoo, surviving especially in the Caribbean and South America, survived in America as only a practice within Christianized communities. Civil religious orientations were divided in the same way that humanist traditions were divided, that is, along competing conceptions of moral commitment, self-conceptions, justifiable methods of change, visions of possible futures, explanations, predictions, and conceptions of instrumental strategies to effect change.

By the early twentieth century, tremendous numbers of nearly every ethnic and racial population in the world became urbanized, compelled to join the industrial working class, and watch folk cultures transformed by commercialism and commodification.

Black soldiers returned to America after World War I as victors, having participated in segregated units, paid far less than White soldiers, never promoted on merit, and denied any substantive leadership roles in combat or in ordering White soldiers. They were American soldiers and victors nonetheless. "What is liberation?" had to be answered in terms of what it is to be liberated for a race, an ethnic group, and every class and status shared with all other Americans. Approaches to this question were thus peppered with numerous background assumptions about moral commitments to community and visions of the future. These background assumptions were foregrounded when irreconcilable competing commitments had to be faced.

The "Garvey Must Go" campaign was an example of irreconcilable moral commitments. Socialist parties and numerous liberals such as Du Bois contributed to destroying the UNIA by cooperating with various government investigations of mail fraud charges against Garvey. The nuances of how "community" should be defined and what moral and nonmoral commitments were due were foregrounded—whether, for example, community entailed a nodal commitment to racial/ethnic kind, class, or nation; whether the goal of social action should be a conscious effort to create a civilization of separate kinds or a radical cosmopolitanism; and whether the destruction of self-deprecation required romantic racialism, the negation of racial categories, or the embedding of racial identity within a notion of multicultural diversity.

The working class for socialists and communists, whether Richard Wright, Harrison, or A. Philip Randolph's version, is the instrument for universal human liberation. The possibility of the negation of racism is contingent for socialists and communists on the ascendancy of the working class to power. The "African American community" is not, *mutatus mutandis*, the source of its own liberation. Rather, the empowerment of the working class, of which African Americans were a central component (but only a component) within its historical course, holds the key to the liberation of all African Americans. Liberation is not as a separate community but as a community of workers in pursuit of the destruction of substantive class, status, racial, and ethnic distinctions. What counts as liberation is not equity in the sense that African Americans would have similar incomes, rights, powers, and privileges as Whites per their class and status position, but in the destruction of significant class and status distinctions as well as the destruction of divisive racial and ethnic distinctions.

If class is universally salient, then there are good reasons to be morally committed to working-class liberation even if it does not automatically ensure the end of racism. There is a choice to be made between the uplift of the least well off (decreasing their exposure to illness, premature death, unjust long-term incarceration, risks of homicide, and increasing control of their labor, income, ability to transfer assets, and availability of mates) and the demise of insults and equalizing of income and wealth between races. If a raciated ethnicity is liberated from the scourge of racism, the working class of the raciated ethnicity remains oppressed as a class. This is so unless one believes something like one of the following: that people are essentially racial kinds and liberation is a matter of realizing racial authenticity; or that racial parity is adequate to make class and status differences irrelevant to appropriate moral commitments.

Discussions of community are always parasitic on suspending what we know about the social position of people in terms of class and status. That is, we must suspend discussion of such distinctions and treat "communities" as ubiquitous.

The brutality suffered by Blacks from the criminal justice system is one way to think about the distinction between community, raciated ethnicities, and classes that I am trying to capture. At least one in four Blacks are involved in the criminal justice system on any given day. They are on trial, imprisoned, or on probation, and may or may not receive fair representation by Black police officials, judges, and juries. When Black people find themselves in prison, which may be located in cities headed by a Black mayor, they are likely goaded by Black and White prison guards, they may be raped by Black, White, or Hispanic gang members operating with relative impunity, and they will eat food sold to the prison by White-owned companies and probably prepared by underpaid, single, Black women. Prisoners are housed in concrete and steel buildings built by Black and White construction workers under contracts that include minority-owned construction and supply companies. To think that the "Black community" exists outside of deep class and status differences is to miss the multiple forms of brutalization suffered by the least well off and avoid substantive distinctions that might recommend different types and degrees of moral commitment.

When we think of the "Black community," we must suspend everything we know about how Blacks are linked to everyone else, for example, that Black Americans have a commitment to promoting Protestant or Baptist forms of Christianity that far outweighs commitment to the "African world" that is predominately non-Christian, at least, and anti-Christian implicitly. We are likely to focus on variables that reveal how excluded Blacks are from the ownership and control of massive capital assets, for example, ownership of patents on computer products and of precious metal mines, hotels, restaurant chains, shipbuilding companies, and airplane parts contractors. The variables tell us that White-owned assets dominate Black life even until death—funeral home products, cemeteries, and Black churches mortgaged by White-owned financial institutions. They also tell us that Whites do not trust Blacks—Blacks are constantly overpoliced each time they enter a store or drive down the street or take an exam in school. No matter what African traits exist in the Black American community, and no matter what role Blacks have played in creating modernity, as a people, the world of Blacks is a world subjugated under the yoke of White supremacy. For example, the real wages of American Blacks in the 1990s averaged three-quarters of what Whites made at all educational levels. Black men's wages declined by 5.7 percent between 1989–1997. In 1997, 37.2 percent of all Black children lived in poverty; more specifically, 8.4 percent of White-headed households lived in poverty, as opposed to 23.6 percent of Black-headed households. The vast majority of Black children are raised by single mothers. Out of all ethnic/racial groups in the United States, Blacks have the least amount in retirement assets and trust funds and transfer the least real wealth growth across generations.

Simultaneously, Black Americans are culturally, religiously, and materially members of the modern capitalist world. Black Americans, for example, are the wealthiest Black population in the world. The first language of Black Americans is English. Black Americans produce within Western capitalism— rap music is exported and missionaries carry evangelical emotivism to orthodox African Christian communities and traditional faiths. Black spies, Agents P-138 and P-800, helped the Federal Bureau of Investigation destroy the UNIA. Even many of the ideals, such as the Afrocentric belief in a common African set of character or cultural traits, is a modernist conception of Africa such that all internal African conflicts, differences, and influences are treated as less than significant causal variables in deference to common character or cultural traits. Moreover, ethnic enclave economies and cultural traits, whether African continuities, Chinese religious practices, or Irish dances, have always been features of American society. The Black community is thus a curious patchwork quilt.

A fallacy occurs when we abstract from the existence of the Black community as an association that is divided in numerous ways and suppose that common salient causes that influence the behavior of all persons do not influence Blacks. Supposing, for example, that class interests motivate Whites but not Blacks, that religious faith motivates Whites to be authoritarian imperialists but not Black missionaries, or that dedication to military protocol motivates Whites but is an irrelevant variable for Blacks.

Imagine that Palo Mayombe, Santeria, Candomble, and voodoo religious faiths are all explained as African adaptations satisfying needs of displaced, enslaved, and exploited Africans in the New World. Such an explanation would not tell us the obvious—that these people believe their religious views are actually true; that they are motivated, at least in part, by the same motivation of European Christians, including those Blacks who are Quakers, Puritans, Protestants, or Episcopalians; and that persons of common faith share information, grant loans, trust one another, and raise their children to hold beliefs that conflict with opposing faiths and pursue common missionary projects. Thinking of "Blacks" and "Whites" as absolute "Others" arguably has no way of seeing the deeply common projects of Christians of which, at best, ethnic or racial forms of faith expressions legitimately occur under the institutional and religious rubric of the faith.

Imagine that the Black American community is described as culturally African and motivated by deep senses of faith in the spirituality of the cosmos, define wealth in terms of personal relationships rather than material goods, and are communal. If these are considered general cultural traits that motivate Black cultural behavior—that is, *if the descriptions are used to explain*—the described cultural traits reflect an extremely Western definition of "African." As such, nearly all of Islamic Africa must be excluded; almost all of East Africa is influenced by North Africa and the Middle East; the Black world of the Middle East does not share the precepts of Western evangelical or racialized Christianity; and all orthodox Christian Africans and everyone that has a deep sense of national or tribal identity such that others are considered immigrants, enemies, or infidels. Magically, a massively complex people—bound together by geography, family heritages, religious conflicts, and victimization by racist stereotypes; entrapped in lower classes because of the recurring asset accumulated by inheritors of past generations of upper/ruling-class oppressors; and survivors of diverse forms of colonial histories and the use of terror of evolving into and through modernity—is reduced to explanatory stereotypical traits. (Any manager of Caterpillar International knows better, especially if he or she wants to sell a single earthmover to diverse populations with local currencies, interests, and needs.)

In addition, it is necessarily true that one, if not all, of the previously mentioned religious faiths hold false beliefs. To think of the Black community without thinking of what people believe as true—given vast differences in beliefs—is to think of the Black community as peopled by stereotypical kinds rather than dynamic, empowered, struggling, exploited, excluded, and yet conquering people. However, if these descriptive traits are seen not as overly explanatory or causal, but as descriptive generalizations to be adjudicated for locations, then they can be very useful.

The Black community is simply not well explained by a singular set of "authentically Black or African" values; rather, it at least evinces, if it is not best explained, by multiple strategies to secure income, assets, dignity, and control over labor and labor time.

What if Marx was right: What and how we produce shapes who and what we are, independent of any romantic ideal of ethnic, racial, or national ideals. Then, who and what we are now, in late capitalist postmodern global villages and African diasporic communities, must be different than who and what we were 200 years ago. Thus, it can be true that Blacks are a hybrid people, as in Paul Gilroy's sense in *Black Atlantic*, and also an African people, as in Cedric J. Robinson's sense in *Black Marxism* or Alain Locke's in *The New Negro*. Code shifting and identity sliding are hardly unique, dangerous, or indicative of an inauthentic character or bad faith of any sort. Embedded identities are platforms that we negotiate, use, create, and maintain to help form social locations to extend prima facie trust, shared experiences, and information. It is these platforms of identity wherein our deepest moral commitments to mates, children, relatives, lovers, friends, coworkers, and physical surroundings are constituted. What moral commitments we make, especially in cases of conflict between loyalty to class or racial liberation and their accompanying competing definitions of liberation, should take into serious account the importance of predictions that rely on causal variables.

Communities, rather than simple ubiquitous ontological entities, are groups whose future is contingent on variables that shape their character. Rather than disjointed aggregates, there are ties that bind, but not invariably. Admittedly, the ways I offer of categorizing and seeing communities and classes is speculative. However, the approach is offered in hopes of finding ways of seeing and discussing topics that avoid the absolutism of romantic racial ontology and also color-blind images.

African Americans are a raciated ethnicity, and liberation, I venture, will depend on freedom from forces that prevent African Americans, as a raciated ethnic group, from amassing assets and transferring wealth across generations; from the racism that creates systemic humiliation and denial of trust and honor; from the lowly status of human worth attributed to Blacks; and from the terror of massive class exploitation and vicious class differences between the wealthy and the poor. It will require that Blacks trust themselves and that others trust Blacks in the multiple ways that formal and informal contracts are constituted and insider information shared. Such perspectives are difficult to arrive at if communities in general and the Black community in particular are conceived in a Manichean fashion—"us" and "the others"—rather than complicated and interlaced associations.

It is hoped that we will find motivation to sustain and create the sort of commitments needed to help destroy the terror of super exploitation and racial humiliation ravaging Black lives—the sort of commitments that are coterminous with explanations that allow us to see the structures that need to be changed and the forces likely to influence hoped-for realities.

NOTES

1. Alain Locke, ed., *The New Negro* (1925; reprint, New York: Maxwell Macmillan, 1992); Leonard Harris, "Prolegomenon to Race and Economics," in *A Different Vision: African American Economic Thought*, ed. Thomas Boston (New York: Routledge, 1997); and Leonard Harris, *Racism* (New York: Humanity, 1999).

2. Charles Wagley, "On the Concept of Social Race in the Americas," in *Contemporary Cultures and Societies of Latin America*, ed. Dwight B. Heath and Richard N. Adams (New York: Random House, 1965), 531.

3. See Leonard Harris, "Historical Subjects and Interests: Race, Class and Conflict," in *The Year Left*, ed. Michael Sprinkler et al. (New York: Verso, 1986). I have argued elsewhere that no one has a legitimate interest in perpetually sustaining racial categories.

4. Charles Tilly, *Durable Inequality* (Berkeley: University of California Press, 1999).

5. Harris, "Historical Subjects and Interests."

6. Harris, "Historical Subjects and Interests"; Harris, *Racism*; and Victor Anderson, *Beyond Ontological Blackness* (New York: Continuum, 1999).

7. V. Y. Mudimbe, *Africa: Gnosis, Philosophy and the Order of Knowledge* (Bloomington: Indiana University Press, 1988).

REFERENCES

Adeleke, Tunde. *Un-African Americans*. Cambridge, Mass.: Harvard University Press, 1993.

Anderson, Victor. *Beyond Ontological Blackness*. New York: Continuum, 1999.

Bell, Derrick A. *Faces at the Bottom of the Well*. New York: Basic, 1992.

Blyden, Edward W. *Islam, Christianity and the Negro Race*. Edinburgh: Edinburgh University Press, 1967.

Chaudhuri, Nupur. *Western Women and Imperialism*. Lexington: University Press of Kentucky, 1998.

Dilthey, Wilhelm. *W. Dilthey: Selected Writings*. Ed. H. P. Rickman. 1883. Reprint, Cambridge: Cambridge University Press, 1976.

Du Bois, W. E. B. *Biography of a Race*. New York: Henry Holt, 2000.

Durkheim, Émile. *The Division of Labor in Society*. Trans. George Simpson. 1933. Reprint, New York: The Free Press, 1964.

Foner, Philip S. *American Socialism and Black Americans*. Westport, Conn.: Greenwood, 1977.

Garvey, Marcus. *The Marcus Garvey and Universal Negro Improvement Association Papers*. Ed. Robert A. Hill and Barbara Bair. Berkeley: University of California Press, 1987.

Gilroy, Paul. *The Black Atlantic: Modernity and Double Consciousness.* Blooming-ton: Indiana University Press, 1992.

Harris, Leonard. "Historical Subjects and Interests: Race, Class and Conflict." In *The Year Left,* ed. Michael Sprinkler et al. New York: Verso, 1986.

——, ed. *Philosophy Born of Struggle: Anthology of Afro-American Philosophy from 1917.* Dubuque: Kendall-Hunt, 1983.

——. "Prolegomenon to Race and Economics." In *A Different Vision: African American Economic Thought,* ed. Thomas Boston. New York: Routledge, 1997.

——. *Racism.* New York: Humanity, 1999.

Harvey, David. *The Condition of Postmodernity.* Cambridge: Blackwell, 1989.

Herder, Johannes G. *Reflections on the Philosophy of the History of Mankind.* Chicago: University of Chicago Press, 1968.

Hutchinson, George. *The Harlem Renaissance in Black and White.* Cambridge, Mass.: Belknap, 1995.

Lewis, David Levering. *When Harlem Was in Vogue.* New York: Knopf, 1981.

Locke, Alain, ed. *The New Negro.* 1925. Reprint, New York: Maxwell Macmillan, 1992.

——. *Race Contacts and Interracial Relations.* Washington, D.C.: Howard University Press, 1992.

Mannheim, Karl. *Man and Society in an Age of Reconstruction.* New York, Harcourt, Brace, 1940.

——. *Ideology and Utopia.* New York: Harcourt, Brace, 1953.

Martin, Tony. *Race First.* Westport, Conn.: Greenwood, 1976.

Merton, Robert K. *Social Theory and Social Structure.* New York: The Free Press, 1968.

Mishel, Lawrence, J. Bernstein, and J. Schmit. *The State of Working America.* Armonk, N.Y.: Sharpe, 1993.

Mudimbe, V. Y. *Africa: Gnosis, Philosophy and the Order of Knowledge.* Blooming-ton: Indiana University Press, 1988.

Robinson, Cedric J. *Black Marxism.* New York: Routledge, 1997.

Smith, Adam. *The Wealth of Nations.* New York: Modern Library, 1994.

Spencer, Herbert. *The Principles of Ethics.* 2 vols. New York: D. Appleton and Co., 1897.

Stewart, Jeffrey C. *Race Contacts and Interracial Relations.* Washington, D.C.: Howard University Press, 1992.

Tilly, Charles. *Durable Inequality.* Berkeley: University of California Press, 1999.

Veblen, Thorstein. *Theory of the Leisure Class.* 1965. Reprint, New York: A. M. Kelley, 1965.

Wagley, Charles. "On the Concept of Social Race in the Americas." In *Contemporary Cultures and Societies of Latin America,* ed. Dwight B. Heath and Richard N. Adams. New York: Random House, 1965.

Weber, Max. *Sociological Writing.* Ed. Wold Heyderbrand. New York: Continuum, 1994.

14

Theorizing Black Community

Richard A. Jones

> There is an invisible book of life that faithfully records our vigilance or our neglect. "The moving finger writes, and having writ moves on. . . ." We still have a choice today: nonviolent coexistence or violent coannihilation. This may well be mankind's last chance to choose between chaos and community.
>
> —Martin Luther King Jr., *Where Do We Go from Here: Chaos or Community?*[1]

What *is* community? From communities of discourse to communities of dominance and subjugation, the concept of "community" describes many human associations. Do African Americans, historically denied access to "communities of the good" from slavery to Jim Crow to the present, desire only assimilation with majoritarian White communities? Or do Black Americans desire more than the repetitious strip-malls, tract-housing, and alienated fragmented lived realities majoritarian Americans build their anticommunities on (in the anonymity of a nation of strangers)? What are the visions, dreams, theories, and strategies that lead from the shadows of postmodern "quietism" and despair to the bright sunlight of practical, livable, material communities? Without our own utopian visions are we destined, as African Americans, when we "succeed" (I use this term ironically), to the coercive and seductive assimilation of *suburbicide?* What *are* the possibilities for new visions of Black community? If neither utopian nor canonical political conceptualizations for Black community can be posited during late postindustrial capitalism, what are the possibilities for transformative Black politics? With the fragmentation of majoritarian White community formation processes, how might Blacks pursue sustainable community? Are Black community formation processes, and the discourses that make these formation processes possible, the transformative strategy behind cultural and political Black nationalism? How would we begin to theorize Black community without the linked exploitations of race (racism), gender (patriarchy), and class (capitalism)? Class interests and race are particularly perplexing. Greg Moses writes, "The race–class question, for all its delineation of the contours of oppression, frustrates clear analysis. Is the significance of race increasing or declining? How much effort shall the black community spend in struggle with whites compared with energy that could be directed toward a group economy?"[2] I investigate these questions in this chapter.

Since the passage of the Civil Rights Bill in 1964 and the Voting Rights Act in 1965, Black public intellectuals and philosophers have explored various ideological models for the African American community. Martin Luther King Jr. provides the foundation for this discussion with "Beloved Community" in his penultimate book *Where Do We Go from Here: Chaos or Community?* This chapter traces the evolution of visions for "community" from the "second reconstruction"[3] (1945–1982) to the present. After outlining King's argument, I survey Cornel West's vision for community in *Prophesy Deliverance! An Afro-American Revolutionary Christianity.* I subsequently examine Lucius Outlaw's *On Race and Philosophy* as a possible third moment between King's and West's positions.

No investigation of Black community would be complete without examining whether community solidarity (Black or White) in a postmodern world is even possible. Given the accelerating disjointed existences in the Black "community's" wealthy entrepreneurial class, traditional religious, intelligentsia, petit bourgeois, alienated suburbanites, middle-class and neoliberals, urban underclass, feminists, socialists, homosexual and lesbian agendas, and revolutionary national separatists—Black identity is increasingly fragmented. Is the possibility of community also lost with this fragmentation? *It is unclear, given the pluralism and stratification within Black community, whether "community" in its traditional modern sense is even possible.* Finally, *what* theoretical moves remain if King's and West's formulations for community are inadequate, and Outlaw's synthesis of liberalism and socialism ("in an axial shift") fails to produce sustainable Black community?

"CHAOS OR COMMUNITY": MARTIN LUTHER KING JR.

This discussion begins with King's "Beloved Community." Important questions King raises are: (1) How might existing legal freedoms help produce a sustaining human community?; (2) Why are Blacks essential for transforming community?; and (3) Why is nonviolent action a superior strategy for building community? Within King's responses, we must try to understand whether "Beloved Community" remains feasible in subsequent theoretical constructs.

King approaches the problem of building community from four perspectives. He writes:

> One positive response to our dilemma is to develop a rugged sense of somebodyness. This sense of somebodyness means the refusal to be ashamed of being black. . . . A second important step that the Negro must take is to work passionately for group identity. This does not mean group isolation or group exclusivity. . . . [A] third thing that the Negro must do to grapple with this dilemma . . . [is to] make full and constructive use of the freedom we already possess. . . . The fourth challenge we face is to unite around powerful action programs to eradicate the last vestiges of racial injustice.[4]

King realizes that community building from within depends on spiritually, economically, and politically healthy individuals. Internal community building from self-identification with others possessing "somebodyness" leads to the criterion for employing external factors in building community—existing laws. "In his vision of the 'World House' King elaborates upon the larger question of values: 'The good and just society is neither the thesis of capitalism nor the antithesis of Communism, but a socially conscious democracy which reconciles the truths of individualism and collectivism."[5] Finally, we achieve "beloved community" in the peaceful, concerted exercise of juridical law. For King, Christian spirituality is the expression of love for others in the "beloved community's" secular church.

At the end of the "second reconstruction," King's vision for community continued to be valorized by African American social strategists. But, increasingly, many theorists came to believe that racism, liberalism, and capitalism were inseparable, and that liberalism's methodology for "beloved community" integration had failed. The postcivil rights legacy romanticized Black nationalism[6] and increasingly romanticized notions of King's "beloved community" generated new theories for community. These new ideas substantively altered utopian and practical theories for Black "community."

Moses argues convincingly that King initiated a new era in Western sociopolitical thought. He writes, "To state my guiding thesis, I think that King establishes grounds for a new age of social and political philosophy, superseding both tired schools of thought that sought to legitimize cold war antagonism, namely, Marxist-Leninism and what I dub 'cowboy capitalism.'"[7] As we will see in West's analysis of the inadequacies of Marxism and capitalist-influenced liberalism, King seeks new alternatives to "tired schools of thought." Like West, King realizes the inherent humanistic appeal of communism, but also realizes communism's incompatibility with Christianity. "If communism, for King, has smothered the individual, then it is also true that capitalism, with its profiteering values, fails to nurture a healthy community."[8]

In tracing the social and political practices that have shaped the realities of life for American Black people, King quotes from *The Peculiar Institution,*

Kenneth Stampp's book on the institutions of slavery. Stampp relates the following "rules" provided by slaveholders to "produce a perfect slave":

1. Accustom him to rigid discipline.
2. Demand from him unconditional submission.
3. Impress on him a sense of his innate inferiority.
4. Develop in him a paralyzing fear of white men.
5. Train him to adopt the master's code of good behavior.
6. Instill in him a sense of complete dependence.[9]

King quotes Stampp to reacquaint his readers with the historical tactics used to induce submission and inculcate inferiority in African Americans. King also locates racism,[10] as practiced in contemporary America, within Stampp's "guidelines" for "producing perfect slaves." But, while many in the Black community, when King wrote *Where Do We Go from Here*, were advocating militancy and "Black Power," King maintained that overcoming the mental enslavement produced by the slaveholders' rules required *The Strength to Love*. King's philosophy is based on nonviolence and positive racial essentialism. Cornel West writes:

> King seemed to believe that Afro-Americans possess a unique proclivity for nonviolence, more so than do other racial groups, that they have a certain bent toward humility, meekness, and forbearance, hence are quite naturally disposed toward nonviolent action. In King's broad overview, God is utilizing Afro-Americans this community of *caritas* (other-directed love) to bring about "the blessed community." . . . He was the drum major of "this mighty army of love."[11]

To overcome the negative racial essentialism embodied in the guidelines for "perfect slaves," King understands that the construction of a positive racialized essentialism is required for a new humanism to emerge.

The praxis King undertook to transform society was self-reflective action intended not only to free and unite the community, but also to free and unite the individual spirit within a multidimensional community of selves. In this "World House," individual identity was as important as group identity. Moses states, "Nonviolent movements demand a context of healthy nurture that must be provided by struggling communities. King is serious about his efforts to make the most of various energies that thrive in a multidimensional community. One dimensional struggle is no answer worthy of life."[12] Is integration to be construed as the integration of individuals into groups (ethnicities), or the integration of groups into coequal national community status? Moses writes, "black group identity is something cherished by King, even as he works to formulate ties with other exploited groups. This group reality becomes problematic, however, depending upon the way which integration is used as a value."[13] In King's "World House," are individuals to be integrated (made one) as individuals, or integrated by ethnicities, or both? Consequently, King's theorizing of "beloved community" is also a theorizing of individual identity. For King, the negative freedom *from* interference is not enough; true freedom is only to be found in the *self*. He writes: "The Negro will only be truly free when he reaches down to the inner depths of his own being and signs with the pen and ink of assertive selfhood his own emancipation proclamation. With a spirit straining toward true self-esteem, the Negro must boldly throw off the manacles of self-abnegation and say to himself and the world: 'I am somebody. I am a person. I am a man with dignity and honor.'"[14]

He realizes, however, that, well paved by legislated laws' goodwill, the paths to "absolute selfhood" and individual "freedom" can only come from the spiritual riches of the self. This emphasis on "self" is easily traced to the contemporary existential political traditions of West, Lewis Gordon, and Martin J. Beck Matuštík. King really believes that gradual progress, inspired by laws, will allow society's teleological emergence in a state where "dignity and honor" are actual possibilities for every individual. He writes: "This is no time for romantic illusions and empty philosophical debates about freedom. This is a time for action. What is needed is a strategy for change, a tactical program that will bring the Negro into the mainstream of American life as quickly as possible."[15] Perforce, the question becomes "what went wrong?" with King's strategy for social change.

If we take the 1960s as the decade of the civil rights movement, the 1970s and 1980s while effecting some positive social transformation did not yield King's vision of "beloved community." Fueled by what King himself labeled "white backlash," the final decade of the twentieth century witnessed profound negative changes in the legal, economic, and social realities for African Americans. Despite King's positive essentialism, altruistic philosophy, and great love for humanity, Black nationalists deemed King's politics a failure, even while praising him.

Without citing the voluminous supporting statistics, although 40 percent of African Americans have now entered the middle class, an urban underclass remains mired in poverty, unemployment, drug abuse, crime, and welfare. While these social dislocations continue, there are currently more African American men in prisons than in colleges, and the percentages of African Americans beneath federal poverty guidelines have grown in the thirty years since the civil rights movement ended. Not only have two cultures emerged in America—one Black and one White—two subclasses—one middle class and the other underclass—have emerged among African Americans.

In *When Work Disappears: The World of the New Urban Poor*, William Julius Wilson argues that the changing global economy has radically altered the American workplace. Wilson believes that losses of manufacturing jobs and the increases in service sector jobs have dislocated African American workers. Additional dislocations have been caused by urban employers increasingly moving their businesses to the suburbs. Wilson provides an economic, instead of moral, framework for the factors leading to the "pathological" Black community Daniel P. Moynihan reports in his 1965 *The Negro Family: The Case for National Action*. In this often cited report, Moynihan points to statistics on the Black family, including teen pregnancies and the break up of the African American family, as primary causes of crime and ghetto poverty. If the Moynihan report blames American economic discrimination[16] for African American family and community dislocation, then Wilson's observations suggest that the ghetto underclass has been further victimized by a new global economy that eliminates manufacturing jobs, while liberal politicians move to more conservative "centrist" political positions eliminating social welfare programs.

My criticisms of King as an integrationist should not be taken as an indictment that he was mistaken. To the contrary, King was an extremely important philosophical figure in his expression of agape, universal classlessness, racelessness, nationless love for humanity, and politically important for initiating a *revolution of conscience*. A reading of *Where Do We Go from Here?* and Moses's *Revolution of Conscience: Martin Luther King, Jr., and the Philosophy of Nonviolence* will convince almost any reader that King's contributions to sociopolitical philosophy were and are enormous.[17] King's philosophy is deep in *nommo* (Molefi Asante's term for the Black tradition of rhetoric that forms a community of listeners), active commitment to the downtrodden, and a deep spirituality that all Americans might only envy. If King's vision of integration leading to "beloved community" failed, it is not because of a failure of King's *Dream*, rather, it is because America (Black and White) has failed. The next section addresses the transition period between what I call the postcivil rights movement's *integrationist* and *isolationist* eras. These brief eras, spanning the mid-1970s to the mid-1980s, are best characterized by West's early writings.

THE POLITICIZATION OF "BELOVED COMMUNITY": CORNEL WEST

Even with King's many successes in the campaign for eliminating segregation in the southern United States, it soon became apparent to many that the passage of the Civil Rights Act of 1964 was not enough to produce a color-blind society. As more African Americans entered the middle class, socioeconomic conditions for middle-class membership evaporated. The jobs, housing, and educational opportunity King sought in integration became a miasma of unemployment, urban decay, and renewed debates concerning Black intelligence. Whereas King's integrationist–assimilationist strategy assumed that racism and White supremacy would be assuaged by the familiarity of increased contact between the races, the 1980s rearticulated (if not recreated) familiar historical racial discord. If anything, racism morphed—that is, changed shape—while the majority community continued to withhold the privileged status of full citizenship. The consensus was growing within the White and Black communities that integration had failed. But this "failure" was not solely one race's intolerance for the other,[18] because as Wilson insists, America's socioeconomic changes also contributed.

Tom Wicker writes: "From 1967 to 1976 more than a million manufacturing, wholesale, and retail jobs, the kind best suited to most blacks of that era, disappeared from New York, Chicago, Philadelphia, and Detroit—in which cities, not incidentally, by 1982 more than a quarter of the nation's poor were living. Between 1979 and 1985, as if the loss of old jobs were not bad enough, nearly half of all *newly created* jobs paid no more than poverty-level wages."[19] Wicker's observation, that changing global socioeconomics led to the "pathological" social condition in the Black ghetto "underclass," is the presupposition that shifts the terrain from King's absolute integrationist perspective to West's critical political theory. Whereas King seeks "beloved community" in law's practical power, West seeks to postulate the conditions for Black community in transcending the normative political conditions that impede it. If King's methodology emphasizes the *individual* and *institutional* levels of racism and power, West's methodology continues King's growing awareness of the *structural* aspects, with *individual* racism being the racist act or remark; *institutional* racism being the biases in schools, jobs, and housing; and *structural* racism being the economic–political system (i.e., liberal market capitalism) that provides support for the normativity of racism's other two levels.

In *Prophesy Deliverance! An Afro-American Revolutionary Christianity*, West explores the evolution of African American critical thought. Essentially, West's pragmatist program begins where King's ends. Whereas King's interpretation for Black community is entailed by Christian theology, West's analysis entails Christian theology within both Marxism and American pragmatism. Working out how these disparate approaches to community can coexist becomes West's central project. Even beyond the realities of racism, White supremacy, changing socioeconomic global conditions, and the ideological dialectics between socialism and capitalism, West views the important element as the emergence of Black critical thought: African American philosophy.

West perceives deeper problems with American capitalism than King. While also acknowledging Marxism's abuses, paralleling them with the "countless calamities perpetrated by Christian churches," West reinterprets King's "secular church" in Marxian terms of the "workers' struggles for dignity." In Marxian class struggle, the opposition of workers and owners, in a material historical dialectic, ultimately yields a "kingdom of freedom" from a "kingdom of necessity."[20] West recognizes King's "beloved community" in Marx's "kingdom of freedom," where the individual is allowed ultimate self-realization by being freed from material necessity. West writes, "The quite similar fundamental thrust of Marxism, despite the numerous brutalities per-petuated by Marxist regimes, is the self-fulfillment, self-development, and self-realization of harmonious personalities."[21]

Pragmatist methodology bridges marked binary oppositions by stressing their interrelatedness. The primary capitalist interrelation is economic com-petition. But in Marxian ideology, individuals cooperating in harmonious in-terrelatedness collectively decide the community. "The worm of individuality reinforces the importance of community, common good, and the harmonious development of personality. And it stands in stark contrast to those doctri-naire individualisms which promote human selfishness, denigrate the idea of community, and distort the wholistic development of personality."[22] West in-scribes the individual's right to develop "harmonious personality" within the context of community as a guaranteed right of both Christianity and Marxism. After analyzing the strengths and weaknesses of both doctrines, West con-cludes that the similarities outweigh the differences: "In my view, . . . an al-liance between prophetic Christianity and progressive Marxism—both casti-gated remnants within their own worlds—lies the hope of Western civilization."[23]

More germane to this discussion is West's analysis of the role postmod-ernism plays in the construction of African American social reality. Grounded in the "construction of community," West's remarks are particularly com-pelling. "The paradox of Afro-American history is that Afro-Americans fully enter the modern world precisely when the postmodern period commences; that Afro-Americans gain a foothold in the industrial order just as the postin-dustrial order begins; and that Afro-Americans procure skills, values, and mores efficacious for survival and sustenance in modernity as the decline of modernity sets in, deepens, and yearns to give birth to a new era and epoch."[24]

Against this background, West offers equally compelling arguments that White Americans' struggles in a historical effort to break cultural–political–religious ties with Europe had not subsided when African slaves began their own struggle for freedom in the New World. West argues that because Euro-pean Americans' entanglements with Europe had not been resolved when African American's entanglements with European Americans in America be-gan, a double dislocation for African Americans resulted from liberalism's decline into postmodernity. While European emigrants in North America sought cultural and political autonomy from Europe, African Americans si-multaneously sought a similar autonomy from them. Also, as European Americans globalized markets and lost faith in science, African Americans sought opportunities in domestic markets and gained faith in science.[25] The idea is that African Americans, motivated by the Enlightenment's promises of continuous "progress" and absolute egalitarianism, continued to pursue un-fashionable paradigms long after European Americans had abandoned them as unworkable. African Americans' pursuit of community is the pursuit of a nineteenth-century chronotope.[26]

Without African American dislocations brought on by the crises in moder-nity, West argues, valid African American philosophical practices might not have arisen. In his own words, "Let it suffice to say that a noteworthy prod-uct of the dispersive practices of Afro-Americans in post-industrial cosmo-politan American culture is the advent of Afro-American philosophy."[27] Leonard Harris echoes this belief that African American philosophy is indeed a "Philosophy Born of Struggle."[28]

For the purposes of this chapter, the central chapters in West's *Prophesy De-liverance!* are those that discuss the integration–assimilation–isolation–sepa-ration continuum. West characterizes this continuum in terms of African American "exceptionalist," "assimilationist," "marginalist," and "humanitarian" traditions. West resolves the elements of African American's responses to racism into:

> *The Afro-American exceptionalist tradition lauds the uniqueness of Afro-American culture and personality. . . . The Afro-American assimilationist tradition considers Afro-American culture and personality to be pathological. . . . The Afro-American marginalist tradition posits Afro-American culture to be restrictive, constraining, and confining. . . . The Afro-American human-ist tradition extols the distinctiveness of Afro-American culture and person-ality. . . .* My conception of these four traditions in Afro-American thought and action assumes that culture is more fundamental than politics in regard to Afro-American self-understanding . . . culture and politics are inseparable, but, as I believe Antonio Gramsci has shown, any political consciousness of an op-pressed group is shaped and molded by the group's cultural resources and re-siliency as perceived by individuals in it.[29]

Ultimately, then, it is within these *traditions* that West grapples with the har-monization of King's "beloved community" with Marxian and socialist in-strumentalities for constructing material and transcendent "communities." West's analyses of identity formation, political and social community, and racial essentialism and assimilation in the postcivil rights era are central to any discussion of Black community formation.

On West's interpretation, King's interests are *exceptionalist* and *humanist*; because as the "drum major" of "a mighty army of love," King views African Americans as essentially different from Whites: African Americans will mod-ify American society (and the communities it contains) by providing a supe-rior example of nobility, long-suffering, tolerance, and Christian love. King exemplifies West's *exceptionalist* tradition. Moses, quoting from King's first book, *Stride toward Freedom*, states, "Since the white man's personality is greatly scarred, he needs the love of the Negro. The Negro must love the white man, because the white man needs his love to remove his tensions, insecurities, and fears. . . . 'Agape' is a willingness to go to any length to restore community. It doesn't stop at the first mile, but it goes the second mile to restore community. It is a willingness to forgive, not seven times, but seventy times seven to restore community."[30] West also holds that cultural uniqueness and distinctiveness are important, but questions King's assumption that these characteristics might flourish within a liberal–capitalist political system that denies minority groups *power*. *Power* resides in more than a society's written laws; as Antonio Gramsci argues, power also resides in culture. But power is more than agency to transform law or culture, it is interwoven—reticulated—in a society's ontology, epistemology, axiology, and politics.

West argues that the *exceptionalist* tradition "claims a *sui generis* status for Afro-American life in regard to form and content."[31] The *assimilationist* tradition[32] considers the African American culture and personality to be pathological. The *marginalist tradition* essentializes culture and locates the source of African American powerlessness within its own community. Finally, West posits the universality, rather than *exceptionalist* particularity of African American culture, in the *humanist* tradition.

By endorsing the *humanist* tradition in African American thought, West minimizes the racial essentialism King employs to justify community building. Furthermore, he provides new necessary conditions for rearticulating Black community formation on political and economic grounds beyond liberalism and capitalism. I take this to be a positive evolution in the theoretics of Black community formation. What West proposes for universally human African American community is vested in the expression of rights as autonomous beings that best supports their "special hopes for the future."

There are those who knew King who argue that toward the end of his life he was moving in the same direction as West. Because of his understanding of the Vietnam War and the economic exploitation of Memphis sanitation workers, increasingly King was shifting toward socialism. King had begun to understand how racism, capitalism, and war were linked exploitations. Manning Marable writes:

> Quietly, King was beginning to articulate a democratic socialist vision for American society: the nationalization of basic industries; massive federal expenditures to revive central cities and to provide jobs for ghetto residents; a guaranteed income for every adult American. King had concluded, like Malcolm X, that America's political economy of capitalism had to be transformed, that the Civil Rights Movement's old goals of voter education, registration, and desegregated public facilities was only a beginning step down the road towards biracial democracy.[33]

Slowly, repeated evidences of unemployment, higher infant mortality rates, drug abuse, alcoholism, and crime began to create a context where most African Americans were willing to entertain the real possibility that the individualistic puritan ethic was not enough; there were no boots, much less bootstraps by which to pull oneself up. By the time West had published *Prophesy Deliverance!* and Marable had written *Race, Reform, and Rebellion*, the pessimism West regarded as "warranted" had seriously undermined the good intentions of integrationism's "with all deliberate speed." Yet West, despite his own good intentions and persuasive arguments, *knew* that there was nothing to unite a primarily foreign socialist agenda with the traditional Black church. Despite this knowledge, he continued advocating this synthesis because he also *knew* that there were few viable alternatives: "By claiming that the Marxist tradition is indispensable yet inadequate, my social analytical perspective is post-Marxist without being anti-Marxist or pre-Marxist; that is, it incorporates elements from Weberian, racial, feminist, gay, lesbian, and ecological modes of social analysis and cultural criticism."[34]

The need for an initiative to launch a third reconstruction leading to more stability for Black community has been evident since the mid-1980s. Answering important questions about which direction this initiative should take has been more difficult. African American social and political theorists need to reconceptualize the core cluster of ideas surrounding "community." Theorists must rearticulate terms of discourse such as "race," "ethnicity," "assimilation," "racism," and "power," among others, as they enjoin the problems of a third reconstruction. Inscribing the problem of "community," these concepts themselves need to be reinscribed within postmodern efforts to provide social meaning in a rapidly changing global community.

One philosopher who addresses these issues is Lucius Outlaw. In the next part of this chapter, I will explicate his thinking in *On Race and Philosophy*. In this book, Outlaw provides the theoretical philosophical development that questions majoritarian normativity, posits the connections between African Americans and all people, and initiates the rearticulation of the terms of community formation discourse.

"CRITICAL SOCIAL THEORY": LUCIUS OUTLAW

On my view, one of the important questions Outlaw raises in *On Race and Philosophy* is the *role* philosophers *should* play in social transformations. Like C. L. R. James, he is skeptical that any elite or vanguard group, including professional philosophers, *can* lead the masses to social transformation. He is also highly critical of philosophers' elitist academic aloofness. His arguments are tempered by the balanced need for the philosophers' personal praxis (living the philosophy) and realizing the philosophers' limited role (providing analytical clarity) in the politics of social transformation. For philosophers like James, Outlaw believes that ordinary people[35] are capable of arriving at their own transformative politics. Paul Gilroy addresses this feature of James's thought: "Its best feature is an anti-hierarchical tradition of thought that probably culminates in C. L. R. James's idea that ordinary people do not need an intellectual vanguard to help them to speak or tell them what to say."[36] I also believe these are central concepts Joy James develops in *Transcending the Talented Tenth: Black Leaders and American Intellectuals*. Also, Anna Grimshaw and Keith Hart state in the introduction to James's *American Civilization*, "His vision was now founded on recognition that the fate of humanity lay in the hands of ordinary men and women, that intellectuals would play no decisive role in the working out of society's future."[37] Outlaw, like James, understands the limited role the African American philosopher qua philosopher plays in social transformation, and the unlimited role the Black philosopher plays qua citizen.

By limiting the professional philosopher's role in motivating social transformation, Outlaw returns political discourse to Earth. He grounds theorizing in concrete particularity instead of abstract universality, and restores the professional philosopher to the traditional role of analyzing and rearticulating the conceptional grounds for action. In doing so, Outlaw traces a new direction to neopragmatist philosophy. He writes:

> I take it to be the case that at least some professional philosophers, myself included, along with thoughtful persons in other walks of life, can contribute to the clarifying work of developing social and political philosophies and policies that might help us to fashion communities in which racism and invidious ethnocentrism have been minimized and curtailed (I do not expect either ever to be eliminated completely and for good), even while races and ethnicities are both conserved and nurtured, without chauvinism, to the enrichment of us all.[38]

In the debate over race as an essential or accidental property, Outlaw understands the racial concept's sociocultural material necessity and usefulness. In answering W. E. B. Du Bois's famous question, "What *is* race?" he writes, "For, I think, it is in and through this world-making, driven by survival needs and competition for resources, that raciation and ethnicization develop as responses to the need for life-sustaining and meaningfully acceptable *order* of various kinds (conceptual, social, political)."[39] In understanding *how* and *why* people use "race" and "ethnicity" in world-making, Outlaw can redefine and reorder these terms. He continues, "Understanding these aspects of our species-being (to re-invoke a central notion from the early Karl Marx) will enable us, I think, to understand better how racial and ethnic groups come to be and go about defining and identifying themselves."[40]

Discussing racial essentialism, Outlaw introduces the term "ethnie." The dialectic concerning race as an essential property or a socially constructed property is resolved in this definition as distinguished *from* race. For Outlaw, *ethnicity*[41] and *race* as distinguishable properties, the former cultural and the later biological, are both necessary and useful: "Race continues to function as a critical yardstick for the rank-ordering of human groups both 'scientifically' and sociopolitically, the latter with support from the former. At bottom, then, 'race'—sometimes explicitly, quite often implicitly—continues to be a major fulcrum of struggle over the acquisition and exercise of power and distribution of social goods."[42] Charles W. Mills also locates the disjunction of race and ethnicity as central to reinterpreting identity. "To the extent 'race' is assimilated to 'ethnicity,' white supremacy remains unmentioned, and the historic Racial Contract—prescribed connection between race and personhood is ignored, these discussions, in my opinion, fail to make the drastic theoretical correction."[43] The drastic correction Outlaw makes is to maintain the importance of race as a property of personhood, while simultaneously remaining mindful of the term's nontotality in discourse.

> But I also believe that it is very important that we continue to make use of the concepts race and ethnie (or ethnic groups) and their derivatives (raciality, ethnicity) as important resources for continuing efforts to critically (re-)construct and maintain social realities. For in complex societies in which race and ethnicity continue to be factors at the heart of social conflict, it is urgent as ever that we engage in such projects with careful mindfulness of biologically and culturally constituted social groupings of races and ethnies, though sometimes it will also be important to have little or no regard for a person's or people's raciality and/or ethnicity. The delicate, complicated, but crucial task is to find ways of having appropriate regard for raciality and ethnicity while being guided by norms that we hope—and our best judgments lead us to believe—will help us to achieve stable, well-ordered, and just societies, norms bolstered by the combined best understanding available in all fields of knowledge that have to do with human beings and that are secured by democratically achieved consensus.[44]

That Outlaw's preoccupation with Black community formation processes overlaps King's and West's is undeniable. He writes, "I shall turn to a question that is constantly before us, and generally follows any consideration of the legacy of Martin Luther King Jr., and what we might or ought do in the future to realize 'the beloved community': the prospects and basis—the theoretical and practical dimensions and foundations—of a new black social movement."[45] What distinguishes Outlaw's reasoning for a new Black social movement is that he is calling for it within an original African American philosophical experience. However, unlike West, Outlaw does not map original Black philosophy onto existing systems, rather, he calls for a new logic centered on the marginalized. Czechoslovakian philosopher Martin J. Beck Matuštík,[46] quoting Outlaw, writes, "Note Outlaw's suspicion: 'Neither the full nature and extent of our oppression, nor our historical–cultural being as

African and African-descended peoples, has been comprehended adequately by the concepts and logics involved in Marxian projects of modernity in societies in Europe and Euro-America."[47] Outlaw asks, "How does our theorizing stack up against the history of black thought and the complexities of different traditions and programs carried by different organizations and institutions that include assimilation, accommodation, bourgeois–capitalist pluralist integration, left-nationalism, separatism, Marxist–Leninist proletarian internationalism, Nkrumahist and other forms of Pan-Africanism, and religious nationalism of various sorts?"[48]

He argues that theoretical progress can occur "only if we recognize the difference between theorizing practice and phronesis, and understand and act in accord with that understanding which situations are appropriate for which."[49] By calling for *phronesis*—that is, "practical wisdom, or knowledge of the practical ends of life, distinguished by Aristotle from theoretical knowledge and mere means–end reasoning"[50]—Outlaw not only reinvests African American theoretical social philosophy in the traditions of western philosophy, but also demonstrates the necessity that

> require[s] that new structural arrangements be realized if the possibilities are to be liberated. . . . The struggle for cultural integrity and economic justice on the part of African-Americans indicates just such a situation: only the achievement of an economic, social, political, and cultural democracy—based on principles and practices that preserve bourgeois liberalism and institute cultural, racial/ethnic, and sexual democracy that secures group identity and integrity—will provide the necessary conditions for both. Theoretical insights into these necessary conditions are preserved in the traditions of humanistic Marxism, democratic socialism, the contemporary women's movement, critical hermeneutics, and Black Nationalism, among others.[51]

Outlaw elevates prior political discourse by recognizing the positive contributions from discourses that have been traditionally marginalized by being the negatively marked poles of binary oppositions. He senses that the moment for synthesizing discourses at a higher level of harmonization is at hand. With *phronesis*, Outlaw understands that *verstand* (the analytical reasoning of examining parts) must also be combined with *vernunft* (the common, practical reasoning of examining the whole). Social reality cannot be mapped entirely into a Marxian economic space of stratified classes without an analysis of racial and sexual stratifications. Nor can communal social reality be traced to a political matrix of individual rights, minimal states, and hypothetically contracted liberties. Cultural mappings, while preserving racial and ethnic affiliations, are worthless unless they allow life choices that lead to positive identity formation and world-making. What Outlaw offers is the possibility for a positive critique unencumbered by the negative reactionary terms of extant critiques. He provides the initial premises for a social philosophy of "nonvictims," moving from a negative critique in the logic of victimology[52] to a positive critique in the logic of human political practicality. By decreasing the theoretical distance between liberalism and socialism, he initiates discourse for a new politics of "inclusion, power, and difference."

Lacking adequate theories that predict, explain, or posit the realities of Black community, Outlaw goes "Against the Grain of Modernity,"[53] by asking crucial questions that require new principles. He writes:

> Should different groups live *together* in the same communities, or should they live in geographically as well as politically distinct and more or less separate social unities, whether these be neighborhoods, federated regions, or nation states? Can knowledge of processes that give rise to and condition the formation of human groupings provide answers to these questions? Are there any principles, inherent, perhaps in the social–natural history of human groups that we can recover and deploy to resolve conflictual racial and ethnic relations? Or must we *invent* the principles we need as bases for forms of social order that can be sufficiently satisfying for enough persons in all groups affected to ensure social stability with justice? . . . *Who* will do the inventing? *Who* will administer the principles? On what terms and in the context of what kind of social formation?[54]

These are central questions that do not depend on established fixed-point ideologies such as Christianity, Marxism, or liberalism. Outlaw's proposal calls for balanced utilization of all theoretical resources for conceptualizing and transforming sociopolitical concepts. He concludes, "What I desire is a new form of 'liberalism,' what Novak terms a *cosmopolitan* rather than *universalist* liberalism, which should rest on two pillars: 'a firm commitment to the laborious but recurring enterprise of full, mutual, intellectual understanding'; and a respect for differences of nuance and subtlety, particularly in the area of 'lived-values'; that have lain until now, in all cultures, so largely unarticulated."[55] Elsewhere, Outlaw observes, "The elaboration of this new liberalism in its possible socio-political realizations would be an important contribution from philosophy, something those of us involved in the discipline have not yet worked out as fully as we might."[56]

Outlaw's critique "limits reason to make room for faith," but Outlaw's faith is in practical humanity rather than theological humility. Building Black community on its own foundations requires more than inherited failed traditions. Black community formation requires original African American theoretical philosophy. Community is not *causa sui*. Community, or its absence, is created by individuals, their institutions, and the structural ideologies that guide them as they choose their lived realities. If Black community is to exist as more than imagined, African American philosophy must flourish.

Outlaw's nuanced and highly articulated standpoint exemplifies how African American philosophy is integral to transformative political practices leading to community. He writes that

> [t]he challenge that is the focus of my concern is part of a much larger complex of practical and intellectual struggles, spanning many years, that recently have been grouped under the heading "the politics of difference." Examples include efforts to include persons from once excluded groups in educational, social and occupational settings through the targeting practices of affirmative action programs; various struggles emerging from the contemporary women's movement; and, in general, the use of racial, ethnic, gender, and sexual lifestyle identifiers as the organization focus for politics and the bases for fashioning terms of justice.[57]

Outlaw also understands how and why group-centered coalitions are necessary rallying centers in postmodern struggles against anti-Black racism. Matuštík characterizes this standpoint as,

> [Outlaw], like West, situates critical theory and praxis in their historical contexts. Yet more emphatically than West and hooks, he suggests that the liberation movements of African-Americans might require adopting "the struggle from the level of a group, i.e. ethnic (or nationalistic . . .) position." Outlaw, thus, considers the "group-centered politics" as strategically necessary, given the American, if not worldwide, macroscopic evidence of anti-black racism.[58]

The key to understanding how Outlaw uses epistemology in this postmodern legerdemain is his recognition of the centrality of each particular self. His philosophy is premised on individual identity politics and across lines of group differences and identities. Yet, Outlaw also situates the self within a broadly based context of transcategorical coalitional community. Discussing Outlaw's collapse of race with class, Matuštík states, "When analyses of political economy are joined with other multiple faces of oppression, there arises Outlaw's possibility of 'a multinational movement' for a democracy across the lines of difference and identity. Blurring such lines turns liberation into the conquests of marginalized difference or marginalized identity by dominant identity."[59]

TOWARD THE POSTMODERN BLACK COMMUNITY

Except for King, the thinkers who provide the critical context for this chapter have all written extensively on the regnant ideas surrounding issues of Blackness and postmodernity. Next, I briefly comment on the fragmentary forces of cultural, political, and racial balkanization, and the counterbalancing force of Black identity politics. Overcoming "fragmentation" of nations, classes, races, and genders is an important motivation for community. Yet, in the postmodern world of nations without fixed boundaries, classes with internal subclassifications (internal class minorities), races with fragmented ethnicities, fragmented selves, and the economics of globalization, communities can only aspire to imagined stabilities. I argue that the irony of community, and the problems attached to the African American struggle to form community across so many intersections, propel African Americans into a "postmodern" trajectory. Although at best only a suggestive analysis, I propose a conception of political philosophy that imports Outlaw's structuring rearticulations of neoliberalism into a Marable–West socialist schema allowing African American "beloved community" within a truly national community of communities. For only within healthy communities is liberty important and freedom possible. Without true community, our associations as citizens, Black or White, are mutually carceral.[60]

Very early on, bell hooks identifies the crisis in African American identity as a function of the postmodern critique. She observes how the new criticism has bypassed the ghetto like a new freeway, and argues that postmodernist thinking is important in formulating Black identity:

> Criticisms of directions in postmodern thinking should not obscure insights it may offer that open up our understanding of African-American experience. The critique of essentialism encouraged by postmodernist thought is useful for African-Americans concerned with reformulating outmoded notions of identity. We have too long had imposed upon us from both the outside and the inside a narrow, constricting notion of blackness. Postmodern critiques of essentialism which challenge notions of universality and static over-determined identity within mass culture and mass consciousness can open up new possibilities for the construction of self and the assertion of agency.[61]

For my purposes, the importance of hooks's analysis is her skillful articulation of the importance of postmodernist thought for Black Americans to produce critique or be the object of critique. Define or be defined. The production of knowledge (analyses of critiques) becomes the *work* in a postindustrial, information age the production of signs, and the participation in the "Great Conversation" becomes the mark of agency; without semiotic agency there is no possibility for the social construction of reality (or counterconstructions of counterrealities). However, deepening the pull in opposing directions—between modernity and postmodernity—Black people faced with the social realities of the material construction of homes, families, identities, and communities resist the emerging postmodernist cyberspace realities of home(pages), Web sites, communities of interest ("chat rooms"), and net surfing.[62]

How is it possible, locally (i.e., within the African American community) or globally (i.e., in the marginalized "other" Second and Third Worlds of exploited, oppressed labor), to bypass progress and modernity for the playful exteriority and glitz of postmodernity? If anything, the creation of language games for the sheer joy of it (philosophy as the criticism of criticism)—which ignore the suffering and violence (actual and symbolic) that are caused by liberalism and capitalism—is not a "game." From this perspective, postmodernist ludism is the excess production of hegemonic linguistic practices that exploit humanity in celebrating *différance* (Jacques Derrida's marking of the coequality of differences[63]) while ignoring similarities in hegemonic political oppressions.

So what is the importance of postmodernism for African Americans? hooks's "new possibilities for the construction of self and the assertion of agency" is an affirmation for creating habitable new communities. But, as pure critique, in a world, as Matuštík reminds us, where violence, suffering, desperation, immiseration, and exploitation affect more people than at any other time in history, postmodernism has particular importance for African American lived realities. Gilroy writes,

> It can be argued that much of the supposed novelty of postmodernism evaporates when it is viewed in the unforgiving historical light of the brutal encounters between Europeans and those they conquered, slaughtered, and enslaved. The periodosation of the modern and postmodern is thus of the most profound importance for the history of blacks in the West and for chronicling the shifting relations of domination and subordination between Europeans and the rest of the world. It is essential for our understanding of the category of "race" itself and of the *genesis* and development of successive forms of racist ideology.[64]

It is of as great interest to African American philosophers *how* postmodern racism differs (endlessly deferring) from modern racism and how ideals of modern communities differ from those of postmodern communities.

> In keeping with the spiritual components which also help to distinguish them from modern secular rationality, the slaves' perspectives deal only secondarily in the idea of rationally pursued utopia. Their primary categories are steeped in the idea of a revolutionary or eschatological apocalypse—the jubilee. They provocatively suggest that many of the advances of modernity are in fact insubstantial or pseudo-advances contingent on the power of the racially dominant grouping and that, as a result, the critique of modernity cannot be satisfactorily completed from within its own philosophical and political norms, that is immanently.[65]

Modernity, construed not only as the promise of scientific progress or *grand récits*, can also be seen as an attack on the rational self. Emile Foucault, in *Discipline and Punish*, understands how totalitarian power is extracted from individual self-fragmentation. Gilroy expresses a deep sensitivity to the tenuous relationships among social fragmentation, individual self-fragmentation, and the necessity given the impossibility to build community if the "essential black subject" no longer exists. He writes, "the pursuit of social and political autonomy has turned away from the promise of modernity and found new expression in a complex term that is often understood to be modernity's antithesis. This can be explained partially through the threat which the maelstrom of modernity poses to the stability and coherence of the self. That self can be safely cultivated and remain secure behind the closed shutters of black particularity while the storms rage outside."[66]

On the face of it, all that is being written on postmodern Blackness is intertextual. That is, it is written in the academy by academics for consumption by other academics (despite what hooks claims). Yet, we have also seen in this chapter a "turning away" from the new critique's "ludic" elements for a "resistance" politics of coalition, dissent, and renewed activism. In a context of continued immiseration and hopeless nihilism, the construction of positive self-identity for Blacks has become increasingly difficult. West portrays this decadent postmodern culture in "Learning to Talk of Race" in the following words: "Postmodern culture is more and more a market culture dominated by gangster mentalities and self-destructive wantonness. This culture engulfs all of us yet its impact on the disadvantaged is devastating, resulting in extreme violence in everyday life. Sexual violence against women and homicidal assaults by young black men on one another are only the most obvious signs of this empty quest for pleasure, property, and power."[67]

Beyond the empty quest for endless pleasure, more property, and greater power lie either the barren nihilistic emptiness of the politics of representation as immiseration flourishes, or the abundances of spirit, individuality, and freedom in actual communities where people live. Postmodern pluralism is more than politically correct multiculturalism. Harris's profound essay "Postmodernism and Utopia" provides devastating evidence for his agreement with West's negative portrayal of postmodern culture's affect on the Black urban underclass:

> The wealth of urban centers depends, in part, on the wealth generated from the proliferation of illegal drugs; the sale of discarded, out dated, and dangerous pharmaceuticals; the sale of foodstuffs to prison systems; and the sale and resale of cheap weapons commonly used in petty crimes. As renters, under-employed service workers, or unemployed, welfare-dependent persons, the underclass does not represent persons who enjoy the architecture which mixes Gregorian columns with mirrored glass windows, or the ease with which persons move from museums with seventeenth-century Italian art to neon light advertisements; it all stands as alien and impenetrable power.[68]

Harris's remarks are an indictment of ludic postmodernism and an acknowledgment of Matuštík's pleas for repoliticization, coalition, and dissent.

Harris's solution is invested in postmodernist relativism, in that he argues for the instantiation of *metautopian* forms, that is, societies where all visions of utopia coexist. Yet, Harris is critical of postmodernism because, "[t]he concept of postmodernism, I argue, is associated with such a vision—a vision which renders the immiserated irrelevant and blacks, in particular, as ornaments without agencies or resistance."[69] Regaining agency is achieved, in Harris's view, by gaining metautopian normativity, where all utopian forms coexist, making room for an African American utopian vision of community unconditioned by majoritarian influence. Theorizing Black community becomes community.

Simply put, my argument is that the mainstream traditions in canonical Western social and political philosophy have failed to provide the ideals (practical and utopian) necessary to promote sustainable, flourishing African American communities. I argue on substantive and theoretical grounds that liberalism, communitarianism, and socialism are inadequate for the realization of future African American political communities. At the same time, I argue that inherited African American models for community, from Black nationalism to "Beloved Community" are also inadequate motivations for producing practical, politically viable civil associations valorizable by the majority community. These theoretical inadequacies, both externally mainstream and internally African American, result in a politically postmodern nihilistic malaise that prevents activism and impedes progress.

I defend the view that sociopolitical ideals—from ideal discourse communities to utopian political speculations—are necessary, if insufficient, criteria for achieving actual political communities. Because both mainstream and minority traditions have had limited success in producing the desired outcomes, original African American sociopolitical critique and theory are urgently required. The ongoing struggle for African American self-identity, community, freedom, and justice demand empowering critique and radically original social ideals. What is required is a renaissance in African American social and political thought.

Assumptions by mainstream theorists that canonical Western sociopolitical forms are the preferred end-states for African Americans are naive at best and condescendingly arrogant at worst. This assumption is either coercively assimilativist or a negative judgment concerning the abilities of African Americans to originate theory. African American social and political philosophers, drawing from all traditions, must seek transformative theories and practices leading to transcendent communities.

In "achieving our community," contemporary African American philosophers must employ syntheses of feminist, socialist, pragmatist, postmodernist, liberal, radical, and critical traditions. The quest is for a nonassimilative, nonseparatist, "redemptive," and transformative Black nationalism that allows African Americans to flourish beyond the pale of a shallow politics of representation in cultural distinctiveness.

In the main, African Americans—philosophers and citizens—do not seek separation from the majority community. The status of African Americans in the United States is unique and perilous. This uniqueness, tempered by historical slavery and an ongoing subaltern social status, also provides a particularly unique opportunity. The opportunity, in overcoming the liabilities of an unfortunate historical moment, is knowledgeable and transformative political engagement. African American efforts to achieve community transforms individuals, the communities in which they live, and the communities to which they aspire. For it is in achieving structurally transformed, redemptively nationalistic, politically practical, and livable communities that revolutionary visions for moral community exist and are imagined.

NOTES

1. Martin Luther King Jr., *Where Do We Go from Here: Chaos or Community?* (New York: Harper and Row, 1967), 191.

2. Greg Moses, *Revolution of Conscience: Martin Luther King, Jr., and the Philosophy of Nonviolence* (New York: Guilford, 1997), 84.

3. I use "second reconstruction" as Manning Marable does. See Manning Marable, *Race, Reform, and Rebellion: The Second Reconstruction in Black America, 1945–1982* (Jackson: University Press of Mississippi, 1986). In the prologue, Marable writes: "The first [reconstruction] was developed before the seminal conflict in American history, the Civil War (1861–65), and came to fruition in the twelve-year period of reunion, reconstruction and racial readjustment which followed (1865–77). Almost a century later, the 'Second Reconstruction' occurred. Like the former period, the Second Reconstruction was a series of massive confrontations concerning the status of the Afro-American and other national minorities (e.g., Indians, Chicanos, Puerto Ricans, Asians) in the nation's economic, social, and political institutions." See Marable, *Race, Reform, and Rebellion*, 1.

4. King, *Where Do We Go from Here*, 122–128.

5. Moses, *Revolution of Conscience*, 201.

6. Marable quotes Malcolm X's article "Separation or Integration: A Debate": "Malcolm X made the simple distinction between desegregation and integration which . . . Negro leaders could never grasp. 'It is not a case of [dark mankind] wanting integration or separation, it is a case of wanting freedom, justice, and equality. It is not integration that Negroes in America want, it is human dignity.'" See Marable, *Race, Reform, and Rebellion*, 62; see also Malcolm X, "Separation or Integration: A Debate," *Dialogue Magazine* 2 (May 1962): 14–18. Whereas King conjectured that the path to human dignity remained within the liberal–contractarian capitalistic structure, by 1965 many African Americans were beginning to believe that other paths to dignity existed. The civil rights movement's legacy increasingly was the militant rhetoric of cultural and political nationalism, including Pan-Africanism.

7. Moses, *Revolution of Conscience*, 2.

8. Moses, *Revolution of Conscience*, 89.

9. King, *Where Do We Go from Here*, 39–40. King quotes Stampp's reference to guidelines published for slaveholders. It is interesting to speculate how postslavery African American self-identity formation processes depended upon constructing and internalizing the contraries to these propositions.

10. According to Fred L. Pincus, "racism" is individual, institutional, or structural. See Fred L. Pincus, "From Individualism to Structural Discrimination," in *Race and Ethnic Conflict*, ed. Fred L. Pincus and Howard J. Ehrlich (Boulder, Colo.: Westview, 1994), 82–87. But many scholars, like Byron Roth, argue that modern racism has changed into "symbolic" forms. I would argue that "symbolic" racism is entirely structural, because the structural level *is* the sociopolitical ideology that supports the institutional and individual levels. However, as the symbolic and ideological features of racism become less overt, their structural imbrication also becomes less obvious. This is a recurring theme in Charles W. Mills's *Racial Contract*, where racism is so structurally embedded in the foundations of liberalism that the social contract is constructed in the interstices of the racial contract and vice versa. See Charles W. Mills, *The Racial Contract* (Ithaca, N.Y.: Cornell University Press, 1997).

11. Cornel West, *Prophesy Deliverance! An Afro-American Revolutionary Christianity* (Philadelphia: Westminster Press, 1982), 75.

12. Moses, *Revolution of Conscience*, 146–147.

13. Moses, *Revolution of Conscience*, 194.

14. King, *Where Do We Go from Here?*, 43.

15. King, *Where Do We Go from Here?*, 59.

16. "One-third of today's Black families are considered middle class compared to two-thirds of White families. When King died, Black families earned 59¢ for every $1 earned by White families. Today, the figure is 58¢." See David Walters and Cornell Christon, "MLK Dream: Alive or Dead 25 Years Later?" *Rocky Mountain News*, 17 January 1993, 18.

17. Having been present at the 1963 March on Washington, I can attest to the fact that this single event galvanized Black revolutionary and transformative struggle.

18. In an interesting monograph, Michael Walzer writes that there is a *continuum of toleration*, "resignation, indifference, stoical acceptance, curiosity, and enthusiasm." He asks, "What exactly do we do when we tolerate difference?" See Michael Walzer, *On Toleration* (New Haven, Conn.: Yale University Press, 1997), 12–13. While *enthusiastic toleration* for integration appears an inappropriate characterization for either race's view of the results of integration or assimilation, *enthusiastic toleration* appears a necessary criterion for a truly multicultural "community."

19. Tom Wicker, *Tragic Failure: Racial Integration in America* (New York: William Morrow, 1996), 124. Wicker's statistics and analyses are very analogous to those by William Julius Wilson. Both writers are in accord that, as much as any other factor, changing conditions in the global economy hastened the crisis in American racial integration. See William Julius Wilson, *When Work Disappears: The World of the New Urban Poor* (New York: Vintage, 1996).

20. Karsten Struhl writes: "'the kingdom of freedom' . . . This Promethean idea derives from Marx's insistence on drawing a boundary line between the 'kingdom of necessity' and the 'kingdom of freedom.' The latter to be continuously expanded as the former declines." See Karsten Struhl, "Capitalist Ethics, Socialist Ethics, Economic Ethics" (unpublished), 13. The "kingdom of necessity" represents the drudgery of ma-

terial disenfranchisement, while the "kingdom of freedom" represents the reinfranchisement of the individual by way of shared ownership and production.

21. West, *Prophesy Deliverance!*, 16.
22. West, *Prophesy Deliverance!*, 17.
23. West, *Prophesy Deliverance!*, 23.
24. West, *Prophesy Deliverance!*, 44.
25. Here, "science" refers not only to "mechanistic" sciences like physics, but also to "practical" sciences like sociopolitical theorizing. This is "science" used in the German sense of *Wissenschaft*, which is the science of any organized attempt to gain knowledge and is not totally identified with physical science. The point is, African American philosophers are not impressed by the hierarchies of knowledge, including the narrow view of science as physical science. In the finest tradition of philosophical epistemology, African American philosophers *know* that there are several ways of knowing (e.g., the *knowing x* [objects], *knowing how* [empirical], and *knowing that* [propositional]), including feminist standpoint epistemologies, like Patricia Hill Collins's "particular sociological or experiential location from which woman-centered knowledge about the world can proceed." See Paul Gilroy, *The Black Atlantic: Modernity and Double Consciousness* (Cambridge, Mass.: Harvard University Press, 1993), 51. African American philosophers seek similar "standpoint" epistemologies, or ways of knowing, from which Africana-knowledge can proceed.

26. Like Gilroy, I use M. M. Bakhtin's term "chronotope" instead of "paradigm" (with its scientistic baggage) in describing "community" as a nineteenth-century "optic." Chronotope also calls attention to the intertextuality of a term like "community"—marking its use as textual instead of a reified ontological reality. Gilroy quotes Bakhtin's definition of chronotope: "A unit of analysis for studying texts according to the ratio and nature of the temporal and spatial categories represented. . . . The chronotope is an optic for reading texts as x-rays of the forces at work in the cultural system from which they spring." See Gilroy, *Black Atlantic*, 225n2.

27. West, *Prophesy Deliverance!*, 44.
28. See Leonard Harris, ed., *Philosophy Born of Struggle: Anthology of Afro-American Philosophy from 1917* (Dubuque: Kendall-Hunt, 1983).
29. West, *Prophesy Deliverance!*, 70–71.
30. Moses, *Revolution of Conscience*, 207.
31. West, *Prophesy Deliverance!*, 70.
32. The "assimilationist" tradition has been analyzed in great detail. Sociologists Robert E. Park and Milton Gordon resolve "assimilation" into a finer-grained structure than West presents. Park and Gordon discuss *assimilation* in seven contexts: "*cultural, structural, marital, identification, attitude-receptional, behavior-receptional, and civic.*" See Joe R. Feagin and Clarence Booher Feagin, "Theoretical Perspectives in Race and Ethnic Relations," in *Race and Ethnic Conflict*, ed. Fred L. Pincus and Howard J. Ehrlich (Boulder, Colo.: Westview, 1994), 30–31. The important point here is that West's analysis of "assimilation" has far fewer dimensions than the complex sociocultural situation for African Americans may demand.

33. Marable, *Race, Reform, and Rebellion*, 115.
34. Cornel West, *Keeping Faith: Philosophy and Race in America* (New York: Routledge, 1993) 133.
35. Here, "ordinary people" is not used pejoratively. From the Wittgensteinian "Ordinary Language" tradition in philosophy, where philosophers are seen as mystifying

agents because they attack ordinary language as inadequate to express their private insights into the great mysteries, to socialism, as a system where the people are equal and equally share in the decisions of power, "ordinary people" are the highest expressions of humanity. A philosopher (I cannot recall who) once described the socialist community as "a place where the brain surgeon waves a good morning greeting to his garbage collector neighbor without any elitism." In other words, my conception of socialism is completely egalitarian, all persons are equally valued, respected, and consulted in matters of power.

36. Gilroy, *Black Atlantic*, 79.

37. Anna Grimshaw and Keith Hart, preface to *American Civilization*, by C. L. R. James (Cambridge: Blackwell, 1993), 16.

38. Lucius Outlaw, *On Race and Philosophy* (New York: Routledge, 1996), 2.

39. Outlaw, *On Race and Philosophy*, 8.

40. Outlaw, *On Race and Philosophy*, 8.

41. I especially like the definition of "ethnicity" given by Bob Blauner: "An ethnic group is a group that shares a belief in its common past. Members of an ethnic group hold a set of common memories that make them feel that their customs, culture, and outlook are distinctive. In short, they have a sense of peoplehood. Sharing critical experiences and sometimes a belief in their common fate, they feel an affinity to one another, a 'comfort zone' that leads to congregating together, even when this is not forced by exclusionary barriers. Thus if race is associated with biology and nature, ethnicity is associated with culture. Like races, ethnic groups arise historically, transform themselves, and sometimes die out." See Bob Blauner, "Talking Past Each Other: Black and White Languages of Race," in *Race and Ethnic Conflict*, ed. Fred L. Pincus and Howard J. Ehrlich (Boulder, Colo.: Westview, 1994), 25.

42. Outlaw, *On Race and Philosophy*, 322.

43. Mills, *Racial Contract*, 125.

44. Outlaw, *On Race and Philosophy*, 2.

45. Outlaw, *On Race and Philosophy*, 44.

46. Martin J. Beck Matuštík's analyses are an important contribution to coalitional politics in the postmodern political era. He is acutely aware of the importance of African American sociopolitical community formation processes. See Martin J. Beck Matuštík, *Specters of Liberation: Great Refusals in the New World Order* (Ithaca: SUNY Press, 1998).

47. Matuštík, *Specters of Liberation*, 14.

48. Outlaw, *On Race and Philosophy*, 46–47.

49. Outlaw, *On Race and Philosophy*, 49.

50. This definition is from Simon Blackburn, *Oxford Dictionary of Philosophy* (New York: Oxford University Press, 1984), 287.

51. Outlaw, *On Race and Philosophy*, 50.

52. Orlando Patterson describes the landscape of "victimology" as "racist determinists of the right who see them [Blacks] as victims of their genetic destiny, from liberal and other determinists of the left who see them as victims of their socioeconomic surroundings, and from conservative determinists of the center, who see them as victims of culture." See Orlando Patterson, *The Ordeal of Integration* (Washington, D.C.: Civitas, 1997), 92.

53. This is also the title of chapter 6 in Outlaw, *On Race and Philosophy*. The complete chapter title is "Against the Grain of Modernity: The Politics of Difference and the Conservation of 'Race.'"

54. Outlaw, *On Race and Philosophy*, 139.

55. Outlaw, *On Race and Philosophy*, 177. Here, Outlaw quotes from Michael Novak, *Pluralism: A Humanistic Perspective* (Cambridge, Mass.: Belknap, 1980), 775.

56. Outlaw, *On Race and Philosophy*, 325.

57. Outlaw, *On Race and Philosophy*, 306.

58. Matuštík, *Specters of Liberation*, 234–235.

59. Matuštík, *Specters of Liberation*, 245.

60. I purposely choose Foucault's term "carceral" to suggest that constructing modern communities proceeds from that analysis. Foucault rightly sees the relationship between the "panoptic" central gaze and prisons. Community as "prison" is the postmodern equivalent to the "carceral" space Foucault delineates when individual perspectival ("panoptical") views relieve the state of responsibility for exercising punitive power. Each perspective as an exercise of power *disciplines* and *punishes*. See Michel Foucault, *Discipline and Punish: The Birth of the Prison* (New York: Vintage, 1995). bell hooks notes the similarities between the American educational system and language itself, with the *carceral* state. I am interested in the tensions between communities as liberating or confining, and the purposes for—the *ghetto* as *confining*, the *suburbs* as *liberating*—the construction of the hegemonic false consciousnesses that maintain these illusions.

61. bell hooks, "Postmodern Blackness," in *Yearning: Race, Gender, and Cultural Politics* (Boston: South End, 1990), 28. Note that while hooks's essay is not itself a "new criticism," it is a call for "new criticism." Also note the ludic quality of changing identities in hooks's name change (from Gloria Watkins to her grandmother's lower-cased name) and her refusal to use footnotes. Her name has the ludic semiotic image of a "bell" on its "hooks" ready to be struck by Zarathustra's hammer—this is not to demean hooks, however, as I respect her work.

62. Holly Sklar writes: "We cannot build communities on economic quicksand. It is time to start using technological advances to free human labor for leisure, family, community and more socially productive work, culture, learning, and so on. Technology can help us build real and 'virtual communities' within neighborhoods and across local and national boundaries. Or it can destroy real communities while promoting cyberspace communities of people increasingly afraid to leave their homes or gated enclaves. Without a change of course, the high-tech world will be a high-oppression world. . . . A world in which some people live in futuristic splendor, and millions live in medieval squalor. A violent world of crumbling cities sprinkled with high-tech gadgets. A world of voice-mail mazes and fewer interactions with real people. A world where children are free to explore their computers, if they have one, but not their neighborhoods." See Holly Sklar, *Chaos or Community* (Boston: South End, 1995), 176–177.

63. Jacques Derrida states: "we will designate as *différance* the movement according to which language, or any code, any system of referral in general, is constituted ('historically' as a weave of differences)." See Jacques Derrida, *Margins of Philosophy* (Chicago: University of Chicago Press, 1982), 12.

64. Gilroy, *Black Atlantic*, 44.
65. Gilroy, *Black Atlantic*, 55–56.
66. Gilroy, *Black Atlantic*, 187–188.
67. Cornel West, "Learning to Talk to Race," in *I Am Because We Are: Readings in Black Philosophy*, ed. Fred Lee Hord and Jonathan Scott Lee (Amherst: University of Massachusetts Press, 1995), 353.
68. Leonard Harris, "Postmodernism and Utopia, an Unholy Alliance," in *I Am Because We Are: Readings in Black Philosophy*, ed. Fred Lee Hord and Jonathan Scott Lee (Amherst: University of Massachusetts Press, 1995), 376.
69. Harris, "Postmodernism and Utopia," 371.

REFERENCES

Blackburn, Simon. *Oxford Dictionary of Philosophy*. New York: Oxford University Press, 1984.
Blauner, Bob. "Talking Past Each Other: Black and White Languages of Race." In *Race and Ethnic Conflict*, ed. Fred L. Pincus and Howard J. Ehrlich. Boulder, Colo.: Westview, 1994.
Derrida, Jacques. *Margins of Philosophy*. Chicago: University of Chicago Press, 1982.
Dyson, Michael Eric. *I May Not Get There with You*. New York: The Free Press, 2000.
———. *Race Rules: Navigating the Color Line*. New York: Vintage, 1997.
Feagin, Joe R., and Clarence Booher Feagin. "Theoretical Perspectives in Race and Ethnic Relations." In *Race and Ethnic Conflict*, ed. Fred L. Pincus and Howard J. Ehrlich. Boulder, Colo.: Westview, 1994.
Foucault, Michel. *Discipline and Punish: The Birth of the Prison*. New York: Vintage, 1995.
Gilroy, Paul. *The Black Atlantic: Modernity and Double Consciousness*. Cambridge, Mass.: Harvard University Press, 1993.
Gordon, Lewis. *Bad Faith and Antiblack Racism*. Highlands, N.J.: Humanities, 1995.
———. ed. *Existence in Black: An Anthology of Black Existential Philosophy*, New York: Routledge, 1997.
Grimshaw, Anna, and Keith Hart. Preface to *American Civilization*, by C. L. R. James. Cambridge: Blackwell, 1993.
Harris, Leonard, ed. *Philosophy Born of Struggle: Anthology of Afro-American Philosophy from 1917,* Dubuque: Kendall-Hunt, 1983.
———. "Postmodernism and Utopia, an Unholy Alliance." In *I Am Because We Are: Readings in Black Philosophy*, ed. Fred Lee Hord and Jonathan Scott Lee. Amherst: University of Massachusetts Press, 1995.
hooks, bell. *Outlaw Culture*. London: Routledge, 1994.
———. *Yearning: Race, Gender, and Cultural Politics*. Boston: South End, 1990.
hooks, bell, and Cornel West. *Breaking Bread*. Boston: South End, 1991.
Hord, Fred Lee, and Jonathan Scott Lee, eds. *I Am Because We Are: Readings in Black Philosophy*. Amherst: University of Massachusetts Press, 1995.
James, C. L. R. *American Civilization*. Cambridge: Blackwell, 1993.
James, Joy. *Resisting State Violence in U.S. Culture*. Minneapolis: University of Minnesota Press, 1996.

———. *Transcending the Talented Tenth: Black Leaders and American Intellectuals.* New York: Routledge, 1997.

King, Martin Luther, Jr. *The Strength to Love.* New York: Harper and Row, 1963.

———. *Stride toward Freedom: The Montgomery Story.* New York: Harper and Row, 1964.

———. *Where Do We Go from Here: Chaos or Community?* New York: Harper and Row, 1967.

Lawson, Bill E., ed. *The Underclass Question.* Philadelphia: Temple University Press, 1992.

Lott, Tommy. "Marooned in America." In *The Underclass Question*, ed. Bill E. Lawson. Philadelphia: Temple University Press, 1992.

———. ed. *Subjugation and Bondage: Critical Essays on Slavery and Social Philosophy.* Lanham, Md.: Rowman & Littlefield, 1998.

Malcolm X. "Separation or Integration: A Debate." *Dialogue Magazine* 2 (May 1962): 14–18.

Marable, Manning. *How Capitalism Underdeveloped Black America: Problems in Race, Political Economy and Society.* Boston: South End, 1983.

———. *Race, Reform, and Rebellion: The Second Reconstruction in Black America, 1945–1982.* Jackson: University Press of Mississippi, 1986.

Matuštík, Martin J. Beck. *Specters of Liberation: Great Refusals in the New World Order.* Ithaca: SUNY Press, 1998.

Mills, Charles W. *Blackness Visible: Essays on Philosophy and Race.* Ithaca, N.Y.: Cornell University Press, 1998.

———. *The Racial Contract.* Ithaca, N.Y.: Cornell University Press, 1997.

Moses, Greg. *Revolution of Conscience: Martin Luther King, Jr., and the Philosophy of Nonviolence.* New York: Guilford, 1997.

Novak, Michael. *Pluralism: A Humanistic Perspective.* Cambridge, Mass.: Belknap Press of Harvard University, 1980.

Omi, Michael, and Howard Winant. *Racial Formation in the United States.* 2nd ed. New York: Routledge, 1994.

Outlaw, Lucius. *On Race and Philosophy.* New York: Routledge, 1996.

———. "Philosophy, Ethnicity, and Race." In *I Am Because We Are: Readings in Black Philosophy*, ed. Fred Lee Hord and Jonathan Scott Lee. Amherst: University of Massachusetts Press, 1995.

Patterson, Orlando. *The Ordeal of Integration.* Washington, D.C.: Civitas, 1997.

Pincus, Fred L. "From Individualism to Structural Discrimination." In *Race and Ethnic Conflict*, ed. Fred L. Pincus and Howard J. Ehrlich. Boulder, Colo.: Westview, 1994.

Sklar, Holly. *Chaos or Community.* Boston: South End, 1995.

Sleeper, Jim. "Toward an End of Blackness: An Argument for the Surrender of Race." *Harper's Magazine* (May 1997).

Smith, Kenneth L., and Ira G. Zepp. *Searching for the Beloved Community: The Thinking of Martin Luther King, Jr.* Lanham, Md.: University Press of America, 1986.

Walzer, Michael. *On Toleration.* New Haven, Conn.: Yale University Press, 1997.

West, Cornel. *Keeping Faith: Philosophy and Race in America.* New York: Routledge, 1993.

———. "Learning to Talk of Race." In *I Am Because We Are: Readings in Black Philosophy*, ed. Fred Lee Hord and Jonathan Scott Lee. Amherst: University of Massachusetts Press, 1995.

———. *Prophesy Deliverance! An Afro-American Revolutionary Christianity.* Philadelphia: Westminster Press, 1982.

Wicker, Tom. *Tragic Failure: Racial Integration in America.* New York: William Morrow, 1996.

Wilson, William Julius. *When Work Disappears: The World of the New Urban Poor.* New York: Vintage, 1996.

Zepp, Ira G., Jr. *The Social Vision of Martin Luther King, Jr.* Brooklyn: Carlson, 1971.

Selected Bibliography

Dyson, Michael Eric. *I May Not Get There with You.* New York: The Free Press, 2000.
———. *Race Rules: Navigating the Color Line.* New York: Vintage, 1997.
Foucault, Michel. *Discipline and Punish: The Birth of the Prison.* New York: Vintage, 1995.
Gilroy, Paul. *The Black Atlantic: Modernity and Double Consciousness.* Cambridge, Mass.: Harvard University Press, 1993.
Gordon, Lewis. *Bad Faith and Antiblack Racism.* Highlands, N.J.: Humanities, 1995.
———. ed. *Existence in Black: An Anthology of Black Existential Philosophy.* New York: Routledge, 1997.
Harris, Leonard, ed. *Philosophy Born of Struggle: Anthology of Afro-American Philosophy from 1917.* Dubuque: Kendall-Hunt, 1983.
———. "Postmodernism and Utopia, an Unholy Alliance." In *I Am Because We Are: Readings in Black Philosophy,* ed. Fred Lee Hord and Jonathan Scott Lee. Amherst: University of Massachusetts Press, 1995.
hooks, bell. *Outlaw Culture.* London: Routledge, 1994.
———. *Yearning: Race, Gender, and Cultural Politics.* Boston: South End, 1990.
hooks, bell, and Cornel West. *Breaking Bread.* Boston: South End, 1991.
Hord, Fred Lee, and Jonathan Scott Lee, eds. *I Am Because We Are: Readings in Black Philosophy.* Amherst: University of Massachusetts Press, 1995.
James, C. L. R. *American Civilization.* Cambridge: Blackwell, 1993.
James, Joy. *Resisting State Violence in U.S. Culture.* Minneapolis: University of Minnesota Press, 1996.
———. *Transcending the Talented Tenth: Black Leaders and American Intellectuals.* New York: Routledge, 1997.
King, Martin Luther, Jr. *The Strength to Love.* New York: Harper and Row, 1963.
———. *Where Do We Go from Here: Chaos or Community?* New York: Harper and Row, 1967.

Lawson, Bill E., ed. *The Underclass Question*. Philadelphia: Temple University Press, 1992.

Lott, Tommy. "Marooned in America." In *The Underclass Question*, ed. Bill E. Lawson. Philadelphia: Temple University Press, 1992.

————, ed. *Subjugation and Bondage: Critical Essays on Slavery and Social Philosophy*. Lanham, Md.: Rowman and Littlefield, 1998.

Marable, Manning. *How Capitalism Underdeveloped Black America: Problems in Race, Political Economy and Society*. Boston: South End, 1983.

————. *Race, Reform, and Rebellion: The Second Reconstruction in Black America, 1945–1982*. Jackson: University Press of Mississippi, 1986.

Matuštík, Martin J. Beck. *Specters of Liberation: Great Refusals in the New World Order*. Ithaca: SUNY Press, 1998.

Mills, Charles W. *Blackness Visible: Essays on Philosophy and Race*. Ithaca, N.Y.: Cornell University Press, 1998.

————. *The Racial Contract*. Ithaca, N.Y.: Cornell University Press, 1997.

Moses, Greg. *Revolution of Conscience: Martin Luther King, Jr., and the Philosophy of Nonviolence*. New York: Guilford, 1997.

Omi, Michael, and Howard Winant. *Racial Formation in the United States*. 2nd ed. New York: Routledge, 1994.

Outlaw, Lucius. *On Race and Philosophy*. New York: Routledge, 1996.

————. "Philosophy, Ethnicity, and Race." In *I Am Because We Are: Readings in Black Philosophy*, ed. Fred Lee Hord and Jonathan Scott Lee. Amherst: University of Massachusetts Press, 1995.

Sleeper, Jim. "Toward an End of Blackness: An Argument for the Surrender of Race Consciousness." *Harper's Magazine* (May 1997).

Smith, Kenneth L., and Ira G. Zepp. *Searching for the Beloved Community: The Thinking of Martin Luther King, Jr.* Lanham, Md.: University Press of America, 1986.

West, Cornel. *Keeping Faith: Philosophy and Race in America*. New York: Routledge, 1993.

————. "Learning to Talk of Race." In *I Am Because We Are: Readings in Black Philosophy*, ed. Fred Lee Hord and Jonathan Scott Lee. Amherst: University of Massachusetts Press, 1995.

————. *Prophesy Deliverance! An Afro-American Revolutionary Christianity*. Philadelphia: Westminster Press, 1982.

Wilson, William Julius. *When Work Disappears: The World of the New Urban Poor*. New York: Vintage, 1996.

Zepp, Ira G., Jr. *The Social Vision of Martin Luther King, Jr.* Brooklyn: Carlson, 1971.

Index

287

About the Contributors

Robert E. Birt teaches philosophy at Morgan State University. His research interests include Africana philosophy, existential philosophy, critical theory, and philosophical anthropology. His articles have appeared in *International Philosophical Quarterly, Man and World, Social Science Information, Quest: Journal of African Philosophy,* and *Philosophical Forum,* and he is presently engaged in further philosophical research exploring the quest for community.

Rod Bush is an assistant professor of sociology at St. John's University in New York City. He has a long activist history in the Black Power and other radical movements since 1965 and is author of *We Are Not What We Seem: Black Nationalism and Class Struggle in the American Century.*

George Carew has taught philosophy at Spelman College, with a specialization in political philosophy and Africana philosophy.

Kevin Cokley is an assistant professor of counseling psychology at Southern Illinois University at Carbondale. His research examines racial identity development. He is currently studying the relationship between racial identity and internalized racialism.

Arnold Farr is an assistant professor of philosophy at St. Joseph's University in Philadelphia. He is coeditor and coauthor of *Marginal Groups and Mainstream American Culture.* He has recently completed a book titled *Reading Farrakhan/Reading America.*

Patrick Goodin is an assistant professor of philosophy at Howard University. His research interests include ancient Greek philosophy and Africana philosophy, especially the emerging field of Afro-Caribbean philosophy.

Lewis R. Gordon is chairperson of Africana studies and professor of Africana studies, contemporary religious thought, and modern culture and media at Brown University. He is also ongoing visiting professor of political thought at the University of the West Indies at Mona, Jamaica. He is author of several books, including *Her Majesty's Other Children*, which won the Gustavus Myer Award for Outstanding Work on Human Rights.

Leonard Harris is a member of the graduate faculty, department of philosophy and African American studies program at Purdue University. He is a former director of Purdue's African American studies program. He has published several books, including *Philosophy Born of Struggle, Exploitation and Exclusion: Race and Class in Contemporary US Society,* and *The Critical Pragmatism of Alain Locke.*

Clevis Headley is an associate professor of philosophy at Florida Atlantic University. His current research focuses on the question of Black subjectivity and its relation to postmodernism and deconstruction. His publications include articles on race, Frege, and Africana philosophy and an article in a critical volume about Cornel West, edited by George Yancy.

Paget Henry is professor of sociology and Africana studies at Brown University, where he teaches courses on critical theory and Afro-Caribbean philosophy. His most recent book is *Caliban's Reason.* He is also the editor of *The C. L. R. James Journal.*

Joy James is professor of Africana studies at Brown University. She is author of numerous books, including *Resisting State Violence, Transcending the Talented Tenth,* and *States of Confinement: Policing, Detention and Prisons.* She has edited *The Angela Davis Reader* and coedited (with T. Denean Sharpley-Whiting) *The Black Feminist Reader.*

Richard A. Jones teaches philosophy at Howard University. His research areas include critical race theory and philosophy of science.

Tracy Denean Sharpley-Whiting is the director of the African American Studies and Research Center and associate professor of French, film studies, comparative literature, and women's studies. She received her B.A. from the University of Rochester, M.A. from Miami University in Oxford, Ohio, and Ph.D. from Brown University. She is the author of five books and is presently working on a book about Negritude women writers from the 1920s to the 1940s.

Eddy Souffrant teaches ethics, social and political philosophy, and Francophone/Caribbean philosophy at Marquette University. He has written a book and numerous articles in those areas. He is currently working on a project that explores the contemporary conceptions of identity.

DATE DUE